Cisco CCNP Remote Access
Exam Certification Guide

Brian Morgan, CCIE #4865, and Craig Dennis

Cisco Press

Cisco Press
201 W 103rd Street
Indianapolis, IN 46290 USA

Cisco CCNP Remote Access Exam Certification Guide

Brian Morgan, CCIE #4865, and Craig Dennis
Copyright © 2001 Cisco Systems, Inc.
Cisco Press logo is a trademark of Cisco Systems, Inc.

Published by:
Cisco Press
201 West 103rd Street
Indianapolis, IN 46290 USA

Printed in the United States of America 3 4 5 6 7 8 9 0   03 02 01
Third Printing May 2001

Library of Congress Cataloging-in-Publication Number: 00-105171
ISBN: 1-58720-003-1

Warning and Disclaimer

This book is designed to provide information about the Cisco CCNP Remote Access Exam #640-505. Every effort has been made to make this book as complete and as accurate as possible, but no warranty or fitness is implied.

The information is provided on an "as is" basis. The authors, Cisco Press, and Cisco Systems, Inc. shall have neither liability nor responsibility to any person or entity with respect to any loss or damages arising from the information contained in this book or from the use of the discs or programs that may accompany it.

The opinions expressed in this book belong to the author and are not necessarily those of Cisco Systems, Inc.

Trademark Acknowledgments

All terms mentioned in this book that are known to be trademarks or service marks have been appropriately capitalized. Cisco Press or Cisco Systems, Inc. cannot attest to the accuracy of this information. Use of a term in this book should not be regarded as affecting the validity of any trademark or service mark.

Feedback Information

At Cisco Press, our goal is to create in-depth technical books of the highest quality and value. Each book is crafted with care and precision, undergoing rigorous development that involves the unique expertise of members from the professional technical community.

Readers' feedback is a natural continuation of this process. If you have any comments regarding how we could improve the quality of this book, or otherwise alter it to better suit your needs, you can contact us through email at feedback@ciscopress.com. Please make sure to include the book title and ISBN in your message.

We greatly appreciate your assistance.

Publisher	John Wait
Editor-In-Chief	John Kane
Cisco Systems Program Manager	Bob Anstey
Executive Editor	Brett Bartow
Acquisitions Editor	Amy Lewis
Managing Editor	Patrick Kanouse
Development Editor	Christopher Cleveland
Copy Editor	Jill Batistick
Technical Editors	Jorge Aragon, Bill Wagner, Steve Wisniewski
Team Coordinator	Tammi Ross
Book Designer	Gina Rexrode
Cover Designer	Louisa Klucznik
Production Team	Octal Publishing, Inc.
Indexer	Tim Wright

About the Authors

Brian Morgan, CCIE #4865, is a CCSI for Mentor Technologies (formerly Chesapeake Network Solutions) teaching the ICRC, ACRC, ICND, BSCN, CVOICE, and CATM courses.

Brian has been an instrutor for nearly four years and in the networking industry for over ten years. During that time he's been teaching Cisco Dial Access Solutions boot camp classes for the Service Provider Solutions Tiger Team, the upper echelon of Cisco's technical support structure.

Prior to teaching, Brian spent a number of years with IBM in Network Services where he attained MCNE and MCSE certifications. He was involved with a number of larger LAN/WAN installations for many of IBM's Fortune 500 clients.

Brian is the proud father of five year-old fraternal twin girls (Emma and Amanda) and husband to Beth. His greatest hobby is spending time with the family.

Craig Dennis is an instructor for Mentor Technologies and lives in Fairfax, Virginia. He is a CCSI and CCDP. Craig has taught CMTD and then BCRAN over the last two years. Craig is an avid, but not good, golfer and is currently working toward his CCIE certification. Craig worked for Texaco, Inc., in their Houston Research Lab for 11 years and as a consultant for the Marine Corps for four years as a Network Administrator. He spent about three years as an independent consultant and has taught Cisco classes for the last four years.

About the Technical Reviewers

Jorge Aragon, CCIE #5567, is a Network Engineer with Perot Systems Corporation (PSC) in Dallas, Texas. He holds a BS in Electrical Engineering from the National Polytechnic Institute in Mexico and a Master of Science in Telecommunications from the University of Pittsburgh. He also holds a MCSE certification and several Cisco specializations. Jorge is part of PSC Global Infrastructure Team where he designs, implements, and troubleshoots LAN/WAN networks for clients in multiple industries across the globe. He enjoys spending time with his wife and children, reading, jogging, and practicing martial arts. Jorge can be reached at jorge.aragon@ps.net

Bill Wagner works as a Cisco Certified System Instructor for Mentor Technologies. He has 22 years of computer programming and data communication experience. He has worked for corporations and companies such as Independent Computer Consultants, Numerax, Mc Graw-Hill/Numerax, and Standard and Poors. His teaching experience started with the Chubb institute, Protocol Interface, Inc., and Geotrain. Currently he teaches at Mentor Technologies.

Steve Wisniewski is CCNP certified, has a Masters of Science in Telecommunications Management from Stevens Institute of Technology. Steve is a Senior Implementation Specialist for Lehman Brothers. Steve has authored a book titled *Network Administration* from Prentice Hall due to be released in October of 2000 and has edited several other Cisco Press books. Steve is married to wife Ellen and resides in East Brunswick, New Jersey.

Dedications

Brian Morgan—This book is dedicated to Beth, Emma, and Amanda. Thank you for making me complete.

Craig Dennis—This book is dedicated to my family, which is my most cherished treasure. Jacob, Sandy, Joseph, and David thank you again and again for being as understanding as you are when Dad has to ignore you while he's at the keyboard. To Sharon, my wife, I thank you most of all for providing the glue that holds the family together while I'm on the road and buried in the latest endeavor.

Acknowledgments

Brian Morgan: I'd like to thank my wife, Beth, and kids, Emma and Amanda, for putting up with me during the time this book was being produced. It has taken me away from them more than I'd like to admit. Their patience in temporarily setting some things aside so I could get the book done has been incredible.

I'd like to give special recognition to Bill Wagner for providing his expert technical knowledge in editing the book. As usual, he's not afraid to tell you when you're wrong. He's also been as good a friend as anyone could hope to have.

Thanks to Kale Wright for taking on additional workload to allow me to spend the necessary time writing and researching this book.

A big "thank you" goes out to the production team for this book. John Kane, Amy Lewis, and Christopher Cleveland have been incredibly professional and a pleasure to work with. I couldn't have asked for a finer team.

Last, and possibly least (just kidding), I'd like to thank my co-author Craig Dennis. I approached him with this project at the very last minute and he's worked very hard to keep the book on time, while not sacrificing technical depth or content.

Craig Dennis:

I want to thank Amy Lewis, John Kane, and Chris Cleveland from Cisco Press for keeping this whole thing on track. Amy, I really, really was almost on time with some of the stuff! Thanks also to Brian Morgan my co-author who always kept the project in focus and pushed me to keep the deadlines that we had. I should also thank all the technical and grammatical editors that took the pieces that were delivered and made a book out of it.

Also, thanks go to my parents, as it will every time I accomplish anything. Through their guidance, encouragement, and love I managed to get an education and develop into a reasonable human being. Thank you Pearl and Rally. I can only hope that I can provide at least a reasonable facsimile of your guidance to my family.

And last a thank you to my wife, Sharon, who kept reminding me of the project at hand and rearranging her schedule so I would have "quiet" times to work. As with all projects of this nature I almost feel guilty to have my name on the cover when, without so many others this book would have never been written.

Contents at a Glance

Introduction xxi

Chapter 1 **All About the Cisco Certified Network and Design Professional Certifications 3**

Chapter 2 **Cisco Remote Connection Products 19**

Chapter 3 **Assembling and Cabling WAN Components 43**

Chapter 4 **Configuring Asynchronous Connections with Modems 67**

Chapter 5 **Configuring PPP and Controlling Network Access 97**

Chapter 6 **Using ISDN and DDR to Enhance Remote Connectivity 125**

Chapter 7 **Configuring the Cisco 700 Series Router 193**

Chapter 8 **Establishing an X.25 Connection 221**

Chapter 9 **Establishing Frame Relay Connections and Controlling Traffic Flow 251**

Chapter 10 **Managing Network Performance with Queuing and Compression 291**

Chapter 11 **Scaling IP Addresses with Network Address Translation 331**

Chapter 12 **Using AAA to Scale Access Control in an Expanding Network 367**

Appendix A **Answers to the "Do I Know This Already?" Quizzes and Q&A Sections 397**

Index 445

Contents

Introduction   xxi

Goals and Methods   xxi

Who Should Read This Book?   xxi

Strategies for Exam Preparation   xxii

How This Book Is Organized   xxii

Approach   xxiv

Icons Used in This Book   xxv

Command Syntax Conventions   xxvi

Chapter 1   All About the Cisco Certified Network Professional and Design Professional Certification   3

How This Book Can Help You Pass the CCNP Remote Access Exam   4

Overview of Cisco Certifications   5

The Remote Access Exam and the CCNP and CCDP Certifications   6

Exams Required for Certification   7

Other Cisco Certifications   8

What Is on the Remote Access Exam?   9

Topics on the Exam   9

Recommended Training Path for CCNP and CCDP   11

How to Use This Book to Pass the Exam   13

One Final Word of Advice   14

You Have Passed Other CCNP Exams and Are Preparing for the Remote Access Exam   14
    Scenario 1: You Have Taken the BCRAN Course   14
    Scenario 2: You Have NOT Taken the BCRAN Course   14

You Have Passed the CCNA and Are Preparing for the Remote Access Exam   15
    Scenario 1: You Have Taken the BCRAN Course   15
    Scenario 2: You Have NOT Taken the BCRAN Course   16

You Have Experience and Want to Skip the Classroom Experience and Take the Remote Access Exam   16
    Scenario 1: You Have CCNA Certification   16
    Scenario 2: You DO NOT Have a CCNA Certification   17

Chapter 2   Cisco Remote Connection Products   19

How to Best Use This Chapter   20

"Do I Know This Already?" Quiz   21

Foundation Topics   23

Router Selection Criteria for Remote Access Purposes   23

Selecting a WAN Connection Type for Remote Access Purposes   25

Determining the Site Requirements   26
    Central Site Installations   26
    Branch Office Installations   26
    Remote Office or Home Office Installations   27

Hardware Selection   27
    Product Families: Capabilities and Limitations   27

Foundation Summary   34

Q&A   36

Scenarios   39

Scenario 2-1   39

Scenario 2-2   39

Scenario Answers   40

Scenario 2-1 Answers   40

Scenario 2-2 Answers   40

Chapter 3   Assembling and Cabling the WAN Components   43

How to Best Use This Chapter   43

"Do I Know This Already?" Quiz   44

Foundation Topics   47

Choosing WAN Equipment   48
    Central Site Router Selection   48
        3600 Router Series   49
        4000 Router Series   50
        AS5X00 Router Series   50
        7200 Router Series   51
    Branch Office Router Selection   51
        1600 Router Series   52
        1700 Router Series   52
        2500 Router Series   52

2600 Router Series   52

Small Office/Home Office (SOHO) Router Selection   53

700 Router Series   53

800 Router Series   53

1000 Router Series   53

Assembling and Cabling the Equipment   54

Available Connections   54

Verifying the Installation   55

Central Site Router Verification   56

3600 Router LEDs   56

Branch Office Router Verification   57

1600 Router LEDs   57

SOHO Router Verification   58

Foundation Summary   60

Q&A   61

Scenarios   63

Scenario 3-1   63

Scenario Answers   64

Scenario 3-1 Answers   64

Chapter 4   Configuring Asynchronous Connections with Modems   67

How to Best Use This Chapter   67

"Do I Know This Already?" Quiz   68

Foundation Topics   72

Modem Signaling   72

Data Transfer   73

Data Flow Control   73

Modem Control   73

DTE Call Termination   74

DCE Call Termination   74

Modem Configuration Using Reverse Telnet   74

Router Line Numbering   75

Basic Asynchronous Configuration   78

Logical Considerations on the Router   79

Physical Considerations on the Router   80

Configuration of the Attached Modem   82

Modem Autoconfiguration and the Modem Capabilities Database   82

Chat Scripts to Control Modem Connections   84
    Reasons for Using a Chat Script   85
    Reasons for a Chat Script Starting   85
    Using a Chat Script   85

Foundation Summary   87

Q&A   90

Scenarios   95

Chapter 5   **Configuring PPP and Controlling Network Access   97**

How to Best Use This Chapter   97

"Do I Know This Already?" Quiz   98

Foundation Topics   101

PPP Background   101
    PPP Architecture   101
        PPP Components   102
        PPP LCP   104
        Dedicated and Interactive PPP Sessions   104

PPP Options   105
    PPP Authentication   105
        PAP   106
        CHAP   107
    PPP Callback   109
    PPP Compression   111
    Multilink PPP   112

PPP Troubleshooting   112

Foundation Summary   114

Q&A   115

Scenarios   118

Scenario 5-1   118

Scenario 5-2   119

Scenario 5-3   119

Scenario Answers   120

Scenario 5-1 Answers   120

Scenario 5-2 Answers   121

Scenario 5-3 Answers   122

Chapter 6   Using ISDN and DDR Technologies   125

How to Best Use This Chapter   125

"Do I Know This Already?" Quiz   126

Foundation Topics   130

POTS Versus ISDN   130

BRI and PRI Basics   131

Basic Rate Interface   131
    BRI Protocols   133
        ISDN Layer 1   133
        ISDN Layer 2   135
        ISDN Layer 3   138
    ISDN Call Setup   139
    ISDN Call Release   141

Implementing Basic DDR   141
    Step 1: Setting the ISDN Switch Type   142
    Step 2: Specifying Interesting Traffic   143
        Specifying Interesting Traffic with Access Lists   144
    Step 3: Specifying Static Routes   145
    Step 4: Defining the Interface Encapsulation and ISDN Addressing Parameters   146
        Configuring ISDN Addressing   146
    Step 5: Configuring Protocol Addressing   147
    Step 6: Defining Additional Interface Information   148
        SPIDs   148
        Caller ID Screening   148
        Configuring Additional Interface Information   148
    Passive Interfaces   149
    Static Route Redistribution   150
    Default Routes   151
    Rate Adaptation   152
    Bandwidth on Demand   153
    Multilink PPP   153
        Troubleshooting Multilink PPP   155

Advanced DDR Operations   157
    Using Dialer Profiles   157
    Rotary Groups   159
    Dial Backup   161
        Alternative Backup   163
        Dynamic Backup   163
        Static Backup   164

Snapshot Routing   165

Primary Rate Interface   166
    ISDN Switch Type   167
    T1/E1 Framing and Line Coding   167
        T1 Framing   168
        T1 Line Code   170
    E1 Framing   171
    E1 Line Code   172
    PRI Layers   172
    PRI Configuration   172
    PRI Incoming Analog Calls on Digital Modems   174

Foundation Summary   177

Q&A   178

Scenarios   183

Scenario 6-1   183

Scenario 6-2   185

Scenario 6-3   185

Scenario 6-4   186

Scenario Answers   187

Scenario 6-1 Answers   187

Scenario 6-2 Answers   188

Scenario 6-3 Answers   189

Scenario 6-4 Answers   190

Chapter 7   Configuring a Cisco 700 Series Router   193

How to Best Use This Chapter   193

"Do I Know This Already?" Quiz   194

Foundation Topics   197

Cisco 700 Series Router Key Features and Functions   197
    Networking   197
    Routing and WAN   198
    ISDN and Telephony   198

Cisco 700 Series Router Profiles   198
    LAN Profile   199

Standard Profile   199
Internal Profile   199
System Profile   199
Profile Use Guidelines   199

Configuring the Cisco 700 Series Router for IP Routing   200
Profile Configuration Commands for the Cisco 700 Series Routers   203
Profile Management Commands for the Cisco 700 Series Routers   205

Routing with the Cisco 700 Series Router   205

DHCP Overview   207

Using the Cisco 700 Series Router as a DHCP Server and Relay Agent   208

Foundation Summary   *210*

Q&A   *213*

Scenarios   *217*

Scenario 7-1   217

Scenario Answers   *218*

Scenario 7-1 Answers   218

Chapter 8   Establishing an X.25 Connection   221

How to Best Use This Chapter   221

"Do I Know This Already?" Quiz   222

Foundation Topics   *226*

X.25 Basics   226
DTE and DCE   228

X.25 Layered Model   229
X.25 Layer   229
X.121 Addressing   231
LAPB Layer   232
X.25 Physical Layer   233

Configuring X.25   233
Step 1: Setting the Interface Encapsulation, Specifying DCE or DTE   234
Step 2: Configuring the X.121 Address   234
Step 3: Mapping the Appropriate Next Logical Hop Protocol Address to its X.121
Address   234
X.25 Configuration Examples   235
Additional Configuration Options   237

Configuring the Range of Virtual Circuits   237
Configuring Packet Size   238
Configuring Window Size   238
Configuring Window Modulus   239
X.25 Final Configuration   239

Foundation Summary   *240*

Q&A   *241*

Scenarios   *245*

Scenario 8-1: X.25 Initial Configuration   245

Scenario 8-2: X.25 Options   246

Scenario Answers   *247*

Scenario 8-1 Answers   247

Scenario 8-2 Answers   248

Chapter 9   **Frame Relay Connection Controlling Traffic Flow   251**

How to Best Use This Chapter   251

"Do I Know This Already?" Quiz   252

Foundation Topics   *257*

Understanding Frame Relay   257
Device Roles   257
Frame Relay LMI   258

Frame Relay Topologies   259
Issues When Connecting Multiple Sites Through a Single Router Interface   260
Resolving Split Horizon Problems   261

Frame Relay Configuration   263
Step 1: Determine the Interface to Be Configured   263
Step 2: Configure Frame Relay Encapsulation   264
Step 3: Configure Protocol-Specific Parameters   264
Step 4: Configure Frame Relay Characteristics   264
Verifying Frame Relay Configuration   266
show frame-relay pvc Command   267
show frame-relay lmi Command   268
debug frame-relay lmi Command   268
show frame-relay map Command   269

Frame Relay Traffic Shaping   270
Frame Relay Traffic Parameters   270

FECN and BECN   271

Using Frame Relay Traffic Shaping   272

Frame Relay Traffic Shaping Configuration   272

Foundation Summary   276

Q&A   279

Scenarios   284

Scenario 9-1   284

Scenario 9-2   285

Scenario 9-3   285

Scenario Answers   286

Scenario 9-1 Answers   286

Scenario 9-2 Answers   287

Scenario 9-3 Answers   287

Chapter 10   Managing Network Performance with Queuing and Compression   291

How to Best Use This Chapter   291

"Do I Know This Already?" Quiz   292

Foundation Topics   296

Queuing Overview   296

FIFO   298

Weighted Fair Queuing   298

Configuring WFQ   299

Priority Queuing   300

Configuring Priority Queuing   301

Custom Queuing   306

Configuring Custom Queuing   308

Verifying Custom Queuing   312

Compression Overview   312

Link Compression   314

STAC   314

Predictor   314

Payload Compression   315

TCP Header Compression   315

Compression Issues   316

Configuring Compression   316

Foundation Summary   317

Q&A   319

Scenarios   324

Scenario 10-1   324

Scenario 10-2   325

Scenario 10-3   325

Scenario 10-4   326

Scenario Answers   327

Scenario 10-1 Answers   327

Scenario 10-2 Answers   327

Scenario 10-3 Answers   328

Scenario 10-4 Answers   329

Chapter 11   Scaling IP Addresses with NAT   331

How to Best Use This Chapter   331

"Do I Know This Already?" Quiz   332

Foundation Topics   336

Characteristics of NAT   336

Simple NAT Translation   338

Overloading   338

Overlapping Networks   339

TCP Load Distribution   340

NAT Definitions   342

NAT Configurations   343
Simple Dynamic NAT Configuration   344
Static NAT Configuration   345
NAT Overloading Configuration   346
NAT Overlapping Configuration   347
NAT TCP Load Distribution Configuration   349

Verification of NAT Translation   350

Port Address Translation   352

Foundation Summary   355

Q&A   356

Scenarios   361

Scenario 11-1   361

Scenario 11-2   361

Scenario 11-3   362

Scenario Answers   363

Scenario 11-1 Answers   363

Scenario 11-2 Answers   364

Scenario 11-3 Answers   364

Chapter 12 Using AAA to Scale Access Control in an Expanding Network   367

How to Best Use This Chapter   367

"Do I Know This Already?" Quiz   368

Foundation Topics   372

AAA Overview   372
  Authentication   372
  Authorization   373
  Accounting   373

Interface Types   373

AAA Configuration   374
  Enabling AAA   374
  AAA Authentication   375
    AAA Authentication Login   376
    AAA Authentication Enable   377
    AAA Authentication ARAP   378
    AAA Authentication PPP   379
    AAA Authentication NASI   380

AAA Authorization   381

AAA Accounting   382

Virtual Profiles   385

Foundation Summary   387

Q&A *389*

Scenarios *393*

Scenario 12-1   393

Scenario Answers *394*

Scenario 12-1 Answers   394

**Appendix A Answers to the "Do I Know This Already?" Quizzes and
             Q&A Sections   397**

Index   445

Professional certifications have been an important part of the computing industry for many years and will continue to become more important. Many reasons exist for these certifications, but the most popularly cited reason is that of credibility. All other considerations held equal, the certified employee/consultant/job candidate is considered more valuable than one who is not.

Goals and Methods

The most important and somewhat obvious goal of this book is to help you pass the Remote Access exam (#640-505). In fact, if the primary objective of this book was different, then the book's title would be misleading; however, the methods used in this book to help you pass the CCNP Remote Access exam are designed to also make you much more knowledgeable about how to do your job. While this book and the accompanying CD together have more than enough questions to help you prepare for the actual exam, the method in which they are used is not to simply make you memorize as many questions and answers as you possibly can.

One key methodology used in this book is to help you discover the exam topics that you need to review in more depth, to help you fully understand and remember those details, and to help you prove to yourself that you have retained your knowledge of those topics. So this book does not try to help you pass by memorization but helps you truly learn and understand the topics. The Remote Access exam is just one of the foundation topics in the CCNP certification and the knowledge contained within is vitally important to consider yourself a truly skilled routing/switching engineer or specialist. This book would do you a disservice if it didn't attempt to help you learn the material. To that end, the book will help you pass the Remote Access exam by using the following methods:

- Helping you discover which test topics you have not mastered

- Providing explanations and information to fill in your knowledge gaps

- Supplying exercises and scenarios that enhance your ability to recall and deduce the answers to test questions

- Providing practice exercises on the topics and the testing process via test questions on the CD

Who Should Read This Book?

This book is not designed to be a general networking topics book, although it can be used for that purpose. This book is intended to tremendously increase your chances of passing the CCNP Remote Access exam. Although other objectives can be achieved from using this book, the book is written with one goal in mind: to help you pass the exam.

So why should you want to pass the CCNP Remote Access exam? Because it's one of the milestones towards getting the CCNP certification; no small feat in itself. What would getting the CCNP mean to you? A raise, a promotion, recognition? How about to enhance your resume? To demonstrate that you are serious about continuing the learning process and that you're not content to rest on your laurels. To please your reseller-employer, who needs more certified employees for a higher discount from Cisco. Or one of many other reasons.

Strategies for Exam Preparation

The strategy you use for CCNP Remote Access might be slightly different than strategies used by other readers, mainly based on the skills, knowledge, and experience you already have obtained. For instance, if you have attended the BCRAN course, then you might take a different approach than someone who learned switching via on-the-job training. Chapter 1, "All About the Cisco Certified Network Professional and Design Professional Certification," includes a strategy that should closely match your background.

Regardless of the strategy you use or the background you have, the book is designed to help you get to the point where you can pass the exam with the least amount of time required. For instance, there is no need for you to practice or read about IP addressing and subnetting if you fully understand it already. However, many people like to make sure that they truly know a topic and thus read over material that they already know. Several book features will help you gain the confidence that you need to be convinced that you know some material already and to also help you know what topics you need to study more.

How This Book Is Organized

Although this book could be read cover-to-cover, it is designed to be flexible and allow you to easily move between chapters and sections of chapters to cover just the material that you need more work with. Chapter 1 provides an overview of the CCNP and CCDP certifications, and offers some strategies for how to prepare for the exams. Chapters 2 through 12 are the core chapters and can be covered in any order. If you do intend to read them all, the order in the book is an excellent sequence to use.

The core chapters, Chapters 2 through 12, cover the following topics:

- **Chapter 2, "Cisco Remote Connection Products"**—This chapter discusses analyzing criteria for placing a Cisco router in a network, selection of the WAN connection type for remote access purposes, determining site requirements in a central office, branch office and small/remote or home office, and selecting the proper Cisco network devices given a set of site requirements.

- **Chapter 3, "Assembling and Cabling WAN Components"**—This chapter discusses the basic ideas behind selection of routers for specific deployments, covers some of the possible types of physical connections that may be necessary for individual deployments, and explains how to confirm the physical connectivity of the WAN devices.

- **Chapter 4, "Configuring Asynchronous Connections with Modems"**—This chapter covers modem signaling, modem cofiguration using reverse Telnet, router line numbering, basic asynchronous configuration, configuration of the attached modem, and controlling modem connections with chat scripts.

- **Chapter 5, "Configuring PPP and Controlling Network Access"**—This chapter examines the underlying technology of the Point-to-Point Protocol (PPP) and its components; how to configure various options available with PPP such as authentication, PPP Callback, compression and PPP Multilink; and troubleshooting with the **show** and **debug** commands to deal with issues arising with PPP .

- **Chapter 6, "Using ISDN and DDR to Enhance Remote Connectivity"**—This chapter examines the underlying technology of ISDN and its components, the technologies relating to BRI specific implementation of ISDN technology, implementing basic DDR and advanced DDR options, as well as the concepts of and differences between T1 and E1 PRI-based implementations .

- **Chapter 7, "Configuring the Cisco 700 Series Router"**—This chapter covers Cisco 700 router key features and functions, Cisco 700 router profiles, configuring the Cisco 700 router for IP routing, the 700 series capability to be used as a router in a very small network, Dynamic Host Configuration Services (DHCP) from the perspective of a 700 series router, and configuration of the 700 series router as a DHCP server or helper agent

- **Chapter 8, "Establishing an X.25 Connection"**—This chapter covers the basics, layered model, and configuration options of X.25 technology.

- **Chapter 9, "Establishing Frame Relay Connections and Controlling Traffic Flow"**—This chapter examines the underlying technology of Frame Relay and its components; explores some of the implementation options available in Frame Relay deployments; covers configuration of Frame Relay including basic configuration, subinterfaces, point-to-point and multipoint options; discusses rate enforcement and traffic behavior modification capabilities in Frame Relay; and covers covers the configuration of the traffic shaping options available for Frame Relay.

- **Chapter 10, "Managing Network Performance with Queuing and Compression"**—This chapter discusses when to use queuing and assist in the decision of which queuing technique to use in the event that queuing is deemed necessary; examines Weighted Fair Queuing (WFQ), Custom Queuing, and Priority Queuing; and addresses the need for compression in today's enterprise network.

- **Chapter 11, "Scaling IP Addresses with Network Address Translation"**—This chapter covers the fundamentals of Network Address Translation (NAT); examines how a simple NAT translation replaces the outbound or inbound destination address with another address; discusses how to overload an address space with NAT, how to overlap networks using the same IP addresses, and how to do a simple TCP load distribution with NAT. In addition, this chapter defines the four NAT address classes, discusses four different NAT configurations and how to verify them, and concludes with a discussion of port address translation, which is a form of NAT that translates the port address as well as the network layer address.

- **Chapter 12, "Using AAA to Scale Access Control in an Expanding Network"**—This chapter covers the fundamentals of and configuration of authentication, authorization, and accounting (AAA). More specifically, this chapter covers how to discriminate interface types which AAA must be able to discern to operate effectively. Also covered are virtual profiles, which are the next generation of a dialer profile.

Example test questions and the testing engine on the CD allow simulated exams for final practice.

Each of these chapters uses several features to help you make best use of your time in that chapter. The featrues are as follows:

- **"Do I Know This Already?" Quiz and Quizlets**—Each chapter begins with a quiz that helps you determine the amount of time you need to spend studying that chapter. The quiz is broken into subdivisions, called "quizlets," that correspond to a section of the chapter. Following the directions at the beginning of each chapter, the "Do I Know This Already?" quiz will direct you to study all or particular parts of the chapter.

- **Foundation Topics**—This is the core section of each chapter that explains the protocols, concepts, and configuration for the topics in the chapter.

- **Foundation Summary**—Near the end of each chapter, a summary collects the most important tables and figures from the chapter. The "Foundation Summary" section is designed to help you review the key concepts in the chapter if you score well on the "Do I Know This Already?" quiz, and they are excellent tools for last-minute review.

- **Q&A**—These end-of-the-chapter questions focus on recall, covering topics in the "Foundation Topics" section by using several types of questions. And because the "Do" I Know This Already?" quiz questions can help increase your recall as well, they are restated in the Q&A sections. Restating these questions, along with new questions, provides a larger set of practice questions for when you finish a chapter and for final review when your exam date is approaching.

- **Scenarios**—Located at the end of most chapters, the scenarios allow a much more in-depth examination of a network implementation. Rather than posing a simple question asking for a single fact, the scenarios let you design and build networks (at least on paper) without the clues inherent in a multiple-choice quiz format.

- **CD-based practice exam**—The companion CD contains a large number of questions not included in the text of the book. You can answer these questions by using the simulated exam feature, or by using the topical review feature. This is the best tool for helping you prepare for the test-taking process.

Approach

Retention and recall are the two features of human memory most closely related to performance on tests. This exam preparation guide focuses on increasing both retention and recall of the topics on the exam. The other human characteristic involved in successfully passing the exam is intelligence; this book does not address that issue!

Adult retention is typically less than that of children. For example, it is common for four-year-olds to pick up basic language skills in a new country faster than their parents. Children retain facts as an end unto itself; adults typically either need a stronger reason to remember a fact or must have a reason to think about that fact several times to retain it in memory. For these reasons, a student who attends a typical Cisco course and retains 50 percent of the material is actually quite an amazing student.

Memory recall is based on connectors to the information that needs to be recalled—the greater the number of connectors to a piece of information, the better chance and better speed of recall.

Recall and retention work together. If you do not retain the knowledge, it will be difficult to recall it. This book is designed with features to help you increase retention and recall. It does this in the following ways:

- By providing succinct and complete methods of helping you decide what you recall easily and what you do not recall at all.

- By giving references to the exact passages in the book that review those concepts you did not recall so that you can quickly be reminded about a fact or concept. Repeating information that connects to another concept helps retention, and describing the same concept in several ways throughout a chapter increases the number of connectors to the same pices of information.

- By including exercise questions that supply fewer connectors than multiple-choice questions. This helps you exercise recall and avoids giving you a false sense of confidence, as an exercise with only multiple-choice questions might do. For example, fill-in-the-blank questions require you to have better recall than multiple-choice questions.

- Finally, accompanying this book is a CD-ROM that has exam-like, multiple-choice questions. These are useful for you to practice taking the exam and to get accustomed to the time restrictions imposed during the exam.

Icons Used in This Book

Router

Bridge

Hub

DSU/CSU

Catalyst
switch

Multilayer switch

ATM
switch

ISDN switch

Communication
server

Gateway

Access server

PC

PC with
software

Sun
Workstation

Mac

Terminal

File server

Web
server

CiscoWorks
Workstation

Printer

Laptop

IBM
mainframe

Front End
Processor

Cluster Controller/
3274 or 3174

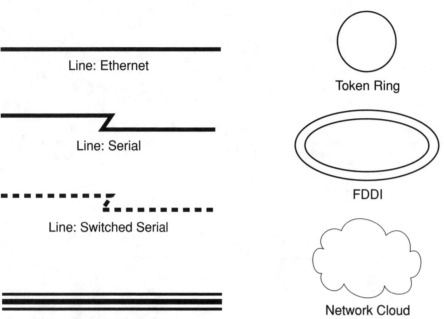

Line: Ethernet

Line: Serial

Line: Switched Serial

Frame Relay Virtual Circuit

Token Ring

FDDI

Network Cloud

Command Syntax Conventions

The conventions used to present command syntax in this book are the same conventoins used in the IOS Command Reference. The Command Reference describes these conventions as follows:

- Vertical bars (|) separate alternative, mutually exclusive elements.

- Square brackets [ ] indicate optional elements.

- Braces { } indicate a required choice.

- Braces within brackets [{ }] indicate a required choice within an optional element.

- **Boldface** indicates commands and keywords that are entered literally as shown. In actual configuration examples and output (not general command syntax), boldface indicates commands that are manually input by the user (such as a **show** command).

- *Italics* indicate arguments for which you supply actual values.

All About the Cisco Certified Network Professional and Design Professional Certification

The Cisco Certified Network Professional (CCNP) and the Cisco Certified Design Professional (CCDP) certifications prove that an individual has completed rigorous testing in the network arena. In addition, the CCNP and CCDP certifications are becoming more important than ever because Cisco is providing greater and greater incentives to their partners that have employees with CCNP- and CCDP-level expertise.

The CCNP and CCDP tracks require the candidate to be comfortable with advance routing techniques, switching techniques, and dial-up or Remote Access Server (RAS) technology. On top of those areas, the CCNP must be able to, without a book, configure and troubleshoot a routed and switched network. In addition, the CCDP must digest a vast quantity of user requirements and prepare a scalable design that fits the customer needs and requirements.

The CCNP is a hands-on certification that requires a candidate to pass the Cisco Internetwork Troubleshooting exam, which is also called the Support exam. The emphasis in the exam is on troubleshooting the router if the configuration for it has failed. CCNP is currently one of the most sought after certifications, short of the Cisco Certified Internetworking Expert (CCIE).

The CCDP track focuses on designing scaleable networks using routing and switching technologies. The exam places heavy emphasis on the interplay between routed and routing protocols. This track has a more theoretical final exam—the Cisco Internetwork Design (CID) exam. This certification is very important to the pre-sales engineer and the design engineer who want to prepare a network on paper, but who do not want to focus on the minor details of the syntax within the router.

Because both the CCNP and CCDP certifications are the same except for the final test, it should not be suprising that a CCNP can produce a solid, scalable design and that a CCDP can configure a router. The core issue between the certifications is the focus that the candidate wants to take into the business world.

The CCNP and CCDP tracks are daunting at first glance because they both require a number of tests. To become a CCNP or CCDP, a candidate must first be a Cisco Certified Network Associate (CCNA). The CCNP and CCDP certifications require study and proficiency in the three areas of advanced routing, in switching and RAS, and a specialization in either design or troubleshooting.

Neither CCNP or CCDP certification is a "one test and I'm home" exam. Each exam for these certifications is difficult in its own right because of the depth of understanding needed for each area of concentration. The focus of this book is the preparation for and passing of the CCNP/CCDP Remote Access Exam.

Some of the information in this book overlaps with information in the routing field, and you may have seen some of this book's information while studying switching. In addition, there are other certification books that specifically focus on advanced routing and switching. You might find some overlap in those manuals also. This is to be expected—all the information taken as a whole is what produces a CCNP or CCDP.

The exam is a computer-based exam that has multiple choice, fill-in-the-blank, and list-in-order style questions. The fill-in-the-blank questions are filled in using the complete syntax for the command, including dashes and the like. For the fill-in-the-blank questions, a tile button is given to list commands in alphabetical order. This is a real life saver if you can't remember if there is a dash or an "s" at the end of a command. Knowing the syntax is key, however, because the list contains some bogus commands as well as the real ones.

The exam can be taken at any Sylvan Prometric testing center (1-800-829-NETS or www.2test.com). The test has 62 randomly generated questions, and you have 90 minutes to complete it. As with most Cisco exams, you cannot mark a question and return to it. In other words, you must answer a question before moving on, even if this means guessing. Remember that a blank answer is scored as incorrect.

Most of the exam is straightforward; however, the first answer that leaps off the page can be incorrect. You must read each question and each answer completely before making a selection. If you find yourself on a question that is incomprehensible, try restating the question a different way to see if you can understand what is being asked. Very few candidates score 100 percent in all catagories—the key is to pass. Giving up just one question because of lack of diligence can mean the difference between passing and failing because there are so few questions. Four questions one way or the other can mean a change of 10–20 percent!!

Many people do not pass on the first try, but success is attainable with study. This book includes questions and scenarios that are designed to be more difficult and more in depth than most questions on the test. This was not done to show how much smarter we are, but to allow you a certain level of comfort when you have mastered the material in this book.

The CCNP and CCDP certifications are difficult to achieve, but the rewards are there, and will continue to be there, if the bar is kept where it is.

How This Book Can Help You Pass the CCNP Remote Access Exam

The primary focus of this book is not to teach material in the detail that is covered by an instructor in a five-day class with hands-on labs. Instead, we tried to capture the essence of each topic and to present questions and scenarios that push the envelope on each topic that is covered for the Remote Access test.

The audience for this book includes candidates that have successfully completed the Building Cisco Remote Access Networks (BCRAN) class and those that have a breadth of experience in this area. The **show** and **debug** commands from that class are fair game for questions within the Remote Access exam, and hands-on work is the best way to commit those to memory.

If you have not taken the BCRAN course, the quizzes and scenarios in this book should give you a good idea of how prepared you are to skip the class and test out based on your experience. On the flip side, however, you should know that although having the knowledge from just a classroom setting can be enough to pass the test, some questions assume a CCNA-level of internetworking knowledge.

Overview of Cisco Certifications

Cisco fulfills only a small portion of its orders through direct sales; most times, a Cisco reseller is involved. Cisco's main motivation behind the current certification program was to measure the skills of people working for Cisco Resellers and Certified Partners.

Cisco has not attempted to become the only source for consulting and implementation services for network deployment using Cisco products. In 1996 and 1997 Cisco embarked on a channel program in which business partners would work with smaller and midsized businesses with whom Cisco could not form a peer relationship. In effect, Cisco partners of all sizes carried the Cisco flag into these smaller companies. With so many partners involved, Cisco needed to certify the skill levels of the employees of the partner companies.

The CCIE program was Cisco's first cut at certifications. Introduced in 1994, the CCIE was designed to be one of the most respected, difficult-to-achieve certifications. To certify, a written test (also at Sylvan Prometric) had to be passed, and then a two-day hands-on lab test was administered by Cisco. The certifications were a huge commitment for the smaller resellers that dealt in the commodity-based products for small business and home use.

Cisco certified resellers and services partners by using the number of employed CCIEs as the gauge. This criterion worked well originally, partly because Cisco had only a few large partners. In fact, the partners in 1995–1997 were generally large integrators that targeted the midsized coporations with whom Cisco did not have the engineering resources to maintain a personal relationship. This was a win-win situation for both Cisco and the partners. The partners had a staff that consisted of CCIEs that could present the product and configuration with the same adroitness as the Cisco engineering staff and were close to the customer.

Cisco used the number of CCIEs on staff as a criterion in determining the partner status of another company. That status in turn dictated the discount received by the reseller when buying from Cisco. The number of resellers began to grow, however, and with Cisco's commitment to the lower-tier market and smaller-sized business, it needed to have smaller integrators that could handle that piece of the market.

The CCIE certification didn't help the smaller integrators who were satisfying the small business and home market; because of their size, the smaller integrators were not able to attain any degree of discount. Cisco, however, needed their skills to continue to capture the small business market, which was—and is—one of the largest markets in the internetworking arena today.

What was needed by Cisco was a level of certification that was less rigorous than CCIE but that would allow Cisco more granularity in judging the skills on staff at a partner company. So Cisco created several additional certifications, CCNP and CCDP included.

Two categories of certifications were developed—one to certify implementation skills and the other to certify design skills. Service companies need more implementation skills, and resellers working in a pre-sales environment needed more design skills. So the CCNA and CCNP are implementation-oriented certifications; whereas, the Cisco Certified Design Associate (CCDA) and CCDP are design-oriented certifications.

Rather than just one level of certification besides CCIE, Cisco created two additional levels— Associate and Professional. CCNA is more basic, and CCNP is the intermediate level between CCNA and CCIE. Likewise, CCDA is more basic than CCDP.

Several certifications require other certifications as a prerequsite. For instance, CCNP certification requires CCNA first. Also, CCDP requires both CCDA and CCNA certification. CCIE, however, does not require any other certification prior to the written and lab tests. This is mainly for historical reasons.

Cisco certifications have become a much needed commodity in the internetworking world as companies scramble to position themselves with the latest e-commerce, e-business, and e-life that is out there. Because Novell, Windows NT, Linux, or any other routed protocols generally need to be routed somewhere, the integrators want a piece of that business as well. Because Cisco cannot form a relationship with every new startup business, it looks for certified partners to take on that responsibility. The CCNP and CCDP certifications are truly another win-win situation for resellers, integrators, you, and Cisco.

The Remote Access Exam and the CCNP and CCDP Certifications

The Remote Access exam proves mastery of the features used in larger corporate dial-in facilities and Internet service provider (ISP) operations. Skills required for CCNP and CCDP certifications include the ability to install, configure, operate, and troubleshoot remote access devices in a complex WAN environment. Specifically, the remote access skills required ensure that the CCNP or CCDP candidate can ensure minimal WAN costs to the customer or client using the Cisco IOS features.

The Cisco features that are critical to this endeavor include dial-on-demand, bandwidth-on-demand, dial backup, snapshot routing, dialer-maps, and dialer profiles. In addition, successful candidates should be comfortable with Frame Relay, ISDN, PSTN, and X.25.

The target audience for CCNP and CCDP certification includes the following:

- Gold- or Silver-certified partners

- CCNAs who want increased earning power, professional recognition, job promotions, and so on

- Level 1 network support individuals that want to progress to level 2

- ISP professionals who want to gain a larger understanding of the Internet picture and its intricacies

A CCNP's training and experience enables him or her to accomplish the following:

- Install and configure a network to minimize WAN costs and to ensure connectivity from remote sites

- Maximize performance over a WAN link

- Improve network security

- Provide access to remote customers or clients

- Configure queuing for congested links to alleviate occasional congestion

- Provide dial-up connectivity over analog and digital networks

- Implement DDR backup services to protect against down time

Exams Required for Certification

You are required to pass a group of exams for CCNP or CCDP certification. The exams generally match the same topics that are covered in one of the official Cisco courses. Table 1-1 outlines the exams and the courses with which they are most closely matched.

Table 1-1   *Exam-to-Course Mappings*

Certification	Exam Number	Name	Course Most Closely Matching the Exam's Requirements
CCNA	640-507	CCNA	Interconnecting Cisco Network Devices (ICND)
CCDA	640-441	CCDP	Designing Cisco Networks
CCNP	640-503	Routing	Building Scalable Cisco Networks (BSCN)
	640-504	Switching	Building Cisco Multilayer Switched Networks (BCMSN)

continues

Table 1-1   *Exam-to-Course Mappings (Continued)*

	640-505	Remote Access	Building Cisco Remote Access Networks (BCRAN)
	640-509*	Foundation	BSCN, BCMSN, and BCRAN
	640-506	Support	Cisco Internetwork Troubleshooting (CIT)
CCDP	640-503	Routing	Building Scalable Cisco Networks (BSCN)
	640-504	Switching	Building Cisco Multilayer Switched Networks (BCMSN)
	640-505	Remote Access	Building Cisco Remote Access Networks (BCRAN)
	640-509*	Foundation	BSCN, BCMSN, and BCRAN
	640-025	CID	Cisco Internetwork Design (CID)

* Passing exam 640-509 meets the same requirements as passing these three exams: 640-503, 640-504, and 640-505.

Other Cisco Certifications

The certifications mentioned so far are oriented toward routing and LAN switching. Cisco has many other certifications, which are summarized in Table 1-2. Refer to Cisco's web site at www.cisco.com/warp/public/10/wwtraining/certprog/index.html for the latest information.

Table 1-2   *Additional Cisco Certifications*

Certification	Purpose, Prerequisites
CCNA-WAN	Basic certification for Cisco WAN switches
CCNP-WAN	Intermediate certification for Cisco WAN switches; requires CCNA-WAN
CCDP-WAN	Design certification for Cisco WAN switches; requires CCNP-WAN
CCIE-WAN	Expert level certification for Cisco WAN switches; no prerequisite; requires exam and lab
CCIE-ISP Dial	CCIE-level certification for Internet Service Provider (ISP) and dial-up network skills; no prerequisite; requires exam and lab
CCIE-SNA-IP	Expert level certification for Cisco products and features used for melding SNA and IP networks; no prerequisite; requires exam and lab
CCNP and CCDP specializations	Several specialized certifications are available for CCNP and CCDP (routing/switching); see www.cisco.com/warp/public/10/wwtraining/certprog/special/course.html for more details

What Is on the Remote Access Exam?

The Remote Access exam evaluates the knowledge of network administrators and specialists who must configure and maintain a RAS and the associated peripheral components that accompany it. Candidates attempting to pass the Remote Access exam must perform the following tasks:

- List and describe the remote access alternatives available and discuss the inherent advantages and disadvantages of each access method

- Configure the RAS for ISDN BRI and PRI access and asynchronous modem connectivity

- Use the appropriate debugging utilities to troubleshoot a connection

- Connect remote office routers to central office routers by dial-up WAN connections and demonstrate end-to-end connectivity

- Implement simple (local router) security and centralized (AAA) security methods

- Distinguish the correct router platform for various sites relating to growth, throughput, and performance

- Configure dial-on-demand and bandwidth-on-demand functions to minimize WAN costs

- Establish backup dial links to protect against primary line loss

- Configure and troubleshoot a Frame Relay connection using subinterfaces

- Configure a reverse Telnet session and maintain the modems used for the RAS device

- Provide queuing for congested links, and quality of service (QOS) for the customer

Topics on the Exam

Table 1-3 outlines the various topics that you are likely to encounter on the exam. The topics represent a detailed list for areas of focus, but are not intended as a list of test question topics. In fact, each listed topic can have subitems. For example, knowing that ISDN BRI stands for "Integrated Services Digital Network Basic Rate Interface" might not be enough knowledge for the test!

Table 1-3 lists the exam topics in the order in which they are found within this book.

Table 1-3 *CCNP/CCDP Remote Access Exam Topics*

Chapter	Topics
Chapter 2, "Cisco Remote Connection Products"	Protocols Overview, Selecting WAN Type and Site Considerations, Cisco Remote Access Solutions, Determining the Appropriate Interfaces, and Cisco Product Selection Tools
Chapter 3, "Assembling and Cabling the WAN Components"	Central/Branch Office/Telecommuter Site Equipment, Assembling and Cabling the Network, and Verifying Installation
Chapter 4, "Configuring Asynchronous Connections with Modems"	Asynchronous Signaling Methods, Reverse Telnet, Configuration of the Router Interface to Communicate Through a Modem, Configuration of a Chat-Script, Assignment of IP Addresses to a Remote Device, and Configuration of the Physical and Logical Parameters for Modem Communication
Chapter 5, "Configuring PPP and Controlling Network Access"	PAP and CHAP Configuration, Remote-Node Connection Overview, PPP Architecture, NCP Options, PPP Authentication, Callback, Compression, Multilink, and PPP Verifying and Troubleshooting
Chapter 6, "Using ISDN and DDR Technologies"	ISDN Overview, ISDN Services, Monitoring ISDN Connections, ISDN BRI and DDR, ISDN BRI Optional Configurations, DDR Overview, Rotary Groups, Dialer Profiles, ISDN PRI Configurations, PRI Incoming Analog Calls on Digital Modems, Backup Overview, Configuring Dial Backup, Using Dialer Interfaces, and Routing with Load Backup, Load Sharing
Chapter 7, "Configuring a Cisco 700 Series Router"	Overview and Features, IOS-700 Features, Profiles, Configuring the Cisco 700 Series, Routing with the Cisco 700 Series, Dynamic Host Configuration Protocol (DHCP) Overview, and Cisco 700 Series as DHCP Server and Relay Agent
Chapter 8, "Establishing an X.25 Connection"	X.25 Protocol, Virtual Circuits, Configuring X.25, and Setting up the Router as a X.25 Switch

Table 1-3   *CCNP/CCDP Remote Access Exam Topics (Continued)*

Chapter	Topics
Chapter 9, "Frame Relay Connection Controlling Traffic Flow"	Frame Relay Operations, Frame Relay Signaling, Configuring Frame Relay, Verifying Frame Relay Operations, Frame Relay Subinterfaces Overview, Configuring Frame Relay Subinterfaces, Frame Relay Traffic Shaping Overview and Terminology, Configuring Traffic Shaping, and Verifying Frame Relay Traffic Shaping
Chapter 10, "Managing Network Performance with Queuing and Compression"	Choosing a Queuing Method, Weighted and Priority Fair Queuing, Custom Queuing, Verifying Queuing Operations, Optimizing Traffic Flow with Data Compression, and Configuring Data Compression
Chapter 11, "Scaling IP Addresses with NAT"	NAT Overview and Terminology, NAT Operations, NAT Overloading, NAT Load Balancing, NAT Overlapping Addresses, Configuring, Verifying and Troubleshooting NAT, PAT Porthandler Operation, and Configuring and Monitoring PAT
Chapter 12 "Using AAA to Scale Access Control in an Expanding Network"	Overview of Cisco Access Control Solutions, Understanding and Configuring Authentication, Authorization and Accounting (AAA), and Using AAA with Virtual Profiles

Recommended Training Path for CCNP and CCDP

The recommended training path for the Cisco professional level certifications is, of course, the instructor-led courses:

- **Building Scalable Cisco Networks (BSCN)**—The BSCN class covers the advanced routing protocols and the scaling issues involved with a large routed network with multiple protocols.

- **Building Cisco Multilayer Switched Networks (BCMSN)**—The BCMSN class covers the switch infrastructure and the configuration in a large network environment.

- **Building Cisco Remote Access Networks (BCRAN)**—The BCRAN class covers the dial-up and RAS issues involved in large scale remote access designs and implementations.

After these courses, the CCNP requires Cisco Internetwork Troubleshooting as the final course. The CCDP requires Cisco Internetwork Design as the final course.

The previously listed courses are the recommended training events for passing the exams for the CCNP or CCDP track. However, as Cisco evolves the testing, the tests might not necessarily correlate to the given class. In other words, the tests can cover material that is germane to the material in the class but that might not have been covered per se. In essence, Cisco is looking for each test to be less a fact-stuffing event and more a gauge of how well you know the technology.

Figure 1-1 illustrates the training track for CCNP and CCDP, as of September 2000.

Figure 1-1   *CCNP/CCDP 2.0 Training and Exam Track*

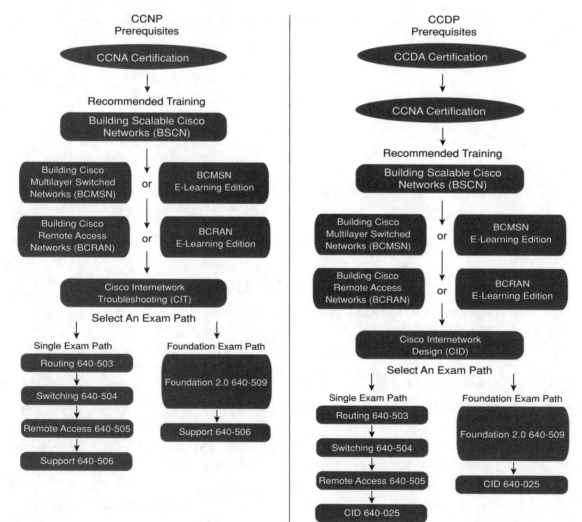

How to Use This Book to Pass the Exam

There are five sections in each chapter: a short pre-assessment quiz, the main topics of the chapter, a summary of the key points of the chapter, a test to ensure that you have mastered the topics in the chapter, and finally (when applicable), a scenario section with scenario-related questions and exercises.

Each chapter begins with a quiz, which is broken into "quizlets." If you get a high score on these quizlets, you might want to review the "Foundation Summary" section at the end of the chapter and then take the chapter test. If you score high on the test, you should review the summary to see if anything else should be added to your crib notes for a final run-through before taking the live test.

The "Foundation Summary" section in each chapter provides a set of "crib notes" that can be reviewed prior to the exam. These notes are not designed to teach, but merely to remind the reader what was in the chapter. Each "Foundation Summary" section consists of charts and raw data that complement an understanding of the chapter information.

If you score well on one quizlet, but low on another, you are directed to the section of the chapter corresponding to the quizlet on which you scored low. You'll notice that the questions in the quizlet are not multiple-choice in most cases. This testing format requires you to think through your answer to see if the information is already where you need it—in your brain! If you score poorly on the overall quiz, it is recommended that you read the whole chapter because some of the topics build on others.

At the end of most chapters are scenarios that require a compilation of all information in the chapter to complete. Much like an English teacher requiring you to write a sentence using a newly learned word because the word is no good if it cannot be applied, the scenarios provide an opportunity to apply the chapter data.

All quizlet and end-of-chapter questions, with answers, are in Appendix A, "Answers to the 'Do I Know This Already?' Quizzes and Q&A." These conveniently located questions can be read and reviewed quickly prior to taking the live test. The CD has testing software, as well as many additional questions similar to the format of the Remote Access exam. These questions should be a valuable resource when making final preparations for the exam.

Anyone preparing for the Remote Access exam can use the guidelines at the beginning of each chapter to guide his or her study. However, if you would like some additional guidance, the final parts of this chapter give additional strategies for study, based on how you have prepared before buying this book. So, find the section that most closely matches your background in the next few pages, and then read some additional ideas to help you prepare. There is a section for the reader who has passed other CCNP exams and is ready for the Remote Access Exam, one for the reader who has passed the CCNA and is starting the CCNP track, and one for the reader that has no Cisco certifications and is starting the CCNP track.

One Final Word of Advice

The "Foundation Summary" section and your notes are your "crib note" knowledge of Remote Access. These pieces of paper are valuable when you are studying for the CCIE or Cisco recertification exam. You should take the time to organize them so that they become part of your paper "long term memory."

Reviewing information that you actually wrote in your own handwriting is the easiest data to put back into your brain RAM. Gaining a certification but losing the knowledge is of no value. For most people, maintaining the knowledge is as simple as writing it down.

You Have Passed Other CCNP Exams and Are Preparing for the Remote Access Exam

Scenario 1: You Have Taken the BCRAN Course

Because you have taken other Cisco exams and have taken the BCRAN course, you know what you are up against. The Remote Access exam is like all the others. The questions are "Sylvanish" and the answers are sometimes confusing if you read too much into them.

The best approach with this book is to take each chapter "Do I Know This Already?" quiz and focus on the parts that draw a blank. It is best not to jump to the final exam until you have given yourself a chance to review the entire book. You should save it to test your knowledge after you have mentally checked each section to see that you have an idea of what the whole test could be. Remember that the CD testing engine spools out a sampling of questions and might not give you a good picture the first time you use it; the test engine could spool a test that is easy for you, or it could spool one that is very difficult.

Before the test, make your own notes using the "Foundation Summary" sections and your own handwritten notes. Writing something down, even if you are copying it, makes it easier to remember. Once you have your bank of notes, study them, and then take the final exam three or four times. Each time you take the test, force yourself to read each question and each answer, even if you have seen them before. Again, repetition is a super memory aid.

Scenario 2: You Have NOT Taken the BCRAN Course

Because you have taken other Cisco exams, you know what you are up against in the test experience. The Remote Access exam is like all the others. The questions are "Sylvanish," and the answers are sometimes confusing if you read too much into them.

The best approach with this book, because you have not taken the class, is to take each chapter's "Do I Know This Already?" quiz as an aid for what to look for as you read the chapter. Once you have completed a chapter, take the end-of-chapter test to see how well you have assimilated the material. If there are sections that do not seem to gel, you might want to consider buying a copy of the Cisco Press book *Building Cisco Remote Access Networks*, which is a hard copy of the material found in the BCRAN course.

Once each chapter has been completed, you should go back through the book and do the scenarios to verify that you can apply the material you have learned. At that point, you should then use the CD testing engine to find out where you are in your knowledge.

Before the test, make notes using the "Foundation Summary" sections and your own additions. Writing something down, even if you are copying it, makes it easier to remember. Once you have your bank of notes, study them, and then take the final practice exam on the CD testing engine three or four times. Each time you take the test, force yourself to read each question and each answer, even if you have seen them before. Again, repetition is a super memory aid.

You Have Passed the CCNA and Are Preparing for the Remote Access Exam

Scenario 1: You Have Taken the BCRAN Course

Because you have taken other Cisco exams and have taken the BCRAN course, you know what you are up against. The Remote Access exam is like all the others. The questions are "Sylvanish," and the answers are sometimes confusing if you read too much into them.

The best approach with this book is to take each chapter's "Do I Know This Already?" quiz and focus on the parts that draw a blank. It is best not to jump to the final exam until you have given yourself a chance to review the entire book. Save the final to test your knowledge after you have mentally checked each section to see that you have an idea of what the whole test could be. The CD testing engine spools out a sampling of questions and might not give you a good picture the first time you use it; the test engine could spool a test that is easy for you, or it could spool one that is very difficult.

Before the test, make your own notes using the "Foundation Summary" sections and your own additions. Writing something down, even if you are copying it, makes it easier to remember. Once you have your bank of notes, study them, and then take the final practice exam on the CD testing engine three or four times. Each time you take the test, force yourself to read each question and each answer, even if you have seen them before. Again, repetition is a super memory aid.

Scenario 2: You Have NOT Taken the BCRAN Course

Because you have taken other Cisco exams, you know what you are up against from the perspective of the test experience. The Remote Access exam is like the others. The questions are "Sylvanish," and the answers are sometimes confusing if you read too much into them.

The best approach with this book, because you have not taken the class, is to take each chapter's "Do I Know This Already?" quiz to determine what to look for as you read the chapter. Once you have completed a chapter, take the end-of-chapter test to see how well you have assimilated the material. If there are sections that do not seem to gel, you might consider buying a copy of the Cisco Press book *Building Remote Access Networks*, which is a hard copy of the material found in the course.

Once each chapter has been completed, you should go back through the book and do the chapter scenarios to see that you can apply the material you have learned. At that point, you should then use the CD testing engine to find out where you are.

Before the test, make your own notes using the "Foundation Summary" sections and your own additions. Writing something down, even if you are copying it, makes it easier to remember. Once you have your bank of notes, study them, and then take the final practice exam on the CD testing engine three or four times. Each time you take the test, force yourself to read each question and each answer, even if you have seen them before. Again, repetition is a super memory aid.

You Have Experience and Want to Skip the Classroom Experience and Take the Remote Access Exam

Scenario 1: You Have CCNA Certification

Because you have taken other Cisco exams, you know what you are up against in the test experience. The Remote Access exam is like the others. The questions are "Sylvanish," and the answers are sometimes confusing if you read too much into them.

The best approach with this book, because you have not taken the course, is to take each chapter's "Do I Know This Already?" quiz to determine what to look for as you read the chapter. Once you have completed a chapter, take the end-of-chapter test to see how well you have assimilated the material. If there are sections that do not seem to gel, you might want to buy a copy of the Cisco Press book *Building Remote Access Networks*, which is a hard copy of the material found in the course.

Once each chapter has been completed, you should go back through the book and do the chapter scenarios to see if you can apply the material you have learned. At that point, you should use the CD testing engine to find out where you are.

Before the test, make your own notes using the "Foundation Summary" sections and your own additions. Writing something down, even if you are copying it, makes it easier to remember. Once you have your bank of notes, study them, and then take the final practice exam on the CD testing engine three or four times. Each time you take the test, force yourself to read each question and each answer, even if you have seen them before. Again, repetition is a super memory aid.

Scenario 2: You DO NOT Have a CCNA Certification

Why don't you have the certification? The prerequisite for the CCNP certification is to be certified as a CCNA, so you really should pursue your CCNA certification before tackling the CCNP certification. Beginning with the Remote Access exam gives you a skewed view of what is needed for the Cisco Professional certification track.

That being said, if you *must* pursue the certifications out of order, follow the spirit of the book. Read each chapter and then do the quiz at the front of the chapter to see if you caught the major points. After you have completed all 12 chapters, do the scenarios and see if you can apply the knowledge. Once that is done, try the test and pay particular attention to the Sylvan-way of testing so that you are prepared for the live test.

Good luck to all!

This chapter covers the following topics that you need to master as a CCNP:

- **Identifying Selection Criteria for Router Placement**—This section addresses the questions raised when planning a Cisco network: Is the router going to be used at a central office facility, a branch office, or in support of telecommuters? What are the cost factors and how volatile is the proposed location?

- **Selecting a WAN Connection Type for Remote Access Purposes**—The WAN connection type directly affects the current and future needs of the customer and influences his or her level of satisfaction. This section addresses the selection process.

- **Determining Site Requirements**—The three sites described are central office, branch office, and the small office/home office (SOHO) or remote office (RO). The successful CCNP candidate should be aware of these sites and their associated requirements.

- **Hardware Selection**—If the site requirements and the WAN connection options are fully considered, the selection of the right product becomes an outgrowth of the design. The Cisco product selection guide can easily narrow the product selection to a short-list with the information gleaned from the site, application uses, bandwidth needs, backup requirements, and so on.

CHAPTER 2

Cisco Remote Connection Products

This chapter covers the selection of products for the central office, the branch office, and the SOHO or RO. The key is to know where product families fit, not to memorize individual product part numbers or codes. For instance, you can get by knowing the capabilities of the 3600 product family as compared to the 1600 product family, without getting into the granular details of either.

The bulk of the information in this chapter leads the engineer to ask the right questions when embarking on a new design. The points to consider include the following:

- **Availability**—The key question here is "Is there ISDN or DSL in my area, and can I get it?" Because we are talking about Remote Access, it is not a given that the service we might want is available.

- **Bandwidth**—What speed is needed for the applications that will use the link? It is important that the bandwidth handle the client's requirements. In general, clients who are extremely cost-conscience might look for solutions that are doomed to failure.

- **Cost**—This is one of the final selection criteria for an implementation. You must explore *all* the WAN options available because costs can vary between regions. In general, cost is directly related to the bandwidth requirement.

- **Ease of management**—Given any installation at any site, the cost of moves, adds, and changes should be factored into the design. CiscoWorks is a good choice for management software, but it is not your only choice.

- **Applications and traffic patterns**—This can be the most difficult task; however, it is by far the most critical. For example, a remote law office repeatedly uploading and downloading thousand-page documents can require a different solution than a remote insurance agency that sends a few pages of client information and that accesses a SQL database. The traffic patterns and needs define the bandwidth requirement, which in turn drives the cost.

- **Backup needs and Quality of Service (QoS)**—The need for backup links and QoS are important. For instance, what is the cost of downtime? If the cost is high, your high-speed Frame Relay circuit should be backed up by a low-cost ISDN line. Another consideration is the cost of loss of service if a dial link fails. If this happens, backup needs and costs should be weighed against the track record of the suppliers in the area for a given access technique.

- **Access control requirements**—In implementations for Remote Access, security is a major consideration. Because the users are not "local" to the location, it is imperative that you consider access control. This can be as simple as a local username/password database or as complex as using an AAA server in a firewall environment. The core issue is knowing the volume of security needed and the sensitivity of the data. For example, Joe and Bob's Tire Shop might require a simple password scheme for security, where Einstein's Genetic Research Corporation would want an environment that provides more control.

Cisco has categorized the locations in which a dial-up situation might be needed. These locations, central, branch, and remote/home office, are detailed in the following list:

- **Central office**—A central site should provide room for growth so that remote or branch sites can be added without a wholesale change at the aggregation site or central office. Considerations for a central site should include which bandwidths are required by each remote or branch and the additional bandwidth needed for growth. The cost of WAN services is also a central office concern because it supplies the bulk of the bandwidth needed for the enterprise. In addition, security and access control are other concerns at the central site.

- **Branch office**—A branch office is smaller than a central site and gives a presence to the company in a specific region. The branch office considerations involve connecting to the central site while knowing the value/cost ratio of the bandwidth. In addition, the availability of the central site connection should be considered. Is backup needed? Does dial-on-demand suffice for this connection? What kind of data will be transferred? Like the central site, costs need to be controlled in the branch office site, but money is not the overriding concern.

- **SOHOs and ROs**—CCDPs implementing SOHOs and ROs are generally more cost-conscious because of the number of the offices in a given situation. The small SOHO or RO must have the capability to connect using the WAN service selected and available, but maintaining multiple unlike devices is not a good idea. For instance, it is best to use the 1600 family at all remotes sites, including the home sites, even if some sites don't need that much power. The placement of unneeded power is balanced by the fact that the engineer must maintain only a few configuration plans.

How to Best Use This Chapter

By taking the following steps, you can make better use of your study time:

- Keep your notes and answers for all your work with this book in one place for easy reference.

- Take the "Do I Know This Already?" quiz and write down your answers. Studies show retention is significantly increased through writing facts and concepts down, even if you never look at the information again.

- Use the diagram in Figure 2-1 to guide you to the next step.

Figure 2-1   *How to Use This Chapter*

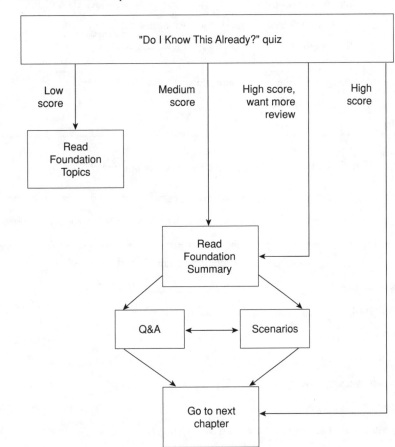

"Do I Know This Already?" Quiz

The purpose of the "Do I Know This Already?" quiz is to help you decide which parts of this chapter to use. If you already intend to read the entire chapter, you do not necessarily need to answer these questions now.

The six-question quiz helps you determine how to spend your limited study time. The quiz is sectioned into smaller "quizlets," each of which corresponds to the four major topic headings in the chapter. Use the scoresheet in Table 2-1 to record your scores.

Table 2-1   *Scoresheet for Quizlets and Quiz*

Quizlet Number	Foundation Topics Section Covered by These Questions	Questions	Score
1	Identifying Selection Criteria for Router Placement	1–2	
2	Selecting a WAN Connection Type for Remote Access Purposes	3	
3	Determining the Site Requirements	4	
4	Hardware Selection	5–6	
All questions		1–6	

1   What are the selection criteria for selecting a router platform?

_____

_____

_____

2   Which of the following does not affect the installation of a router?

   a. availability

   b. reliability

   c. cost

   d. router port density

   e. security requirements

   f. bandwidth usage

3   In routing, what is meant by the term *availability*?

_____

_____

_____

Generally speaking, the information you must consider to select the appropriate piece of network hardware consists of the following:

- **Availability**—Ask yourself if you can get the service in your area, and what are the geographic restrictions to this technology, who are service providers and what is the backhaul network or infrastructure that will carry your data past the last mile? Availability is the most critical criterion for many out-of-the-way ROs and SOHOs. Remember that telecommuting from a ranch in Big Bend might sound fantastic, but determining the modes of communication that are available is the key consideration behind the implementation.

- **Reliability and QoS**—Will voice or video be added at a later time? How critical is the traffic? If it is a brokerage house or online banking institution, the aspect of reliability may override all other factors. If it is a local tire shop, which checks inventory at the warehouse, the reliability of the link may not be mission critical. The loss of this link during a bad storm or local power outage may be a minor concern to the tire shop. If there is no local power then you probably can't install any tires anyway. Is a backup link needed? Is the link critical enough to warrant backup services for it? If you are a home user and you lose your phone or ISDN service do you need a backup?

- **Cost**—WAN fees must be paid every month. This parameter is the driving force behind many decisions, as it should be. The Cisco DDR feature enables the WAN link to be present when interesting traffic, as defined by the administrator or customer, warrants it. The bandwidth-on-demand (BoD) feature is another method to reduce WAN costs but maintain speed.

- **Security requirements and access control**—Today many companies are embracing the idea of e-commerce. Consumers, customers, and outsiders are given access to different parts of the internal corporate network. To protect the internal network, you should know what type of control is in place, what type can be put in place, and how much each type costs. A small biotechnical research firm, whose only asset is the information on the network, might be willing to expend a great deal of effort to ensure protection. On the other hand, a small tire shop might be willing to expend only a small amount.

- **Bandwidth usage**—*Speed* is a better way to describe this issue. You should know how much information can be received and how much must be received. Not enough bandwidth leads to congestion and frustration for the SOHO, RO, or branch office. In fact, too little bandwidth can be the same as none.

- **Ease of management**—Any solution must be palatable to the customer. If the administrative overhead of a solution outweighs the viability of the solution it may be more costly. A solution that continually needs to be fixed, upgraded, changed, or tweaked is a poor choice in terms of time. On the other hand, any solution that is totally free from management worries generally costs too much. The issue is to offer the right management solution for each situation.

4 In routing, what is meant by the term *reliability*?

_____

_____

5 Name two important issues that you must consider when selecting a product for a SC

_____

_____

_____

6 What product would you select for a central office facility that had to support three to fiv branch offices using Frame Relay circuits from 64–256 Kbps and that had 20–30 occasional dial-up users?

_____

_____

The answers to the "Do I Know This Already?" quiz are found in Appendix A, "Answers to the 'Do I Know This Already?' Quizzes and Q&A Sections," on page 397. The suggested choices for your next step are as follows:

- **You correctly answered four or fewer questions overall**—Read the chapter. This includes the "Foundation Topics," "Foundation Summary," and "Q&A" sections, as well as the scenarios at the end of the chapter.

- **You correctly answered five or more questions overall**—If you want more review on these topics, skip to the "Foundation Summary" section, and then go to the "Q&A" section and the scenarios at the end of the chapter. Otherwise, move to the next chapter.

Foundation Topics

Router Selection Criteria for Remote Access Purposes

The selection of a hardware product for Remote Access usage is an art form to some extent, and the biggest router possible is not always the best router. For instance, information gathered about the site is also critical.

- **Application traffic**—You should know the type of traffic that is carried on the link. Is the link primarily used for file transfer or email? What are the packet sizes? What type of delay is acceptable? For example, if a file transfer takes two seconds over a LAN but ten minutes over a WAN link, is this acceptable? Application traffic and the actions of your customers are critical to your decision.

Once each piece of information has been gathered, router selection is easy because knowing what needs to be done and how much has to be done by the router helps you select the right router for the job.

Much of the information in the previous bulleted list could be considered common sense; however, many consumers of WAN technology buy a big router because it is better than a small router. The cost of any networking equipment is small compared to the monthly cost to maintain the WAN service. The decision process should focus strictly on the usage and needs.

This section discussed that there is no one answer to what a customer needs. Each installation and each design is unique to the situation that is being solved. The value-added reseller (VAR) or integrator must focus on the business of the customer rather than the business of selling the same router to each customer.

Selecting a WAN Connection Type for Remote Access Purposes

Once you define customer needs, you must select carrier technology to support the applications that are identified. For Remote Access, the choices (in descending order of speed and control) are as follows:

- **Leased line**—A leased line gives the consumer complete control of the facility in terms of what data is to be put on it. The customer effectively owns the bandwidth of the link. This ownership offers high security and control to the customer; however, this is probably the highest cost solution available. Although lease facilities with very high data rates (up to multiple megabit) can be obtained, the issue is how much bandwidth, and at what cost, the consumer is willing to purchase.

- **Frame Relay**—Frame Relay service probably carries the majority of business circuits in the United States. With this service, the customer somewhat controls the resources being used by specifying a Committed Information Rate (CIR) or guaranteed rate of delivery. The Frame Relay provider, however, controls the latency or delay through the network, and speed is a function of the provider's offerings. Speeds can range up to multiple megabit transfer rates; however, they are generally available only up to T1 (1.544 Mbps). With Frame Relay, the issue of cost is lessened because many companies share the circuits.

- **ISDN**—Integrated Services Digital Network (ISDN) offers more bandwidth than a simple dial-up link; however, it is a circuit-switched connection and is subject to availability of the remote end. The control of the circuit is given over to the provider. Speed for ISDN is limited to 128 Kbps for a remote user using a Basic Rate Interface (BRI).

- **Asynchronous dialup**—Simple modem connectivity such as asynchronous dialup is sometimes all that is needed for communication. Speeds are limited to 53 kbps or slower, depending on the type of connection and the modem being used. Dialup is the most inexpensive of all communication methods and is available almost everywhere.

Once you settle on the criteria of need and availability, your next step is to determine the requirements for installing the hardware at various sites.

Determining the Site Requirements

In general, each company site can be placed into one of three categories: central, branch, or SOHO or RO. Each type of site provides different opportunities for growth. The sections that follow provide insight into which platforms would be used at each site.

Central Site Installations

If the installation is taking place in a central or corporate headquarters site, room for growth should be a strong consideration. Room for growth is important because remote or branch sites can be added or deleted over time and the hardware platform should be flexible so that a "fork-lift" upgrade is not needed every time a change in corporate strategy occurs.

Decisions for the central office should include evaluation of speeds and feeds. The speeds should be sufficient to aggregate the information flows from the branch and remote sites. With speeds, cost is a major consideration because the recurring WAN charges are the dominant cost factor. In fact, hardware costs pale in comparison to the ongoing costs for WAN charges. Firewalls and access control (feeds) are also top considerations because the central site must maintain and enable outside communication, but protect against unauthorized access.

Branch Office Installations

If the installation is to be done in a branch office, there is less need for flexibility than with the central site. This does not mean that a fixed configuration device is acceptable, however. It still might be more palatable for the router to contain enough ports for expansion. Branch office support generally includes access to smaller single function remote offices or remote users.

Considerations at the branch office include the WAN connection type and the monthly costs. Additionally, the branch office must be able to authenticate itself to the central site.

The issue of availability is another critical factor in the branch office. You must know how often and how long a connection will be needed and if a backup is necessary. The central office generally uses links that are always available or highly reliable, whereas the branch office might not want to pay for that reliability.

Remote Office or Home Office Installations

An installation at either of these locations is likely to have a fixed function device that was chosen with cost as a main factor. Once the election of the access method is made, it is unlikely to change in the near term.

The traffic or data that exits the RO or HO can usually be categorized very neatly. An example of this categorization would be a remote salesperson who must gain download corporate pricing and upload sales data and email.

The overriding consideration at these offices is generally cost. In addition, the RO must maintain a method for authentication to the branch or central site and justify the connection time to a central or branch office. In general, these offices would use a dial-on-demand methodology to minimize WAN charges.

Hardware Selection

When the research is done and the location is selected, the last step is to select a router that meets the specifications created.

Cisco is continually updating the product line for all types of WAN scenarios. The best way to stay current with the offerings available for RAS solutions is at the Cisco web site at www.cisco.com.

The products in the following section represent some of the current offerings for Remote Access environments. The successful CCNP or CCDP candidate should be aware of the capabilities and limitations of each product family and where the devices from each family can be implemented.

Product Families: Capabilities and Limitations

The Cisco 700 series family of routers supports IP and IPX routing over ISDN. Routers from this family have no scalability for adding ports and were designed for ROs and SOHOs.

A 700 series router is an inexpensive ISDN access device. Figure 2-2 illustrates a Cisco 700 series router.

Figure 2-2 *Cisco 700 Series Router*

The Cisco 800 series family of routers is the lowest priced entry-level router that runs the IOS software. Because the base operating system for the 800 series router is the same as for the higher end router platforms, this platform enables the corporate staff to use the same language to configure the remote device. The Cisco 800 series router is ideal for the RO or SOHO.

The WAN options for the 800 series are the same as for the 700 series. Figure 2-3 illustrates a Cisco 800 series router.

Figure 2-3 *Cisco 800 Series Router*

One of the older device families, the Cisco 1000 series family of routers provides either ISDN or serial connections for the branch office or RO. A router from this family can be used for X.25 or Frame Relay and is sometimes called an end-node router.

The key feature of this router family is that it provides an expanded set of WAN options. It is a fixed configuration router, so the selection of the WAN option must be made prior to purchase.

Figure 2-4 shows a Cisco 1000 series router.

Figure 2-4   *Cisco 1000 Series Router*

The Cisco 1600 series is relatively new and offers a modular construction that enables the WAN interfaces to be changed by the customer as needed.

The WAN cards in a 1600 series router can be shared with routers from the 2600 and 3600 router series. This enables the maintenance of only a small set of hot-spare boards.

The 1600 uses the trademark IOS and is generally positioned at a branch office site and not at a RO or SOHO.

Figure 2-5 illustrates a Cisco 1600 series router.

Figure 2-5   *Cisco 1600 Series Router*

The Cisco 2500 router series is the oldest router platform mentioned so far. A router from this series is a fixed configuration router that offers a wide range of options for the branch or central office.

This router series is not modular. If a different port configuration is needed, a new 2500 is required.

Figure 2-6 illustrates a Cisco 2500 series router.

Figure 2-6   *Cisco 2500 Series Router*

The Cisco 2600 series router is replacing the current 2500 router due to its flexibility with the WAN card design. The 2600 can support many different hardware configurations in a single chassis. In fact, the customer can mix and match both LAN and WAN resources by simply changing boards on the chassis. The 2600 series router is generally positioned in a branch office site or small central facility.

Figure 2-7 illustrates a Cisco 2600 series router.

Figure 2-7   *Cisco 2600 Series Router*

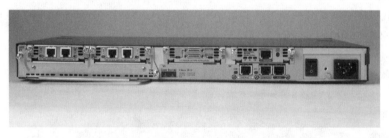

The Cisco 3600 series provides two, four, or six module slots, depending on the model. The 2600 series router provides only two. A 3600 series router is considered a central office piece of equipment because the flexibility and port density are so high.

Figure 2-8 illustrates a Cisco 3600 series router.

Figure 2-8   *Cisco 3600 Series Router*

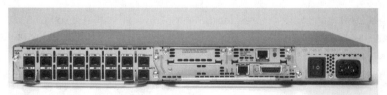

The Cisco 4500 and 4700 series router models are being eclipsed by the 3600; however, they are still viable products.

The 4500 and 4700 series provide a modular design similar to the 3600 and are intended for large regional offices and central office facilities that require a high rate of throughput.

Figure 2-9 illustrates the Cisco 4xxx series router.

Figure 2-9   *Cisco 4xxx Series Router*

The Cisco AS5000 series routers (specifically, the 5200 and 5300 routers) provide a high port density and are typically found at an Internet service provider's (ISP) Point-of-Presence (POP).

The AS5000 chassis incorporates the functions of modems, switches, routers, and channel banks into a single platform. In addition, the AS5000 series can support serial, digital, ISDN, and asynchronous access through a single physical interface. This support of mixed media makes this router very useful for a central office environment in which many different branch offices and ROs must be supported.

Figure 2-10 illustrates a Cisco AS5300 series router.

Figure 2-10   *Cisco AS5300 Series Router*

The Cisco 7200 series router is used in a RAS environment. The 7200 series can provide a central site with many high-speed interfaces in which many branch offices can be aggregated.

Figure 2-11 shows several Cisco 7200 series routers.

Figure 2-11   *Cisco 7200 Series Router*

The preceding router descriptions represent much of the Cisco product line. To properly install this equipment, you should consult Cisco's web site (www.cisco.com) to gain the most up-to-date information.

Although it is possible to review the entire suite of Cisco products before making a product decision for an installation, to do so would be time consuming. To help with the selection task, you should use the Cisco Product Selection Tool, which is available on CD-ROM and Cisco's web site. This tool enables the user to quickly narrow a selection to a small handful of router platforms by paring down the Cisco product line so that only the router platforms that match the search criteria are displayed.

In addition to using the Product Selection Tool, the customer or consumer can simply provide the requirements to a Cisco-certified VAR or to a Cisco sales engineer and ask which products satisfy the requirements. This advice might sound a bit trite, but Cisco is truly focused on ensuring that the right solution is provided in every instance in which their products are used. The emphasis that Cisco has placed on the certification process for their VARs is just one piece of evidence that supports this statement.

Foundation Summary

The section is a collection of information that provides a convenient review of many key concepts in this chapter. For those of you already comfortable with the topics in this chapter, this summary could help you recall a few details. For those of you who just read this chapter, this review should help solidify some key facts. For any of you doing your final preparation before the exam, these tables and figures will hopefully be a convenient way to review the day before the exam.

The selection of router products should be based on the following criteria:

- Availability

- Bandwidth

- Cost

- Ease of management

- Applications and traffic patterns

- Backup needs and QoS

- Access control requirements

In general, each company site can be placed into one of three categories: central, branch, or remote. Table 2-2 outlines considerations for each type of site.

Table 2-2   *Site Considerations*

Site	Major Considerations
Central	Cost of WAN services
	Bandwidth growth
	Flexibility
	Access control
Branch	WAN availability
	Backup needs
	Ease of management
	Application traffic patterns
RO or SOHO	Cost of equipment
	Ease of management

Table 2-3   *Router Model Usage Location Table*

Router Model	Site Usage	Notes
700	Home office	Inexpensive ISDN access router
800	Remote office/Branch office	IOS software; ISDN access router
1000	Remote office/Branch office	ISDN/serial LAN extender
2500/2600	Branch office	Medium flexibility with mid-range cost; supports a variety of LAN/WAN technologies
3600	Central office	High-flexibility, high-cost modular configuration that supports any office configuration
5000	Central office	Specifically targeted at high-density RAS sites that support a large number of dial-up users over both analog and ISDN lines
7000	Central office	Provides high-powered, high-cost, core router functionality

Table 2-4   *WAN Connection Options Table*

Method	Speeds	Notes
Leased Lines	All speeds	High control; high bandwidth
	Up to T1/T3	High-cost, enterprise network usage
Frame Relay	Up to T1 speed	Medium-control, shared-bandwidth, branch office usage
X.25	Up to T1 speed	Low-control shared bandwidth that is generally considered to be old technology
ISDN	PRI-T1 speed; BRI-128 kbps	Low-control shared bandwidth that is faster than asynchronous dialup
Asynchronous	Up to 53 kbps	Low control and variable cost that is effective for limited usage environments

Q&A

The questions and scenarios in this book are more difficult than what you will experience on the actual exam. The questions do not attempt to cover more breadth or depth than the exam; however, they are designed to make sure that you know the answer. Rather than enabling you to derive the answer from clues hidden inside the question itself, the questions challenge your understanding and recall of the subject.

Questions from the "Do I Know This Already?" quiz from the beginning of the chapter are repeated here to ensure that you have mastered the chapter's topic areas. Hopefully, mastering these questions will help you limit the number of exam questions on which you narrow your choices to two options and then guess.

The answers to these questions can be found in Appendix A, on page 397.

1 What are the selection criteria for selecting a router platform?

_____

_____

_____

2 Which of the following does not affect the installation of a router?

a. availability

b. reliability

c. cost

d. router port density

e. security requirements

f. bandwidth usage

3 Of the 3600, 4800, 5300, and 7100 series routers, which provides a high dial-up port density for an ISP?

_____

_____

_____

4   Which of the following statements is true?

   a. All interface cards used in the 2600 can be used in the 1600.

   b. All interface cards used in the 1600 can be used in the 2600.

   c. All interface cards used in the 3600 can be used in the 1600.

   d. All interface cards used in the 3600 can be used in the 2600.

5   In routing, what is meant by the term *availability*?

   _____

   _____

   _____

6   In routing, what is meant by the term *reliability*?

   _____

   _____

   _____

7   Backup is a consideration when looking at which of the following criteria: availability, reliability, traffic patterns, or QoS?

   _____

   _____

   _____

8   What WAN connection method affords the most control for the consumer?

   _____

   _____

   _____

9   Name two important issues in the selection of a product for a SOHO.

   _____

   _____

   _____

10 What WAN methods offer the least control to the customer?

_____

_____

_____

11 What product would you select for a central office facility that had to support three to five branch offices using Frame Relay circuits from 64–256 Kbps and that had 20–30 occasional dial-up users?

_____

_____

_____

12 What router would be appropriate for a SOHO user who is using ISDN and who is very cost-conscious?

_____

_____

_____

13 A branch office must connect to the central site over Frame Relay at 64 kbps. No growth is expected for the next two years, at which time Frame Relay connectivity for two satellite sites will be added at 64 kbps. What router platform would you recommend?

_____

_____

_____

14 The administration is considering supplying routers for all their ISDN dial-up users. The network administrators are comfortable with the IOS and must implement the dialup for 20 users over the next few months. What equipment would you propose for the central office and the SOHOs?

_____

_____

_____

Scenarios

The following scenarios and questions are designed to draw together the content of the chapter and exercise your understanding of the concepts. There is not necessarily a right answer. The thought process and practice in manipulating each concept in the scenario is the goal of this section.

Scenario 2-1

You have decided to use a 3640 router for the central office to support 15 dial-up users and two Frame Relay connections attached to your corporate Ethernet.

1 What modules would be needed for your router?

2 Would you offer BoD to your dial-up users?

3 How can you offer ISDN dial-up service?

Scenario 2-2

You provide leased-line connectivity (T1s) from your central office to three branch offices that supply time-critical information for your customers. In addition, the central site maintains an ISP connection for the branch office users to do research. The branch office has less than 10 users who constantly upload small files to the corporate data warehouse. In addition, they use the leased line for e-mail and Web surfing.

1 What backup plans would you consider?

2 What controls might you place on the backup links?

3 What router would you recommend for the branch offices?

Scenario Answers

The answers provided in this section are not necessarily the only possible correct answers. They merely represent one possibility for each scenario. The intention is to test your base knowledge and understanding of the concepts discussed in this chapter.

Should your answers be different (as they likely will be), consider the differences. Are your answers in line with the concepts of the answers provided and explained here? If not, go back and read the chapter again, focusing on the sections related to the problem scenario.

Scenario 2-1 Answers

1 An Ethernet module, a channelized T1, a MICA modem bank, and a multiport serial card are recommended. The Ethernet module provides connectivity to the local LAN. The T1 and MICA bank fulfill the dial-up needs, and the serial card enables Frame Relay.

2 Given the fact that you have 24 channels and 15 occasional dial-up users, multilink or BOD should be considered to improve the service.

3 The question should be "How can I offer analog service?" because MICA modems require analog service. This question requires you to think about how termination is done for both analog and digital in the same device.

Scenario 2-2 Answers

1 ISDN would be a good choice because of the higher speed. You might consider making sure that the service is divergent into your branch office so that if the frame fails due to a "back-hoe attack," the ISDN line has a chance of being uninterrupted.

2 Access control is a major issue. If the primary link fails, the backup link should block all noncritical traffic such as HTTP so that the mission critical information is not lost. It is assumed that the reason for the T1 is that the bandwidth is needed. If an ISDN BRI is used for backup, the highest possible link would be 128 kbps, hence the need for strict control.

3 A 1600 router should be sufficient, although a 2600 router would also work. Given the fact that there are only three remotes, you might want to go with the 1600 router and buy two for each location so that in the event of a hardware failure, a hot swap could be done.

This chapter covers the following topics that you need to master as a CCNP:

- **Choosing WAN equipment**—This section discusses the basic guidelines behind the selection of routers for specific deployments.

- **Assembling and cabling the equipment**—This section goes over some of the possible types of physical connections that can be necessary for individual deployments.

- **Verifying the installation**—This section explains how to confirm the physical connectivity of the WAN devices.

CHAPTER 3

Assembling and Cabling the WAN Components

The CCNP Remote Access Exam requires you to have an in-depth understanding of various WAN technologies. This chapter focuses on the cabling requirements of various technologies.

Although individual WAN topologies can require specific cabling variances and Frame Relay implementations require little or no variance from implementations of High-Level Data Link Control (HDLC), the physical cabling is virtually identical. However, other technologies can have different requirements depending on the location (internal or external) of WAN devices, such as CSU/DSU's or NT1's.

This chapter explores the basics behind racking and cabling the remote access devices discussed in this book. The discussion in this chapter focuses on routers.

How to Best Use This Chapter

By taking the following steps, you can make better use of your study time:

- Keep your notes and answers for all your work with this book in one place for easy reference.

- Take the "Do I Know This Already?" quiz and write down your answers. Studies show retention is significantly increased through down writing facts and concepts, even if you never look at the information again.

- Use the diagram in Figure 3-1 to guide you to the next step.

Figure 3-1 *Do I Know This Already?*

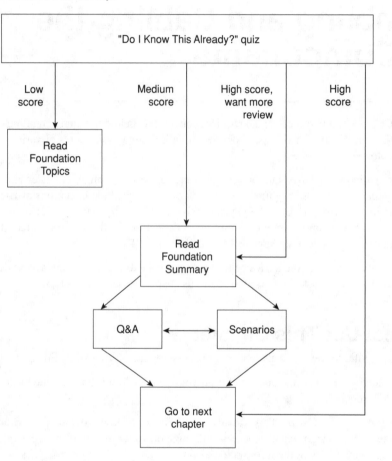

"Do I Know This Already?" Quiz

The purpose of the "Do I Know This Already?" quiz is to help you decide what parts of this chapter to use. If you already intend to read the entire chapter, you do not necessarily need to answer these questions now.

The six-question quiz helps you make good choices about how to spend your limited study time. The quiz is sectioned into smaller, two-question "quizlets," each of which corresponds to the three major topic headings in the chapter. Use the scoresheet in Table 3-1 to record your scores.

Table 3-1   *Scoresheet for Quizlets and Quiz*

Quizlet Number	Foundation Topics Section Covered by These Questions	Questions	Score
1	Choosing WAN Equipment	1–2	
2	Assembling and Cabling the equipment	3–4	
3	Verifying the Installation	5–6	
All questions		1–6	

1 Which router is best used as a central site router: 2611, 3640, or 1004?

_____

_____

_____

2 Which router best serves as a small office or home office (SOHO) router for telecommuters: 7200, 700, or 7500?

_____

_____

_____

3 Which WAN technology is best suited for providing high-density dial-up access for remote users?

_____

_____

_____

4 Which WAN technology is best suited for variable bandwidth (low-speed to high-speed) deployments that enable the connection of multiple branch offices to a central site?

_____

_____

_____

5 What does a green LINK LED signify on an Ethernet interface?

_____

_____

_____

6 On a 1600 router, what is the CD LED?

_____

_____

_____

The answers to the "Do I Know This Already?" quiz are found in Appendix A, "Answers to the 'Do I Know This Already?' Quizzes and Q&A," on page 397. The suggested choices for your next step are as follows:

- **You correctly answered four or fewer questions overall**—Read the chapter. This includes the "Foundation Topics," "Foundation Summary," and "Q&A" sections, as well as the scenarios at the end of the chapter.

- **You correctly answered one or fewer questions on any quizlet**—Review the subsections of the "Foundation Topics" part of this chapter, based on the information that you entered in Table 3-1. Then move into the "Foundation Summary" and "Q&A" sections and the scenarios at the end of the chapter.

- **You correctly answered five or more questions overall**—If you want more review on these topics, skip to the "Foundation Summary" section, and then go to the "Q&A" section and the scenarios at the end of the chapter. Otherwise, move to the next chapter.

Foundation Topics

The discussions in this chapter revolve around a fictitious, albeit typical, network topology. Figure 3-2 depicts that topology.

Figure 3-2   *Network Topology for Chapter Discussion*

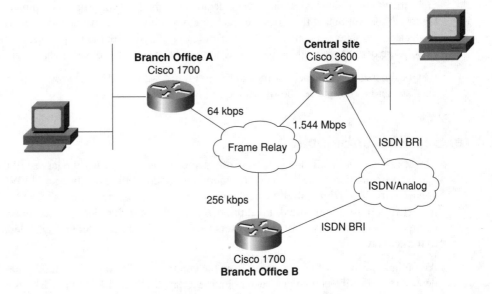

Figure 3-2 depicts a number of technologies in the network. These technologies (ISDN, Frame Relay, X.25, and so on) are discussed in this book at various times and are not discussed in this chapter.

You must understand the concepts and components involved in properly connecting WAN devices. Frame Relay, ISDN (BRI and PRI), and other Layer 2 technologies are necessary implementation in your WAN deployment. Choosing the proper technology is a decision that is based on the goals of the network at each step.

The goals of the network must be laid out ahead of time. Some of the questions you should consider include

- What do you wish to gain from this specific deployment?
- How many users must it support?
- How much bandwidth is necessary to support the applications in use at each site?
- Which router model(s) support the needs of the site?

- Has future growth been taken into account?

- Will the selected WAN components support an upgrade, or will a new component be necessary?

Choosing WAN Equipment

Once the goals of the network have been decided on, the hunt for proper equipment begins. Choosing the equipment that goes into each site is always an interesting endeavor. Vendors are contacted, and sales personnel visit and relentlessly tell you that their equipment is the best. Wisely, the decision is made to go with Cisco products (as if there were ever a doubt).

Obviously, the needs of each individual site in Figure 3-2 vary. The next few sections focus on each site and its unique technological requirements.

Central Site Router Selection

The central site is usually the corporate office site and is also usually the largest of the sites. With this distinction comes the need for more diverse capabilities with regard to WAN connectivity. Many times, multiple technologies must be supported at this site, and all facets of the network must be supported. In addition, each of the branch offices connects back to the central site, and remote and/or mobile users need to be able to connect through telephone lines to the network.

All of these needs must be supported from the central site. To do so, you must simultaneously deploy a number of technologies, such as Frame Relay, ISDN BRI/PRI (T1 or E1), asynchronous modems, network authentication, serial connections, bandwidth issues, and the list goes on. Many times the solution involves a combination of the options listed here, and then some.

For serial connections as well as T1/E1 PRI, you should know that inside of North America, the customer (that is, your company) is responsible for providing a CSU/DSU for the installation of the network. For BRI connections, the customer must provide the NT1. Outside of North America, however, these devices are generally telco-provided.

The issue of the point of demarcation (demarc) arises when setting up the central site. The demarc is the point at which responsibility for the line changes from the telco to customer or vice versa.

The demarc is placed in the section of the premises at which the telephone equipment is installed. Many times, however, this is not the desired location of the router, so a choice must be made. Should you have the demarc extended, or extend it yourself? Usually, it's much easier (although slightly more expensive) to have the telco installer extend the demarc for you. On the customer side of the demarc, the devices installed are known as customer premises equipment (CPE). Extending the point of responsibility transfer saves you a great number of headaches.

Obviously, all the possibilities for a central site router cannot be discussed at this time. There are too many variables (and the exam doesn't even touch on all of them anyway). However, you should know that many mid- to high-range routers, including WAN access and Access server routers, support multiple technologies and port densities for the central site router.

In this chapter we discuss the 36X0, 4000, AS5X00, and 7200 series routers. Keep in mind that there are high-end routers, such as the 7500 series, 12000 series, and so on. However, these high-powered routers are beyond our scope at the moment.

3600 Router Series

The 3600 series is a versatile family of routers; for variations of supported technologies, it is hard to beat. It is a multifunctional platform that enables routing of data, voice, video, and dial access capabilities in a single chassis.

The 3600 series offers three chassis variants: 3620, 3640, and the new 3660. The 3620 has two module slots, the 3640 has four module slots, and the 3660 has six module slots. Each module slot can contain MICA modems for dial-in access, voice network modules for telephone connectivity directly to the router, and data network modules.

The beauty of this series is that all these technologies can be implemented simultaneously in one chassis. All the interface components can be removed, serviced, and inserted without taking the chassis out of the rack. In addition, all the modules use spring screws that won't detach from the component, so there is no more looking for that dropped screw.

NOTE   The modules for this router are not hot-swappable! You must turn off the power before inserting or removing any component.

The 3620 probably is not the best choice for a central installation. Although it is a highly versatile and capable router, it simply doesn't have the port density necessary for deploying a wide spectrum of technologies simultaneously.

The 3640 and 3660 shine in their support of the varying technologies and speeds in the typical Enterprise deployment. These two models combine mix and match capabilities with the horsepower necessary to support a wide array of variables. For instance, these two routers can provide dial-up access (through MICA modem modules), ISDN, Frame Relay, and X.25 services in a single chassis. In any central site deployment, this type of flexibility is imperative.

4000 Router Series

The 4000 series is tried and tested. The routers in this series are established models. This router family makes use of Network Processing Modules (NPM) to implement different technologies. These individual cards can be mixed and matched to some degree for various technologies. LAN and WAN NPMs can be installed simultaneously at varying line speeds and encapsulations.

Although this series is somewhat versatile, any changing of components requires the removal of the entire motherboard tray. Care should be taken here. Many 4000 routers have been destroyed at this point because although there is a handle on the tray that facilitates its removal, most people are not ready for the sudden weight change when the end of the tray clears the chassis and the whole thing drops. Newer 4000 chassis have a clip built in that stops the tray to get your attention; when the tray stops, you have to move the clip aside to continue removing the board.

A router in the 4000 series is a good choice for a central site. However, the technological advances and added features of the 3600 series tend to make them more attractive.

AS5X00 Router Series

This family of routers is an Access Server line (hence the AS in the name). The available models in the line are the AS5200, the AS5300, and the AS5800. The series also includes a very high-end model known as the AccessPath. It consists of a number of AS5300s operating together in a single integrated rack with a Catalyst switch collocated.

The AS5X00 family of devices can provide carrier class service scalability as well as multiprotocol routing services. These devices are usually deployed in an ISDN installation to provide remote users dial-up access to internetwork resources. The AS5300 is Voice-over-IP capable with the proper line cards installed.

This family of routers is designed to perform best in dial-up access environments. The routers offer high-density voice and data solutions. The AS5200 is an older model and is quickly being replaced by the AS5300. The AS5300 can terminate both digital and analog data calls. There are three slots in an AS5300. It supports four or eight T1/E1 ports in a single slot, with MICA modems or VOIP feature cards in the other two slots, which are typically PRI ports. With eight T1s, the incoming call volume can reach 192 calls (240 with E1s). With the other two slots populated with MICA modem blades, that capacity can easily be supported.

For extremely high call volume, the AS5800 model is available. It can handle six 12-port T1/E1 trunk cards (72 T1/E1 ports). This means it can handle up to 1728 B channels at T1 or 2160 B channels at E1. This density enables hot sparing.

The AS5800 model has the capability to support 10 MICA modem line cards, each of which is capable of handling 72 calls (720 total). With only 14 line card slots, it obviously cannot do both T1/E1 and MICA modem cards at the same time; however, this combination is very common.

Inbound calls to an AS5800 router can be digital from another ISDN device or analog from a dial-up user. Therefore, this router is a good choice for central site dial-up facilities. In a mixed technology environment with multiple WAN technologies, this router probably isn't the best choice, but for dial-up deployments, it's hard to beat.

7200 Router Series

This family of routers has been around for a while and represents a wide install base. These devices provide high-power core LAN/WAN routing capabilities as well as voice integration capabilities. ATM, ISDN, and circuit emulation services are just a few of the available options supported.

If an AS5800 solution is being put in place, this router is absolutely necessary. It provides the router shelf function for the AS5800. Without the 7200, the AS5800 does not function.

The 7200 has a six-slot chassis. The port modules can be mixed and matched for varying degrees of connectivity and bandwidth. The newer VXR version of the 7200 includes a TDM bus, which provides better performance than its predecessors. This router is a great choice for the central site, based on its flexibility and overall power.

Branch Office Router Selection

Branch office sites are the source of many debates when the time comes to connect them to the central site through a WAN implementation. The amount of bandwidth necessary to adequately support the site is a crucial factor in the decision-making process. The technology implemented to provide the necessary bandwidth is equally important.

Consider a small branch office of three users with low bandwidth needs. ISDN BRI might be a good fit for the installation. However, what if the office grows to 20 users in a short time? At that point, the 128 kbps can be inadequate to support them, and ISDN BRI has no additional bandwidth to offer.

If the bandwidth becomes inadequate, a technology and/or router change becomes necessary. However, the time and costs involved may not be feasible at the current time. Would adequate planning and an alternate choice of technology have prevented the issue? Yes, they may have prevented the issue, if there were any indication that this particular office was going to grow as it did. Overall, it's sometimes a guessing game.

This section of the chapter focuses on some router families that meet the needs of the small- to medium-sized branch office. These are the 1600, 1700, 2500, and 2600 series routers. Note that the 3620 can also be a good choice for the branch office, when flexibility is needed. However, it was discussed in the previous section and need not be revisited.

1600 Router Series

This family of routers is generally meant to extend networks to small offices. These routers are flexible in their physical configuration options, but cannot support high port densities. The 1600 has a small footprint (read: not rack mountable), so it fits just about anywhere in the wiring closet. If it is to be placed in a rack, it requires a shelf to sit on.

All 1600 router implementations include one or two LAN ports and a single WAN port. For dedicated connectivity back to the central site, this router would provide a solid base.

1700 Router Series

This router family is designed for the small- to medium-sized office. It can support one to four WAN connections and Ethernet or Fast Ethernet connectivity. It is quite similar in some regards to its 1600 router cousin. However, it tends to be a higher horsepower device.

A 1700 series router is seen in some circles as the replacement to the 2500 series router. It can provide multiple WAN connections simultaneously and is a strong, stable router. It has a small footprint and is easy to work with. This flexibility and growth capacity make it an ideal choice for a small- to medium-sized branch office. If it is to be placed in a rack, it requires a shelf to sit on.

2500 Router Series

The 2500 is the workhorse of the product line. Its chassis is arguably the most deployed router model in the world. It has a seemingly endless array of configuration options. Typically, 2500 series routers are mission-specific; that is, they are usually fixed configuration chassis. They can support almost any technology in some form or fashion.

The 2500 is the most deployed router model in Cisco's line. With the varying interface configurations it offers, it's proven itself very valuable. Its downfall has been the introduction of devices with higher speeds and lower costs. It's well known that this router works well in almost any situation. However, it may not work as quickly as its newer counterparts. If speed is the issue (as it usually is), the 1700 or 2600 probably are better choices.

2600 Router Series

A cousin to the 3620 series, the 2600 series can support multiservice offerings of voice, video, and data in a single chassis. Analog or digital telephony are options for this box. Traditional LAN/WAN routing options are, of course, available as well.

This router too is seen as a viable replacement for the 2500 series routers. It is rack mountable and flexible in its configuration. It combines high-speed processing capabilities with mix and match port types.

For branch offices with integrated voice and data, the 2600 series router would be a good choice. However, in a data only environment, it cannot offer the port density necessary for a medium-sized branch office.

Small Office/Home Office (SOHO) Router Selection

This is a somewhat newly emerging market. The growing needs of the telecommuter are a very real aspect of today's internetwork deployments. Cisco offers a couple options with regard to SOHO deployments. Depending on the company and the needs of the telecommuter, a 2500 or 2600 router could be utilized. However, Cisco's 700, 800, and 1000 series routers can be a more manageable and ideal solution.

700 Router Series

The options available here are the 760 or 770. These are primarily low-cost ISDN routers. It should be noted that although these routers are easily managed, they do not run the Cisco IOS. Therefore, the rules and methods of configuring other Cisco routers do not apply to this one. This could be a good thing or a bad thing, depending on the preferences of the person performing the configuration. Users who prefer the IOS command-line interface (CLI) may not like it as well because it does not respond to the same command structure.

This router is well suited to SOHO use; however, it is limited to ISDN. If ISDN is not the technology of choice, this may not be the solution for you. The 700 router is addressed in detail later in this book.

800 Router Series

The 800 series connects small offices and corporate telecommuters to the Internet or to a corporate LAN through ISDN, serial connections (Frame Relay, leased lines, X.25, or asynchronous dial-up), IDSL, and ADSL. It also enables customers to take advantage of value-added services, such as differentiated classes of service, integrated voice/data, business class security, and virtual private networks (VPNs).

The routers in the 800 series run the Cisco IOS and are a good choice if the needs of the SOHO include low port density with flexible WAN technology options.

1000 Router Series

The 1000 router series is the LAN extender router series. Routers in this series run Cisco IOS Software and are capable of implementing technologies other than ISDN. The 1004 router is used with ISDN, and the 1003 router is used with Frame Relay.

The 1000 series routers provide a single LAN and a single WAN interface. The 1004 includes a single ISDN BRI (S/T or U) interface. The 1003 includes a single serial interface. The 1600 and 800 series routers are seen as replacements to the 1000 series because routers in the 1000 series are nearing their end of life.

Assembling and Cabling the Equipment

There are a number of types of physical connectivity options available based on the technologies being implemented. This section touches on the basics behind these connections. Much of what this section holds is review for most people with any significant time in the industry. For more in depth information regarding physical connectivity, pinouts for individual cables, and other requirements, check out www.cisco.com.

Available Connections

For this section, refer to Figure 3-3, which represents a number of technologies. Note that if all the labels are removed from the figure, the various connectivity possibilities become numerous.

Figure 3-3 *Connection Types*

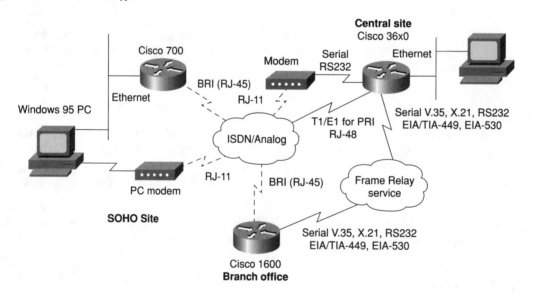

A few of the connection options in Figure 3-3 come up on a regular basis:

- **Frame Relay**—Frame Relay connections are serial connections only. EIA/TIA-232, EIA/TIA-449, V.35, and X.21 are the supported serial connections for Cisco routers. V.35 is the most common connection type for most areas; however, popularity varies. These connections make use of electrically specific transition cables that should be purchased along with the router.

- **ISDN BRI**—BRI connections are known as 2B+D connections. However, 1B+D and 0B+D implementations are available for deployment. An ISDN BRI connection makes use of Category 5 cabling to connect to the demarc. It may be necessary to provide an external NT1 if one is not integrated into the router. You can tell whether one is integrated by the label on the interface. A BRI interface with an integral NT1 is labeled as *BRI U*, and a BRI interface without an integral NT1 is labeled as *BRI S/T*. These connections make use of RJ-45 cables, which are typically Category 4 or 5 in quality.

- **ISDN PRI**—This implementation varies, based on geographic location. Based on ISDN technology, PRI makes use of T1 or E1 characteristics. Outside of North America, you will very likely encounter E1 PRI. Inside of North America, you will encounter T1 PRI. The primary difference between the two is the number of bearer channels. T1 PRI makes use of 23B+D connectivity, and E1 PRI makes use of 30B+D connectivity. E1 PRI obviously has a significantly higher bandwidth capacity than T1 PRI. These connections make use of category 4 or 5 RJ-45 cables.

- **Asynchronous**—These connections make use of RJ-11 cables. They are dial-up connection interfaces designed to accept calls from remote users. If utilizing external modems, EIA/TIA-232 cables are necessary to connect the modem to the router. It is feasible to have all modems internal to the router as well.

Verifying the Installation

The task of verifying physical connectivity is usually an easy one. If all is well, there is an LED on the front of the router (or on the back by the interface in question) that is green. If it's not green, it's time to figure out why.

During the boot process, the LEDs may flash green. This is completely normal. Other models of Cisco devices have an amber colored light during the boot sequence. However, once the router has booted, all active and functioning LEDs should turn to solid green. You'll hear the phrase "Green is good" over and over in many Cisco classes and environments.

For most routers, identifying the LEDs is the difficult part. This section focuses on some of the routers discussed in previous sections to give you some idea of where to find the proper LEDs for your specific needs. For additional information, refer to the installation guide that came with your specific router.

Central Site Router Verification

Each router model has its own set of LEDs. They're usually located in the same places. Overall status LEDs, such as *Enabled* and *Active* LEDs, are usually on the front of the chassis. The interface specific LEDs are on the back of the chassis, adjacent to the interface in question.

The rule with LEDs is simple: "Green is good." Any other color should be investigated. With the model by model differences in mind for individual routers, this discussion focuses on only a couple chassis models, rather than all the models that have been discussed in this chapter.

3600 Router LEDs

The 3600 series chassis architecture was a departure from the traditional router chassis architecture in that the CON and AUX ports are on the front of the box. This has received mixed reviews overall. The LEDs that share the front of the box with the CON and AUX ports enable the administrator to monitor at a glance the status of the router. The Ready LED (located on the front of the router) indicates that a functional network module is in the indicated slot. As traffic traverses the router, the Activity LED blinks according to the volume of the traffic. The Enable LED specifies whether the module has passed the power on self-test (POST). Obviously, if no module has been inserted into a particular slot, the appropriate LEDs remain dark. Figure 3-4 illustrates the positioning of the LEDs on the 3640 router.

Figure 3-4   *3640 Router LEDs*

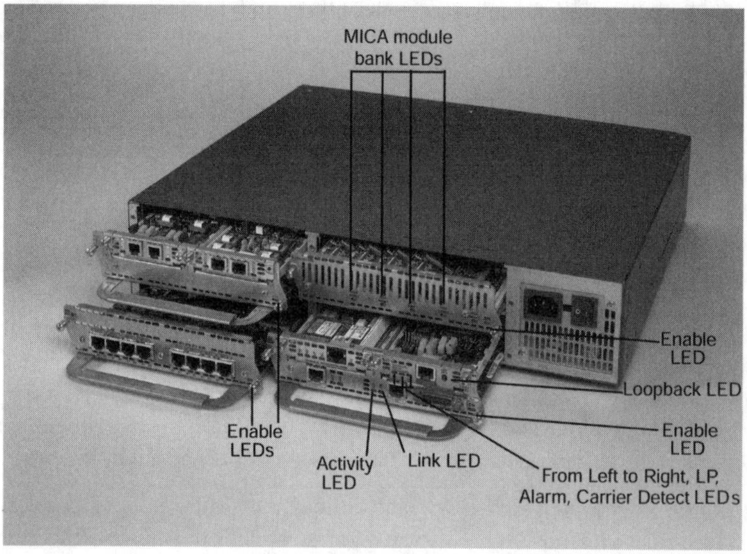

Each interface on each network module in a 3600 has its own LEDs to provide status. Ethernet (two LEDs), Serial (five LEDs), PRI (four LEDs), and so on all have interface-specific LEDs. Each type of interface can have a different number of LEDs to communicate status and activity. Ethernet interfaces, for example, have only two LEDs: Link and Activity. The Link LED specifies that the cable is properly connected to the hub or switch. The Activity LED specifies that LAN traffic has been detected on the wire.

Branch Office Router Verification

LEDs are LEDs. The "Green is good" rule still applies no matter the type of router with which you are dealing. Each branch office router has its own set of LEDs, as was the case with the central site routers. Again, all models discussed previously are not mentioned; only a single chassis is discussed.

1600 Router LEDs

The 1600 router is a mission-specific router. It's capable of sustaining one WIC, one BRI, and one LAN interface. LEDs on the router consist of those appropriate to each type of interface as well as two system LEDs. Refer to Figure 3-5 for the 1600 LEDs.

Figure 3-5   *1600 Router LEDs*

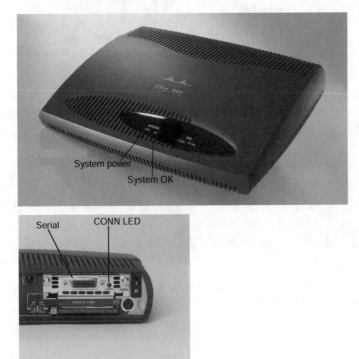

The system LEDs are PWR and OK. They are fairly self-explanatory. The PWR LED should be green if the router is powered on. The OK LED should be green if the router has passed the POST. The OK LED flashes during the router boot sequence.

The BRI interface LEDs consist of one LED for each B channel (B1 and B2). Each is green only when that B channel is connected to a remote site.

There are two WIC LEDs. The CD LED is green once an active connection is established on the serial interface. The ACT (Activity) LED is green once traffic is detected on the WAN interface. On the back of the router, the WIC itself has an LED (CONN) indicating that data is traversing the link.

SOHO Router Verification

These routers are generally quite small. Many of them are not much larger than the old Hayes and US Robotics modems of the 1980s. There is only so much that can be said about LEDs before the point is over emphasized. As in the two previous sections, this discussion focuses on a single router chassis, in this case, the 770 router. Figure 3-6 depicts the LEDs in this discussion.

Figure 3-6   *770 Router LEDs*

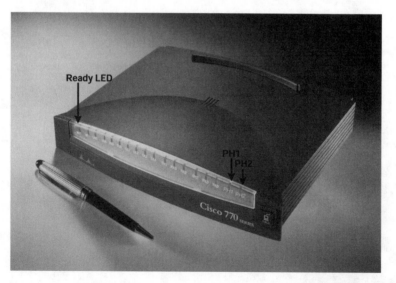

As you can see in the figure, there are a number of LEDs on this box. Table 3-2 analyzes the relevant LEDs, from left to right.

Table 3-2   *770 Router LEDs*

LED	What the LED Indicates
RDY	This LED is the Ready indicator. It is green when the router is powered up.
NT1	This LED indicates that the internal NT1 (an ISDN device that provides the basic functionality of a CSU/DSU in an ISDN environment) in the 770 is active. While synchronizing with ISDN terminal devices, the LED blinks once per second. When synchronizing with telco switching equipment, it blinks 5 times per second.
LINE	This LED indicates synchronization between the ISDN S interface and the ISDN terminal device(s).
LAN	This LED indicates that a frame has been sent or received on the interface in the last minute.
LAN RXD	This LED signifies that traffic has been received on the Ethernet interface.
LAN TXD	This LED signifies that traffic has been sent from the Ethernet interface.
CH1	This LED is the indicator for the first ISDN B channel. Once a connection has been established on the first B channel, this LED lights.
CH1 RXD	This LED indicates the receipt of traffic on the first ISDN B channel.
CH1 TXD	This LED indicates the transmission of traffic on the first ISDN B channel.
CH2	This LED is the indicator for the second ISDN B channel. Once a connection has been established on the first B channel, this LED lights.
CH2 RXD	This LED indicates the receipt of traffic on the second ISDN B channel.
CH2 TXD	This LED indicates the transmission of traffic on the second ISDN B channel.
PH1, PH2	These LEDs are analog POTS (plain old telephone service) ports that are green only when the attached devices (such as a phone, fax, and so on) are in use.
LINK	Located on the back of the router near the Ethernet interface, this LED indicates physical connectivity to the Ethernet segment.

Foundation Summary

Overall, this chapter dealt with physical connectivity for the router. Most cables are interface-specific in that they can be attached at only one place on the router. That is not always the case, however. For example, Category 5 UTP cable can be used with Ethernet, T1/E1 WIC, and ISDN interfaces. You should take the time to ensure that the correct cable is attached in the appropriate place. A straight-through Ethernet cable does not work in a T1/E1 WIC connection. The pinouts are dissimilar.

LEDs are an important part of the router. They provide a quick status of the router and its interfaces. A red or amber LED is worthy of investigation. Remember, green is good.

Table 3-3 documents the site types and the Cisco router options applicable to each location type.

Table 3-3   *Cisco Routers Applicable to Central, Branch, and SOHO Locations*

Site	Applicable Routers
Central	3600, 4000, AS5X00, 7200
Branch	1600, 1700, 2500, 2600
SOHO	700, 800, 1000

Q&A

The questions and scenarios in this book are more difficult than what you will experience on the actual exam. The questions do not attempt to cover more breadth or depth than the exam; however, they are designed to make sure that you know the answer. Rather than enabling you to derive the answer from clues hidden inside the question itself, the questions challenge your understanding and recall of the subject.

Questions from the "Do I Know This Already?" quiz from the beginning of the chapter are repeated here to ensure that you have mastered the chapter's topic areas. Hopefully, mastering these questions will help you limit the number of exam questions on which you narrow your choices to two options and then guess.

If you incorrectly answer one of the following questions, review the answer and ensure that you understand the reason(s) why your answer is incorrect. If you are confused by the answer, refer to the text in the chapter to review.

The answers to these questions can be found in Appendix A, on page 397.

1   Which router is best used as a central site router: 2611, 3640, or 1004?

_____

_____

_____

2   Which router best serves as a small office or home office (SOHO) router for telecommuters: 7200, 700, or 7500?

_____

_____

_____

3   Which WAN technology is best suited for providing high-density dial-up access for remote users?

_____

_____

_____

4 Which WAN technology is best suited for variable bandwidth (low-speed to high-speed) deployments that enable the connection of multiple branch offices to a central site?

_____

_____

_____

5 What does a green LINK LED signify on an Ethernet interface?

_____

_____

_____

6 On a 1600 router, what is the CD LED?

_____

_____

_____

7 List four routers that would be suitable for use as central site routers.

_____

_____

_____

8 List three routers that would be suitable for use as branch office routers.

_____

_____

_____

9 List a possible cause of an OK LED not being green on a 1600 router.

_____

_____

_____

10 List a possible cause of a LINK LED not being lit on an Ethernet interface.

_____

_____

_____

Scenarios

The following scenarios and questions are designed to draw together the content of the chapter and exercise your understanding of the concepts. There is not necessarily a right answer to each scenario. The thought process and practice in manipulating the related concepts is the goal of this section.

Scenario 3-1

Consider Figure 3-7 for the purposes of this scenario.

Figure 3-7   *Scenario 3-1 Topology*

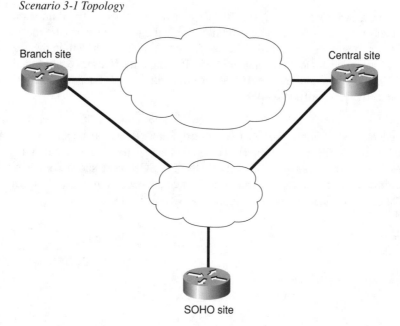

The goal in this case is to adequately deploy the proper technologies and line speeds to support the sites in the figure. Complete the scenario by meeting the needs of each step specified in the tasks that follow.

1   Make the decision as to which types of routers should be deployed at each site. For the central site, assume 100+ users and that the number is growing. For the branch site, assume 10 users, and for the SOHO site, assume a single user.

2   Based on your router choices, deploy WAN topology appropriate to your choices.

Scenario Answers

The answers provided in this section are not necessarily the only possible correct answers. They merely represent one possibility for the scenario. The intention is to test your base knowledge and understanding of the concepts discussed in this chapter.

Should your answers be different (as they likely will be), consider the differences. Are your answers in line with the concepts of the answers provided and explained here? If not, go back and read the chapter again, focusing on the sections related to the problem scenario.

Scenario 3-1 Answers

1 For the growing central site, with 100+ users, it can be necessary to implement a 7200 router or higher. A 3640 could certainly handle the job. However, care must be taken in regards to future growth. If the site has few or no plans for growth in the near future, the 3640 is a good choice. The branch office site with only 10 users could function with a 1700, 2600, or similar router. The SOHO site with a single user will likely use ISDN for connectivity and a 1004 or 700 router.

2 For the central site connecting to the branch site, a single dedicated circuit can be implemented. If future sites are to be added, Frame Relay can be appropriate. According to Figure 3-7, there is a secondary connection between the central and branch sites. Secondary connections are typically ISDN. The SOHO site shows connectivity to the same cloud as the secondary central-to-branch connection. Also, with the selection of a 700 or 1004 router, the obvious connectivity choice is ISDN.

This chapter covers the following topics that you need to master as a CCNP:

- **Modem signaling**—This section covers the transfer of data, the flow control for the signal and the modem, and the call termination methods that are defined by the modem signal pins.

- **Modem configuration using reverse Telnet**—This section describes reverse Telnet, which provides a method to communicate with a device that is attached to an asynchronous port on the router.

- **Router line numbering**—In this section, each router asynchronous interface has an associated line number where the physical and datalink parameters are configured. The line numbering is different between the fixed and nonfixed configuration router models.

- **Basic asynchronous configuration**—This section covers the configuration of the physical interface so that it can communicate with the attached device. In the same way that you configure a COM port to talk to a modem on a PC, you must declare to a router the parameters that match the modem settings.

- **Configuration of the attached modem**—In this section, you learn that a modem must be configured to answer a call and to provide the correct signalling for the telephone company. This is done using the modem command language, which uses the AT command set.

- **Chat scripts to control modem connections**—This section covers chat scripts, which provide a way to dictate to the modem how to place a call, answer an incoming call, and handle a current connection.

CHAPTER 4

Configuring Asynchronous Connections with Modems

To successfully configure an asynchronous modem connection, the following must occur:

1 The modem itself must be configured to respond correctly to the telephone company circuit.

2 The physical aspects of the router link to the modem must be correctly defined to match the modem parameters.

3 The logical parameters must be established to provide a network-layer end-to-end connection.

The modem must be configured so that it understands the signalling on both the telephone-line side and the router-connection side. This information includes the line rate and the number of bits used for data and other physical settings for the modem. The particulars for the modem are discussed in the body of this chapter.

The second and third pieces of an asynchronous modem connection are configured on the router and provide both physical and logical aspects for a connection. The physical properties are configured on the *line*. These parameters include the line rate, the data link-layer protocols supported on the line, and so on. These parameters are needed for the router line to communicate with the attached modem.

The last piece of an asynchronous modem connection is configuring the logical information on the router *interface*. The logical information includes the Layer 3 addresses, the network-layer protocol, the authentication methods, and so forth.

How to Best Use This Chapter

By taking the following steps, you can make better use of your study time:

• Keep your notes and answers for all your work with this book in one place for easy reference.

• Take the "Do I Know This Already?" quiz and write down your answers. Studies show retention is significantly increased through writing facts and concepts down, even if you never look at the information again.

• Use the diagram in Figure 4-1 to guide you to the next step.

Figure 4-1   *How to Use This Chapter*

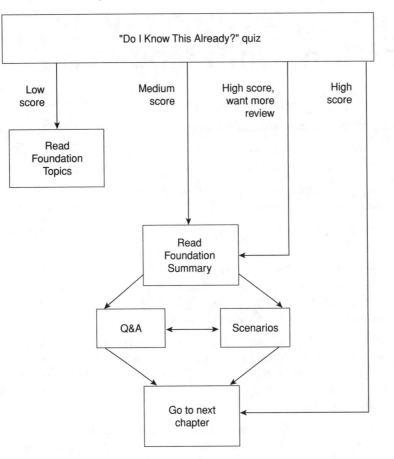

"Do I Know This Already?" Quiz

The purpose of the "Do I Know This Already?" quiz is to help you decide what parts of this chapter to use. If you already intend to read the entire chapter, you do not necessarily need to answer these questions now.

The twelve-question quiz helps you determine how to spend your limited study time. The quiz is sectioned into smaller, two-question "quizlets," each of which corresponds to the six major topic headings in the chapter. Use the scoresheet in Table 4-1 to record your scores.

Table 4-1   *Scoresheet for Quizlets and Quiz*

Quizlet Number	Foundation Topics Section Covered by These Questions	Questions	Score
1	Modem Signaling	1–2	
2	Modem Configuration Using Reverse Telnet	3–4	
3	Router Line Numbering	5–6	
4	Basic Asynchronous Configuration	7–8	
5	Configuration of the Attached Modem	9–10	
6	Chat Scripts to Control Modem Connections	11–12	
All questions		1–12	

1   What pins are used for modem control?

_____

_____

_____

2   What is the standard for DCE/DTE signaling?

_____

_____

_____

3   In character mode using reverse Telnet, what is the command to connect to the first async port on a 2509 router that has a loopback interface of 192.168.1.1?

_____

_____

_____

4   What port range is reserved for accessing an individual port using binary mode?

_____

_____

_____

5   If a four-port serial (A/S) module is in the second slot on a 3640 router, what are the line numbers for each port?

_____

_____

_____

6   What is the AUX port line number on a 3620 series router?

_____

_____

_____

7   What does the **physical-line async** command do and on what interfaces would you apply it?

_____

_____

_____

8   In what configuration mode must you be to configure the physical properties of an asynchronous interface?

_____

_____

_____

9   When should **modem autoconfigure discovery** be used? What happens when you use it?

_____

_____

_____

10   Which of the following commands would you use to add an entry to a modemcap database called newmodem?

a. **edit modemcap newmodem**

b. **modemcap edit newmodem**

c. **modemcap edit type newmodem**

d. **modemcap add newmodem**

11 List four reasons why you would use a chat script.

_____

_____

_____

_____

12 Which of the following would trigger a chat script start?

a. Line reset

b. DDR

c. Line activation

d. Manual

The answers to the "Do I Know This Already?" quiz are found in Appendix A, "Answers to the 'Do I Know This Already?' Quizzes and Q&A," on page 397. The suggested choices for your next step are as follows:

- **6 or fewer overall score**—Read the chapter. This includes the "Foundation Topics," the "Foundation Summary," Q&A, and scenarios at the end of the chapter.

- **7, 8, or 9 overall score**—Begin with the "Foundation Summary," then go to the Q&A and scenarios at the end of the chapter.

- **10 or more overall score**—If you want more review on these topics, skip to the "Foundation Summary," then go to the Q&A and scenarios at the end of the chapter. Otherwise, move to the next chapter.

Foundation Topics

Modem Signaling

This chapter covers the signaling of the modem and the configurations for a Remote Access Server (RAS) connection. The successful CCNP or CCDP candidate should be able to describe the signaling and pins used by the cabling and not just the syntax that is required for the connection. The signaling is just as important because it provides the basis for the physical-layer troubleshooting that can be needed to establish a connection.

Asynchronous data communications technology occurs when an end device, such as a PC, calls another end device, such as a server, to exchange data. In asynchronous data communications, end devices are called data terminal equipment (DTE). These devices communicate through data circuit-terminating equipment (DCE). DCE devices clock the flow of information. In our case, the modem provides the DCE function to the PC and server.

The Electronic Industries Association/Telecommunications Industry Association (EIA/TIA) defines a standard for the interface between DCE and DTE devices. This standard is the EIA/TIA-232 and was previously referred to as the RS-232-C standard (where the RS stood for "recommended standard").

It is unwise to think of a PC-to-server connection that uses asynchronous communications as a single circuit. The PC using a modem is one DTE to DCE path end. The far end DCE to DTE (modem to server) is another path. Each DTE–DCE or DCE–DTE connection must be made prior to data transfer.

With asynchronous communication, eight pins are used in a DB25 to transfer data and control the modem, as listed in Table 4-2. The table shows the pins and their definitions. As you read the table, note the direction of the signal and whether DCE or DTE controls or signals on the pin.

Table 4-2   *Standard EIA/TIA-232 Definitions and Codes*

Pin Number	Designation	Definition	Description
2	TD	Transmits data	DTE-to-DCE data transfer
3	RD	Receives data	DCE-to-DTE data transfer
4	RTS	Request to send	DTE signal buffer available
5	CTS	Clear to send	DCE signal buffer available
6	DSR	Data set ready	DCE is ready.
7	GRD	Signal ground	
8	CD	Carrier detect	DCE senses carrier.
20	DTR	Data terminal ready	DTE is ready.

Pins 2, 3, and 7 enable data transfer, pins 4 and 5 enable flow control of data, and pins 6, 8, and 20 provide modem control.

Data Transfer

The pins used for data transfer are pin 2, 3, and 7. The DTE device raises the voltage on the RTS when it has buffer space available to receive from the DCE device. Once a call is established and the DTE device sees the DCE raise the voltage on the CTS, the DTE device transmits data on pin 2. Conversely, the DTE device will raise the voltage on the RTS when it has buffer space available to receive from the DCE device. The need for the ground pin is such that a positive or negative voltage can be discerned.

Data Flow Control

The RTS pin and the CTS pin control the flow of information. The DTE device controls the RTS pin (as shown in Tabel 4-2), which, when seen by the DCE, alerts the DCE that it can receive data. It might help you to think of the RTS as the ready-to-receive pin. The DCE device controls the CTS pin, which in turn signals the DTE that it has buffer available. These definitions are critical to a CCNP or CCDP candidate.

Modem Control

DSR and DTR are signal pins used to control how the modem operates. The DSR pin is raised when the modem is powered on. This raising lets the DTE device know that the modem is ready for use. The DTR pin is raised when the DTE device is powered and ready to receive information from the DCE.

In most cases, when the DTE device is powered on, the DTR pin is raised; however, there are cases in which the DTR pin is raised only if a software package begins to run. This might sound like a minor point, but when you are troubleshooting, it is important to know if the DTE has signaled the modem that it is ready. In fact, just because the PC is on does not necessarily mean that DTR is asserted, and whether your DTE device raises the DTR when powering up or when you turn on your communication software, DTR is needed for a two-way conversation between the DCE and DTE device.

Note that the CD pin is also a signal pin. When two DCE devices establish a connection, the CD pin is asserted to indicate that a carrier signal has been established between the DCE devices. Note also that because two devices constitute the DTE (PC) and DCE (modem) connection, either must be allowed to terminate the connection.

DTE Call Termination

When the DTE is ready to terminate the connection because the user has completed the call and signaled the PC to go back on-hook, the DTR is dropped. For this to happen, the modem must be configured to interpret the loss of the DTR as the end of a conversation. When the DTE drops the DTR, the modem is alerted that the carrier is no longer needed.

This configuration is done when the modem is first installed. This can be manually done for each call, or it can be scripted in a chat script that is sent to the modem each time a call is terminated. Each time a call is terminated, the router resets (rescripts) the modem. This low level configuration is done on the modem to prepare the modem for reuse. In many cases, accepting the default configuration for a modem allows it to function properly.

Even accepting the default configuration provides a "configuration" to the modem. The details of each modem parameter are discussed in the section, "Configuration of an Attached Modem," later in this chapter.

DCE Call Termination

If a far-end modem drops the CD because the remote DTE has ended the transmission, the near-end modem must signal the near-end DTE that the transmission has been terminated. The modem must be programmed to understand and signal this termination. In other words, the modem must be told how to handle the loss of carrier detection. By default, most modems understand that this signal loss is an indication that the call is to be terminated. However, it is a configuration parameter that the modem must understand.

Modem Configuration Using Reverse Telnet

In order to configure a modem, a router must be set up to talk to it. Cisco refers to this as a *reverse Telnet connection*. A host that is connected to a router can Telnet to a Cisco reserved port address on the router and establish an 8-N-1 connection to a specific asynchronous port. An *8-N-1* connection declares the physical signaling characteristics for a line.

Table 4-3 shows reserved port addresses. The router must have a valid IP address on an interface and an asynchronous port. To establish a connection to the modem connected to the asynchronous port, you can Telnet to any valid IP address on the router and declare the Cisco reserved port number for the asynchronous interface. You can do this only, however, from the router console or a remote device that has Telnet access to the router.

Most modem consoles operate using eight data bits, zero parity bits, and one stop bit. In addition, the use of reverse Telnet enables the administrator to configure locally attached devices. For example, suppose you want to set up an 8-N-1 connection to the first asynchronous interface on a router, which has the 123.123.123.123 address assigned to its E0 port. To connect in character mode using Telnet, you would issue the following command:

```
telnet 123.123.123.123 2001
```

where **123.123.123.123** is the router's E0 port and **2001** is the Cisco reserved port number for the first asynchronous port on the router. Table 4-3 shows the Cisco reserved port numbers for all port ranges.

Table 4-3   *Reverse Telnet Cisco Reserved Port Numbers*

Connection Service	Reserved Port Range For Individual Ports	Reserved Port Range For Rotary Groups
Telnet (character mode)	2000–2xxx	3000–3xxx
TCP (line mode)	4000–4xxx	5000–5xxx
Telnet (binary mode)	6000–6xxx	7000–7xxx
Xremote	9000–9xxx	10000–10xxx

The use of the rotary group reserved port number connects to the first available port that is in the designated rotary group. If a specific individual port is desired, the numbers from the first column of Table 4-3 are used.

You can establish a session with an attached modem using reverse Telnet and the standard **AT** command set (listed later in Table 4-4) to set the modem configuration. This, however, is the hard way because once a modem connection has been established using reverse Telnet, you must disconnect from the line for the modem to be usable again. In addition, to exit the connection, you would have to press Ctrl+Shift+6 and then x to suspend the session, and then issue the **disconnect** command from the router prompt. It is important to remember this simple sequence because the modem does not understand the **exit** command as does a router!

Router Line Numbering

The line numbers on a router are obtained in a methodical manner. The console port is line 0. Each asynchronous (TTY) port is then numbered 1 through the number of TTY ports on the router. The auxiliary port is given the line number LAST TTY + 1, and the virtual terminal (vty) ports are numbered starting at LAST TTY + 2.

Example 4-1 has the **show line** output for a Cisco 2511 router, which has eight asynchronous ports available. Notice that the AUX port is labeled in line 17 and the vty ports are labeled in lines 18–22.

Example 4-1   **show line** *Output for Cisco 2511 Router*

```
2511Router>show line
  Tty Typ     Tx/Rx     A Modem  Roty AccO AccI   Uses   Noise  Overruns   Int
*   0 CTY               -    -      -    -    -      0      1     0/0        -
*   1 TTY    9600/9600  -    -      -    -    -      7     23     0/0        -
*   2 TTY    9600/9600  -    -      -    -    -      5      1     0/0        -
*   3 TTY    9600/9600  -    -      -    -    -     14     63     0/0        -
*   4 TTY    9600/9600  -    -      -    -    -      4      3     0/0        -
```

continues

Example 4-1 show line *Output for Cisco 2511 Router (Continued)*

*	5	TTY	9600/9600	-	-	-	-	-	16	6	0/0	-
*	6	TTY	9600/9600	-	-	-	-	-	12	7	0/0	-
	7	TTY	9600/9600	-	-	-	-	-	3	1	0/0	-
	8	TTY	9600/9600	-	-	-	-	-	0	9	0/0	-
*	9	TTY	9600/9600	-	-	-	-	-	12	0	0/0	-
*	10	TTY	9600/9600	-	-	-	-	-	16	0	0/0	-
*	11	TTY	9600/9600	-	-	-	-	-	25	2	0/0	-
*	12	TTY	9600/9600	-	-	-	-	-	5	0	0/0	-
*	13	TTY	9600/9600	-	-	-	-	-	0	0	0/0	-
	14	TTY	9600/9600	-	-	-	-	-	0	2	0/0	-
	15	TTY	9600/9600	-	-	-	-	-	0	0	0/0	-
	16	TTY	9600/9600	-	-	-	-	-	3	0	0/0	-
	17	AUX	9600/9600	-	-	-	-	-	0	0	0/0	-
	18	VTY		-	-	-	-	-	0	0	0/0	-
	19	VTY		-	-	-	-	-	0	0	0/0	-
	20	VTY		-	-	-	-	-	0	0	0/0	-
	21	VTY		-	-	-	-	-	0	0	0/0	-
	22	VTY		-	-	-	-	-	0	0	0/0	-

The numbering scheme for interfaces was expanded for the 3600 series routers. The console is still line 0 and the vty ports are similarly counted after the TTYs. However, Cisco chose to use reserved numbering for the available slots. Thus, slot 0 has reserved lines 1–32, slot 1 has reserved lines 33–64, slot 2 has reserved lines 65–97, and so on. Each slot is given a range of 32 line numbers, whether they are used or not.

Figure 4-2 shows the rear of the chassis for a 3620 and 3640 router and the line numbers associated with each slot.

Figure 4-2 *Line Numbers for 3620 and 3640 Routers*

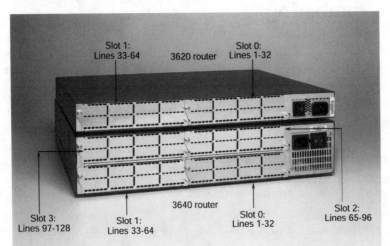

The line-numbering scheme is important when configuring a router. In the case of the 3600 and 2600 routers with the new modular interfaces, the line numbers are based on the slot that the feature card is in. For illustration, consider the output in Example 4-2, which is from a 3640 series router with a modem card in slot 2. Notice that the line numbers for the internal modems are 65–70 because only one MICA card is installed in the slot.

Example 4-2   **show line** *Output from a 3640 Series Router with a Modem Card in Slot 2*

```
router#show line
 Tty Typ      Tx/Rx       A Modem  Roty AccO AccI   Uses   Noise   Overruns   Int
*   0 CTY                 -   -      -    -    -      0       0       0/0       -
I  65 TTY                 - inout    -    -    -      0       0       0/0       -
I  66 TTY                 - inout    -    -    -      0       0       0/0       -
I  67 TTY                 - inout    -    -    -      0       0       0/0       -
I  68 TTY                 - inout    -    -    -      0       0       0/0       -
I  69 TTY                 - inout    -    -    -      0       0       0/0       -
I  70 TTY                 - inout    -    -    -      0       0       0/0       -
I  97 TTY 115200/115200   - inout    -    -    -      0       0       0/0       Se3/0
*129 AUX    9600/9600     -   -      -    -    -      0       0       0/0       -
 130 VTY                  -   -      -    -    -      0       0       0/0       -
 131 VTY                  -   -      -    -    -      0       0       0/0       -
 132 VTY                  -   -      -    -    -      0       0       0/0       -
 133 VTY                  -   -      -    -    -      0       0       0/0       -
 134 VTY                  -   -      -    -    -      0       0       0/0       -
The following lines are not in asynchronous mode or are without hardware support:
1-64, 71-96, and 98-128.
```

To properly configure a router, you must know the association between the line and interface numbers. The AUX port on the modular routers is the last line number, which would be the number of slots multiplied by 32, plus 1. In the case of the 3640 router shown in Example 4-2, the AUX port number is 129, and the vty ports are 130–134 by default.

In Example 4-3, the configuration for a 3640 router has physical characteristics configured on line 97 for the asynchronous interface in slot 3/0. The remaining IOS commands are discussed in detail later in this chapter, but are presented here for completeness.

Example 4-3   *3640 Router Configuration*

```
interface Serial3/0
 physical-layer async
 ip unnumbered Ethernet0/0
 no ip directed-broadcast
 encapsulation ppp
 async mode interactive
 peer default ip address pool TESTPOOL
 no cdp enable
 ppp authentication chap
!
line 97
 password cisco
```

continues

Example 4-3 *3640 Router Configuration (Continued)*

```
 autoselect during-login
 autoselect ppp
 login local
 modem InOut
 transport input all
 stopbits 1
 speed 115200
 flowcontrol hardware
line aux 0
line vty 0 4
 login local
!
```

Basic Asynchronous Configuration

To configure the modem (the DCE) from the router (the DTE), you must set up the logical and physical parameters for the connection. The logical parameters include the protocol addressing, the authentication method, and the encapsulation, all of which are configured on the asynchronous interface. The physical configuration is done on the line. The physical parameters include the flow control, the DTE-DCE speed, and the login request. It is important for the successful CCNP or CCDP to be aware of the command mode needed for configuration.

The configuration in Example 4-4 demonstrates which commands are used on each line or interface.

Example 4-4 *Configuration for a Serial Interface in Asynchronous Mode*

```
interface Serial3/0      !logical parameters go on the interface
    physical-layer async
    ip unnumbered Ethernet0/0
    no ip directed-broadcast
    encapsulation ppp
    async mode interactive
    peer default ip address pool remaddpool
    no cdp enable
    ppp authentication chap
line 97    !physical parameters go on the line
    autoselect during-login
    autoselect ppp
    login
    modem InOut
    modem autoconfigure type usr_sportster
    transport input all
    stopbits 1
    rxspeed 115200
```

Example 4-4 shows the distinction between the physical and logical parameters and where they are defined in the router configuration file.

Three types of router interfaces can be configured for serial communication:

- Asynchronous interfaces

- Synchronous/asynchronous interfaces (A/S)

- Synchronous interfaces

Router interfaces that are synchronous only cannot be used for modem or asynchronous communication. On the router models with A/S ports, the serial ports default to synchronous, and the interface must be declared for asynchronous usage using the **physical-layer async** command.

The configuration in Example 4-4 is for the first (port 0) synchronous/asynchronous interface on a four-port A/S card in the third slot of a 3600. The **physical-layer async** is needed because this device has A/S ports. Hence, the **physical-layer async** command is entered at the **router(config-if)#** prompt for Serial 3/0. On the other hand, in the case of those routers that have ports designated as asynchronous, only the **physical-layer async** command is not used.

Logical Considerations on the Router

Logical considerations are configured on the interface of the router. These include the network-layer addressing, the encapsulation method, the authentication, and so on. The configuration in Example 4-5 is for a serial interface that is used to receive an inbound call.

Example 4-5 *Router Configuration for Serial Interface Receiving Inbound Calls*

```
interface Serial2
  physical-layer async
  ip unnumbered Ethernet0
  ip tcp header-compression passive
  encapsulation ppp
  bandwidth 38
  async mode interactive
  peer default ip address pool remaddpool
  no cdp enable
  ppp authentication chap
```

In Example 4-5, the **physical-layer async** command places the serial 2 interface in asynchronous mode. Once this command is issued, the router treats the interface as an asynchronous port. This can be done on ONLY those interfaces that are defined as A/S.

The **ip unnumbered Ethernet0** command declares that the interface assume the address of the E0 interface. This enables the saving of IP addresses but makes the interface non-SNMP manageable. This command could be replaced with the desired IP address of the interface (refer to the discussion in this section that covers **ip address pool**). Note that it is quite common for a large number of asynchronous interfaces to a common physical interface to be unnumbered and to use an address pool to assign the network-layer addresses to the dial-up users.

The **ip tcp header-compression passive** command states that if the other DCE device sends packets with header-compression, the interface understands and sends in kind but does not initiate the compression.

The **encapsulation ppp** command declares the encapsulation method for the interface.

The **bandwidth 38** command tells the routing protocol and the router (for statistics) the speed of the line. This command has no affect on the actual negotiated speed of the modem or the speed at which the DTE talks to the modem.

The **async mode interactive** command enables, once a connection is made, the dial-up user access to the EXEC prompt.

The **peer default ip address pool remaddpool** command specifies that the IP address assigned to the dial-up user be from the address grouping or pool defined by the label **remaddpool**. The syntax for the pool definition, defined in global configuration mode, is as follows:

```
ip local pool remaddpool low-ip-pool-address high-ip-pool-address.
```

A unique address from the pool of addresses is given to a dial-up user for the duration of the session. The address is returned to the pool when the dial-up user disconnects the session. In this fashion, it is not necessary to associate an IP address with each asynchronous interface. Each asynchronous interface to another interface on the router is unnumbered and the pool is created from part of that interface's subnet. For more information and examples on the use of address pools and unnumbering, refer to Chapter 6, "Using ISDN and DDR Technologies."

The **no cdp enable** command turns off the Cisco Discovery Protocol for the interface. By default, this protocol is on, and because the interface is likely connected to a dial-up user who does not understand CDP, the bandwidth it would use is saved.

The **ppp authentication chap** command specifies that the Challenge Handshake Authentication Protocol (CHAP) be used on this link. Failure of the client to honor CHAP results in the link not being established.

Physical Considerations on the Router

Physical characteristics are configured in line mode. These include the speed, the direction of the call, modem setup, and so on. Example 4-6 shows a configuration used to connect to a USR Sportster modem on physical line 2.

Example 4-6 *Router Configuration Connecting USR Sportster Modem on Physical Line 2*

```
line 2
        autoselect during-login
        autoselect ppp
        login local
        modem InOut
        modem autoconfigure type usr_sportster
        transport input all
        stopbits 1
        rxspeed 115200
        txspeed 115200
        flowcontrol hardware
```

The **login local** command is the same for this line as it is for the console and AUX ports. The **Login local** command tells the physical line to request a username/password pair when a connection is made and to look locally on the router for a matching **username** *xxxx* **password** *yyyy* pair that has been configured in global mode (*xxxx* and *yyyy* represent a freely chosen username and password combination).

The **autoselect during-login** and **autoselect ppp** commands automatically start the PPP protocol and issue a carriage return so that the user is prompted for the login. This feature became available in IOS Software Release 11.0. Prior to this "during-login" feature, the dial-up user was required to issue an exec command or press the Enter key to start the session.

The **modem InOut** command enables both incoming and outgoing calls. The alternative to this command is the default **no modem inout** command, which yields no control over the modem.

The **modem autoconfigure type usr_sportster** command uses the **modemcap database usr_sportster** entry to initialize the modem. We further discuss this initialization later in the chapter.

The **transport input all** command enables the processing of any protocols on the line. This command defines which protocols to use to connect to a line. The default command prior to 11.1 was **all**; the default with 11.1 is **none**.

In the router configuration, the number of **stopbits** must be the same for both communicating DCE devices. Remember that the physical-layer parameters must match for the physical layer to be established. Failure to do so prevents the upper layers from beginning negotiation.

In Example 4-6, **rxspeed** and **txspeed** are shown as separate commands. The **speed** command, however, sets both transmit and receive speeds and locks the speed between the modem and the DTE device. Failure to lock or control the DTE-to-DCE speed allows the speed of local communication to vary with the line speed negotiated between the DCE devices. This limits the capability of the DTE-to-DCE flow control.

The **flowcontrol hardware** command specifies that the RTS and CTS be honored for flow control.

Example 4-6 provides the basic configuration for an asynchronous line. Once the DTE device has been configured, you must set the DCE device to communicate with the modem by using the AT commands.

Configuration of the Attached Modem

In the early modem days, the Hayes command set was the de facto standard; however, there was never a ratified industry command set. Today, rather than converging to a general standard, the modem industry has actually diverged. Nonetheless, the AT commands documented in Table 4-4 are considered "standard" and should work on most modems.

Table 4-4 *Standard* AT *Commands*

COMMAND	Result
AT&F	Loads factory default settings
ATS0=n	Auto answers
AT&C1	CD reflects the line state
AT&D2	Hangs up on low DTR
ATE0	Turns off local echo
ATM0	Turns off the speaker

A CCNP or CCDP should be familiar with these commands. For many modems on the market today, commands not in this table are used to configure the modem fall into the category of not standard.

The correct initialization string must be sent to the modem for proper operation. You can do this by using a chat script or the **modem autoconfigure** command. The former method is the most common.

Modem Autoconfiguration and the Modem Capabilities Database

Modem autoconfiguration is a Cisco IOS software feature that enables the router to issue the modem configuration commands, which frees the administrator from creating and maintaining scripts for each modem. The general syntax for modem autoconfiguration is as follows:

```
modem autoconfigure [discovery | type modemcap-entry-name]
```

The two command options for the **modem autoconfigure** command are as follows:

* **type**—This option configures modems without using modem commands, or so it is implied. The **type** argument declares the modem type that is defined in the modem capabilities database so that that the administrator does not have to create the modem commands.

- **discovery**—Autodiscover modem also uses the modem capabilities database, but in the case of **discover**, it tries each modem type in the database as it looks for the proper response to its query.

As you can see, the **modem autoconfigure** command relies on the modem capabilities database, also known as the *modemcap*. The modem capabilities database has a listing of modems and a generic initialization string for the modem type. The discovery of a modem using the **autoconfigure** feature uses the initialization strings from each modem in the modem capabilities database to discover the installed modem. If the modem is not in the database, it fails, and the administrator has to manually add the modem to the database.

The use of the discovery feature is not recommended because of the overhead on the router. Each time the line is reset, the modem is rediscovered. However, the discovery feature can be used to initially learn the modem type if you are not geographically near the router and cannot gather the information any other way. After discovery has taken place, the administrator should use the **type** option to specify the entry in the modem capabilities database to use.

To discover a modem, the syntax would be as follows:

```
modem autoconfigure discovery
```

Again, once the modem type is determined, the final configuration for the router interface should be as follows:

```
modem autoconfigure type entry_name_from_modemcap
```

This configuration eliminates unnecessary overhead on the router.

Use the **show modemcap** command to see the entries in the modemcap database. Example 4-7 demonstrates the output from the **show modemcap** command.

Example 4-7   **show modemcap** *Command Output Reveals Modemcap Database Entries*

```
BCRANrouter#show modemcap

default
codex_3260
usr_courier
usr_sportster
hayes_optima
global_village
viva
telebit_t3000
microcom_hdms
microcom_server
nec_v34
nec_v110
nec_piafs
cisco_v110
mica
```

To view the detailed settings for a particular entry in the modem capabilities database, the entry name is added as an argument to the **show modemcap** command. The database has most models of modems. If your entry is not in the database, it can be added by editing the database.

Editing the database requires creating your own entry name and specifying the AT commands for the initialization string. This must be done for any modem that is not in the database. This might sound time-consuming or tedious, but it has to be done only once. The added information to the database is stored in NVRAM as part of the router configuration and can be copied to other routers that have the same modems.

Common practice dictates that multiple modem types not be used at a single RAS facility. Instead, the administrator should use a single modem type and maintain spares of that particular type so that constant manipulation of the modem capabilities database is not necessary.

Let's take a look at how a modem is added to the database. If an attached modem is a Viva plus that is not listed in the database, but another Viva modem is in the database, you could create a new entry and name it whatever you want. The AT commands that are unique to the Viva plus modem would be added to the local configuration in NVRAM and the additional AT commands that are the same for all Viva modems would be obtained from the database.

To add the modem, you would use the following global commands:

```
modemcap edit viva_plus speed &B1
modemcap edit viva_plus autoanswer s0=2
modemcap edit viva_plus template viva
```

These commands use the initialization string from the entry **viva** and enable the administrator to alter the newly created **viva_plus**. All changes and additions to the modemcap are stored in the configuration file for the router. Because of this, Cisco can add to the modemcap at any release because the local NVRAM changes override the modemcap.

The overview of all this is that you bought some modems that you, as the administrator, feel are the best for your application. The modemcap database may, or may not, have these particular modems defined. If the modem is defined in the modemcap then you can simply use the **type** option to the **modem autoconfigure** command. If the modem is not in the database then it must be added. Once it is added, all future modem connections on this router can simply point to the added entry.

Chat Scripts to Control Modem Connections

Chat scripts enable us to talk to or through a modem to a remote system using whatever character strings or syntax is needed. A chat script takes the form of

Expect-string - send-string - expect-string - send-string

where the *expect* strings are character strings sent from or through the modem to the DTE device and the *send* strings are character strings sent from the DTE device to or through the modem.

Reasons for Using a Chat Script

As a CCNP or CCDP, you should be aware that chat scripts are used for the following goals:

- **Initialization**—To initialize the modem
- **Dial string**—To provide the modem with a dial string
- **Logon**—To log in to a remote system
- **Command execution**—To execute a set of commands on a remote system

Reasons for a Chat Script Starting

A chat script can be manually started on a line using the **start-chap** command; they can also be configured to start for the following events:

- **Line activation**—CD trigger (incoming traffic)
- **Line connection**—DTR trigger (outgoing traffic)
- **Line reset**—Asynchronous line reset
- **Startup of an active call**—Access server trigger
- **Dialer startup**—From a dial-on-demand trigger

Using a Chat Script

The primary use of a chat script is to provide the dial number for the connection. The following line shows an example of this chat script:

```
Router(config)#chat-script REMDEVICE ABORT ERROR ABORT BUSY "" "ATZ" OK "ATDT \T"
TIMEOUT 30 CONNECT \c
```

Care should be taken with the character case used in this command. **ABORT ERROR** and **ABORT BUSY** cause the modem to abort if it sees **ERROR** or **BUSY**. Both arguments might be easier understood if read as "abort if you see ERROR" and "abort if you see BUSY," respectively. If **error** or **abort** are entered in lowercase, the modem never sees these conditions because its search is case-sensitive. The **\T** inserts the called number from the **dial string** or **map** command into the chat script. A **\t** causes the script to look for a "table character"; hence, case is important here as well.

NOTE   Detailed information on the **dial string** and **map** commands are provided in Chapter 6.

The **REMDEVICE** chat script has been configured to drop the connection if the modem declares a busy or error condition. If no busy or error condition is declared, the router does not wait for anything except string = " ". The router then issues the **ATZ**, or modem reset, command, using a send string. The router waits for the modem to respond OK, which is the normal modem response to **ATZ**. The router then sends the **ATDT** command and replaces the \T with the phone number to make the call. Last, the **TIMEOUT 30** declares that the call is considered "not answered" if no carrier is obtained in 30 seconds. Once the connection is made, the chat script sends a **c**, which is a carriage return.

Provided that the router, the modem, and the phone number are correct, the physical layer should now be established! Congratulations! You can now move on to the upper layer protocols, such as PPP (see Chapter 5, "Configuring PPP and Controlling Network Access") and advanced uses (see Chapter 6).

Foundation Summary

The Foundation Summary is a collection of tables and figures that provides a convenient review of many key concepts in this chapter. For those of you already comfortable with the topics in this chapter, this summary could help you recall a few details. For those of you who just read this chapter, this review should help solidify some key facts. For any of you doing your final preparation before the exam, these tables and figures will hopefully be a convenient way to review the day before the exam.

Table 4-5   *Standard EIA/TIA-232 Definitions and Codes*

Pin Number	Designation	Definition	Description
2	TD	Transmits data	DTE-to-DCE data transfer
3	RD	Receives data	DCE-to-DTE data transfer
4	RTS	Request to send	DTE signal buffer available
5	CTS	Clear to send	DCE signal buffer available
6	DSR	Data set ready	DCE is ready.
7	GRD	Signal ground	
8	CD	Carrier detect	DCE senses carrier.
20	DTR	Data terminal ready	DTE is ready.

Table 4-6   *Cisco Reserved Port Numbers Used with Reverse Telnet*

Connection Service	Reserved Port Range for Individual Ports	Reserved Port Range for Rotary Groups
Telnet (character mode)	2000–2xxx	3000–3xxx
TCP (line mode)	4000–4xxx	5000–5xxx
Telnet (binary mode)	6000–6xxx	7000–7xxx
Xremote	9000–9xxx	10000–10xxx

Figure 4-3   *3600 Line Numbers*

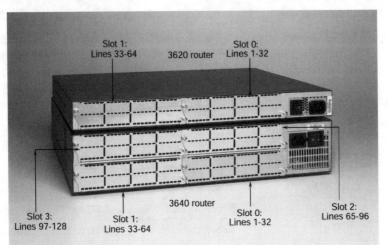

Table 4-7   **modem autoconfigure** *Commands*

Command	What It Does
modem autoconfigure discovery	Discovers the modem
modem autoconfigure type *entry_name_from_modemcap*	Creates the final configuration for the router interface, which eliminates unnecessary overhead on the router
show modemcap	Displays the entries in the modemcap database

Table 4-8   *Standard* AT *Commands*

Command	Result
AT&F	Loads factory default settings
ATS0=n	Auto answers
AT&C1	CD reflects the line state
AT&D2	Hangs up on low DTR
ATE0	Turns off local echo
ATM0	Turns off the speaker

Reasons for using a chat script:

- **Initialization**—To initialize the modem
- **Dial string**—To provide the modem with a dial string
- **Logon**—To log in to a remote system
- **Command Execution**—To execute a set of commands on a remote system

A chat script can be manually started on a line using the **start-chap** command; they can also be configured to start for the following events:

- **Line activation**—CD trigger (incoming traffic)
- **Line connection**—DTR trigger (outgoing traffic)
- **Line reset**—Asynchronous line reset
- **Startup of an active call**—Access server trigger
- **Dialer startup**—From a dial-on-demand trigger

Q&A

The questions and scenarios in this book are more difficult than what you will experience on the actual exam. The questions do not attempt to cover more breadth or depth than the exam; however, they are designed to make sure that you know the answer. Rather than enabling you to derive the answer from clues hidden inside the question itself, the questions challenge your understanding and recall of the subject.

Questions from the "Do I Know This Already?" quiz from the beginning of the chapter are repeated here to ensure that you have mastered the chapter's topic areas. Hopefully, mastering these questions will help you limit the number of exam questions on which you narrow your choices to two options and then guess.

The answers to these questions can be found in Appendix A, on page 397.

1 What pins are used for modem control?

_____

_____

_____

2 What is the standard for DCE/DTE signaling?

_____

_____

_____

3 If the user wants to terminate a call, what pin does the DTE device drop to signal the modem?

_____

_____

_____

4 What must be done to terminate a reverse Telnet session with an attached modem?

_____

_____

_____

5 In character mode using reverse Telnet, what is the command to connect to the first async port on a 2509 router that has a loopback interface of 192.168.1.1?

_____

_____

_____

6 Which interface is line 97 on a 3640 series router?

a. S 0/97

b. S 3/1

c. S 2/1

d. S 097

7 What port range is reserved for accessing an individual port using binary mode?

_____

_____

_____

8 When flow control is enabled, which pins are used?

_____

_____

_____

9 If a four-port serial (A/S) module is in the second slot on a 3640 router, what are the line numbers for each port?

_____

_____

_____

10   What is the **AT** command to return a router to factory default settings?

   a. **AT Default**

   b. **AT@F**

   c. **AT&F**

   d. **ATZ**

11   What is the AUX port line number on a 3620 series router?

   _____

   _____

   _____

12   Which of the following commands configure a router for use with a Viva modem?

   a. **modem autoconfigure viva**

   b. **modem configure type viva**

   c. **modem autoconfigure type viva**

   d. **modem autoconfigure discovery type viva**

13   What does the **physical-line async** command do and on what interfaces would you apply it?

   _____

   _____

   _____

14   In what configuration mode must you be to configure the physical properties of an asynchronous interface?

   _____

   _____

   _____

15   What does it mean when the signal pin RTS is asserted?

   _____

   _____

   _____

16 What is the command to manually begin a chat script named remcon?

_____

_____

_____

17 When should **modem autoconfigure discovery** be used, and what are the ramifications of doing so?

_____

_____

_____

18 What command would you use to add an entry to the modemcap database called newmodem?

_____

_____

_____

19 Which interface type provides clocking for a line?

_____

_____

_____

20 List four reasons why you would use a chat script.

_____

_____

_____

21 What command can be used to determine whether Serial 0 is the DCE or DTE?

_____

_____

_____

22 What command lists the transmit and receive speeds for the asynchronous ports on the router?

_____

_____

_____

23 On which pins does the DTE device send and receive?

_____

_____

_____

24 Which of the following would trigger a chat script start?

a. Line reset

b. DDR

c. Line activation

d. Manual

Scenarios

There are no scenarios for this particular chapter. The key issues and concepts here are syntax, syntax, and syntax. For further review, you should practice creating a configuration for a router and include all parts necessary for an asynchronous setup. The parts should include:

- Line configuration (physical)
- Interface configuration (logical)
- A new modemcap entry (your choice)
- An alias to address the modem locally (Reverse Telnet)
- A chat script for the connection (no phone number needed!)

This chapter covers the following topics that you need to master as a CCNP:

- **PPP background**—This section examines the underlying technology of the Point-to-Point Protocol (PPP) and its components.

- **PPP options**—This section discusses how to configure various options available with PPP. These options include authentication, PPP Callback, compression, and PPP Multilink.

- **PPP troubleshooting**—This section details some of the **show** and **debug** commands useful in dealing with issues arising with PPP.

Configuring PPP and Controlling Network Access

The CCNP Remote Access Exam requires you to have an in depth understanding of various WAN technologies. In this chapter the discussion focuses on Point-to-Point Protocol (PPP). The typical implementation of PPP has traditionally been in dial-up and/or ISDN deployments.

The growing need of corporations to include dial-up access to network resources for remote users has created a high demand for point-to-point technologies. Telecommuting personnel require access to network devices and information that looks and feels as it would at the office (albeit at slower access rates). PPP and its options enable this type of access to become a reality. The capabilities of PPP give it the versatility to remain flexible, yet viable, in many situations.

Most remote access technology implementations center on PPP as the core access method. Dial-up clients require a means of accessing the network. Windows 95, Windows 98, Windows 2000, and so forth include dial-up networking client software as part of a standard installation. In addition, many companies have created proprietary dial-up clients. PPP is the underlying architecture that makes it all work.

PPP creates a single connection over which multiple protocols can be multiplexed. IP, IPX, and AppleTalk, for example, can all traverse PPP links. The actual configuration of the dial-up client is not discussed here. The discussions in this chapter center on the Access Server configuration. Whether the Access Server is a 3640 router or an AS5x00 router, the configuration is essentially the same.

Authentication plays a vital role in PPP connections. Having dial-up lines with no user authentication is a dangerous game to play. Password Authentication Protocol (PAP) and Challenge Handshake Authentication Protocol (CHAP) authentications provide varying degrees of security.

How to Best Use This Chapter

By taking the following steps, you can make better use of your study time:

- Keep your notes and answers for all your work with this book in one place for easy reference.

- Take the "Do I Know This Already?" quiz and write down your answers. Studies show retention is significantly increased through writing down facts and concepts, even if you never look at the information again.

- Use the diagram in Figure 5-1 to guide you to the next step.

Figure 5-1 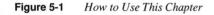 *How to Use This Chapter*

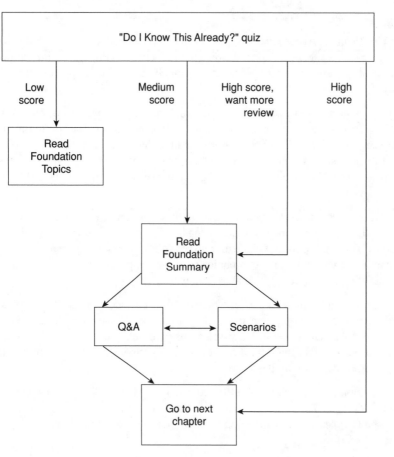

"Do I Know This Already?" Quiz

The purpose of the "Do I Know This Already?" quiz is to help you decide what parts of this chapter to use. If you already intend to read the entire chapter, you do not necessarily need to answer these questions now.

The nine-question quiz helps you make good choices about how to spend your limited study time. The quiz is sectioned into smaller, three-question "quizlets," each of which corresponds to the three major topic headings in the chapter. Use the scoresheet in Table 5-1 to record your scores.

Table 5-1   *Scoresheet for Quiz and Quizlets*

Quizlet Number	Foundation Topics Section Covered by These Questions	Questions	Score
1	PPP Background	1–3	
2	PPP Options	4–6	
3	PPP Troubleshooting	7–9	
All questions		1–9	

1 Where is PPP typically implemented?

_____

_____

_____

2 What is the function of the LCP?

_____

_____

_____

3 What is the difference between interactive and dedicated asynchronous implementations?

_____

_____

_____

4 List the four PPP LCP negotiable options.

_____

_____

_____

5 List the two supported authentication types with PPP.

_____

_____

_____

6 In PPP Callback implementations, which router is in charge of the authentication challenge as well as the disconnect of the initial call?

_____

_____

_____

7 What command shows the status of individual B channels at any given time?

_____

_____

_____

8 What command enables the real-time viewing of CHAP communications?

_____

_____

_____

9 What command enables the real-time viewing of dial events?

_____

_____

_____

The answers to the "Do I Know This Already?" quiz are found in Appendix A, "Answers to the 'Do I Know This Already?' Quizzes and Q&A Sections," on page 397. The suggested choices for your next step are as follows:

- **You correctly answered four or fewer questions overall**—Read the chapter. This includes the "Foundation Topics," "Foundation Summary," and "Q&A" sections, as well as the scenarios at the end of the chapter.

- **You correctly answered one or fewer questions on any quizlet**—Review the subsections of the "Foundation Topics" part of this chapter, based on the information that you entered in Table 5-1. Then move into the "Foundation Summary" and "Q&A" sections and the scenarios at the end of the chapter.

- **You correctly answered five or more questions overall**—If you want more review on these topics, skip to the "Foundation Summary" section, and then go to the "Q&A" section and the scenarios at the end of the chapter. Otherwise, move to the next chapter.

Foundation Topics

PPP Background

RFC 1661 defines PPP. PPP's basic function is to encapsulate network layer protocol information over point-to-point links. The mechanics of PPP are as follows:

Step 1   To establish communications, each end of the PPP link must first send Link Control Protocol (LCP) packets to configure and test the data link.

Step 2   After the link has been established and optional facilities have been negotiated as needed, PPP must send Network Control Protocol (NCP) packets to choose and configure one or more network layer protocols.

Step 3   Once each of the chosen network layer protocols has been configured, traffic from each network layer protocol can be sent over the link.

Step 4   The link remains configured for communications until explicit LCP or NCP packets close the link down, or until some external event occurs (such as the expiration of an inactivity timer expires or the intervention of a network administrator). In other words, PPP is a pathway that is opened for multiple protocols simultaneously.

PPP was originally developed with IP in mind; however, it functions independently of the Layer 3 protocol that is traversing the link.

PPP Architecture

As mentioned, PPP encapsulates the network layer protocol(s) that are configured to traverse a PPP-configured link. PPP has a number of capabilities that make it flexible and versatile, including:

- Multiplexing of network layer protocols
- Link configuration
- Link quality testing
- Authentication
- Header compression
- Error detection
- Link parameter negotiation

PPP supports these functions by providing an extensible LCP and a family of NCPs to negotiate optional configuration parameters and facilities. The protocols to be transported, the optional capabilities, and the user authentication type are all communicated during the initial exchange of information when a link between two points is set up.

PPP Components

PPP can operate across any DTE/DCE interface. The only absolute requirement imposed by PPP is the provision of a duplex circuit, either dedicated or switched, that can operate in either an asynchronous or synchronous bit-serial mode, transparent to PPP link layer frames. Other than those imposed by the particular DTE/DCE interface in use, PPP does not impose any restrictions regarding transmission rates.

In just about every type of WAN technology in internetworking, a layered model is shown to provide a point of reference to the OSI model and to illustrate where each particular technology operates. PPP is not much different from other technologies. It too has its own layered model to define form and function. Figure 5-2 depicts the PPP layered model.

Figure 5-2   *PPP Layered Model*

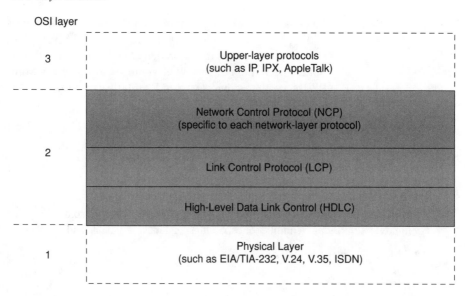

As with most technologies, PPP has its own framing structure. This structure enables the encapsulation of virtually any Layer 3 protocol. Because PPP is, by nature, point-to-point, no mapping of protocol addresses is necessary. Figure 5-3 shows the PPP frame format.

Figure 5-3   *PPP Frame Format*

1	1	1	2	Variable	2 or 4
Flag	Address	Control	Protocol	Data	FCS

The frame structure fields for PPP are as follows:

- *Flag*—A single byte that indicates the beginning or end of a frame. The flag field consists of the binary sequence 01111110.

- *Address*—A single byte that contains the binary sequence 11111111, the standard broadcast address. PPP does not assign individual station addresses.

- *Control*—A single byte that contains the binary sequence 00000011, which calls for transmission of user data in an unsequenced frame.

- *Protocol*—Two bytes that identify the protocol encapsulated in the information field of the frame. The most up-to-date values of the protocol field are specified in the most recent *Assigned Numbers* RFC. At press time, this was RFC 1700. For more information, see www.isi.edu/in-notes/rfc1700.txt.

- *Data*—Zero or more bytes that contain the datagram for the protocol specified in the Protocol field. The end of the Data field is found by locating the closing flag sequence and allowing 2 bytes for the FCS field. The default maximum length of the information field is 1500 bytes. By prior agreement, consenting PPP implementations can use other values for the maximum Data field length.

- *Frame Check Sequence* (**FCS**)—Normally 16 bits (2 bytes). By prior agreement, consenting PPP implementations can use a 32-bit (4-byte) FCS for improved error detection.

The LCP can negotiate modifications to the standard PPP frame structure. Modified frames, however, are always clearly distinguishable from standard frames.

PPP LCP

The PPP LCP provides a method of establishing, configuring, maintaining, and terminating the point-to-point connection. LCP goes through four distinct phases:

1 A link establishment and configuration negotiation occurs. Before any network layer datagrams (for example, IP) can be exchanged, LCP first must open the connection and negotiate configuration parameters. This phase is complete when a configuration-acknowledgment frame has been both sent and received.

2 A link-quality determination is made. LCP allows an optional link-quality determination phase following the link-establishment and configuration-negotiation phase. The link is tested to determine whether the quality is sufficient to initialize the network layer protocols. Transmission of network layer protocols can be held until this phase is complete.

3 The network layer protocol configuration negotiation occurs. Network layer protocols can be configured separately by the appropriate NCP and can be initialized and taken down at any time.

4 Link termination then occurs at the request of the user or a predefined inactivity timer, loss of carrier occurrence, or some other physical event.

Three classes of LCP frames are used to accomplish the work of each of the LCP phases:

- Link-establishment frames are used to establish and configure a link.

- Link-termination frames are used to terminate a link.

- Link-maintenance frames are used to manage and debug a link.

Dedicated and Interactive PPP Sessions

Asynchronous interfaces on an access server can be configured to accept inbound calls from remote users. There are two modes that can be used in this situation, interactive and dedicated. In interactive mode, users who dial into the network are able to access the user mode prompt. The user must enter the command **ppp connect** to initiate the connection. If access to the router prompt is unacceptable, dedicated mode should be used. Dedicated mode forces the connection into a PPP session once the call setup is complete. The command to implement interactive or dedicated mode for dial-up connections is as follows:

```
RouterA(config-if)#async mode [dedicated | interactive]
```

IP addressing on serial interfaces can be done statically or dynamically. If assigned statically, the **ip address** command is used on the interface just as any other interface. To enable dynamic addressing, the **ip unnumbered** command is used:

```
RouterA(config-if)#ip unnumbered interface-type interface-number
```

Asynchronous interfaces can assign predefined IP addresses to dial-up clients using the following command:

```
RouterA(config-if)#peer default ip address {ip-address | dhcp | pool poolname}
```

The **dhcp** and **pool** options require global configuration of a pool of addresses using the following command:

```
RouterA(config)#ip local pool poolname start-address end-address
```

The *poolname* must match the *poolname* in the **peer default ip address** command.

It is possible for the dial-up client to assign his or her own address. To do this, use the **async dynamic address** command at the interface level.

PPP Options

As mentioned, LCP negotiates a number of parameters. This section goes into more detail regarding those parameters.

LCP negotiation enables you to add features to your PPP configuration. The additional options are as follows (more details are in upcoming sections of this chapter):

- **Authentication**—By using either PAP or CHAP (discussed later) to authenticate callers, this option provides additional security. Implementation of this option requires that individual dial-up clients identify themselves and provide a valid username and password.

- **Callback**—This option can be used to provide call and dial-up billing consolidation. A user dials into the network and disconnects; then, the access server dials the user back and a connection is established.

- **Compression**—Compression is used to improve throughput on slower-speed links. Care should be taken when implementing compression. The topic of compression is discussed later in this book.

- **Multilink PPP**—This option takes advantage of multiple ISDN B channels. Multilink is a standardized method of bundling B channels to aggregate their bandwidth. Data is transmitted across multiple links and reassembled at the remote end.

PPP Authentication

The topic of authentication has been touched on throughout this chapter. At this point, it is finally time to get down to specifics.

PPP authentication offers two options—PAP and CHAP. These two protocols offer differing degrees of protection. Both protocols require the definition of usernames and accompanying passwords. This can be done on the router itself or on a TACACS or RADIUS authentication server. The examples we deal with in this book are those in which the router itself is configured with all usernames and passwords.

PAP

PAP is exactly what its name implies. It is a clear text exchange of username and password information. When a user dials in, a username request is sent. Once that is entered, a password request is sent.

All communications flow across the wire is in clear text form. No encryption is used with PAP. There is nothing stopping someone with a protocol analyzer from gleaning passwords as they traverse the wire. At that point, simply playing back the packet allows authentication into the network. Although it may not provide the level of protection you may be seeking, it's better than nothing. It serves to keep honest people honest. Figure 5-4 depicts the PAP authentication procedure.

Figure 5-4   *PAP Authentication*

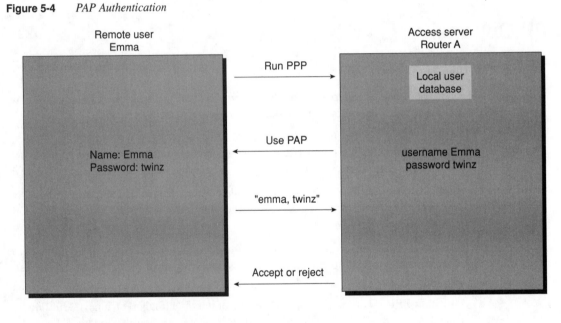

As is clearly seen, PAP is a one-way authentication between the router and the host. Example 5-1 shows a basic PPP PAP configuration.

Example 5-1   *PAP Configuration Example*

```
RouterA(config)#username emma password twinz
RouterA(config)#interface async 0
RouterA(config-if)#enapsulation ppp
RouterA(config-if)#ppp authentication pap
```

CHAP

CHAP is much more secure than PAP. It implements a two-way encrypted authentication process. Usernames and passwords still must exist on the remote router, but they do not cross the wire as they did with PAP.

When a user dials in, the access server issues a challenge message to the remote user after the PPP link is established. The remote end responds with a one-way hash function. This hash is generally an MD5 entity. If the value of the hash matches what the router expects to see, the authentication is acknowledged. If not, the connection terminates. Figure 5-5 depicts CHAP authentication.

Figure 5-5   *CHAP Authentication*

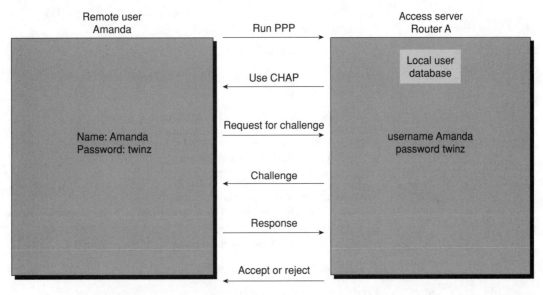

The playback of packets captured by a protocol analyzer is not an issue with CHAP. The use of variable challenge values (that is, unique values) for each authentication attempt ensures that no two challenges are the same. CHAP also repeats a challenge every two minutes for the duration of the connection. If the authentication fails at any time, the connection is terminated. The access server controls the frequency of the challenges. Example 5-2 shows a basic CHAP configuration.

Example 5-2   *CHAP Configuration Example*

```
RouterA(config)#username amanda password twinz
RouterA(config)#interface async 0
RouterA(config-if)#enapsulation ppp
RouterA(config-if)#ppp authentication chap
```

There are specific steps involved in a CHAP negotiation:

Step 1 **Making a call**—The inbound call arrives at the PPP configured interface. LCP opens the CHAP negotiation and the access server initiates a challenge.

Step 2 **Conveying the challenge**—When the access server sends the challenge, a challenge packet is constructed. The packet consists of a challenge packet type identifier, a sequence number for the challenge, a random number (as random as an algorithm can be), and the authentication name of the *called* party.

The calling party must process the challenge packet as follows:

(a)   The ID value from the challenge packet is fed into the MD5 hash generator.

(b)   The random value is fed into the MD5 hash generator.

(c)   The authentication name of the *called* party is used to look up the password.

(d)   The password is fed into the MD5 hash generator.

The resulting value is the one-way MD5 CHAP challenge that is forwarded to the called party in response to the challenge. This value is always 128 bits in length.

Step 3 **Answering the challenge**—Once the reply is hashed and generated, it can be sent back. The response has a CHAP response packet type identifier, the id from the challenge packet, the output from the hash, and the authentication name of the *calling* party.

The response packet is then sent to the *called* party.

Step 4 **Verifying**—The called party processes the response packet as follows:

(a)   The ID is used to find the original challenge packet.

(b)   The ID is fed into the MD5 hash generator.

(c)   The original challenge random number value is fed into the MD5 hash generator.

(d)   The authentication name of the *calling* party is compared to the username/password list in the router or in an authentication server.

(e)   The password is fed into the MD5 hash generator.

(f)   The hash value received in the response packet is compared to the result of the hash value just generated.

The authentication succeeds only if the hash value received from the calling party (from Step 2) matches the calculated hash value (from Step 4).

Step 5   **Constructing the result**—If the values of the hash calculations match, the authentication is successful and a CHAP success packet is constructed. It contains a CHAP success message type and the id from the response packet.

If the authentication fails, a CHAP failure packet is constructed. It contains a CHAP failure message type and the ID from the response packet.

Indication of success or failure is then sent to the calling party.

PPP Callback

The PPP Callback option was developed to provide connectivity to remote users while controlling access and the cost of calls. Callback enables a router to place a call, and then request that the central router call back. Once the request is made, the call disconnects. The central router then dials the router back, which reverses the charges for the call. This callback feature adds another layer of protection because it only dials back authorized numbers. However, callback is not considered to be a security feature.

PPP Callback routers can play two roles, that of the callback client and that of the callback server. The client router passes authentication (PAP or CHAP) information to the server router, which in turn analyzes dial string and hostname information to determine whether callback is authorized.

If authentication is successful, the server disconnects the call and then places the return call. The username of the client router is used as a call reference to associate it with the initial call. For the callback to be successful, the hostname must exist in a **dialer-map** statement; otherwise, the router is unable to determine the proper dial string to use in calling back the client. If the return call fails, there are no retries. The client has to reissue the callback request.

For callback to function, both sides of a PPP link must be configured to support it. As mentioned, a server and a client must be specified. The client issues the initial call and the server places return calls. There is a catch, however. If a call is placed requesting callback, the server disconnects the call after authentication. It is possible that another call will come in on the same B channel during the idle time between disconnect and callback. If it is the last available B channel, callback will not occur. It is also possible that on DDR implementations, interesting traffic can force an outbound call on the last available B channel. Again, if this happens, callback does not occur. Example 5-3 shows a PPP Callback configuration for the client.

Example 5-3 *PPP Callback Client Configuration*

```
Client(config)#username Client password cisco
Client(config)#username Server password cisco
Client(config)#dialer-list 1 protocol ip permit
Client(config)#interface S0
Client(config-if)#ip address 10.1.1.1 255.255.255.0
Client(config-if)#encapsulation ppp
Client(config-if)#dialer map ip 10.1.1.2 name Server 5551212
Client(config-if)#dialer-group 1
Client(config-if)#ppp callback request
Client(config-if)#ppp authentication chap
Client(config-if)#dialer hold-queue timeout 30
```

Example 5-4 shows the PPP Callback configuration for the server.

Example 5-4 *PPP Callback Server Configuration*

```
Server(config)#username Client password cisco
Server(config)#username Server password cisco
Server(config)#dialer-list 1 protocol ip permit
Server(config)#interface S0
Server(config-if)#ip address 10.1.1.1 255.255.255.0
Server(config-if)#encapsulation ppp
Server(config-if)#dialer callback-secure
Server(config-if)#dialer map ip 10.1.1.1 name Client 5553434
Server(config-if)#dialer-group 1
Server(config-if)#ppp callback accept
Server(config-if)#ppp authentication chap
```

The callback client uses the **ppp callback request** command to request that the callback occur. The server router uses the **ppp callback accept** command as an indication that it should accept callback requests and place a call to the phone number configured for the requesting client (in this case, **5553434**).

The **dialer callback-secure** command disconnects calls that are not properly configured for callback. It also forces a disconnect of any unconfigured dial-in users. This command ensures that the initial call is always disconnected at the receiving end and that the return call is made only if the username is configured for callback.

Figure 5-6 illustrates the PPP Callback procedure.

Figure 5-6   *PPP Callback Procedure*

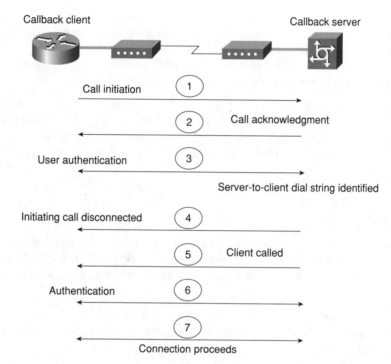

When the client router dials, its hold queue timer begins to count down. No additional calls to the same destination can be made until the time reaches zero. This value is configurable using the **dialer hold-queue** command detailed later in this chapter.

PPP Compression

Compression is covered in Chapter 10, "Managing Network Performance with Queuing and Compression," in more detail. This section is simply an overview of PPP's compression capabilities.

Compression is most useful on slower-speed links. In routing, there comes a point when it is faster to send information outright than it is to compress, send, and decompress it. Compression simply serves to decrease transit time across the WAN.

PPP or Layer 2 compression is determined during LCP negotiation. Therefore, if one side of the call doesn't support it or have it configured, it is not utilized for that call.

Cisco supports a number of compression algorithms. They include STAC, Predictor, MPPC, and TCP header compression. These are discussed in Chapter 10 and are not therefore covered here.

Multilink PPP

Multilink PPP is a specification that enables bandwidth aggregation of multiple B channels into one logical pipe. Its mission is comparable to that of Cisco's bandwidth-on-demand (BOD). More specifically, the Multilink PPP feature provides load-balancing functionality over multiple WAN links, while providing multivendor interoperability, packet fragmentation and proper sequencing, and load calculation on both inbound and outbound traffic.

Cisco's implementation of Multilink PPP supports the fragmentation and packet sequencing specifications in RFC 1717. Multilink PPP enables packets to be fragmented and the fragments to be sent at the same time over multiple point-to-point links to the same remote address. Refer to Chapter 6, "Using ISDN and DDR Technologies," for a more detailed discussion of Multilink PPP.

PPP Troubleshooting

Troubleshooting PPP is similar to troubleshooting many other WAN technologies. However, there is a key difference: The implementation of authentication adds another item to the list of things that can go wrong. This section details some of the commands useful in dealing with PPP issues.

The first step in troubleshooting PPP connections is to remove authentication of any kind from the configuration. If the service functions properly at that point, it's time to rethink your authentication configuration.

The **show dialer** command provides useful information about the current status of B channels. Example 5-5 shows sample output.

Example 5-5 **show dialer** *Command Output Reveals B Channel Status*

```
RouterA#show dialer
Dial String      Successes    Failures    Last called    Last status
4155551212           1           0          00:00:00       successful
4155551213           1           0          00:00:00       successful
0 incoming call(s) have been screened.
BRI0: B-Channel 1
Idle timer (300 secs), Fast idle timer (20 secs)
Wait for carrier (30 secs), Re-enable (15 secs)
BRI0: B-Channel 2
Idle timer (300 secs), Fast idle timer (20 secs)
Wait for carrier (30 secs), Re-enable (15 secs)
```

The **show dialer** command shows status and connection information regarding each B channel and the number to which the channel is connected. It also shows successful and failed calls.

The **debug ppp negotiation** and **debug ppp authentication** commands are useful in enabling the administrator to view the real-time communication between PPP configured devices. They are mentioned together because they are often implemented simultaneously. Example 5-6 shows screen output from the commands.

Example 5-6 *Combined* **debug ppp negotiation** *and* **debug ppp authentication** *Command Output*

```
ppp: sending CONFREQ, type = 3 (CI_AUTHTYPE), value = C223/5
ppp: sending CONFREQ, type = 5 (CI_MAGICNUMBER), value = 28CEEF99
ppp: received config for type = 3 (AUTHTYPE) value = C223 value = 5 acked
ppp: received config for type = 5 (MAGICNUMBER) value = 1E23F5C acked
PPP BRI0: B-Channel 1: state = ACKSENT fsm_rconfack(C021): rcvd id E4
ppp: config ACK received, type. = 3 (CI_AUTHTYPE), value = C223
ppp: config ACK received, type = 5 (CI_MAGICNUMBER), value = 28CEEF99
BRI0: B-Channel 1: PPP AUTH CHAP input code = 1 id = 82 len = 16
BRI0: B-Channel 1: PPP AUTH CHAP input code = 2 id = 95 len = 28
BRI0: B-Channel 1: PPP AUTH CHAP input code = 4 id = 82 len = 21
BRI0: B-Channel 1: Failed CHAP authentication with remote.
Remote message is: MD compare failed
ppp: sending CONFREQ, type = 3 (CI_AUTHTYPE), value = C223/5
ppp: sending CONFREQ, type = 5 (CI_MAGICNUMBER), value = 28CEEFDB
%LINK-3-UPDOWN: Interface BRI0: B-Channel 1, changed state to down
%LINK-5-CHANGED: Interface BRI0: B-Channel 1, changed state to down
%LINK-3-UPDOWN: Interface BRI0: B-Channel 1, changed state to up
%LINK-5-CHANGED: Interface BRI0: B-Channel 1, changed state to up
ppp: sending CONFREQ, type = 3 (CI_AUTHTYPE), value = C223/5
ppp: sending CONFREQ, type = 5 (CI_MAGICNUMBER), value = 28CEF76C
ppp: received config for type = 3 (AUTHTYPE) value = C223 value = 5 acked
ppp: received conf.ig for type = 5 (MAGICNUMBER) value = 1E24718 acked
PPP BRI0: B-Channel 1: state = ACKSENT fsm_rconfack(C021): rcvd id E6
ppp: config ACK received, type = 3 (CI_AUTHTYPE), value = C223
ppp: config ACK received, type = 5 (CI_MAGICNUMBER), value = 28CEF76C
BRI0: B-Channel 1: PPP AUTH CHAP input code = 1 id = 83 len = 16
BRI0: B-Channel 1: PPP AUTH CHAP input code = 2 id = 96 len = 28
BRI0: B-Channel 1: PPP AUTH CHAP input code = 4 id = 83 len = 21
BRI0: B-Channel 1: Failed CHAP authentication with remote.
Remote message is: MD compare failed
```

As is noted in the output, this is an example of a failed CHAP authentication attempt.

Chapter 6 covers additional **show** and **debug** commands for PPP.

Foundation Summary

PPP was developed specifically for point-to-point connectivity, as its name implies. It has become one of the more versatile protocols in use today. ISDN implementations, serial connections, and other dial-up connections now implement PPP.

Configuring PPP is not a difficult process; however, it does have some intricate differences when compared to other WAN technologies.

The options provided by PPP enable a level of control over network resources previously unknown. LCP negotiation of authentication, callback, compression, and PPP Multilink make this granularity possible.

PPP authentication enables the use of PAP or CHAP. PAP makes use of clear text passwords, which could enable packet playback if captured by a protocol analyzer. CHAP implements an MD5 hash challenge and response. Every challenge is unique, as is each response. At periodic intervals (two minutes) during the course of the connection, additional challenges are issued. In the event of a failed authentication, the call is immediately disconnected.

PPP Callback enables the centralization of call related costs. A central site provides callback services to remote clients. Client devices dial it and are authenticated. Upon successful authentication, the server disconnects the call and dials the client back.

PPP Compression enables a reduction in the delay associated with transmission of data over lower-speed links. Care should be taken when using compression because memory utilization on the router is greatly increased.

PPP Multilink enables the bundling of multiple bearer channels into one aggregate pipe. Traffic is broken up and sent across the redundant pathways to the remote side where it is reassembled.

Any protocol can go across a PPP link. The only requirement is that the adjacent interfaces must be configured with the protocols that need to cross the link.

Q&A

The questions and scenarios in this book are more difficult than what you will experience on the actual exam. The questions do not attempt to cover more breadth or depth than the exam; however, they are designed to make sure that you know the answer. Rather than enabling you to derive the answer from clues hidden inside the question itself, the questions challenge your understanding and recall of the subject.

Questions from the "Do I Know This Already?" quiz from the beginning of the chapter are repeated here to ensure that you have mastered the chapter's topic areas. Hopefully, these questions will help you limit the number of exam questions on which you narrow your choices to two options and then guess.

The answers to these questions can be found in Appendix A, on page 397.

1   Where is PPP typically implemented?

_____

_____

_____

2   What is the function of the LCP?

_____

_____

_____

3   What is the difference between interactive and dedicated asynchronous implementations?

_____

_____

_____

4   List the 4 PPP LCP negotiable options.

_____

_____

_____

5   List the two supported authentication types with PPP.

_____

_____

_____

6   In PPP Callback implementations, which router is in charge of the authentication challenge as well as the disconnect of the initial call?

_____

_____

_____

7   What command shows the status of individual B channels at any given time?

_____

_____

_____

8   What command enables the real-time viewing of CHAP communications?

_____

_____

_____

9   What command enables the real-time viewing of dial events?

_____

_____

_____

10   Describe the PPP Callback procedure.

_____

_____

_____

11   What are the supported compression types on Cisco routers?

_____

_____

_____

12   Which command, used with callback, ensures that a callback is made only to a properly configured client?

_____

_____

_____

13 What command informs a router that it is to be a callback client?

_____

_____

_____

14 What command informs a router that it is to be a callback server?

_____

_____

_____

15 What is the default time interval between CHAP challenges?

_____

_____

_____

16 In the event of PPP authentication failure, what happens to the call?

_____

_____

_____

Scenarios

The following case studies and questions are designed to draw together the content of the chapter and exercise your understanding of the concepts. There is not necessarily a right answer to each scenario. The thought process and practice in manipulating the related concepts is the goal of this section.

Scenario 5-1

Refer to Figure 5-7 for this scenario.

Figure 5-7   *Network Environment for Scenario 5-1*

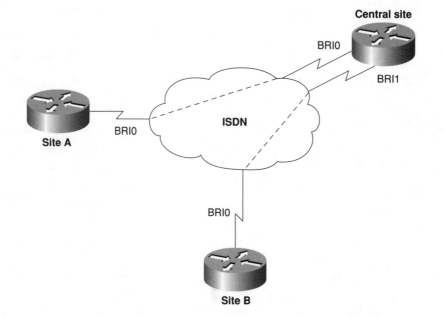

These three routers need to be configured for dial-up access. Varying degrees of configuration are performed on each router. Use the figure as the sole source of information for the following tasks:

1   Configure the Central site router for CHAP authentication. The password in all instances is "cisco". The interfaces in question are BRI 0 and BRI 1. Don't worry about the intricacies of the ISDN configuration. The task here is the PPP configuration only. ISDN is covered in Chapter 6.

  2 Configure the SiteA router for PPP and CHAP authentication on BRI 0. Use "cisco" as the password.

  3 Configure the SiteB router for PPP and CHAP authentication on BRI 0. Use "cisco" as the password.

Scenarion 5-2

It has been determined that a callback implementation is in order. Complete the tasks that follow:

  1 Configure the Central site router to act as a PPP Callback server.

  2 Configure the SiteA router to act as a PPP Callback client.

  3 Configure the SiteB router to act as a PPP Callback client.

Scenario 5-3

The PPP implementation is having problems. Implement appropriate means of troubleshooting to meet the following symptoms:

  1 The call is being completed successfully; however, it is immediately disconnected. List the commands to troubleshoot this issue.

  2 The callback client has issued a callback request and successfully authenticated; however, the callback is not occurring. What is a possible cause?

Scenario Answers

The answers provided in this section are not necessarily the only possible correct answers. They merely represent one possibility for each scenario. The intention is to test your base knowledge and understanding of the concepts discussed in this chapter.

Should your answers be different (as they likely will be), consider the differences. Are your answers in line with the concepts of the answers provided and explained here? If not, go back and read the chapter again, focusing on the sections related to the problem scenario.

Scenario 5-1 Answers

1 The Central site router configuration is as follows:

```
Central(config)#username Central password cisco
Central(config)#username SiteA password cisco
Central(config)#username SiteB password cisco
Central(config)#interface bri0
Central(config-if)#encapsulation ppp
Central(config-if)#ppp authentication chap
Central(config)#interface bri1
Central(config-if)#encapsulation ppp
Central(config-if)#ppp authentication chap
```

2 The SiteA router configuration is as follows:

```
SiteA(config)#username Central password cisco
SiteA(config)#username SiteA password cisco
SiteA(config)#interface bri0
SiteA(config-if)#encapsulation ppp
SiteA(config-if)#ppp authentication chap
```

3 The SiteB router configuration is as follows:

```
SiteB(config)#username Central password cisco
SiteB(config)#username SiteB password cisco
SiteB(config)#interface bri0
SiteB(config-if)#encapsulation ppp
SiteB(config-if)#ppp authentication chap
```

Scenario 5-2 Answers

1   The Central site router configuration is as follows:

```
Central(config)#username Central password cisco
Central(config)#username SiteA password cisco
Central(config)#username SiteB password cisco
Central(config)#dialer-group 1 protocol ip permit
Central(config)#interface bri0
Central(config-if)#encapsulation ppp
Central(config-if)#dialer callback-secure
Central(config-if)#ip address 10.1.1.1 255.255.255.0
Central(config-if)#ppp authentication chap
Central(config-if)#dialer map ip 10.1.1.2 name SiteA 5555656
Central(config-if)#dialer-group 1
Central(config-if)#ppp callback accept
Central(config)#interface bri1
Central(config-if)#encapsulation ppp
Central(config-if)#dialer callback-secure
Central(config-if)#ppp authentication chap
Central(config-if)#ip address 10.2.1.1 255.255.255.0
Central(config-if)#dialer map ip 10.2.1.2 name SiteB 5556767
Central(config-if)#dialer-group 1
Central(config-if)#ppp callback accept
```

2   The SiteA router configuration is as follows:

```
SiteA(config)#username Central password cisco
SiteA(config)#username SiteA password cisco
SiteA(config)#dialer-list 1 protocol ip permit
SiteA(config)#interface bri0
SiteA(config-if)#ip address 10.1.1.2 255.255.255.0
SiteA(config-if)#encapsulation ppp
SiteA(config-if)#ppp authentication chap
SiteA(config-if)#dialer map ip 10.1.1.1 name Central 5559090
SiteA(config-if)#dialer-group 1
SiteA(config-if)#ppp callback request
```

3   The SiteB router configuration is as follows:

```
SiteB(config)#username Central password cisco
SiteB(config)#username SiteB password cisco
SiteB(config)#dialer-list 1 protocol ip permit
SiteB(config)#interface bri0
SiteB(config-if)#ip address 10.2.1.2 255.255.255.0
SiteB(config-if)#encapsulation ppp
SiteB(config-if)#ppp authentication chap
SiteB(config-if)#dialer map ip 10.2.1.1 name Central 5559191
SiteB(config-if)#dialer-group 1
SiteB(config-if)#ppp callback request
```

Scenario 5-3 Answers

1 The symptom listed here is consistent with authentication failure. Show dialer or debug ppp authentication assists in troubleshooting the condition.

2 A callback failure of this sort can sometimes be attributed to busy B channels. If a callback request comes in and authentication is successful, the server disconnects the call. If this is the last available B channel, and a new call comes in, the new call takes the available B channel and callback cannot occur.

This chapter covers the following topics that you need to master as a CCNP:

- **POTS versus ISDN; BRI and PRI Basics**—These introductory sections examine the underlying technology of ISDN and its components.

- **Basic Rate Interface**—This section explores the technologies related to BRI-specific implementations of ISDN technology.

- **Implementing Basic DDR**—This section covers many of the commands used to configure a basic DDR solution (the traditional methodology for deploying ISDN), including the definition of interesting traffic, dialer maps, and static routes. This section helps you understand DDR and the accompanying command structure.

- **Advanced DDR operations**—This section covers a number of variable parameters specific to a DDR implementation, such as the decision to use Cisco's proprietary bandwidth on demand function to load share over multiple bearer channels as well as the standardized PPP Multilink.

- **Primary Rate Interface**—This section explains the concepts of and differences between T1 and E1 PRI-based implementations.

Using ISDN and DDR Technologies

The CCNP Remote Access Exam requires you to have an in depth understanding of various WAN technologies. In this chapter the discussion focuses on ISDN. ISDN is not a new technology by any means. However, it is still widely implemented around the world. Even with the advent of newer (and faster) broadband technologies, ISDN continues to grow in the workplace, albeit at a slower rate than what has been seen in the recent past.

There are two specific implementation types discussed in this chapter: BRI and PRI. Although they are based on the same technologies and use the same protocols, their implementations are very different. This chapter touches on the background information necessary to give you a solid understanding of each technology.

How to Best Use This Chapter

By taking the following steps, you can make better use of your study time:

- Keep your notes and answers for all your work with this book in one place for easy reference.

- Take the "Do I Know This Already?" quiz and write down your answers. Studies show retention is significantly increased through writing down facts and concepts, even if you never look at the information again.

- Use the diagram in Figure 6-1 to guide you to the next step.

Figure 6-1 *How to Use This Chapter*

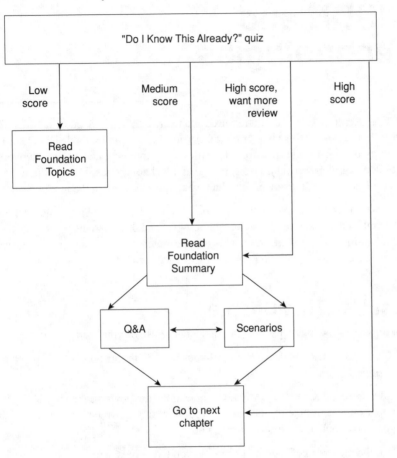

"Do I Know This Already?" Quiz

The purpose of the "Do I Know This Already?" quiz is to help you decide what parts of this chapter to use. If you already intend to read the entire chapter, you do not necessarily need to answer these questions now.

The 15-question quiz helps you determine how to spend your limited study time. The quiz is sectioned into smaller, three-question "quizlets," each of which corresponds to the major topic headings in the chapter. Use the scoresheet in Table 6-1 to record your scores.

Table 6-1   *Scoresheet for Quizlets and Quiz*

Quizlet Number	Foundation Topics Section(s) Covered by These Questions	Questions	Score
1	POTS versus ISDN; BRI and PRI Basics	1–3	
2	Basic Rate Interface	4–6	
3	Implementing Basic DDR	7–9	
4	Advanced DDR Operations	10–12	
5	Primary Rate Interface	13–15	
All questions		1–15	

1 List the two most common implementations of ISDN.

_____

_____

_____

2 List the number of bearer channels for BRI, T1 PRI, and E1 PRI.

_____

_____

_____

3 What type of information is carried over the D channel?

_____

_____

_____

4 List the specifications that define Layer 2 and Layer 3 of ISDN.

_____

_____

_____

5 When is it necessary to use **dialer in-band** in an ISDN BRI configuration?

_____

_____

_____

6 What is the difference between a router with a *BRI S/T* interface and one with a *BRI U* interface?

_____

_____

_____

7 Write out the commands to define only Telnet and FTP as interesting traffic for DDR.

_____

_____

_____

8 List two of the most common encapsulations available for use on BRI interfaces.

_____

_____

_____

9 An interface that has been configured not to send routing updates is known as what type of interface?

_____

_____

_____

10 When using rotary groups, what should determine the dialer interface number?

_____

_____

_____

11 What technology is used to provide redundancy for WAN links?

_____

_____

_____

12 DDR traditionally involves the use of static routes. If static routes are not desired, what technology can be implemented?

_____

_____

_____

13 What information is required of the telco to implement PRI implementations?

_____

_____

_____

14 List the options available for T1 and E1 framing and line code configuration.

_____

_____

_____

15 List the command to have the router forward all incoming voice calls to internal MICA technology modems.

_____

_____

_____

The answers to the "Do I Know This Already?" quiz are found in Appendix A, "Answers to the 'Do I Know This Already?' Quizzes and Q&A Sections," on page 397. The suggested choices for your next step are as follows:

- **You correctly answered six or fewer questions overall**—Read the chapter. This includes the "Foundation Topics," "Foundation Summary," and "Q&A" sections, as well as the scenarios at the end of the chapter.

- **You correctly answered two or fewer questions on any "quizlet"**—Review the subsections of the "Foundation Topics" part of this chapter, based on the information that you entered in Table 6-1. Then move into the "Foundation Summary" and "Q&A" sections and the scenarios at the end of the chapter.

- **You correctly answered seven, eight, or nine questions overall**—Begin with the "Foundation Summary" section and then go to the "Q&A" section and scenarios at the end of the chapter.

- **You correctly answered 10 or more questions overall**—If you want more review on these topics, skip to the "Foundation Summary" section, and then go to the "Q&A" section and the scenarios at the end of the chapter. Otherwise, move to the next chapter.

Foundation Topics

ISDN refers to a set of digital services that has been available to end users for a number of years. It involves the digitizing of the telephone network so that carriers can provide end users with multiple services from a single end-user interface over existing telephone wiring.

ISDN is an effort to standardize subscriber services, user/network interfaces, and network and internetwork capabilities. The goal of standardizing subscriber services is to give some level of international compatibility.

Compatibility between International Carrier networks has long been at the forefront of more than a few heated debates in the global standards committees. Their pain, to a degree, has been good for the technology. This standardization, as it has evolved, has made reality of the myth of multivendor interoperability. By no means is it implied that multivendor interoperability is perfect. It is nowhere near perfect and will never be as long as there are global politics in the technology fields.

The ISDN community would like to ensure that ISDN networks communicate easily with one another. ISDN was developed with the idea that it would be used to transport voice calls, data traffic, and video traffic. The evolution of ISDN as a viable technology moves forward with the needs of those very different traffic types in mind. ISDN applications include high-speed image applications, additional telephone lines in homes to serve the telecommuting industry, high-speed file transfer, and video conferencing. ISDN is also becoming very common in home-based and small offices as many corporations extend their offices into the residential arena.

POTS Versus ISDN

ISDN is the replacement of traditional analog plain old telephone service (POTS) equipment and wiring schemes with higher-speed digital equipment. The transition from POTS to ISDN changes the way connections at the local loop area are processed.

With POTS, a caller would have to dial up the operator and request a call setup. To accomplish this, the calling party telephone was picked up (that is, went off hook) and a crank was turned to generate current on the line that would light up an LED on the operator console. The operator would answer the setup request and begin setting up the call, making a manual connection between the caller and the called party. The manual connection completed the analog local loop (that is, the connection between the telco switch and customer devices).

From the local loop, the call typically went through the central office (CO). Once digital technologies were born and implemented, the operator was replaced with digital facilities, leaving only the local loop as analog. The transition to ISDN completes the digital link by replacing the local loop with digital equipment.

BRI and PRI Basics

ISDN interfaces can be either PRI or BRI. A PRI differs from a BRI mainly due to the number of channels it offers.

ISDN channels are usually divided into two different types—B and D:

- **The bearer channel**—The B channel is the facility that carries the data. Each B channel has a maximum throughput of 64 kbps. B channels can carry encoded pulse code modulation (PCM) digital voice, video, or data. B channels are used mainly for circuit-switched data communications such as High-Level Data Link Control (HDLC) and Point-to-Point Protocol (PPP). However, they can also carry packet-switched data communications.

- **The D Channel**—The D channel is used to convey signaling requests to an ISDN switch. In essence, it provides a local loop to the telephone company's central office. The router uses the D channel to dial destination phone numbers. It has a bandwidth of 16 kbps for BRI or 64 kbps for PRI. Although the D channel is used mainly for signaling, it too can also carry packet-switched data (X.25, Frame Relay, and so on).

Basic Rate Interface

BRI is the most typical ISDN connection and is a native ISDN interface on a router. The basic rate connection consists of two bearer (B) channels and a single (D) channel. When both B channels are active, the aggregate bandwidth becomes 128,000 bps.

You can purchase ISDN service with two, one, or zero B channels. Typical deployments use two B channels. Implementations of one B channel provide cost reduction, and zero B channel implementations enable another technology (such as X.25) to be run across the D channel. In this book, we do not discuss the deployment of zero B channel deployments because such implementations are not typical in most internetworks. Figure 6-2 depicts the typical 2B+D model.

Figure 6-2   *BRI 2B + D*

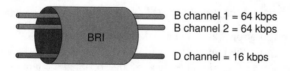

When you have ISDN BRI installed, the telephone company (or telco) places a Category 5 unshielded twisted-pair (UTP) cable at your site. The telco runs the cable to a location within your premises (usually a telephone room). Many times, the base installation charge covers only bringing the line into your premises. In that case, you must decide if you want to extend the cable into your wiring closet or server room. Usually it is well worth the negligible additional charge to enable the telco installer to extend it to a point that is easy to reach from the router with another cable.

When you extend the cable, the extension begins at a 66 block on your premises. A 66 block is merely the location where all the lines coming into your premises are separated into individual pairs. Once the decision has been made regarding where to put the cable and the cable is put in place, the installer attaches an eight-pin modular (RJ-45) jack to the cable and attaches the jack to the wall.

The installer should label the jack with the appropriate service profile identifiers (SPIDs) and a circuit identifier number. This information is necessary if a call for service is needed in the future. In North America, this jack is the *point of demarcation (demarc)*, where responsibility for the line changes hands. The equipment on your side of the point of demarc is known as *customer premise equipment (CPE)*. The jack that the telco installs is a direct interface from the local central office switch to your customer premise equipment.

One important piece of equipment in any ISDN BRI installation is an NT1. The NT1 is a device similar to a channel service unit/data service unit (CSU/DSU), which is used in serial connections. The NT1 terminates the local loop.

The NT1 has at least two interfaces: an S/T interface jack and a U interface. The S/T interface is attached to the router's BRI interface. The U interface is attached to the telco jack. Many of Cisco's BRI-capable routers are now available with an integrated NT1. These interfaces are labeled "BRI U". If this feature is not available on the chassis, the interface is labeled "BRI S/T" and an external NT1 is necessary. This native ISDN interface is the router's *TE1 interface*.

From time to time, it may be necessary to install ISDN, but there is no native BRI interface on your router. In such cases, it is still possible to use ISDN. However, another piece of hardware known as a *terminal adapter* must be used. The terminal adapter is a device that contains the BRI that your router is missing. In recent ISDN hype, telecommunications manufacturers marketed terminal adapters as ISDN modems. Terminal adapters are *not* modems. They do not modulate and demodulate signals. What they do is interface your router's universal I/O serial port. The terminal adapter interfaces the NT1 with a native BRI.

The non-native (that is, non-BRI) ISDN is known as the TE2 interface. The interface between the TE2 and the TA is known as the R interface. It is important to note that a non-native ISDN interface (more specifically, a solution that lacks a D channel) requires you to use the **dialer in-band** command to issue signaling requests to the ISDN switch.

Using the **dialer in-band** configuration, each B channel, in effect, loses 8000 bps of available bandwidth for signaling. Therefore, the bandwidth available per B channel becomes 56,000 bps. In some cases, ISDN facilities are available only at 56,000 bps per B channel, regardless of whether the interface is native ISDN. Check with the telco provider for details for a particular installation. Figure 6-3 shows the ISDN reference points.

Figure 6-3   *ISDN Interface Detail*

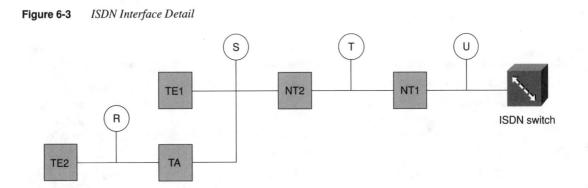

BRI Protocols

As is the standard for implementations in this industry, the ISDN implementation is divided into multiple layers. This division of labor for ISDN is not unlike the OSI model.

ISDN has three layers. Layer 1 deals with signal framing, Layer 2 deals with framing protocols, and Layer 3 deals with D channel call setup and teardown protocols. Each of these protocols has a specific mission to accomplish. Figure 6-4 depicts the ISDN layer model.

Figure 6-4   *ISDN Protocol Layers*

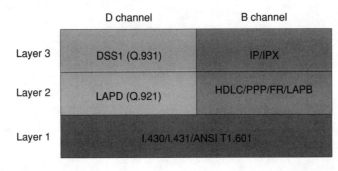

ISDN Layer 1

Layer 1 for ISDN is similar to that of the OSI model. It refers to physical connectivity. This connectivity is obviously an important piece of the picture. Without it, nothing happens.

In order for a router to communicate with an ISDN network, it must be configured for the type of switch to which it is connected. The carrier should provide the type of switch that is to be used. If it was not previously documented, a call should be placed to the carrier to obtain the information.

Manufacturers of ISDN central office switches (also known as *local exchange equipment*) divide the local exchange into two functions: *local termination* and *exchange termination*. The local termination function deals with the transmission facility and termination of the local loop. The exchange termination function deals with the switching portion of the local exchange.

The AT&T 5ESS and the Northern Telecom DMS-100 are the two principle ISDN switches used in North America. The recent release of National ISDN-1 software has corrected most incompatibility issues between the AT&T and Northern Telecom switches. Prior to the release of this software, for example, you could not use AT&T ISDN products with a Northern Telecom switch.

AT&T introduced the 5ESS switch in 1982. It can provide up to 100,000 local loops. Approximately 16000 5ESS switches are in use worldwide, serving close to 40 million lines. In the United States, approximately 85 percent of the BRI lines in service connect to a 5ESS-equipped central office.

By comparison, the Northern Telecom DMS-100 switch family is intended to deliver a wide range of telecommunication services. The DMS-100, introduced in 1978, can terminate up to 100,000 lines. Although AT&T and Northern Telecom have deployed the most ISDN switches, there are other ISDN switch manufacturers. Table 6-2 depicts the various switch types available for BRI implementations.

Table 6-2   *BRI Switch Types*

Switch Type	Description
Basic-1tr6	1TR6 switch type for Germany
Basic-5ess	AT&T 5ESS switch type for the U.S.
Basic-dms100	DMS-100 switch type
Basic-net3	NET3 switch type for UK and Europe
Basic-ni1	National ISDN-1 switch type
Basic-nwnet3	NET3 switch type for Norway
Basic-nznet3	NET3 switch type for New Zealand
Basic-ts013	TS013 switch type for Australia
Ntt	NTT switch type for Japan
vn2	VN2 switch type for France
vn3	VN3 and VN4 switch types for France
Basic-1tr6	1TR6 switch type for Germany

*Check with the provider for the appropriate switch type. A change of switch type requires a reload of the router.

The ISDN Layer 1 is concerned not only with physical connectivity, but also with how the bits traverse the wire. To accommodate transmission, a framing method must be established to enable communication between the NT and the TE as well as between the NT and the Local Exchange (LE).

The framing between the NT and TE is defined in the ITU specification I.430. Figure 6-5 depicts the BRI frame.

Figure 6-5   *ISDN BRI Framing Between NT and TE*

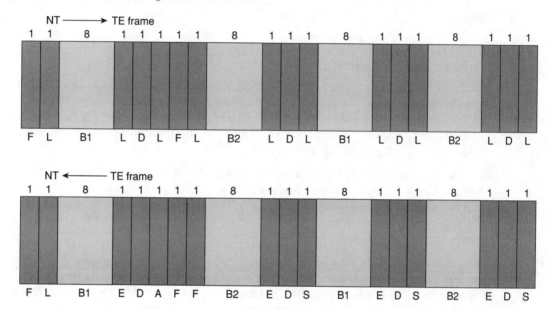

Notice in Figure 6-5 that 16 bits from each B (B1 and B2) channel and 4 bits from the D channel (D) are being time division multiplexed along with framing (F) and alignment (A) bits. Frame transmission is constant regardless of whether data is actually being sent.

Between the NT and the LE, another framing convention is used, ANSI T1.601. The intricacies of ANSI T1.601 are not discussed at this time because they are not covered on the CCNP Remote Access Exam. For more information on this topic, check out www.ansi.org.

ISDN Layer 2

The Layer 2 processes of ISDN are defined in the ITU specifications Q.920 and Q.921. Q.921 defines the actual communication format. Obviously, Layer 2 communication does not take place unless Layer 1 is properly installed and functioning.

Q.921 institutes an addressing scheme similar to many other networking technologies. Just as in LAN implementations, ISDN Layer 2 addressing is meant to provide physical addressing on the network. Because multiple logical devices can exist in a single physical device, it is necessary to correctly identify the source and/or destination process or logical entity when transmitting or receiving data. In communication with the ISDN switch, an identifier must be issued by the switch. This is known as a *Terminal Endpoint Identifier (TEI)*.

The telco has the option of creating a specific profile for your implementation. Should this be the case, the telco will assign a SPID for each of your bearer channels. The use of SPIDs is optional.

Terminal Endpoint Identifier (TEIs)

A terminal endpoint can be any ISDN-capable device attached to an ISDN network. The TEI is a number between 0 and 127, where 0–63 are used for static TEI assignment, 64–126 are used for dynamic assignment, and 127 is used for group assignments. (0 is used only for PRI and is discussed later.) The TEI provides the physical identifier, and the service access point identifier (SAPI) carries the logical identifier.

The process of assigning TEIs differs slightly between North America and Europe. In North America, Layer 1 and Layer 2 are activated at all times. In Europe, the activation does not occur until the call setup is sent (known as "first call"). This delay conserves switch resources. In Germany or Italy, as well as in other parts of the world, the procedure for TEI assignment can change according to local practices.

In other countries, another key piece of information to obtain is the *bus type*. Supported types are point-to-point or point-to-multipoint connection styles. In Europe, if you are not sure, specify a point-to-multipoint connection, which will enable dynamic TEI addressing. This is important if BRI connections are necessary because Cisco does not support BRI using TEI 0, because it is reserved for PRI TEI address 0. If you see a TEI of 0 on a BRI, it means that a dynamic assignment has not yet occurred, and the BRI may not be talking to the switch. In the U.S., a BRI data line is implemented only in a point-to-point configuration.

Example 6-1 shows a typical ISDN Layer 2 negotiation.

Example 6-1 **debug isdn q921** *Output*

```
RouterA#debug isdn q921
BRI0: TX -> IDREQ  ri = 65279  ai = 127
BRI0: RX <- UI sapi = 0  tei = 127 i = 0x0801FF0504038090A218018896250101
BRI0: TX -> IDREQ  ri = 61168  ai = 127
BRI0: RX <- IDASSN  ri = 61168  ai =64
BRI0: TX -> SABMEp sapi = 0  tei = 64
BRI0: RX <- UAf sapi = 0  tei = 64
BRI0: TX -> INFOc sapi = 0  tei = 64  ns = 0  nr = 0  i = x08017F5A080280D1
BRI0: RX <- RRr sapi = 0  tei = 64  nr = 1
BRI0: RX <- INFOc sapi = 0  tei = 64  ns = 0  nr = 1  i = x08007B963902EF01
BRI0: TX -> RRr sapi = 0  tei = 64  nr = 1
```

Example 6-1   **debug isdn q921** *Output (Continued)*

```
BRI0: RX <- INFOc sapi = 0  tei = 64 ns = 1  nr = 1 i = 0x8007B962201013201013B0110
BRI0: TX -> RRr sapi = 0  tei = 64  nr = 2
BRI0: TX -> RRp sapi = 0  tei = 64  nr = 2
BRI0: RX <- RRf sapi = 0  tei = 64  nr = 1
BRI0: TX -> RRp sapi = 0  tei = 64  nr = 2
BRI0: RX <- RRf sapi = 0  tei = 64  nr = 1
```

NOTE   The following paragraphs are a partial explanation of the output listed in Example 6-1. You should take the time to understand this section because the output gives a great deal of troubleshooting information. You may need more than one reading to get it all straight.

The **ri** is a reference indicator. It provides the router and the switch a way to keep straight all the calls they may be processing. Notice in the **IDREQ** and the **IDASSN**, the **ri** value is the same. If the router sends an **IDREQ** and receives no response, it retries every two seconds. Each time the **ri** is different. The **ai** is an association indicator. **ai = 127** is the router's way of requesting a TEI from the switch. The switch reply is **ai = 64**. Therefore, 64 is the assigned TEI.

Notice that all remaining correspondence has **tei = 64** referenced. Once the router has a TEI, it sends a **SABME** (Set Asynchronous Balanced Mode Extended) message with **sapi = 0**. This means that this is a signalling connection (that is, this is all taking place over the D channel).

If no TEI is assigned, Layer 2 does activate and the output from the **debug isdn q921** command renders only **TX->IDREQ** lines. If all the Layer 2 processes are successful, you will see **MULTIPLE_FRAME_ESTABLISHED** under the **Layer 2 Status** section in the output of the **show isdn status** command. See Example 6-3 in the "ISDN Call Setup" section for a demonstration of the **show isdn status** command output.

Service Profile Identifiers (SPIDs)

Another key part of the ISDN BRI Layer 2 is the SPID. SPIDs are used only in BRI implementations. PRI implementations do not require the use of SPIDs. The SPID specifies the services to which you are entitled from the switch and defines the feature set that you ordered when the ISDN service was provisioned.

The SPID is a series of characters manually entered into the router's configuration to identify the router to the switch. This is different from the TEI discussed earlier. The TEI address is dynamically assigned. The SPID is statically assigned to the router based on information provided by the service provider. If needed, two SPIDs are configured, one for each channel of the BRI. Usually, the SPID includes the ten-digit phone number of each B channel followed by four additional digits (sometimes 0101) assigned by the telco.

SPID requirements are dependent on both the software revision and the switch. Many switch manufacturers are moving away from SPIDs, as they have already done in Europe. SPIDs are required only in the U.S., and then are used only by certain switches. 5ESS, DMS-100, and NI-1 support the use of SPIDs; however, it is not necessary to configure them unless it is required by the LEC.

ISDN Layer 3

ISDN Layer 3 does not impose the use of any network layer protocol for the B channels. The use of the D channel is defined in Q.931 and specified in ITU I.451 and Q.931 + Q.932.

Q.931 is used between the TE and the local ISDN switch. Inside the ISDN network, the Signalling System 7 (SS7) Internal Signalling Utility Protocol (ISUP) is used. Link Access Procedure on the D channel (LAPD) is the ISDN data link layer protocol for the D channel. The data link protocol for the B channel, however, can be any of the available protocols because the information can be passed transparently to the remote party. HDLC, PPP, or Frame Relay encapsulations can be used to pass data over the B channel.

LAPD

As mentioned, LAPD is the data link layer protocol for the D channel. It defines the framing characteristics for payload transmission, as illustrated in Figure 6-6.

Figure 6-6 *The LAPD Frame*

Flag	Address					Ctrl	Data	FCS	Flag
	SAPI 6 bits	C/R 1 bit	EA 1 bit	TEI 7 bits	EA 1 bit				
1	2					1	Variable	1	1

The following list defines the subfields of the Address portion of the LAPB frame.

- **SAPI**—Service access point identifier (6 bits)
- **C/R**—Command/response bit (1 bit)
- **EA**—Extended addressing bits
- **TEI**—Terminal Endpoint Identifier

NOTE   All fields are one byte except for the Address field, which has two bytes. Data is variable in length.

ISDN Call Setup

The setup procedure for ISDN calls is very similar to that of other circuit switched technologies. It begins with a request, which is acknowledged. The acknowledging switch then forwards the setup request on to the next switch in the line, and so on. Once the called party is reached, a connect message is sent, which also must be acknowledged. Figure 6-7 depicts the ISDN call setup procedure.

Figure 6-7   *ISDN Call Setup*

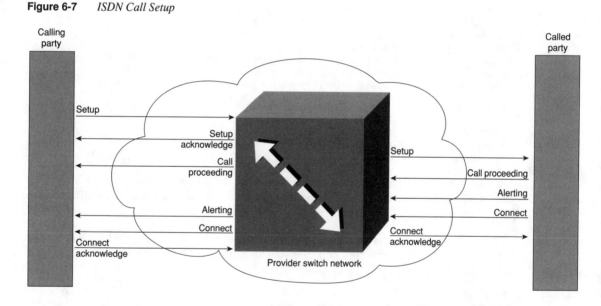

Prior to the actual Connect and the Call Proceeding (CALL PROC) messages, there can be a number of different progress messages indicating call progress. For instance, the calling party sends setup messages to the switch. The switch responds with the Setup Acknowledgement (SETUP ACK) and Call Proceeding messages. The remote switch then sends the setup message to the called party, which acknowledges with a CALL PROC message. Alerting messages can then be sent, although they are optional, depending on carrier implementation. Alerting messages are normally associated with voice traffic and are not usually implemented in data calls.

Connect messages flow from the called party to the calling party when the connection is established and can be followed by a Connect Acknowledgement (CONNECT ACK), which is also optional. Once the calling party receives the CONNECT ACK, the call setup is complete.

Example 6-2 shows the beginning of a call setup. The output is from a **ping** to the remote side while the **debug isdn q931** command is active. Note the **ping** timeout (.), which is followed by a **ping** success (!) after the call setup.

Example 6-2 **debug isdn q931** *Command Output Reveals Call Setup Details*

```
RouterA#debug isdn q931
RouterA#ping 10.12.1.2
Type escape sequence to abort.
Sending 5, 100-byte ICMP Echos to 10.12.1.2, timeout is 2 seconds:
ISDN BR0: TX -> SETUP pd = 8  callref = 0x0E
    Bearer Capability i = 0x8890
    Channel ID i = 0x83
    Keypad Facility i = 0x3935353532303032
ISDN BR0: RX <- SETUP_ACK pd = 8  callref = 0x8E
Channel ID i = 0x89
ISDN BR0: RX <- CALL_PROC pd = 8  callref = 0x8E
ISDN BR0: RX <- CONNECT pd = 8  callref = 0x8E
%LINK-3-UPDOWN:Interface BRI0:1, changed state to up
ISDN BR0: TX -> CONNECT_ACK pd = 8  callref = 0x0E
%LINEPROTO-5-UPDOWN: Line protocol on Interface BRI0:1, changed state to up.!!!
Success rate is 60 percent (3/5), round-trip min/avg/max = 36/36/36 ms
%ISDN-6-CONNECT: Interface BRI0:1 is now connected to 2145553000 RouterB
```

The ICMP traffic falls within the parameters of what has been defined as interesting traffic. The call is placed and interface BRI 0, B channel 1 can be seen initializing and completing the call. The last line of the output states that the call is connected to 2145553000, RouterB.

Once the call is up, you can monitor the call using the **show isdn status** command. This is a useful troubleshooting command because it shows the status of all three layers of ISDN that have been discussed in this chapter.

Example 6-3 shows the output from the **show isdn status** command. Note that both B channels are connected to the remote side. This is visible under the Layer 2 Status section.

Example 6-3 **show isdn status** *Command Output*

```
RouterA#show isdn status
The current ISDN Switchtype = basic-5ess
ISDN BRI0 interface
  Layer 1 Status:
        ACTIVE
  Layer 2 Status:
    TEI = 90, State = MULTIPLE_FRAME_ESTABLISHED
  Layer 3 Status:
        1 Active Layer 2 Call(s)
        Activated dsl 0 CCBs are 2, Allocated = 2
          callid=0, sapi=0, ces=2
          callid=8000, sapi=0, ces=1
```

ISDN Call Release

Any party in the network can release the call for whatever reason. Whether the release of the call is intentional or accidental (that is, due to some type of failure in the network), the call is torn down completely.

When either the calling or called party is ready to disconnect a call, that party issues a disconnect (DISC) message. The disconnect is not negotiable. If necessary, the call can be re-established, but once a disconnect is issued, the call comes down.

When a DISC is issued, it is acknowledged with a release message (RELEASED). The switch forwards the RELEASED message, which should be followed by a Release Complete (RELEASE COMPLETE) message. Figure 6-8 depicts the ISDN call release process.

Figure 6-8   *ISDN Call Release*

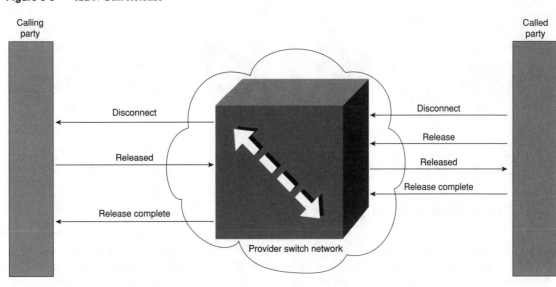

Implementing Basic DDR

Dial-on-demand routing (DDR) is a feature available on ISDN-capable Cisco routers. It was created to enable users to save money on usage-based ISDN. Use-based ISDN occurs when charges are assessed for every minute of ISDN circuit connect time.

Obviously, in a charge-by-the-minute scenario, the connection should be down during no or low-volume traffic times. DDR provides that capability and offers a wide array of commands and configuration variations. Many of those configuration options are covered in the remainder of this chapter.

The configuration tasks for implementing basic DDR are as follows:

Step 1   Set the ISDN switch type.

Step 2   Specify interesting traffic.

Step 3   Specify static routes.

Step 4   Define the interface encapsulation and ISDN addressing parameters.

Step 5   Configure the protocol addressing.

Step 6   Define any additional interface information.

Figure 6-9 depicts the network topology that is referenced throughout this chapter.

Figure 6-9   *Sample ISDN Topology*

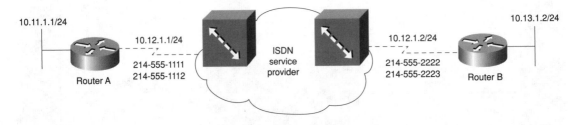

Step 1: Setting the ISDN Switch Type

The telephone company provides you the type of switch to which you are connecting. Manufacturers of ISDN central office switches (also known as *local exchange equipment*) divide the local exchange into two functions: local termination and exchange termination. The local termination function primarily deals with the transmission facility and termination of the local loop. The exchange termination function deals with the switching portion of the local exchange.

To function, the switch type must be specified on the router. Use the **isdn switch-type** command to configure the router for the type of switch to which the router connects. Your telephone company provides you the type of switch that is located in the central office to which your router will connect. For a listing of supported switch types, see Table 6-2.

The **isdn switch-type** command has historically been issued from the global configuration prompt. However, as of IOS version 12.0, this command can be issued from the interface configuration prompt as well. The usage of this command is included in Example 6-4.

Step 2: Specifying Interesting Traffic

The entire configuration of DDR depends on how the traffic types that cause a call setup to occur are triggered. This traffic is known as *interesting traffic*.

Cisco's implementation of DDR allows for as much or as little specificity of interesting traffic as is deemed necessary; interesting traffic is defined by the creation of *dialer-lists* that can specify that an entire protocol suite, no matter the level of traffic, can trigger a call setup.

Dialer-lists can be associated with standard or extended access lists to be specific to various traffic types. Rather than associating an access list with an interface, it is associated with a dialer-list (discussed in the "Specifying Interesting Traffic with Access Lists" section in this chapter).

Example 6-4 shows a basic configuration in which all IP traffic has been specified as interesting. This is specified in the *dialer-list line*. The dialer-list is associated with the proper interface using a *dialer-group* line, as shown.

Note that the list number and the group numbers are identical. This number ties the dialer-list and dialer-group together. This number cannot be re-used by any other dialer-list or dialer-group in the same router.

Example 6-4 *Basic DDR Configuration on RouterA*

```
RouterA(config)#isdn switch-type basic-5ess
!
RouterA(config)#interface BRI0
RouterA(config-if)#ip address 10.12.1.1 255.255.255.0
RouterA(config-if)#encapsulation ppp
RouterA(config-if)#dialer idle-timeout 180
RouterA(config-if)#dialer map ip 10.12.1.2 5552222
RouterA(config-if)#dialer-group 1
!
RouterA(config)#dialer-list 1 protocol ip permit
```

The remote router configuration should be similar. Example 6-5 details the basic configuration of the remote router.

Example 6-5 *Basic DDR Configuration on RouterB*

```
RouterA(config)#isdn switch-type basic-5ess
!
RouterA(config)#interface BRI0
RouterA(config-if)#ip address 10.12.1.2 255.255.255.0
RouterA(config-if)#encapsulation ppp
RouterA(config-if)#dialer idle-timeout 180
RouterA(config-if)#dialer map ip 10.12.1.1 5551111
RouterA(config-if)#dialer-group 1
!
RouterA(config)#dialer-list 1 protocol ip permit
```

Specifying Interesting Traffic with Access Lists

Example 6-4 and 6-5 deal with a blanket statement enabling entire protocol suites. This type of implementation is not always the best, or preferred, method of defining interesting traffic.

To define specific traffic types as interesting traffic, you should use access lists. Any type of access list can be implemented in defining interesting traffic. Rather than being associated with an interface, the access list is associated with the dialer-list.

This access list discussion focuses on IP access lists because the author assumes that you are already familiar with access lists to some degree.

Example 6-6 shows a sample configuration using IP extended access lists to define interesting traffic. The explanation follows the output.

Example 6-6   *Extended Access Lists with Interesting Traffic*

```
RouterA#config t
RouterA(config)#access-list 101 deny tcp any any eq ftp
RouterA(config)#access-list 101 deny tcp any any eq telnet
RouterA(config)#access-list 101 permit ip any any
!
RouterA(config)#interface bri 0
RouterA(config-if)#ip address 10.12.1.1 255.255.255.0
RouterA(config-if)#encapsulation ppp
<output omitted>
RouterA(config-if)#dialer-group 2
!
RouterA(config)#dialer-list 2 protocol ip list 101
```

Example 6-6 implements a more specific definition of interesting traffic. **access-list 101** is denying FTP and Telnet. That is, they are not allowed to trigger a call setup. Any other IP traffic attempting to traverse the link triggers the call. Once the call is up, Telnet and FTP can go across freely.

Notice the dialer-list line highlighted in Example 6-6. Rather than enabling the entire IP protocol suite to trigger the call, this line specifies that all traffic attempting to exit through BRI 0 must be tested against **access-list 101**.

The interface configuration has not changed from our basic configuration model. Only the dialer-list has been altered to point to the access list. The dialer-list still must point to the dialer-group on the interface (that is, the dialer-list and dialer-group numbers must match). The access list number can be any valid standard or extended access list number (Example 6-6 demonstrates IP only). However, as stated earlier, interesting traffic for any protocol can be implemented using the appropriate access list command structure.

Step 3: Specifying Static Routes

In the classic DDR model, dynamic routing protocol updates are not moving across the link, so it is important that static routes be used in place of dynamic updates. To provide bidirectional reachability between the two sites in the absence of routing protocol traffic, static routes should be configured at both the local and remote routers. As demonstrated in Example 6-6, any IP traffic that needs to cross the link has been defined as interesting and will trigger a call setup.

Do not confuse the definition of interesting traffic with the implementation of security measures. DDR defines only what types of traffic can initiate a call, not what can go across it. Once a call has been established, any type of traffic that has been configured on the BRI interface traverses the link freely. This includes routing updates. If the IP network on which the BRI interface exists is included in the routing protocol configuration (and the BRI interface isn't specified as passive), routing updates can flow across the link while it is active. Once static routes have been specified, it is important to make the BRI interface(s) passive. Passive interfaces are discussed later in this chapter.

Static routes are necessary in DDR because the ISDN link is not always active. In a dynamic routing environment, the fact that the link is down could be construed as a network down condition and reachability could be lost. To combat this, the link shows that it's spoofing while it's down. Example 6-7 demonstrates this through the **show interface bri 0** command.

Example 6-7 **show interface bri 0** *Command Output*

```
RouterA#show interface bri 0
BRI0 is up, line protocol is up (spoofing)
Hardware is BRI
MTU 1500 bytes, BW 64 Kbit, DLY 20000 usec, rely 255/255, load 1/255
Encapsulation PPP, loopback not set
Last input 0:00:06, output 0:00:06, output hang never
Last clearing of "show interface" counters never
Input queue: 0/75/0 (size/max/drops); Total output drops: 0
Output queue: 0/64/0 (size/threshold/drops)
   Conversations  0/1 (active/max active)
   Reserved Conversations 0/0 (allocated/max allocated)
5 minute input rate 0 bits/sec, 0 packets/sec
5 minute output rate 0 bits/sec, 0 packets/sec
   359 packets input, 5814 bytes, 1 no buffer
   Received 0 broadcasts, 0 runts, 0 giants
   0 input errors, 0 CRC, 0 frame, 0 overrun, 0 ignored, 0 abort
   70 packets output, 307 bytes, 0 underruns
   0 output errors, 0 collisions, 6 interface resets, 0 restarts
   0 output buffer failures, 0 output buffers swapped out
   5 carrier transitions
```

The first line in the output shows that the interface is up and the line protocol is down, but the line protocol is actually up because the router knows this is a DDR connection and keeps the line protocol state at **up (spoofing)**.

Obviously, while there is no connectivity, routing updates cannot flow. If all IP traffic is defined as interesting and the implementation in question is using a dynamic routing protocol, the routing updates keep the link up at all times. For example, IGRP uses a 90-second update cycle. Previous examples in this chapter placed a **dialer idle-timeout 180** command on the interface. This command states that the link should come down after 180 seconds of idle time. If IGRP updates are sent every 90 seconds, the idle timeout countdown is reset with each update. The very purpose of DDR has been defeated.

Step 4: Defining the Interface Encapsulation and ISDN Addressing Parameters

ISDN installations are capable of employing HDLC or PPP encapsulation (among others). PPP is most often used because of its rich feature set and flexibility. PPP offers the use of a single B channel or the combination of the two B channels in a single aggregate pipe. It enables us to decide when a connection should be dialed, when an additional channel should be brought up and used, when to disconnect the call, and other options that are discussed in the next couple of sections.

As discussed earlier in Chapter 5, PPP encapsulates network layer protocol information over point-to-point links. Although it can be configured on a variety of interfaces, our focus remains on the ISDN-capable interface. To establish communications over an ISDN link, each end of the PPP link must first send Link Control Protocol (LCP) packets to configure and test the data link. After the link has been established and optional facilities have been negotiated as needed, PPP must send Network Control Protocol (NCP) packets to choose and configure one or more network-layer protocols.

Once each of the chosen network layer protocols has been configured, datagrams from each network layer protocol can be sent over the link. The link remains configured for communications until explicit LCP or NCP packets close the link down, or until some external event occurs (for example, a period of inactivity).

Functionally, PPP is simply a pathway opened for multiple protocols to share simultaneously. The call setup is initiated by interesting traffic as defined using access lists and terminated by an external event, such as manual clearing or idle timer expiration. Any interesting traffic that traverses the link resets the idle timer; non-interesting traffic does not.

Configuring ISDN Addressing

ISDN addressing uses phone numbers that are exactly like the phone numbers utilized by millions of people day in and day out. These numbers are telco-designated and locally significant. They usually include an area code, a local exchange, and additional digits.

To function, the router must understand what phone number to dial as well as when to dial it. How does it come to know this information? The same way it knows everything else it knows—the administrator tells it.

The administrator uses dialer maps to tell the router how and when to dial a particular destination. Dialer maps serve the same basic function as does ARP in a LAN: the mapping of network layer addresses to data link layer addresses. In this case, the data link layer address is the phone number. To get to a specific destination, the router must associate the proper destination phone number with the next logical hop protocol address.

Step 5: Configuring Protocol Addressing

Once the encapsulation has been decided upon, you must apply a protocol addressing scheme. You can configure DDR with any routable protocol. Each protocol that must pass across the link must have a configured address.

For IP implementations, you must supply an IP address and subnet mask to the interface. The protocol addressing scheme should be decided upon well in advance of any deployment of any networking technology.

In IPX implementations, you must apply an IPX network number to the BRI interface. The host portion of the address is hard-coded in the global configuration or is taken from the Burned In Address (BIA) of the lowest numbered LAN interface (that is, Ethernet 0). When IPX routing is enabled and IPX network numbers are configured on interfaces, the IPX RIP and the SAP protocols are automatically enabled for those interfaces.

IPX RIP and SAP are broadcast-based updates for routing table information and Novell NetWare service propagation, respectively. These broadcasts are on independent 60-second timers. You might or might not wish for this traffic to go across your ISDN link. To avoid this traffic, you can simply not include RIP and SAP in your interesting traffic definitions. This is accomplished by implementing IPX access lists to filter out RIP and SAP. The access lists are then associated with the dialer list defining interesting traffic. At this point, RIP and SAP go across the link only as long as the link is up because of the transfer traffic that fits the interesting parameters.

You can also define IPX static routes and static SAP entries. Example 6-8 shows the encapsulation as well as the application of an IPX network number and an IP address to the BRI interface.

Example 6-8 *Protocol Addressing*

```
RouterA(config)#interface BRI0
RouterA(config-if)#ip address 10.12.1.1 255.255.255.0
RouterA(config-if)#ipx network number 80fa
RouterA(config-if)#encapsulation ppp
```

Step 6: Defining Additional Interface Information

The purpose of DDR is to bring down the ISDN link when the traffic volume is low or idle. However, at times, the traffic volume can simply be in a short lull. Indeed, LAN traffic is bursty—quiet times followed by an explosion of traffic.

To avoid the link coming down when traffic flow ceases and then being forced to redial, use the **dialer idle-timeout** command. Executing this command dictates that when traffic defined as interesting has ceased to flow across the link for the specified period of time (in seconds), go ahead and bring down the link. For instance, if the command **dialer idle-timeout 180** is used at the interface configuration mode, the link comes down three minutes after the last piece of interesting traffic has traversed the link. Note that only interesting traffic resets the timer. Any non-interesting traffic goes across, but does not contribute to keeping the link up.

SPIDs

As discussed earlier in this chapter, many BRI implementations use SPIDs. The SPID simply informs the switch of the purchased feature set for the particular installation. These SPIDs are not standardized in their format. The telco provider specifies the use of SPIDs and the appropriate values, if necessary.

To apply SPIDs to the interface, use the commands **isdn spid1** and **isdn spid2**. These commands have an optional parameter at the end known as *ldn*. This is the local dial number. As stated, it is optional; however, it has been found that in some implementations, the circuit does not perform optimally in the absence of the *ldn* parameter. In addition, although it doesn't hurt to have the *ldn* parameter on the command line, it can hurt sometimes not to have it.

As noted earlier, PRI does not use SPID information. The *ldn* parameter must be used if the switch is programmed to look for them (the telco will inform you of this). If they are expected and not specified, the circuit may not come up. This lack of coming up can be seen in the **show isdn status** command under the Layer 2 status section. It shows **invalid ldn** and **spid invalid**. Obviously the circuit is not initialized in this state.

Caller ID Screening

Utilizing the features offered by caller ID, the router can be configured to accept calls only from specified callers. The **isdn answer** command is used for this purpose. The configuration is quite simple. Once this command has been issued, the router only accepts calls from numbers that have been specified. Use of this feature combats unauthorized use of the facilities.

Configuring Additional Interface Information

Example 6-9 illustrates the concepts of this section, including SPIDs, the **dialer idle-timeout** command, call screening, and dialer maps.

Example 6-9 *Optional Configuration Parameters*

```
RouterA(config)#interface BRI0
RouterA(config-if)#ip address 10.12.1.1 255.255.255.0
RouterA(config-if)#encapsulation ppp
RouterA(config-if)#dialer idle-timeout 180
RouterA(config-if)#isdn spid1 21455511110101 2145551111
RouterA(config-if)#isdn spid2 21455511120101 2145551112
RouterA(config-if)#isdn answer 2145552222
RouterA(config-if)#isdn answer 2145552223
RouterA(config-if)#dialer map ip 10.12.1.2 2145552222
RouterA(config-if)#dialer map ip 10.12.1.2 2145552223
RouterA(config-if)#dialer-group 1
!
RouterA(config)#dialer-list 1 protocol ip permit
!
RouterA(config)#ip route 10.13.1.0 255.255.255.0 10.12.1.2
```

Passive Interfaces

Static routes used in place of dynamic routing functions also allow the link to be dropped. However, you must take care in your configuration.

To continue the discussion, an IGRP example is used; consider the basic IGRP/DDR configuration in Example 6-10.

Example 6-10 *Passive Interface Justification*

```
RouterA(config)#isdn switch-type basic-5ess
!
RouterA(config)#interface ethernet 0
RouterA(config-if)#ip address 10.11.1.1 255.255.255.0
!
RouterA(config)#interface BRI0
RouterA(config-if)#ip address 10.12.1.1 255.255.255.0
RouterA(config-if)#encapsulation ppp
RouterA(config-if)#dialer idle-timeout 180
RouterA(config-if)#isdn spid1 21455511110101 2145551111
RouterA(config-if)#isdn spid2 21455511120101 2145551112
RouterA(config-if)#isdn answer 2145552222
RouterA(config-if)#isdn answer 2145552223
RouterA(config-if)#dialer map ip 10.12.1.2 2145552222
RouterA(config-if)#dialer map ip 10.12.1.2 2145552223
RouterA(config-if)#dialer-group 1
!
RouterA(config)#access-list 101 permit tcp any any eq telnet
RouterA(config)#access-list 101 permit tcp any any eq ftp
RouterA(config)#access-list 101 permit tcp any any eq ftp-data
!
RouterA(config)#dialer-list 1 protocol ip list 101
!
```

continues

Example 6-10 *Passive Interface Justification (Continued)*

```
RouterA(config)#router igrp 100
RouterA(config-router)#network 10.0.0.0
!
RouterA(config)#ip route 10.13.1.0 255.255.255.0 10.12.1.2
```

There is a stub network on the remote side; this stub network is network 10.13.1.0/24. This configuration has a problem: while the static route is properly defined, IGRP is still sending updates across the link. In addition, because interface BRI 0 is part of the classful network 10.0.0.0, it is included in routing updates. A simple alteration under the IGRP configuration remedies the problem, as demonstrated by Example 6-11.

Example 6-11 *Making the Configuration Work Properly*

```
RouterA(config)#router igrp 100
RouterA(config-router)#network 10.0.0.0
RouterA(config-router)#passive-interface bri 0
```

Making an interface passive lets the routing protocol know that it should not attempt to send updates out the specified interface.

The **passive-interface** command has a slightly different effect, depending on the type of routing protocol used. For RIP and IGRP, the operation is the same. These two protocols do not send updates out the passive interface, although they can receive updates through these interfaces.

OSPF and EIGRP also act the same. These protocols rely on the establishment of communications with neighboring routers. If the interface is passive, this cannot occur. Therefore routing updates are neither sent nor received on the passive interface. If the neighbor relationship cannot be achieved, updates cannot flow.

Static Route Redistribution

An issue arises from time to time with static routes—static routes are just that, static. The dynamic routing protocol does not advertise the static route, so reachability can be affected. To remedy this, the static route can simply be redistributed into the dynamic routing protocol. It is important that a default metric be assigned in the configuration of the redistribution, or the routing protocol will not know how to treat the route. Redistribution is beyond our scope at this time and is not discussed further.

Default Routes

From time to time, a router is faced with a dilemma that it would dread (if it could dread, that is). The dilemma is what to do when it doesn't know what to do. As it stands now, in the absence of a suitable routing table entry to a given destination, a router has no choice but to return an ICMP "Destination Unreachable" message to the sender.

This dilemma, however, is easily remedied. By giving the router a default route, it can forward the traffic on to another router that may have a suitable entry in a routing table to keep the traffic flow alive. This is known as the *gateway of last resort*.

The default route can be entered in a number of different ways. Depending on the routing protocol and its configuration, the default route can even be injected into the routing table automatically.

If the default route must be entered manually (as with RIP), you can issue the **ip default-network** command. There is a catch here, however: The router must have a valid route (either static or dynamic) to the default network. If the routing table does not have an entry for the default network, one must be entered. Example 6-12 illustrates this concept.

Example 6-12 *Static Route with* **ip default-network**

```
RouterB(config)#ip route 10.11.1.0 255.255.255.0 10.12.1.1
RouterB(config)#ip default-network 10.11.1.0
```

As mentioned earlier, you may have the option of performing this function in another way: If the routing protocol supports it, a static default route to the network 0.0.0.0 0.0.0.0 is used. The entry is that of a static route. Example 6-13 illustrates the static default route.

Example 6-13 *Static Default Route*

```
RouterB(config)#ip route 0.0.0.0 0.0.0.0 10.12.1.1
```

Notice that a specific next hop was specified. This is significant in that a static route with a specific next hop is not redistributed automatically. If the overall desire is to have this route automatically redistribute, an outbound interface can be specified. This is true with all static routes, not just the static default route. Example 6-14 illustrates the same configuration, but with one that does have to be manually redistributed.

Example 6-14 *Automatically Redistributed Default Route*

```
RouterB(config)#ip route 0.0.0.0 0.0.0.0 Serial 0
```

In this case, any traffic for which the router does not have a suitable routing entry is forwarded out interface serial 0 to the device on the other side of the link.

Note that the example does not reference BRI 0 as the outbound interface. Although it is a valid command configuration to place BRI 0 at the end of the default route command (that is, the router allows it), this configuration will not function because the routing table entry is the origin of the next hop address information that triggers the call to the other side of the network. In addition, the dialer map association ties a phone number to that next hop address. If there's no routing table entry, the device has no way of knowing the next hop address. Therefore, it does not know which dialer map to utilize for the call and the call fails.

Rate Adaptation

Earlier in the chapter, a solution was discussed that involved the use of non-native ISDN routers being placed into service in an ISDN network. A short discussion described how this is possible using TA.

In this type of implementation, the **dialer in-band** command is a necessary part of the configuration which effectively takes 8 kbps from each B channel for use by the signaling entity. In other words, the 16 kbps that would normally be out-of-band in the D channel now has to be taken from the B channels. Effectively, the throughput is now 56 kbps for each B channel.

Should a native solution dial into a non-native solution with out-of-band signaling, the native solution would need to step down its speed to 56 kbps. This is done with rate adaptation. The implementation of rate adaptation is simply an extension of the **dialer map** command. The **dialer-map** command tells the router that to reach a specific next hop address, a specific phone number must be called. The **dialer-map** command simply associates the destination protocol address with the appropriate phone number to dial to get there. Example 6-15 illustrates the configuration of the router dialing into the non-native 56-kbps installation.

Example 6-15 *Rate Adaptation*

```
RouterA(config)#interface BRI0
RouterA(config-if)#ip address 10.12.1.1 255.255.255.0
RouterA(config-if)#encapsulation ppp
RouterA(config-if)#dialer idle-timeout 180
RouterA(config-if)#dialer map ip 10.12.1.2 speed 56 2145552222
RouterA(config-if)#dialer map ip 10.12.1.2 speed 56 2145552223
RouterA(config-if)#dialer-group 1
!
RouterA(config)#dialer-list 1 protocol ip permit
!
RouterA(config)#ip route 10.13.1.0 255.255.255.0 10.12.1.2
```

Bandwidth on Demand

Bandwidth on demand (BOD) is a Cisco proprietary implementation that allows the aggregation of multiple B channels into a single logical connection. This implementation is widely used in Cisco-centric networks.

The implementation of Cisco's BOD solution is accomplished through the **dialer load-threshold** command. The variable parameter in the command is *load*. When the interface is connected to the remote side, a measurement of *load* is kept and updated continually based on utilization of the link. The load is measured on a scale of 1–255, with 255 representing link saturation. This command is typically utilized in almost every DDR configuration to provide load sharing over both B channels. Example 6-16 demonstrates this concept.

Example 6-16 *Implementing Cisco's BOD Feature*

```
RouterA(config)#interface BRI0
RouterA(config-if)#ip address 10.12.1.1 255.255.255.0
RouterA(config-if)#encapsulation ppp
RouterA(config-if)#dialer idle-timeout 180
RouterA(config-if)#dialer load-threshold 110
RouterA(config-if)#dialer map ip 10.12.1.2 speed 56 2145552222
RouterA(config-if)#dialer map ip 10.12.1.2 speed 56 2145552223
RouterA(config-if)#dialer-group 1
!
RouterA(config)#dialer-list 1 protocol ip permit
!
RouterA(config)#ip route 10.13.1.0 255.255.255.0 10.12.1.2
```

The **dialer load-threshold 110** statement specifies that if the load of the first B channel reaches 110 (about 43 percent utilization), the second B channel should be initialized and, once connected, the traffic should load balance across both channels.

The router recalculates the load of the link every 5 minutes to maintain an accurate picture without unnecessarily using CPU cycles. In a multivendor environment, BOD may not be a viable choice due to its proprietary nature. For such cases, Multilink PPP is more appropriate.

Multilink PPP

Multilink PPP is a specification that enables the bandwidth aggregation of multiple B channels into one logical pipe. Its mission is comparable to that of Cisco's BOD. More specifically, the Multilink PPP feature provides load-balancing functionality over multiple wide area network (WAN) links, while providing multivendor interoperability, packet fragmentation and proper sequencing, and load calculation on both inbound and outbound traffic.

Cisco's implementation of Multilink PPP supports the fragmentation and packet sequencing specifications in RFC 1717. Multilink PPP enables packets to be fragmented and the fragments to be sent (at the same time) over multiple point-to-point links to the same remote address.

As with BOD, the multiple links come up in response to a **dialer load-threshold** command. The load can be calculated on inbound traffic or outbound traffic as needed for the traffic between the specific sites. Multilink PPP provides bandwidth on demand and reduces transmission latency across WAN links. Also, as in BOD, a router running MLPPP recalculates the load every five minutes.

At any time, you can use a **show interface** command to see the current load of the interface. Example 6-17 shows the configuration and the **show interface BRI 0** command output.

Example 6-17 *Multilink PPP*

```
RouterA(config)#interface BRI0
RouterA(config-if)#ip address 10.12.1.1 255.255.255.0
RouterA(config-if)#encapsulation ppp
RouterA(config-if)#ppp multilink
RouterA(config-if)#dialer idle-timeout 180
RouterA(config-if)#dialer load-threshold 110
RouterA(config-if)#dialer map ip 10.12.1.2 speed 56 2145552222
RouterA(config-if)#dialer map ip 10.12.1.2 speed 56 2145552223
RouterA(config-if)#dialer-group 1
!
RouterA(config)#dialer-list 1 protocol ip permit
!
RouterA(config)#ip route 10.13.1.0 255.255.255.0 10.12.1.2
RouterA(config)#end
!
RouterA#show interface bri 0 1
BRI0:1 is up, line protocol is up
 Hardware is BRI with integrated NT1
 MTU 1500 bytes, BW 64 Kbit, DLY 20000 usec, rely 255/255, load 1/255
 Encapsulation PPP, loopback not set, keepalive set (10 sec)
 LCP Open, multilink Open
Open: IPCP
 Last input 00:00:01, output 00:00:01, output hang never
 Last clearing of "show interface" counters never
 Queueing strategy: fifo
 Output queue 0/40, 0 drops; input queue 0/75, 0 drops
 5 minute input rate 0 bits/sec, 0 packets/sec
 5 minute output rate 0 bits/sec, 0 packets/sec
 6148 packets input, 142342 bytes, 0 no buffer
 Received 6148 broadcasts, 0 runts, 0 giants, 0 throttles
 0 input errors, 0 CRC, 0 frame, 0 overrun, 0 ignored, 0 abort
 6198 packets output, 148808 bytes, 0 underruns
 0 output errors, 0 collisions, 0 interface resets
 0 output buffer failures, 0 output buffers swapped out
 9 carrier transitions
```

The preceding **show interface bri 0 1** command shows only the first B channel (hence the **bri 0 1**). If the second B channel were up, the command **show interface bri 0 2** could be entered to view its status. Notice that as highlighted in Example 6-17, the load is currently 1/255. In other words, little or no traffic is flowing across the link.

Troubleshooting Multilink PPP

Multilink PPP can have its share of issues. Fortunately, there are some troubleshooting commands readily available. The following commands are useful in resolving any issues with your PPP connection(s). Each command is followed by sample output.

show ppp multilink Command

Executing the **show ppp multilink** command displays the current status of Multilink PPP sessions. Example 6-18 shows sample output of a call in progress.

Example 6-18 *show ppp multilink Command Output*

```
RouterA#show ppp multilink
Bundle RouterA, 1 member, Master link is BRI 0
Dialer Interface is BRI0
  0 lost fragments, 0 reordered, 0 unassigned, sequence 0x0/0x0 rcvd/sent
  0 discarded, 0 lost received, 1/255 load

Member Link: 1 (max not set, min not set)
BRI0:1
```

show dialer Command

Executing the **show dialer** command displays active calls and status information. Example 6-19 shows sample output of calls in session.

Example 6-19 *show dialer Command Output*

```
RouterA#show dialer
BRI0 - dialer type = ISDN
Dial String      Successes       Failures      Last called      Last status
2145552222       18              0             00:01:12         successful

0 incoming call(s) have been screened.

BRI0:1 - dialer type = ISDN
Idle timer (120 secs), Fast idle timer (20 secs)
Wait for carrier (30 secs), Re-enable (15 secs)
Dialer state is multilink member
Dial reason: ip (s=10.12.1.1, d=10.12.1.2)
Connected to 2145552222 (RouterB)

BRI0:2 - dialer type = ISDN
Idle timer (120 secs), Fast idle timer (20 secs)
Wait for carrier (30 secs), Re-enable (15 secs)
Dialer state is idle
 Idle timer (120 secs), Fast idle timer (20 secs)
Wait for carrier (30 secs), Re-enable (15 secs)
Dialer state is data link layer up
Time until disconnect 93 secs
Connected to 2145552223 (RouterB)
```

debug ppp multilink Command

Executing the **debug ppp multilink** command monitors the PPP connect phase. Example 6-20 shows sample output of a **ping** triggered call.

Example 6-20 debug ppp multilink *Command Output*

```
RouterA#debug ppp multilink
*Apr 14 03:22:10.489: %LINK-3-UPDOWN: Interface BRI0:1, changed state to up
*Apr 14 03:22:10.497:%LINEPROTO-5-UPDOWN: Line protocol on Interface BRI0:1,
changed state to up
*Apr 14 03:22:10.520%LINK-3-UPDOWN: Interface BRI0:2, changed state to up
*Apr 14 03:22:10.554: BR0:1 MLP: O seq 80000000 size 58
*Apr 14 03:22:10.558: BR0:2 MLP: O seq 40000001 size 60
*Apr 14 03:22:10.586: BR0:1 MLP: I seq 80000000 size 58
*Apr 14 03:22:10.590: BR0:2 MLP: I seq 40000001 size 60
*Apr 14 03:22:10.598: BR0:1 MLP: O seq 80000002 size 58
*Apr 14 03:22:10.598: BR0:2 MLP: O seq 40000003 size 60
*Apr 14 03:22:10.629: BR0:1 MLP: I seq 80000002 size 58
*Apr 14 03:22:10.629: BR0:2 MLP: I seq 40000003 size 60!!!
*Apr 14 03:22:10.630:Success rate is 94 percent (47/50), round-trip min/avg/max =
36/41/128 ms
*Apr 14 03:22:10.637: BR0:1 MLP: O seq 80000004 size 58
*Apr 14 03:22:10.641: BR0:2 MLP: O seq 40000005 size 60
%LINEPROTO-5-UPDOWN: Line protocol on Interface BRI0:2, changed state to up
*Apr 14 03:22:10.669: BR0:1 MLP: I seq 80000004 size 58
Apr 14 03:22:11.330:%ISDN-6-CONNECT:InterfaceBRI0:2 is now connected to 2145552223
RouterB
```

debug dialer Command

There are many more commands and command outputs that are useful in troubleshooting the dial process in general. For instance, the **debug dialer** command is one of the best tools to use in figuring out what traffic is attempting to traverse the ISDN link. Example 6-21 shows the **debug dialer** command output.

Example 6-21 *debug dialer Command Output*

```
RouterA#ping 10.12.1.2
%SYS-5-CONFIG_I: Configured from console by console
Type escape sequence to abort.
Sending 5, 100-byte ICMP Echos to 10.12.1.2, timeout is 2 seconds:
BRI0: Dialing cause ip (s=10.12.1.1, d=10.12.1.2)
BRI0: Attempting to dial 2145552222.
%LINK-3-UPDOWN: Interface BRI0:1, changed state to up
%LINEPROTO-5-UPDOWN: Line protocol on Interface BRI0:1, changed state to up.!!!
Success rate is 60 percent (3/5), round-trip min/avg/max = 36/41/52 ms
%ISDN-6-CONNECT: Interface BRI0:1 is now connected to 2145552222 RouterB
```

The troubleshooting section of this book could continue on indefinitely. However, the commands here are only those that stay within the scope of the exam. For more information, go to www.cisco.com/univercd/cc/td/doc/product/software/ios113ed/dbook/index.htm and check out the **debug** command reference.

Advanced DDR Operations

Up to this point, the discussion has been based in the basics of DDR. With a more solid understanding of the technological base of ISDN and DDR implementations, it is now appropriate to discuss some additional, and more advanced, features available with DDR.

DDR installations are capable of utilizing dialer profiles (utilizing virtual dialer interfaces) and rotary groups. The installations also provide redundancy through dial backup and enable the use of dynamic routes across a DDR link while maintaining the routing table and keeping the link idle through snapshot routing.

Using Dialer Profiles

Dialer profiles first became a configuration option in Cisco IOS Release 11.2. The premise behind dialer profiles was to enable flexible design capabilities for deployment of custom profiles that meet users' dial access needs. This feature separates the logical function of DDR from the physical interface that places or receives the calls.

Prior to dialer profiles, B channels had no choice but to take on the configuration options applied to the physical interface. In this type of deployment, all users who dialed into a particular access server received the same configuration, regardless of their access needs. With dialer profiles, each user's needs can be met by customized services and unique interfaces. In other words, each individual profile contains appropriately matched interface definitions and needs.

Dialer profiles enable the configuration of a logical interface to be associated with one or more physical interfaces. With this type of deployment, the logical and physical configurations are dynamically bound call by call. A dialer profile is made up of three components:

- **Dialer interfaces**—Logical entities implementing a dialer profile on a destination-by-destination basis. Destination specific settings are applied to the dialer interface configurations. Multiple phone numbers (that is, dialer strings) can be specified for the same interface. Using a dialer map class, multiple configuration variations can be associated with a single phone number.

- **Dialer map class**—Defines specific characteristics for any call made to the specified dial string. Earlier in this chapter, the issue of rate adaptation was discussed. The configuration examples specified the *speed 56* parameter in the **dialer map** statement. With dialer profiles, the map class can specify the speed based on the destination being dialed. At other times, again based on destination, the map class can specify *speed 64*. The speed can be altered on the fly based on the number being dialed. **dialer map** has an additional keyword, **broadcast**, that specifies that routing updates should be allowed to flow across the link. Without the **broadcast** keyword, routing updates would not reach across the cloud.

- **Dialer pool**—Individual dialer interfaces that make use of a dialer pool. The dialer pool is a group of one or more physical interfaces associated with a logical interface. A physical interface can belong to multiple dialer pools. Contention for a specific physical interface is resolved with a configured priority.

When implementing dialer profiles with PPP, you must define specific parameters for the physical interface. The physical interface definition uses only the **encapsulation**, **authentication**, **ppp multilink**, and **dialer pool** configuration parameters. All other settings are applied to the logical interface and applied to that interface as needed for specific calls. Dialer profiles support both PPP and HDLC encapsulation on the physical interface.

You can create a number of dialer interfaces on each router. Valid interface designations include numbers ranging from 1 through 255. Each logical dialer interface contains the complete configuration for a destination logical network and any networks reached through it. In other words, multiple physical interfaces can be forced to share a common set of characteristics. Example 6-22 shows a sample configuration for dialer profiles.

Example 6-22 *Dialer Profile Configuration Example*

```
RouterA(config)#isdn switch-type basic-5ess
!
RouterA(config)#interface ethernet 0
RouterA(config-if)#ip address 10.11.1.1 255.255.255.0
!
RouterA(config)#interface BRI0
RouterA(config-if)#encapsulation ppp
RouterA(config-if)#dialer pool-member 1
RouterA(config-if)#ppp authentication chap
RouterA(config-if)#ppp multilink
!
RouterA(config)#interface Dialer1
RouterA(config-if)#ip address 10.12.1.1 255.255.255.0
RouterA(config-if)#encapsulation ppp
RouterA(config-if)#dialer remote-name RouterB
RouterA(config-if)#dialer string 2145552222 class remote
RouterA(config-if)#dialer load threshold 50 either
RouterA(config-if)#dialer pool 1
RouterA(config-if)#dialer-group 1
RouterA(config-if)#ppp authentication chap
RouterA(config-if)#ppp multilink
!
RouterA(config)#map-class dialer remote
RouterA(config-map-class)#dialer isdn speed 56
!
RouterA(config)#ip route 10.12.1.2 255.255.255.255 Dialer1
RouterA(config)#ip route 10.13.1.0 255.255.255.0 10.12.1.2
RouterA(config)#dialer-list 1 protocol ip permit
```

In Example 6-22, there are a number of items to note. For instance, notice that there is no **dialer map** statement. The mapping is performed in separate statements. The **dialer string** statement defines the remote phone number as well as the map class (named **remote**) to utilize in dialing that destination. This is why it is possible to use the outbound interface for the static route definition. This particular example also makes use of the rate adaptation capabilities. The **dialer pool** statements bind each interface (both logical and physical) together as a single operating entity.

Dialer profiles are a very useful addition to the configuration arsenal offered by Cisco IOS. However, they also represents a new set of issues and commands for troubleshooting. As with other implementations of ISDN, it is wise to simply utilize the **debug** commands discussed to this point.

To view the status of a dialer interface, the **show dialer interface bri 0** command can be of use, as demonstrated in Example 6-23.

Example 6-23 show dialer interface bri 0 *Command Output*

```
RouterA#show dialer interface bri 0
BRI0 - dialer type = ISDN
Dial String Successes Failures Last called Last status
0 incoming call(s) have been screened.
BRI0: B-Channel 1
Idle timer (120 secs), Fast idle timer (20 secs)
Wait for carrier (30 secs), Re-enable (15 secs)
Dialer state is data link layer up
Dial reason: ip (s=10.12.1.1, d=10.12.1.2)
Interface bound to profile Dialer0
Time until disconnect 102 secs
Current call connected 00:00:19
Connected to 2145552222 (RouterB)
BRI0: B-Channel 2
Idle timer (120 secs), Fast idle timer (20 secs)
Wait for carrier (30 secs), Re-enable (15 secs)
Dialer state is idle
```

The **show dialer interface bri 0** command displays the status of each B channel and its configured settings. It specifies the reason for the call setup as well as the interface to which the physical interface is bound.

Rotary Groups

ISDN *rotary groups* are similar to dialer pools. One primary difference, however, is the lack of map class capabilities in rotary groups. Configuring rotary groups involves the creation of logical dialer interfaces (as is done in dialer pool configurations), the interface designation of which is an important detail.

Example 6-24 shows all the physical BRI interfaces associated with **dialer rotary-group 2**. The number **2** is used as a rotary group number, so it must also be used as our dialer interface number designator.

Example 6-24 *Rotary Group Configuration*

```
RouterA(config)#isdn switch-type basic-5ess
!
RouterA(config)#interface ethernet 0
RouterA(config-if)#ip address 10.11.1.1 255.255.255.0
!
RouterA(config)#interface BRI0
RouterA(config-if)#encapsulation ppp
RouterA(config-if)#dialer rotary-group 2
RouterA(config)#interface BRI1
RouterA(config-if)#encapsulation ppp
RouterA(config-if)#dialer rotary-group 2
RouterA(config)#interface BRI2
RouterA(config-if)#encapsulation ppp
RouterA(config-if)#dialer rotary-group 2
!
RouterA(config)#interface Dialer2
RouterA(config-if)#ip address 10.12.1.1 255.255.255.0
RouterA(config-if)#encapsulation ppp
RouterA(config-if)#dialer remote-name RouterB
RouterA(config-if)#dialer string 2145552222 class remote
RouterA(config-if)#dialer load threshold 50 either
RouterA(config-if)#dialer pool 1
RouterA(config-if)#dialer-group 1
RouterA(config-if)#ppp authentication chap
RouterA(config-if)#ppp multilink
!
RouterA(config)#ip route 10.13.1.0 255.255.255.0 10.12.1.2
RouterA(config)#dialer-list 1 protocol ip permit
```

NOTE   It is important that the dialer interface designator (in this case, **2**) match the **dialer rotary-group** number. If these two numbers do not match, the configuration does not function properly.

Figure 6-10 depicts the concept of rotary groups.

Figure 6-10   *Rotary Groups*

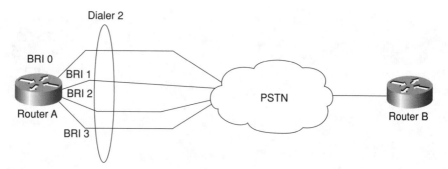

The only protocol or configuration attributes configured on the physical interface are the individual commands that make the BRI interface a part of the rotary group and the encapsulation. On dialer pool interfaces, you can set a priority to specify the order in which the interfaces are used. With rotary groups, that granularity is not possible. All protocol attributes are entered at the logical dialer interface configuration level.

The use of dialer profiles versus rotary groups comes down to one question: "How much control do I want to have over the link?" With dialer profiles, a map class can be created and applied on a per destination basis. This allows a great degree of control over the characteristics of a particular call based on the destination being called. Rotary groups do not make use of the map class featureset. Therefore, they are limited to the characteristics applied to the dialer interface.

Dial Backup

Dial backup provides redundancy for WAN links. Although the ISDN connection may not provide the same amount of bandwidth as a primary link, dial backup provides a maintenance path if the primary link fails. Once the down or overload condition of the primary link is detected, the dial-on-demand configuration is placed into service.

Figure 6-11 illustrates a network in which dial backup could be utilized.

The primary data pathway across the WAN exists between each router's Serial 0 interface. As mentioned, dial backup can be implemented in two ways. The first, and most obvious, manner is to have dial backup function when a primary link fails. This occurs when a "down" condition is detected on the primary interface, and then the secondary, or backup, link is changed to an "up" state and a connection is established.

The backup pathway is used in the absence of the primary, obviously. But, how does the backup link know when it's time to return to the backup state? Simple—you configure the parameters of the "up" and/or "down" state for the backup link.

Figure 6-11 *Dial Backup Scenario*

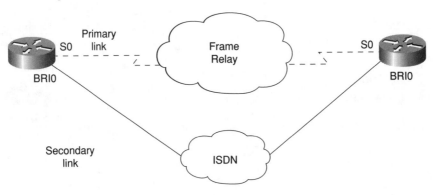

In Example 6-25, notice the **backup delay 5 60** command, which specifies that if there is a failure, the system should wait five seconds to bring up the backup link. Once the failure has passed, the system should wait 60 seconds to bring the backup link back down.

Example 6-25 *Dial Backup Example Configuration*

```
RouterA(config)#isdn switch-type basic-5ess
!
RouterA(config)#interface serial 0
RouterA(config-if)#ip address 10.14.1.1 255.255.255.0
RouterA(config-if)#encapsulation hdlc
RouterA(config-if)#backup interface BRI0
RouterA(config-if)#backup delay 5 60
RouterA(config-if)#backup load 90 5
!
RouterA(config)#interface BRI0
RouterA(config-if)#ip address 10.12.1.1 255.255.255.0
RouterA(config-if)#encapsulation ppp
RouterA(config-if)#dialer idle-timeout 180
RouterA(config-if)#dialer map ip 10.12.1.2 2145552222
RouterA(config-if)#dialer-group 1
!
RouterA(config)#dialer-list 1 protocol ip permit
```

Implementation of these timers is an attempt to compensate for a "bouncing" interface. In other words, the timers exist to compensate for an interface that drops momentarily and then comes right back up.

The backup functionality available with Cisco IOS is not simply for redundancy in the case of a failure. In situations where a WAN link approaches saturation, the ISDN service can be initialized until the period of congestion has passed. The configuration enables the use of a load setting both for the initialization of the link as well as for the termination of the link once the condition is clear.

In the example, note the **backup load 90 5** command, which specifies that the router should monitor the load on the primary interface and bring the link up when the load across the primary link is particularly heavy. The numbers represent the load of the interface as shown by the **show interface s0** command.

The load on an interface is represented by a number between 1 and 255. In the **backup load 90 5** command, **90** is the percentage load at which the backup link is activated (in this case 230/255). The second number (in this case, **5%**) is a measurement of aggregate load. Once the backup link has been initialized, the router continues to monitor the load. Once the load of both interfaces combined reaches a value of 13/255, the secondary link is terminated.

So although dial backup was designed for link redundancy to partially compensate for failure, it can also provide load sharing capabilities to alleviate congestion on the WAN link.

Alternative Backup

Dial backup is not the only method of providing redundancy. In some implementations, ISDN is not available or viable. In such cases, alternative methods may be the only option. If multiple links are available, standard routing protocol operations automatically load balance across equal cost redundant links.

This load balancing usually requires no configuration. From time to time, such as with IPX RIP, it is necessary to define the number of alternative pathways that should be allowed from a specific source to a specific destination. There are even routing protocols that go one step further.

Dynamic Backup

IGRP and EIGRP have a configuration option known as a *variance*. These two Cisco proprietary routing protocols can load balance over a maximum of six redundant pathways. The difference between the protocols is that the redundant pathways do not have to equal the cost pathways. The only real rule in the selection is that the next hop must be closer to the destination (that is, it cannot go back to go forward).

The variance factor determines the amount of traffic to send across these suboptimal routes. For example, a variance of 4 (e.g., issuing the **variance 4** command at the routing protocol configuration mode) tells the router to send data over a particular route if the metric is within four times the value of the best route.

Variance is calculated based on the documentation of your network. It should be evident from the examination of network topological maps exactly how many pathways are available from a particular source to a particular destination.

Static Backup

This section discusses the use of static routes to provide redundant facilities rather than a solution such as dial backup. Static routes were discussed earlier in the chapter and are probably a well-known topic at this point.

Static routes used for redundancy purposes are usually implemented as floating static routes. By default, static routes are the most preferred routes because an administrator defines them. This concept of one route being more preferred than another is known as *administrative distance*. Depending on how it was derived, a particular route (whether static or dynamic) can be more believable than another route derived by a less sophisticated method.

Static routes have a default administrative distance of 0 if they are defined with an outbound interface, or 1 if a next-hop address is defined. This makes them highly believable routes. It is possible to alter administrative distance to make a route less preferred than routes that are dynamically derived.

Administrative distance is a number between 0 and 255. The higher the distance, the less preferred the route. When the administrative distance of a static route is altered to the point where it is less preferred than the dynamic routes derived by a dynamic routing protocol, it becomes a "floating" static route. Example 6-26 illustrates configuring a floating static route.

Example 6-26 *Floating Static Route Example*

```
RouterA(config)#ip route 10.13.1.0 255.255.255.0 10.12.1.2 200
```

The number **200** at the end of the line defines the static route as having an administrative distance of 200. If the dynamic routing protocol being used is RIP (default administrative distance = 120), the static route is now less preferred than the dynamic route. Should the RIP route be lost for some reason, the static route becomes the preferred route until the RIP route returns. Table 6-3 displays the administrative distances of common routing protocols.

Table 6-3 *Administrative Distances*

Routing Protocol	Administrative Distance
Connected	0
Static Route	1
EIGRP Summary	5
External BGP	20
Internal EIGRP	90
IGRP	100
OSPF	110
IS-IS	115

Table 6-3   *Administrative Distances (Continued)*

Routing Protocol	Administrative Distance
RIP	120
EGP	140
External EIGRP	170
Internal BGP	200
Unknown	255

Snapshot Routing

Snapshot routing was developed to save bandwidth utilization across dialup interfaces. With snapshot routing, the routing table is placed in an update restricted (that is, frozen) state. This implementation of DDR utilizes a *quiet* period and an *active* period. The routing table is not updated during the *quiet period*, which is the amount of time that the routing table remains frozen. When the quiet period expires, a dialer interface initiates a call to a remote router. The *active period* is the amount of time the call remains up in order for the two routers to exchange routing updates.

It is important to note that snapshot routing is designed for use only with distance vector routing protocols. In addition, you can configure the router to exchange routing updates each time the line protocol goes from "down" to "up" or from "dialer spoofing" to "fully up."

A router can fill one of two roles in a snapshot relationship: server or client. The *client* router is in charge of the quiet timer countdown. Once the counter reaches zero, the client router dials the *server* router. Snapshot routing enables dynamic distance vector routing protocols to run over DDR lines.

In many implementations, routing broadcasts (including routes and services) are filtered out on DDR interfaces and static definitions are configured instead. With snapshot routing implementations, normal updates are sent across the DDR interface for the short duration of the active period. After this, routers enter the quiet period, during which time the routing tables at both ends of the link remain unchanged. Snapshot routing is therefore a triggering mechanism that controls routing update exchange in DDR scenarios. Only during the active period are the neighboring routers exchanging routing protocol updates. During the quiet period, no updates traverse the link (even if the link is up to enable interesting traffic to cross) and the routing information previously collected is kept in an isolated state in the routing tables.

Snapshot routing is useful in two command situations:

- Configuring static routes for DDR interfaces

- Reducing the overhead of periodic updates sent by routing protocols to remote branch offices over a dedicated serial line

In Example 6-27 and 6-28, RouterA is defined as the server router and RouterB is defined as the client router. In this scenario, the quiet timer is slowly counting down to zero. Once the quiet period timer expires, the client router dials the server router. The defined quiet period is 12 hours (actually 720 minutes). Once the 12 hours have elapsed, the client and server routers "thaw" their routing tables and exchange updates for the duration of the active period, in this case, five minutes.

Example 6-27 *RouterA Snapshot Routing Configuration Example*

```
RouterA(config)#hostname RouterA
RouterA(config)#isdn switch-type basic-5ess
!
RouterA(config)#interface BRI0
RouterA(config-if)#snapshot server 5 dialer
RouterA(config-if)#dialer map snapshot 1 name RouterB 2145552222
```

Example 6-28 *RouterB Routing Configuration Example*

```
RouterB Snapshot Routing Configuration Example
RouterA(config)#hostname RouterB
RouterA(config)#isdn switch-type basic-5ess
!
RouterA(config)#interface BRI0
RouterA(config-if)#snapshot client 5 720 dialer
RouterA(config-if)#dialer map snapshot 1 name RouterA 2145551111
```

The active periods defined must match on both server and client routers. Five minutes is the minimum active period you can configure for any snapshot configuration.

Although the routing tables are frozen, routing updates are still sent at their regular intervals out of any LAN interfaces on the router. For example, if there is an Ethernet segment on the opposite side of a snapshot router, the routing updates still broadcast out of that interface at the normal update interval, while remaining dormant on the BRI interface. It is possible to force the quiet period to expire and start the active period manually using the **clear snapshot quiet-time** command. To monitor snapshot routing processes, use the **show snapshot** command.

Primary Rate Interface

PRI implementations are based on T1/E1 technologies. Although PRI is still ISDN, it is treated differently in regard to framing and signaling. Like BRI, PRI has only one connection to the ISDN network, and the switch type must be specified for the configuration to function. An ISDN PRI T1 implementation has 23 B channels and a D channel. As with BRI, each of the B channels has 64-kbps bandwidth available. The D channel, however, is also a 64-kbps channel (unlike BRI).

In traditional T1 implementations, 24 timeslots exist. Obviously, one of the 24 timeslots (timeslot 23, counting 0–23) is taken way for signaling and framing. With E1 PRI implementations, there are 30 B channels available and one D channel, all having 64-kbps bandwidth available.

In traditional E1 implementations, there are 30 timeslots, leaving 2 timeslots for signaling and framing. Timeslot 0 is used for framing and timeslot 16 is used for signaling (counting 0–31). E1 PRI makes use of this same principal. Timeslot 16 is the D channel, and timeslot 0 is used for framing information. Figure 6-12 depicts T1 and E1 PRI.

Figure 6-12   *T1 and E1 PRI*

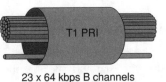

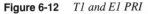

23 x 64 kbps B channels
1 x 64 kbps D channel

30 x 64 kbps channels
1 x 64 kbps D channel (signaling)

ISDN Switch Type

The PRI installation procedure is similar to its BRI counterpart. A service call is placed, and then the demarc is determined and extended, if necessary. The carrier provides the basic information necessary for connectivity, but it will be necessary to configure the router with the appropriate switch type. Table 6-4 shows the Cisco-supported switch types.

Table 6-4   *Cisco-Supported Primary Rate Switch Types*

Switch Type	Description
primary-4ess	AT&T 4ESS switch type for the U.S.
primary-5ess	AT&T 5ESS switch type for the U.S.
primary-dms100	Northern Telecom switch type for the U.S.
primary-net5	European switch type for NET5
primary-ni	National ISDN switch type for the U.S.
primary-ntt	Japanese switch type
primary-ts014	Australian switch type

*Check with the provider for the appropriate switch type. A change of switch type requires a reload of the router.

T1/E1 Framing and Line Coding

Although it is ISDN, PRI uses T1 framing and line coding. These technologies are based on the same model, represented in a number of 64-kbps channels.

The original use of digital facilities was the transport of voice traffic. Because analog technologies were not adequate for long distance transmission due to attenuation, another form of transmission—digitizing—was necessary. Digitizing the voice traffic for transmission enabled it to travel very long distances with no attenuation.

Once the data world was born, it became necessary to also transport data over long distances. Because the digital facilities were already available, it seemed a natural extension to use those facilities. However, it proved to be something of a painful experience for a time. The history of voice and data transmission over T1 and E1 facilities followed the same growing pains.

T1 Framing

The first part of this section focuses on T1 framing and line coding. E1 framing and line coding are discussed afterward.

T1 specifies the physical coding of the signal on the wire, and DS1 specifies the framing of characteristics. So, T1 and DS1 are not the same thing after all, even though the two have been used interchangeably for years and it's certain not to stop because of this book. But, now you know.

A digital signal that is level 1 (DS-1) consists of 24 DS-0s. A DS-0 is a 64-kbps channel. This channel is known as a *timeslot*. One DS0 represents one voice call. The timeslot is derived from the Nyquist theorem. Nyquist said that $f_s = 2(BW)$. Because the voice world had decided that 0–4000 Hz would be the supported range for voice circuits, the number 4000 was plugged into the formula in the BW position. Therefore, $f_s = 2(4000) = 8000$, which is the number of samples we should take of this analog wave per second.

To properly digitize (quantize) analog voice, it is necessary to take samples of the voice wave over time. Sample too fast and you waste resources. Sample too slowly and you allow for aliasing. Aliasing is a condition that occurs when two or more analog waves can match the coordinate points set forth by the samples (a little beyond our scope).

Each of the 8000 samples per second is represented by an eight-bit code word. Without going into too much depth, this code word simply defines the coordinates of the sample (polarity = 1 bit, segment = 3 bits, and step = 4 bits). Figure 6-13 depicts the sampling of the wave and the resulting code word.

The resulting throughput of 8000 eight-bit samples per second is 64,000 bps, or one DS-0.

When one sample has been taken from each of the 24 timeslots, a T1 frame is created. Because this is time division multiplexing (TDM), 8000 eight-bit samples are taken from each timeslot every second. The result is 8000 T1 frames per second.

The telco provider specifies the type of framing that you should use when connecting to their facilities. The choices with T1 are SuperFrame (SF, also known as D4 framing) and Extended SuperFrame (ESF).

SF is the assembly of 12 T1 frames. Each of the T1 frames is separated from adjacent frames by a single framing bit (8000 T1 frames per second, each with an additional bit that is an additional 8000 bps of overhead).

Figure 6-13   *Sampling the Analog Wave*

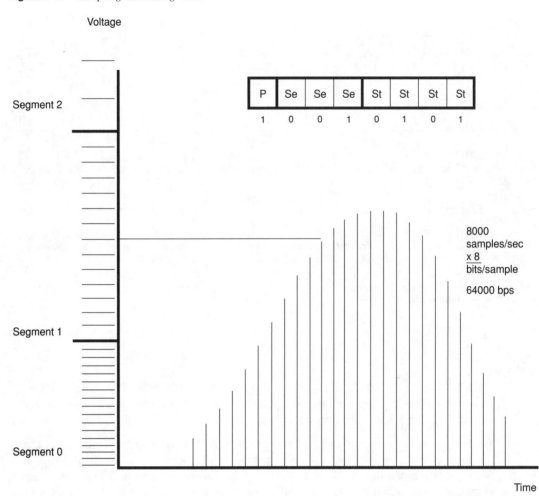

ESF is the assembly of 24 T1 frames. Each frame is still separated by a delineating bit, but not all are used for framing. 2000 bps are used for framing, 2000 bps are used for CRC, and 4000 bps are used for data link control (this gives us many more management capabilities as compared to SF). Figure 6-14 depicts a SuperFrame and an Extended SuperFrame.

Figure 6-14 *SF and ESF*

T1 Frame 1	Framing	T1 Frame 2	Framing	T1 Frame 3	Framing	T1 Frame 4	Framing	T1 Frame 5	Framing	T1 Frame 6	Framing	T1 Frame 7	Framing	T1 Frame 8	Framing	T1 Frame 9	Framing	T1 Frame 10	Framing	T1 Frame 11	Framing	T1 Frame 12	Framing

12 T1 Frames = 1 SuperFrame

T1 Frame 1	DLC	T1 Frame 2	CRC	T1 Frame 3	DLC	T1 Frame 4	Framing	T1 Frame 5	DLC	T1 Frame 6	CRC	T1 Frame 7	DLC	T1 Frame 8	Framing	T1 Frame 9	DLC	T1 Frame 10	CRC	T1 Frame 11	DLC	T1 Frame 12	Framing
T1 Frame 13	DLC	T1 Frame 14	CRC	T1 Frame 15	DLC	T1 Frame 16	Framing	T1 Frame 17	DLC	T1 Frame 18	CRC	T1 Frame 19	DLC	T1 Frame 20	Framing	T1 Frame 21	DLC	T1 Frame 22	CRC	T1 Frame 23	DLC	T1 Frame 24	Framing

24 T1 Frames = 1 Extended SuperFrame

T1 Line Code

Once the framing has been configured, the next step is to configure the line coding. In North America, there are two types of line coding that are dominant: Alternate Mark Inversion (AMI) and Bipolar with 8 Zero Substitution (B8ZS).

AMI is becoming increasingly rare in favor of B8ZS. AMI forces data bandwidth to 56 kbps due to the enforcement of a 1s density rule stating that 12.5 percent of all bits transmitted must be 1s. To enforce the rule, AMI line coded CSU/DSUs force every eighth bit (that is, the least significant bit of each timeslot) to a 1. Effectively, this bit is lost. The rule may or may not actually change the bit, but effective throughput is reduced nonetheless. The end result is that there are still 8000 samples per second, but each sample has been reduced to seven bits, thereby rendering 56000 bits per second.

B8ZS has a more effective way of dealing with the enforcement of 1s density. It alters bits only when necessary, and then changes the affected bits back to their original values at the remote side.

To verify the configuration of the framing and line code being currently in use, type the command **show controllers t1**. Example 6-29 shows a sample output of this command.

Example 6-29 show controllers t1 *Command Output*

```
isdn-14#show controllers t1
T1 0 is up.
  No alarms detected.
  Framing is ESF, Line Code is B8ZS, Clock Source is
    Line Primary.
  Data in current interval (676 seconds elapsed):
    0 Line Code Violations, 0 Path Code Violations
    0 Slip Secs, 0 Fr Loss Secs, 0 Line Err Secs,
    0 Degraded Mins
    0 Errored Secs, 0 Bursty Err Secs, 0 Severely Err Secs,
    0 Unavail Secs
  Total Data (last 46 15 minute intervals):
    0 Line Code Violations, 0 Path Code Violations,
    0 Slip Secs, 0 Fr Loss Secs, 0 Line Err Secs,
    0 Degraded Mins,
    0 Errored Secs, 0 Bursty Err Secs, 1 Severely Err Secs,
    0 Unavail Secs
```

E1 Framing

E1 is based on the same basic foundation as T1. The concept of 64-kbps timeslots created by 8000 eight-bit samples per second still holds true, and the sampling rates and methodologies between T1 framing and E1 framing are very similar. The differences lay in the assembly and multiplexing of the channels.

E1 frames are constructed of 30 timeslots. Therefore, each E1 frame contains 30 eight-bit samples. When 16 E1 frames are assembled, a *multiframe* is created. MultiFrame is the dominant frame type in E1 implementations. Figure 6-15 depicts a multiframe.

Figure 6-15 *E1 Multiframe*

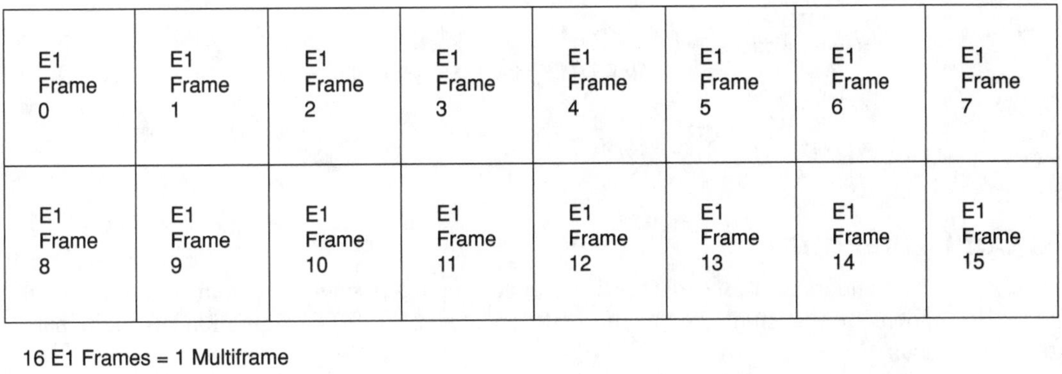

E1 Frame 0	E1 Frame 1	E1 Frame 2	E1 Frame 3	E1 Frame 4	E1 Frame 5	E1 Frame 6	E1 Frame 7
E1 Frame 8	E1 Frame 9	E1 Frame 10	E1 Frame 11	E1 Frame 12	E1 Frame 13	E1 Frame 14	E1 Frame 15

16 E1 Frames = 1 Multiframe

E1 Line Code

E1 deployments can implement AMI; however, the issues with AMI and data transmission still hold true: data transmissions are limited to 56 kbps. To remedy this, high-density bit, level 3 (HDB3) was created. It operates similarly to B8ZS, but in a slightly more efficient manner. If a long string of 0s is detected, a number of them are changed to 1s for the duration of their trip across the provider network. They are then changed back to their original values at the remote CSU/DSU.

Obviously, T1/E1 framing and line coding have not been discussed at length. It is an important topic to understand, however, even though it is not touched on in depth on the CCNP Remote Access Exam. For more information on this topic, check out www.cisco.com.

PRI Layers

PRI is based in the same technologies as BRI. In fact, PRI implements ISDN Q.921 (Layer 2) and Q.931 (Layer 3) in the same manner as BRI. In addition, the call setup messages are identical, as are the call release messages.

There are some basic differences between BRI and PRI, however. PRI relies on the assignment of a TEI. This TEI, however, is always 0 in Cisco's implementation.

Example 6-30 shows sample output of the **show isdn status** command. Notice the TEI and the fact that the state is MULTIPLE_FRAME_ESTABLISHED. This verifies the existence of Layer 2 connectivity.

Example 6-30 **show isdn status** *Command Output*

```
RouterA#show isdn status
 The current ISDN Switchtype = primary-ni
 ISDN Serial0:23 interface
     Layer 1 Status:
         ACTIVE
     Layer 2 Status:
         TEI = 0, State = MULTIPLE_FRAME_ESTABLISHED
     Layer 3 Status:
         No Active Layer 3 Call(s)
     Activated dsl 0 CCBs = 0
```

PRI Configuration

The configuration of the PRI service is quite simple. Although the command variations and options are very similar to that of its BRI counterpart, a PRI configuration has additional requirements.

To meet the needs of the PRI provisioning, the T1 or E1 (whichever is appropriate) must be configured to match telco requirements of framing and line code, as discussed in the preceding sections of this chapter.

The T1/E1 controller is actually an internal CSU/DSU. It must be told which timeslots are included in the PRI configuration. For purposes of controller configuration, the timeslot numbering starts at 1 (1–24 for T1, and 1–30 for E1). The command syntax is mercifully limited in the number of actual parameter choices available. Table 6-5 illustrates the options available for T1 and E1 configuration.

Table 6-5   *T1/E1 Framing and Line Code Options*

Options	Framing*	Line Code*
T1	SF (D4)	AMI
	ESF	B8ZS
E1	CRC4	AMI
	NO-CRC4	HDB3
	CRC4 Australia	
	NO-CRC4 Australia	

*Framing and line code are telco-provided configuration parameters. If the controller configuration does not match what the telco has defined, the line does not function.

Once all the appropriate information is collected, the configuration can be completed. Example 6-31 illustrates a typical T1 controller configuration.

Example 6-31 *T1 PRI Configuration*

```
AS5300A(config)#isdn switch-type primary-ni
!
AS5300A(config)#controller t1 0/0
AS5300A(config-controller)#pri-group timeslots 1-24
AS5300A(config-controller)#framing esf
AS5300A(config-controller)#linecode b8zs
AS5300A(config-controller)#clock source line primary
!
AS5300A(config)#interface serial 0/0:23
AS5300A(config-if)#ip address 10.12.1.1  255.255.255.0
AS5300A(config-if)#isdn incoming-voice modem
```

Note that the switch type has been set. Again, this setting is based on telco-provided information. The **controller t1 0/0** command specifies the controller in slot 0, port 0. All 24 timeslots are active in the configuration. The framing is ESF and the linecode is B8ZS; both pieces of information are telco-provided. If this information is not readily available (that is, not provided by the telco), try using the configuration in Example 6-31.

ESF and B8ZS are the default (and most commonly deployed in North America) settings for the configuration in Example 6-31. For E1 implementations, the most common implementation is CRC4 and HDB3. If it doesn't work, change the line code and framing appropriately. There are a finite number of configuration variables. It is much less time consuming to experiment with the configuration and figure it out than it would be to call the telco and actually get to talk to someone who knows the appropriate settings for your installation.

Once the controller is configured, you must define the characteristics of the D channel. For controller t1 0/0, the D channel (as in Example 6-31) is interface serial 0/0:23. The last timeslot (number 0–23 here) is the D channel in T1 PRI. The D channel in E1 PRI is timeslot 15 (numbered 0–30).

The timeslot numbering scheme has long been the subject of confusion. To aid in dispelling the confusion, the numbering scheme used at each point is specified. Example 6-32 illustrates the E1 equivalent configuration.

Example 6-32 *E1 PRI Configuration*

```
AS5300A(config)#isdn switch-type primary-ni
!
AS5300A(config)#controller e1 0/0
AS5300A(config-controller)#pri-group timeslots 1-30
AS5300A(config-controller)#framing crc4
AS5300A(config-controller)#linecode hdb3
AS5300A(config-controller)#clock source line primary
!
AS5300A(config)#interface serial 0/0:15
AS5300A(config-if)#ip address 10.12.1.1  255.255.255.0
AS5300A(config-if)#isdn incoming-voice modem
```

This interface, in this case serial 0/0:15, carries the protocol specific configuration (that is, the IP address, the IPX network, and so forth) for protocols that need to traverse this link.

The configuration in Example 6-32 was captured from an AS5300 with eight PRI ports and two MICA modem blades with 120 modems each. The **isdn incoming-voice modem** command specifies that any inbound calls originating from modem users be directed to a MICA modem installed in this device rather than treated as if an actual ISDN-capable device were issuing a call setup. This is not to say that a device with bearer capabilities cannot dial into this device for connectivity. It still can. The AS5300 detects the call type and treats it accordingly.

PRI Incoming Analog Calls on Digital Modems

Up to this point, the discussion has focused on data calls. In other words, the topics have centered on B channel to B channel calls.

In remote access deployments, the end user dials into an access server. The incoming lines that provide connectivity from end user to the access server are PRI implementations. These PRI lines are completely digital facilities. Figure 6-16 illustrates the typical deployment of an access server installation.

Figure 6-16 *Network Access Server Deployment*

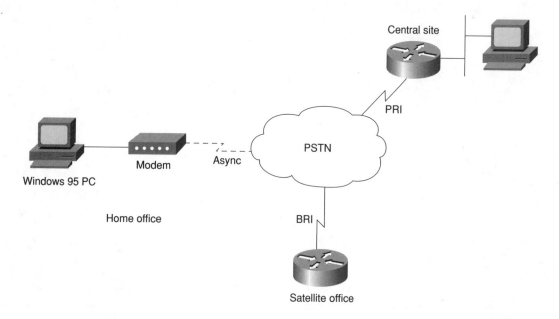

When an end user dials into the network access server (NAS), the router detects that the call is inbound from a modem. In other words, it sees the call as an incoming analog call. If it were a call from another B channel, the call would be completely digital; however, because the call originated from an analog modem, the NAS must answer back in the form expected by the modem. Using the **isdn incoming-voice modem** command, the router passes the call off to one of the internal MICA modems installed in the NAS.

In a traditional modem-to-modem call setup, the call begins as digital communication between the PC and the modem. The modem converts the transmission to analog (that is, modulated) and passes it off to the edge CO switch. Once inside the PSTN, the transmission is again converted to digital format for its journey across the PSTN. Once the transmission arrives at the remote edge switch, it is converted back to analog only to be changed back to digital by the modem (that is, demodulated) at the remote site and forwarded to the receiving party. It all seems a bit redundant.

In the case of PRI incoming lines receiving these "voice" calls, the call process is the same—up to the point where the call is demodulated by the remote modem. In a NAS implementation, the demodulation is not necessary. It is taken, in digital form, and passed to a MICA modem where it is not demodulated, but left in digital form. The MICA modem negotiates the connection just as any other modem.

Once the connection is complete, the calling party machine is assigned an IP address from the IP address pool configured on the NAS, or another configured source. Once an IP address and default gateway are assigned, the calling party machine functions as if it were attached to the LAN on the remote side of the NAS.

Foundation Summary

The Foundation Summary is a collection of tables and figures that provides a convenient review of many key concepts in this chapter. For those of you already comfortable with the topics in this chapter, this summary can still help you recall a few details. For those of you who just read this chapter, this review should help solidify some key facts. For any of you doing your final preparation before the exam, these tables and figures are a convenient way to review the day before the exam.

Table 6-6 summarizes the ISDN service offerings.

Table 6-6   *ISDN Services*

Service	B Channels	D Channel	Bandwidth
BRI	2 x 64 kbps	1 x 16 kbps	144 kbps
T1 PRI	23 x 64 kbps	1 x 64 kbps	1.544 Mbps
E1 PRI	30 x 64 kbps	1 x 64 kbps	2.048 Mbps

Table 6-7 summarizes ISDN protocols.

Table 6-7   *ISDN Protocols*

Layer	Protocol	Description
1	I.430/T1.601	This layer is the physical layer dealing with connectivity. I.430 specifies framing between TE1 and NT1. T1.601 specifies framing between TE and the LE.
2	Q.921	Q.921 institutes an addressing scheme for ISDN.
3	Q.931	Q.931 is used between the TE and the local ISDN switch. Call setup is handled by Q.931 as well.

Q&A

The questions and scenarios in this book are more difficult than what you should experience on the actual exam. The questions do not attempt to cover more breadth or depth than the exam; however, they are designed to make sure that you know the answer. Rather than enabling you to derive the answer from clues hidden inside the question itself, the questions challenge your understanding and recall of the subject.

Questions from the "Do I Know This Already?" quiz from the beginning of the chapter are repeated here to ensure that you have mastered the chapter's topic areas. Hopefully, these questions will help you limit the number of exam questions on which you narrow your choices to two options and then guess.

The answers to these questions can be found in Appendix A, on page 397.

1 List the two most common implementations of ISDN.

2 List the number of bearer channels for BRI, T1 PRI and E1 PRI.

3 What type of information is carried over the D channel?

4 List the specifications that define Layer 2 and Layer 3 of ISDN.

5 When is it necessary to use **dialer in-band** in an ISDN BRI configuration?

6 What is the difference between a router with a BRI S/T interface and one with a BRI U interface?

_____

_____

_____

7 Write out the commands to define only Telnet and FTP as interesting traffic for DDR.

_____

_____

_____

8 List two of the most common encapsulations available for use on BRI interfaces.

_____

_____

_____

9 An interface that has been configured not to send routing updates is known as what type of interface?

_____

_____

_____

10 When using rotary groups, what should determine the dialer interface number?

_____

_____

_____

11 What technology is used to provide redundancy for WAN links?

_____

_____

_____

12 DDR traditionally involves the use of static routes. If static routes are not desired, what technology can be implemented?

_____

_____

_____

13 What information is required of the telco to implement PRI implementations?

_____

_____

_____

14 List the options available for T1 and E1 framing and line code configuration.

_____

_____

_____

15 List the command to have the router forward all incoming voice calls to internal MICA technology modems.

_____

_____

_____

16 Describe the key difference between Cisco's bandwidth on demand and Multilink PPP.

_____

_____

_____

17 Create an access list that specifies HTTP and any ICMP traffic as interesting.

_____

_____

_____

Use Figure 6-17 to answer the remaining questions.

Figure 6-17   *Network Diagram for Use with Q&A*

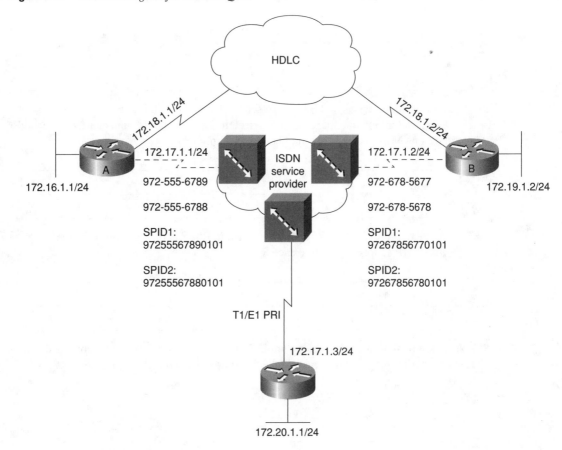

18 Configure router A such that any IP traffic causes an ISDN call to be placed.

_____

_____

_____

19 Configure both routers A and B for dynamic routing using RIP and for static routing
between networks 172.16.1.0 and 172.19.1.0. Assume the use of only the ISDN network
at this time. Make sure no dynamic routes are being sent out the BRI0 interface.

_____

_____

_____

20 Configure both routers A and B for basic DDR connectivity using dialer maps. Use basic-ni1 for the switch type. Include the configuration parameters from Questions 3 and 4.

---

21 Configure both routers A and B so that a second B channel is initialized if the first reaches 50 percent saturation in either direction. Also, the call should disconnect after 30 seconds of idle time. Note: This is not a dial backup situation.

---

22 Configure router C for T1 PRI connectivity using B8ZS and ESF. Configure the appropriate IP addressing on interface S 0:23.

---

23 Now assume that router C is being implemented in an E1 environment using the default settings for framing and linecode. Make the appropriate configuration changes.

---

24 Remove the static routes between A and B. Implement a solution that enables dynamic routing without keeping the link up constantly.

---

25 Configure routers A and B so that the ISDN link is activated only in cases in which the HDLC link is down or has reached 85 percent capacity. The backup timers for failure are at your discretion.

Scenarios

The following case studies and questions are designed to draw together the content of the chapter and exercise your understanding of the concepts. There is not necessarily a right answer to each scenario. The thought process and practice in manipulating the related concepts is the goal of this section.

Scenario 6-1

In Figure 6-18, the Raleigh and Atlanta routers are dialing into the San Francisco router using DDR configurations. Example 6-33 details the configuration of the Raleigh router and Example 6-34 shows the Atlanta router configuration. Examine the figure and the configurations and utilize them in answering the questions that follow.

Figure 6-18   *Scenario 6-1 Topology*

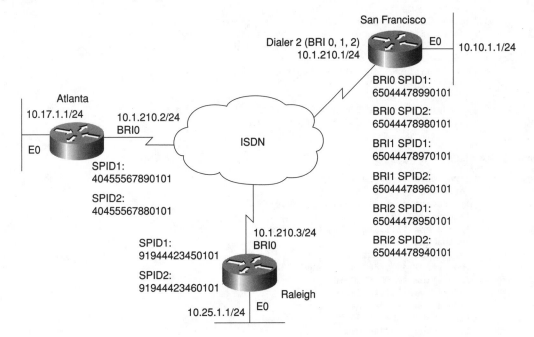

Example 6-33 *Raleigh Configuration*

```
isdn switch-type basic-5ess
interface ethernet 0
ip address 10.25.2.2 255.255.255.0
interface BRI0
ip address 10.1.210.3 255.255.255.0
encapsulation ppp
dialer idle-timeout 180
isdn spid1 91944423450101 9194442345
isdn spid2 91944423460101 9194442346
isdn answer 4045556789
isdn answer 4045556788
dialer map ip 10.210.1.2 4045556789
dialer map ip 10.210.1.2 4045556788
dialer map ip 10.210.1.1 6504447899
dialer map ip 10.210.1.1 6504447898
dialer map ip 10.210.1.1 6504447897
dialer map ip 10.210.1.1 6504447896
dialer map ip 10.210.1.1 6504447895
dialer map ip 10.210.1.1 6504447894
dialer-group 1
access-list 101 permit tcp any any eq telnet
access-list 101 permit tcp any any eq ftp
access-list 101 permit tcp any any eq ftp-data
access-list 101 permit icmp any any
dialer-list 1 protocol ip list 101
router rip
network 10.0.0.0
ip route 10.17.1.0 255.255.255.0 10.210.1.2
ip route 10.10.1.0 255.255.255.0 10.210.1.1
```

Example 6-34 *Atlanta Configuration*

```
isdn switch-type basic-5ess
interface ethernet 0
ip address 10.17.1.1 255.255.255.0
interface BRI0
ip address 10.1.210.2 255.255.255.0
encapsulation ppp
dialer idle-timeout 180
isdn spid1 40455567890101 4045556789
isdn spid2 40455567880101 4045556788
isdn answer 9194442345
isdn answer 9194442346
isdn answer 6504447899
isdn answer 6504447898
isdn answer 6504447897
isdn answer 6504447896
isdn answer 6504447895
```

Example 6-34 *Atlanta Configuration (Continued)*

```
isdn answer 6504447894
dialer map ip 10.210.1.3 9194442345
dialer map ip 10.210.1.3 9194442346
dialer map ip 10.210.1.1 6504447899
dialer map ip 10.210.1.1 6504447898
dialer map ip 10.210.1.1 6504447897
dialer map ip 10.210.1.1 6504447896
dialer map ip 10.210.1.1 6504447895
dialer map ip 10.210.1.1 6504447894
dialer-group 1
access-list 101 permit tcp any any eq telnet
access-list 101 permit icmp any any
dialer-list 1 protocol ip list 101
router rip
network 10.0.0.0
ip route 10.25.1.0 255.255.255.0 10.210.1.3
ip route 10.10.1.0 255.255.255.0 10.210.1.1
```

Answer the following questions:

1 What type(s) of traffic causes a call to set up between Atlanta and Raleigh?

2 Will the Raleigh router have any problems in the event that the San Francisco router attempts to call it?

3 Can both Raleigh and Atlanta be connected to the San Francisco router concurrently?

4 Is it possible for the Atlanta router to dial both the San Francisco and the Raleigh routers at the same time?

5 Write out the IOS commands that enable the San Francisco router to support the configuration depicted by Figure 6-18 by using a dialer profile.

Scenario 6-2

Refer back to Figure 6-18. Now that the basic configuration is in place, expand the configurations to include the use of snapshot routing:

1 Configure the San Francisco router to act as the snapshot server.

2 Configure the Atlanta and Raleigh routers to act as snapshot clients.

Scenario 6-3

The network has been expanded to support higher bandwidth needs. Frame Relay links have been implemented as the primary connection between the sites. Use Figure 6-19 as reference for the questions that follow.

Figure 6-19   *Expanded Network Topology*

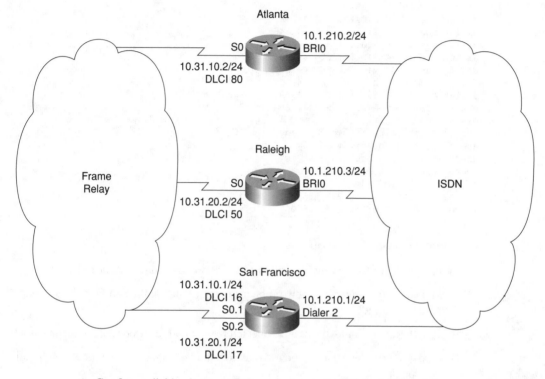

1   Configure dial backup on all three routers to provide redundancy five seconds after a failure until sixty seconds after the failure has cleared.

2   Configure dial backup on all three routers to provide load balancing in the event that the load on the Frame Relay circuit reaches 90 percent. The link should stay active until the aggregate load is reduced to 10 percent.

Scenario 6-4

In the course of testing the configuration of dial backup in Scenario 6-3, you found that the ISDN circuits are not functioning properly.

1   Plan and document your Layer 1 troubleshooting strategy.

2   Plan your Layer 2 troubleshooting strategy. Document the **show** and **debug** commands used at this point.

3   You've found that you are not receiving a TEI from the switch. Layer 1 is down. What are the possible causes?

4   Plan your Layer 3 troubleshooting strategy. Document the **show** and **debug** commands used at this point.

Scenario Answers

The answers provided in this section are not necessarily the only possible correct answers. They merely represent one possibility for each scenario. The intention is to test your base knowledge and understanding of the concepts discussed in this chapter.

Should your answers be different (as they likely will be) consider the differences. Are your answers in line with the concepts of the answers provided and explained here? If not, go back and read the chapter again focusing, on the sections related to the problem scenario.

The key here is for you to gain an understanding of the topics.

Scenario 6-1 Answers

1 Any ICMP or Telnet traffic causes the call setup to occur. This is defined by **access-list 101**.

2 Yes. The Raleigh router has implemented caller ID screening. It has been configured to accept only calls originating from the Atlanta router. To correct the situation, it is necessary to add additional **isdn answer** lines to the configuration on the Raleigh router.

3 Yes. The San Francisco router has an adequate number of B channels available to support inbound calls from both the Raleigh and Atlanta routers.

4 Yes. One B channel can be connected to each site based on the destination of the interesting traffic.

5 Example 6-35 details the configuration that enables the San Francisco router to support the configuration depicted by Figure 6-18 using a dialer profile.

Example 6-35 *Answer to Scenario 6-1, Question 5*

```
isdn switch-type basic-5ess
!
interface ethernet 0
ip address 10.10.1.1 255.255.255.0
!
interface BRI0
encapsulation ppp
dialer pool-member 1
!
interface BRI1
encapsulation ppp
dialer pool-member 1
!
interface BRI2
encapsulation ppp
dialer pool-member 1
```

continues

Example 6-35 *Answer to Scenario 6-1, Question 5 (Continued)*

```
!
interface Dialer1
ip unnumbered Ethernet 0
encapsulation ppp
peer default ip address 10.1.210.2
dialer remote-name Atlanta
dialer string 4045556789
dialer string 4045556788
dialer pool 1
dialer-group 1
ppp multilink
!
interface Dialer2
ip unnumbered Ethernet0
encapsulation ppp
peer default ip address 10.1.210.3
dialer remote-name Raleigh
dialer string 9194442345
dialer string 9194442346
dialer pool 1
dialer-group 1

ppp multilink
!
dialer list 1 protocol ip permit
```

Scenario 6-2 Answers

1 Example 6-36 details the configuration of the snapshot server on the San Francisco router.

Example 6-36 *Snapshot Server Configuration*

```
interface dialer 2
snapshot server 5 dialer
dialer map snapshot 1 name Raleigh 9194442345
dialer map snapshot 1 name Atlanta 4045556789
```

2 Example 6-37 details the configuration of the snapshot client on the Atlanta router. Example 6-38 details the snapshot client configuration on the Raleigh router.

Example 6-37 *Snapshot Client Configuration on the Atlanta Router*

```
interface BRI0
snapshot client 5 720 dialer
dialer map snapshot 1 name SanFrancisco 6504447899
```

Example 6-38 *Snapshot Client Configuration on the Raleigh Router*

```
interface BRI0
snapshot client 5 720 dialer
dialer map snapshot 1 name SanFrancisco 6504447898
```

Scenario 6-3 Answers

1 Example 6-39 shows the dial backup configuration for the San Francisco router. Example 6-40 shows the configuration for the Raleigh router. Example 6-40 shows the configuration for the Atlanta router. Note that in the following configurations, the DDR commands are assumed to be properly implemented.

Example 6-39 *San Francisco Router Dial Backup for Failure Configuration*

```
interface serial 0.1
backup interface bri 0
backup delay 5 60
interface serial 0.2
backup interface bri 0
backup delay 5 60
```

Example 6-40 *Raleigh Router Dial Backup for Failure Configuration*

```
interface serial 0
backup interface bri 0
backup delay 5 60
```

Example 6-41 *Atlanta Router Dial Backup for Failure Configuration*

```
interface serial 0
backup interface bri 0
backup delay 5 60
```

2 Examples 6-42, 6-43 and 6-44 show the commands that need to be added to the configurations specified in Question 1 to provide load balancing in the event that the load on the Frame Relay circuit reaches 90 percent.

Example 6-42 *San Francisco Router Dial Backup for Load Configuration*

```
interface serial 0.1
backup load 90 10
interface serial 0.2
backup load 90 10
```

Example 6-43 *Raleigh Router Dial Backup for Load Configuration*

```
interface serial 0
backup load 90 10
```

Example 6-44 *Atlanta Router Dial Backup for Load Configuration*

```
interface serial 0
backup load 90 10
```

Scenario 6-4 Answers

The answers for this scenario represent a basic troubleshooting guide. By far, they are not the only answers available.

1 Layer 1 represents the physical layer. Make sure the cabling is properly connected. Ensure that the proper cables are being used. Make sure you have the proper switch type configured. Call the telco to ensure the proper setting. Make sure the interface has not been shutdown. With all cables properly connected and the proper switch type, the layer should activate.

2 Layer 2 obviously relies on Layer 1. If Layer 1 is not active, Layers 2 and 3 cannot activate. There are a number of commands useful in troubleshooting Layer 2. Table 6-7 lists some of the privileged EXEC commands:

Table 6-8 *ISDN Layer 2 Troubleshooting Commands*

Command	Explanation
show isdn status	This command is useful in troubleshooting all 3 layers of the ISDN connection. It shows layer by layer the status of the connection. If Layer 2 is active, you will see MULTIPLE_FRAME_ESTABLISHED in the output under the Layer 2 information.
debug isdn q921	This command shows the real-time negotiation (or lack thereof) between the router and the telco switch. TEI negotiation can also be monitored here.
show interface bri0	This command shows a snapshot of the current status (up/down, and so on) of the interface.

3 If the TEI is not being negotiated, check the Layer 1 connectivity and the switch type. If Layer 1 is correctly connected and the switch type is properly configured, there may be a problem with the installation. If the switch type is correct, and the telco hasn't properly installed the line, there is no connectivity. Remember, in Europe, a TEI is not assigned until a call is set up. In North America, there should be on-going communication between the switch and the router, so the TEI should be assigned. Cisco does not support TEI=0

for BRI connections. For PRI, the TEI is 0. If the switch type is incorrect and/or the switch type is changed, save the configuration and reload the router. The new switch type is not activated until a reload is done.

4 Layer 3 connectivity is dependent on Layers 1 and 2. If they are not active, Layer 3 does not activate. Table 6-8 shows only a few of the privileged EXEC commands available to troubleshoot Layer 3.

Table 6-9   *ISDN Layer 3 Troubleshooting*

Command	Explanation
show isdn status	This command is useful in troubleshooting all 3 layers of the ISDN connection. It shows (layer by layer) the status of the connection.
debug isdn q931	This command shows the real-time call setup (or lack thereof). You can monitor the progress of the call in real time.
debug dialer	This enables the real-time dialing and negotiation between the two routers.
show interface bri0	This shows a snapshot of the current status (up/down, and so on) of the interface.

This chapter covers the following topics that you need to master as a CCNP:

- **Cisco 700 series router key features and functions**—The 700 series router relies on profiles as psuedo interfaces for the device. These profiles take on the characteristics of the site to which the router is being connected. The sites that are discussed in the chapter are the remote office (RO), the small office/home office (SOHO), and the ISP. In addition, the Dynamic Host Configuration Protocol (DHCP) functionality of the device is discussed.

- **Cisco 700 series router profiles**—This section describes the use of profiles for the configuration of a Cisco 700 series router. These profiles provide the building blocks for the 700 series router functionality.

- **Configuring the 700 series router for IP routing**—This section details the commands for routing in an IP environment with the 700 series router.

- **Routing with the Cisco 700 series router**—This section describes the 700 series router's capabilities in a very small network. This function is generally not used because the 700 is catagorized as an end-user device.

- **DHCP overview**—This section describes DHCP from the perspective of a 700 series router.

- **Using the 700 series router as a DHCP server and relay agent**—This section presents the 700 series router configured as a DHCP server or helper agent. The ability to configure a 700 series router for DHCP is a necessary skill for a CCNP.

CHAPTER 7

Configuring a Cisco 700 Series Router

The 700 series router was purchased by Cisco from Combinet in 1997. The purchase gave Cisco an ISDN product uniquely suited to the telecommuter and SOHO market. The 700 series provides single Basic Rate Interface (BRI) connectivity and an Ethernet interface for a LAN connection. The 700 series router is compatible with the full Cisco router product line; however, it does not use the same command line structure for configuration.

The command line of the 700 series router uses **set** as the main verb for most of the commands. This has been likened to the switch product line by some; however, there is no similarity except the use of the **set** verb.

For those who are familiar with the IOS command set, the 700 series command language can be less than intuitive. It is important, however, for the successful CCNP candidate to become familiar with the basic concepts of the 700 configuration and the target market. The target market for this product is the telecommuter, the small office, and the home office environment.

How to Best Use This Chapter

By taking the following steps, you can make better use of your study time:

- Keep your notes and answers for all your work with this book in one place for easy reference.

- Take the "Do I Know This Already?" quiz and write down your answers. Studies show retention is significantly increased through writing down facts and concepts, even if you never look at the information again.

- Use the diagram in Figure 7-1 to guide you to the next step.

Figure 7-1   *How to Use This Chapter*

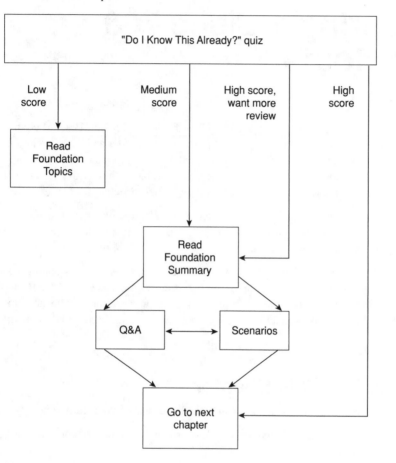

"Do I Know This Already?" Quiz

The purpose of the "Do I Know This Already?" quiz is to help you decide what parts of this chapter to use. If you already intend to read the entire chapter, you do not necessarily need to answer these questions now.

The nine-question quiz helps you determine how to spend your limited study time. The quiz is sectioned into smaller "quizlets," each of which corresponds to four of the major topic headings in the chapter. Use the scoresheet in Table 7-1 to record your scores.

Table 7-1   *Scoresheet for Quizlets and Quiz*

Quizlet Number	Foundation Topics Section Covered by These Questions	Questions	Score
1	Cisco 700 series router key features and functions	1	
2	Cisco 700 series router profiles	2–4	
3	Configuring the 700 series router for IP routing	5–7	
4	Using the 700 series router as a DHCP server and relay agent	8–9	

1 Define the acronyms SOHO and RO.

_____

_____

_____

2 What are the three permanent profiles for the 700 series router?

_____

_____

_____

3 For what is the internal profile used?

_____

_____

_____

4 How many user profiles can be created?

_____

_____

_____

5 Can an ISP support dial-on-demand (DDR) routing and bandwidth-on-demand (BoD) with a 700 series router? If not, why?

_____

_____

_____

6 What is the mechanism that points the 700 to the ISP?

_____

_____

_____

7 What routing protocols can be configured on the 700 series router?

_____

_____

_____

8 How would you configure a 700 series router as a DHCP relay agent?

_____

_____

_____

9 When configuring the 700 series router for a DHCP server, how do you set up the default gateway for the client?

_____

_____

_____

The answers to the "Do I Know This Already?" quiz are found in Appendix A, "Answers to the 'Do I Know This Already?' Quizzes and Q&A," on page 397. The suggested choices for your next step are as follows:

- **You correctly answered five or fewer questions overall**—Read the chapter. This includes the "Foundation Topics," the "Foundation Summary," and the "Q&A" sections, as well as the scenarios at the end of the chapter.

- **You correctly answered six, seven, or eight questions overall**—Begin with the "Foundation Summary" section and then go to the "Q&A" section and the scenario at the end of the chapter.

- **You correctly answered all questions correctly**—If you want more review on these topics, skip to the "Foundation Summary" section, and then go to the "Q&A" section and the scenario at the end of the chapter. Otherwise, move to the next chapter.

Foundation Topics

Cisco 700 Series Router Key Features and Functions

The key features of a 700 router are:

- **Internet access for multiple users over one ISDN line**—The Cisco 700 series router enables multiple PCs to access the Internet simultaneously. This keeps users from having to share a single PC with an Internet connection or rely on server-based hardware and software. A single Cisco 700 series router can make everyone in the office more productive.

- **Affordable Internet connections for SOHOs**—With the Cisco 700 series, there's no need to install a separate ISDN card in every PC to provide Internet access to new users and no need to have multiple ISDN lines or multiple Internet access accounts. The Cisco 700 series router includes everything you need for fast access, without the need for costly added hardware or software in a dedicated PC or central server.

- **High-speed Internet connections**—Unlike ISDN cards, the Cisco 700 series router does not steal performance from a PC's main processor or add work for your central server. Fast call setup with automatic dialup provides quick, automated connections to the Internet and online services.

The functions of the 700 series router can be categorized into three feature sets: networking, routing and WAN, and ISDN and telephony features. All are described in the sections that follow.

Networking

The Cisco 700 series router offers full Point-to-Point Protocol (PPP) support, which includes Password Authentication Protocol (PAP), Challenge Handshake Authentication Protocol (CHAP), and Multilink PPP. The Cisco 700 series router also supports data compression that is compatible with the IOS feature set.

As mentioned, the 700 series router can also function as a DHCP server or relay agent to provide address assignments for the network environment. In addition, the router can provide port address translation (PAT) support for a small office's Internet connectivity.

In a small office environment, using the 700 series router as the DHCP server can offer the small value-added reseller (VAR) the ability to control the address assignment without the need to modify or maintain each client on the local network. This is a major benefit to the small VAR from the standpoint of servicing the account. In addition, the use of PAT would give the small office the necessary access to the Internet without the need for knowledge of the IP addresses assigned locally. Both of these factors make this choice an ideal device for a small (four to ten) node network to access the Internet, where the service is handled by a single VAR-managed device.

Routing and WAN

IP and IPX are the only protocols supported on the Cisco 700 series router; however, the 700 series router can function as a bridge for any other protocol. RIP v1 and RIP v2 are supported for IP, and RIP for IPX is also supported. Support for Cisco's snapshot routing feature is also supported to provide an on-demand method of routing update exchanges. Dial-on-demand routing and bandwidth-on-demand features compatible with the customary IOS features are also configurable on the device.

ISDN and Telephony

The 700 series router provides dial tone for the telephone service on plain old telephone service (POTS) RJ-11 interfaces. On the earlier 700 series models (750/760), the model number defined the ISDN interface type. The 700 series models that ended in an even number provided the built-in network termination 1 (NT1) interface for ISDN. The models that ended in an odd number provided an S/T interface, for which the customer had to supply the NT1 device if it was needed.

In the United States, the built-in NT1 provided a complete solution. The NT1 in the international community, however, is a telephone company device. Thus, there is the need for the different models. The recent models now have both the S/T interface and the U interface on the router.

The 775/776 model types are currently recommended. Again, the even numbered 776 comes with a built-in NT1 and the 775 does not. Both models provide two POTS jacks and a four-port hub.

Cisco 700 Series Router Profiles

The Cisco 700 series router uses different profiles to store the configuration parameters associated with a remote connection or location. This is not unlike the IOS command-line syntax that most engineers associate with an interface dialer on an enterprise-type Cisco router. In a 2500 series router, the phone number, the authentication password, and the addressing could be associated with a dialer interface. The 700 series router, using the same concept, calls the stored information for a connection a *profile*, and stores it in a UNIX subdirectory.

Creating each profile on a 700 series router is similar to creating an **interface dialer** on a Cisco IOS platform. The unique advantage that the 700 provides is that the profiles can be named instead of numbered. For example, on an IOS platform, the connection to the corporate office can be **interface dialer 1**, whereas on the 700, the profile can be called **corp_office**. This simplicity provides a key element in troubleshooting when a configuration has not been viewed for many months.

The 700 series router can store a maximum of 20 profiles. This includes 16 user profiles, or 16 definitions for remote connections. There are also three permanent profiles: *LAN*, *standard*, and *internal*. These, in addition to the *system* profile, make a total of 20. The system profile is also referred to as the *global* profile in some Cisco documentation.

The concept of storage from the standpoint of the IOS is not relevant; **set** commands are immediately stored in the configuration in which they are typed. Some commands require the router to be rebooted to take effect. The general rule of thumb is to reboot following any configuration change.

LAN Profile

The LAN profile defines the connection to the Ethernet port. It is used for routing. The parameters that are set here are similar to the configuration on the E0 using the familiar IOS command strings. Although the parameters are similar, the syntax is not. The parameters are the IP address and mask, the route protocol, and so forth.

Standard Profile

The standard profile is used for inbound ISDN calls that do not have an associated profile. This profile does not support routing. The standard profile is the default profile. If authentication is not required and the destination device you are connecting to does not have a user-defined profile, the router uses the standard profile. If authentication is required and no profile is found, the call is dropped.

Internal Profile

The internal profile is used when routing is enabled and provides the configuration parameters to pass data between the bridge engine and the IP/IPX route engine.

System Profile

The system profile provides a declaration of what protocols can be used by the other profiles. If a routing protocol is turned on in the system profile, it can be used by any profile. An example here tells the story best: if you turn off IPX routing in the system profile, no profile can do IPX routing. If the system profile has IPX routing turned on, a profile can choose to do IPX routing. The system provides a global control for all protocols.

Profile Use Guidelines

Much ado is made about routing in the profiles. Simply stated, an unknown call is not handled with the route engine, and the standard profile does not support routing. On the other hand, a known call, or one with an associated profile, is passed to the internal profile if IP or IPX routing has been declared for the profile and then sent to the route engine for processing to the LAN.

The following guidelines should be known by the successful CCNP candidate:

- **Functions**—LAN and internal profiles provide the same basic function.

- **LAN routing**—Any protocol routed in the LAN must be routed in the user profile. If a user profile does not declare routing, the LAN profile does not route it.

- **Bridging**—Any protocol routed in the internal profile may be routed or bridged in the user profile.

- **Pinging**—If IP or IPX routing is on for the internal profile, the router can be pinged.

The system, LAN, and user profiles must be configured to establish a call. The system level is similar to the IOS *global configuration mode*, and is where the switch type service profile identifiers (SPIDs) (if needed) and local directory numbers are entered.

The IP address and mask for the Ethernet interface and the routing protocol are established in the LAN profile. Again, this is similar to the configuration of **interface E0** using the IOS command **set**. The user profile declares the phone number, frame type, encapsulation, static routing and authentication for this connection.

Once the profiles are created, they must be activated. An active profile is ready to accept a demand call. To activate a profile once it is created, you would use

set active *profile-name*

where the *profile-name* is the freely chosen name of the connection. For example, suppose the profile **my_corp_off** has been created and configured using the **set user my_corp_off** command. The next step would be to activate the profile by issuing this command:

```
set active my_corp_off.
```

A more in-depth discussion of the syntax takes place later in the chapter.

Configuring the Cisco 700 Series Router for IP Routing

There are three sections to configuring a Cisco 700 series router—the system level, the LAN, and the user profile.

The system profile contains that information that is generally found in the global configuration on an IOS router. The information includes the name of the router and the switch type. Additionally, the system level contains the encapsulation type, the authentication type, and the password used by the 700 series router when it connects to another device. This information is placed on the individual WAN interfaces on other router platforms; however, the fact that encapsulation and the authentication type are NOT *interface* level parameters can be explained by noting that that there is only *one* WAN interface on the 700.

The LAN section of the Cisco 700 series router configuration contains the information associated with the Ethernet interface of the router. The IP and/or IPX address and the mask are set in this section. The routing protocol is also turned on in this section. This is similar to the IOS syntax in which routing is turned on as a global parameter, but then the **network** statement is used to enable routing on the interfaces. Again, because there is only *one* LAN interface, this approach makes sense.

The user section of the Cisco 700 series router configuration contains the information associated with the connection or call. The address and mask, the phone number, the routing protocol, and the static route are put into this section. This section is defined as a profile on the router.

Figure 7-2 and Example 7-1 demonstrate a simple configuration for a 700 series router connecting over an ISDN network to a remote access server. Figure 7-2 shows schematically what is being done and Example 7-1 shows the configuration syntax. Note that the System, LAN, and User headers shown in Example 7-1 do not exist as part of the configuration, but are shown to show the parts of the configuration more clearly.

Figure 7-2   *Rem700 Router Connecting to the RAS Router Called CorpOff*

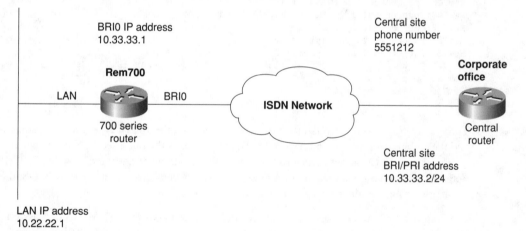

Example 7-1 shows the configuration file for the network setup in Figure 7-2.

Example 7-1   *Configuration File for the Cisco 700 Series Router Labeled Rem700 in Figure 7-1*

```
-----------------------------System section------------------------------------
>set system Rem700
Rem700>set switch 5ess
Rem700>set encapsulation ppp
Rem700>set ppp authentication incoming chap
Rem700>set ppp authentication outgoing chap
Rem700>set ppp secret
prompt for password
prompt for password
Rem700>cd lan
----------------------------LAN section-----------------------------------------
lan>set bridging off
lan>set ip  10.22.22.1
lan>set ip netmask 255.255.255.0
lan>set ip routing on
lan>cd
Rem700>set user CorpOFF
-----------------------------User section---------------------------------------
Rem700:CorpOFF>set bridging off
Rem700:CorpOFF>set ip 10.33.33.1
Rem700:CorpOFF>set ip netmask 255.255.255.0
Rem700:CorpOFF>set ip routing on
Rem700:CorpOFF>set ppp host abc123
Rem700:CorpOFF>set number 5551212
Rem700:CorpOFF>set ip route destination 0.0.0.0/0 gateway 10.33.33.2
Rem700:CorpOFF>cd
Rem700>set active CorpOFF
```

The system commands establish the hostname of the 700, the switch type, the encapsulation, and the authentication type and password. The password is the one used by the 700 when connecting to the Corporate Office router. The authentication has been declared as PPP CHAP both inbound and outbound. This is unique to the 700 IOS whereas in the non-700 IOS, the declaration of authentication does not take on a direction.

The command **cd lan** changes the LAN profile. The commands in the LAN section assign the IP address and mask and enable routing. You may be asking the following: "What routing protocol is turned on?" The answer is RIP Version 1 (RIP-1). The router supports *only* RIP, and by not specifying that RIP Version 2 (RIP-2) is to be used, the router uses RIP-1.

In the last section in Example 7-1, the user CorpOFF is created with the command **set user CorpOFF**. The use of the command **set user** is used *only* to create the profile (subdirectory). After the profile has been created, it can be accessed to alter the configuration by using the command **cd CorpOFF**. This command works with any permanent profile.

The commands in the User section set an IP address for the WAN and turn on routing so that the user profile during this call participates with the LAN profile. The phone number is set, and the default gateway is established. In effect, the static route says if the packet isn't for me, send it to 10.33.33.2, which is the other side of the WAN link. It is important to note that a static route is required on the CorpOFF router to gain access to the Ethernet or LAN of the 700 series router because RIP updates have not been turned on.

To turn on RIP updates, you would need the command **set RIP update periodic**; however, using a distance vector protocol over a dial-on-demand link to maintain route table entries would not be cost effective.

The successful CCNP candidate should understand the profile location of the commands, the interoperability with the IOS command set, and the features available on the router.

Profile Configuration Commands for the Cisco 700 Series Routers

Profile commands are used to establish the basics of the 700 series router configuration. The commands can be categorized for use in the three basic profiles used. Table 7-2 summarizes the commands used for the three basic profiles.

Table 7-2

Profile	Command	Description
System	**set switch**	This command declares the switch type for the 700 series router. Valid choices would be DMS100, 5ESS, NI1, and so on. Because the 700 series router only supports a single BRI interface, there is no need for further definition of the switch type.
	set encapsulation	This command declares the encapsulation method for the BRI connection. The choices here are PPP and CPPP. PPP would be the most common setting.
	set ppp authentication incoming	This command declares the authentication type for an incoming call. The choices are CHAP, PAP, or NONE. This feature is unique to the 700 IOS and enables the authentication to take on a direction.
	set ppp authentication outgoing	This command is similar to the incoming authentication, but declares the method of authentication for calls leaving the 700 series router. Again, the method choices are CHAP, PAP, and NONE.
	set ppp secret	This command declares the password for the 700 series router that is used for all calls leaving the 700. This password would be used by PAP or CHAP as declared by the **set ppp authentication outgoing** command.

continues

Table 7- 2

Profile	Command	Description
	set active	This command activates the profile. This can be accomplished by a router reboot after the configuration is complete.
LAN	**set bridging off**	This command does what it suggests—it turns off bridging on the LAN interface. Only those protocols (IP or IPX) that are routed are passed.
	set ip	This command declares the IP address for the LAN interface.
	set ip netmask	This command declares the IP address mask for the LAN interface.
	set ip routing on	This command turns on IP routing for the interface.
User	**set user CorpOFF**	This command creates the user profile called CorpOFF. This profile name is used (along with the password specified by the **set ppp host** command) for authentication in the inbound direction. This command is not used after the profile has been created. Once a profile is created, the command **cd** is used to change it.
	set bridging off	This device enables bridging to be turned off in the profile for the BRI port.
	set ip 10.33.33.1	The ip address 10.33.33.1 is used for the BRI interface when this profile is used.
	set ip netmask 255.255.255.0	The mask for the IP address is set to 24 bits.
	set ip routing on	This command enables ip routing on the interface. This does not enable the sending of RIP updates; it simply allows routing to take place over the interface.
	set number 5551212	The phone number 5551212 is called when this profile is used.
	set ip route destination 0.0.0.0/0 gateway	This is a default route inside the CorpOFF profile. This route causes this profile to be used whenever an ip packet does not have an explicit route to take.

Profile Management Commands for the Cisco 700 Series Routers

Table 7-3 summarizes the commands used for managing the Cisco 700 series router profiles.

Table 7- 3

Command	Description
set user	This command initially creates the profile (or subdirectory) for the connection called user. Selecting the name "user" for a connection is similar to naming a router "router". Generally, the name of the connection is something that is meaningful to the connection.
upload	This command writes the configuration to the monitor screen. The configuration is presented on the screen without page breaks. It is necessary to use a monitor program (such as hyperterminal) to view the entire configuration by using the scroll arrows on your keyboard.
set default	This command is similar to doing an **erase startup-config** and then issuing a **reload** command on an IOS router. Care should be taken with this command because it does NOT prompt the user that the configuration will be set back to factory defaults. The use of this command could be a career-ending event if there is no saved hardcopy of the configuration.
reset	This command simply reloads and reinitializes the router.

Routing with the Cisco 700 Series Router

Routing over the WAN with the 700 series router is accomplished by using static routes within the profile. Each profile (or subdirectory) has a route associated with it. The router, when looking for a route to satisfy a user request for connectivity to a remote network, finds the profile that can satisfy that request and makes a connection using the configuration parameters associated with that profile.

Routing on the LAN side of the router is done using RIP-1 or RIP-2. Because the router has a directly connected LAN and each profile is pseudo directly connected, the router maintains a route table with these entries. Any other routes that are learned through RIP over the LAN are also reflected in the route table.

It is possible to run RIP over the WAN side; however, because DDR is the general mode for this router, it doesn't make sense to learn routes from a remote side because the connection is not going to remain up to maintain the routes.

The Cisco 700 series router is compatible with the IOS snapshot routing protocol for RIP and can exchange routes on the WAN side, although it would be a rare implementation that would require this. The positioning of this router does not lend itself to being an access router for a large group of users.

Figure 7-3 shows a 700 series router used by a home office user who has a need to connect to a corporate office, another branch, and an Internet service provider. The configuration would consist of multiple profiles, one for each of the connections.

Figure 7-3   *Home Office Configuration to a Corporate Office, a Branch Office, and a Local ISP*

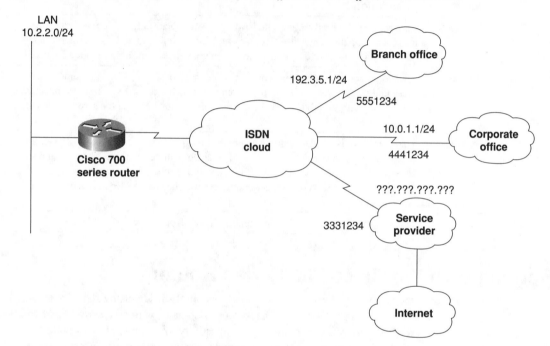

The configuration would have the profiles shown in Example 7-2:

Example 7-2   *Profiles for the Configuration in Figure 7-2*

```
set user BRANCH
set bridging off
set ip 192.3.5.2
set ip netmask 255.255.255.0
set ip routing on
set number 5551234
set ip route destination 192.3.4.0/24 gateway 192.3.5.1

set user CORPORATE
set bridging off
set ip 10.0.1.2
set ip netmask 255.255.255.0
set ip routing on
set number 4441234
set ip route destination 10.0.0.0/24 gateway 10.0.1.1
```

Example 7-2 *Profiles for the Configuration in Figure 7-2 (Continued)*

```
set user MYISP
set bridging off
set ip routing on
set number 3331234
set ip route destination 0.0.0.0/0 gateway 0.0.0.0 propagate on
set ip netmask 0.0.0.0
set bridge off
```

Executing the **show ip route all** command would display the output shown in Example 7-3.

Example 7-3 **show ip route all** *Command Output Displays IP Routes for All Profiles*

```
show ip route all
Profile          Type Destination     Bits Gateway          Prop Cost Source Age
--------------------------------------------------------------------------------
LAN              NET  10.118.0.0      24   DIRECT           ON   1    DIRECT 0
CentralA         NET  0.0.0.0         0    0.0.0.0          OFF  1    STATIC 0
```

With this configuration, when the router receives a packet for the 192.3.4.0 network, the packet would be passed to the BRI0 port and the **BRANCH** profile would be used. If a packet was destined for any 10.0.0.0 network, it would be passed to the BRI0 and the **CORPORATE** profile would be used. All other packets that are destined to non-known networks would be passed to the BRI0 port and the **MYISP** profile would be invoked. Note that bridging has been turned off and IP routing has been turned on in each profile. All non-IP packets will not pass through the router; however, all IP packets will be routed.

It should be noted that the **MYISP** profile has not actually been configured for an IP address. Although it does accept the address assigned by the service provider, this is done by simply declaring the IP netmask as 0.0.0.0, without specifying an IP address.

The successful CCNP candidate is aware of the flexibility of the 700 series router; however, he or she need not be a subject matter expert on each command nuance. In general, he or she should remember that the 700 series router would be used in a SOHO environment in which ISDN is being used to connect to a limited number of locations and to provide higher-than-modem speeds to an ISP.

DHCP Overview

DHCP provides a method for automatically assigning reusable IP addresses to clients. Cisco's implementation of DHCP follows RFC 2131 for DHCP concepts and RFC 2131 for DHCP options.

The 700 IOS DHCP server gives the SOHO administrator a much simpler IP address management scheme. DHCP enables the small office with the capability to provide IP addressing on an as-needed basis for each local client. This method eliminates address management on a PC-by-PC basis, which reduces client configuration tasks and costs. Hosts in remote offices can obtain dynamic IP addresses directly from the local 700 series router.

DHCP has been generally adopted as the standard for assigning addresses to an internal network. This frees the administrator from configuring and maintaining an address scheme on a PC-by-PC basis.

For more information on the inner workings of DHCP, you can turn to the following references (all of which can be accessed from www.isi.edu/in-notes/):

- **RFC 951**—Bootstrap Protocol (BOOTP)
- **RFC 1542**—Clarifications and Extensions for the Bootstrap Protocol
- **RFC 2131**—Dynamic Host Configuration Protocol
- **RFC 2132**—DHCP Options and BOOTP Vendor Extensions

These RFCs can be a bit heady for understanding the average uses of DHCP. Nonetheless, the basic thrust of this technology has been widely implemented and accepted. In fact, all Cisco routers can understand and implement this function per the standards.

Using the Cisco 700 Series Router as a DHCP Server and Relay Agent

The 700 series router is capable of being the DHCP server or functioning as a relay agent to a DHCP server running on another device. To perform the function of a relay agent, the router is configured as follows:

```
set dhcp relay ip-address
```

The use of the 700 series router as a relay agent is very similar to setting an IP helper-address on an IOS router pointing to a DHCP server. Using the **set dhcp relay** command passes only the DHCP request; however, the IP helper-address can pass other broadcast packets if not configured for *only* DHCP requests. The use of the router as a relay agent simply points to another device responsible for the maintenance of the IP addressing.

Using the 700 series router as a DHCP server is also syntactically very simple: the router must be declared as the server and the address pool must be defined. Any DHCP broadcast request received from the LAN interface is satisfied from the pool. The code in Example 7-4 is required on the router shown in Figure 7-4.

Example 7-4 *700 Configuration to Implement the Router as a DHCP Server*

```
set dhcp server
set dhcp address 10.1.1.2 252
set dhcp netmask 255.255.255.0
set dhcp gateway primary 10.1.1.1
set dhcp dns primary 192.168.1.5
set dhcp wins primary 192.168.1.5
set dhcp domain mycompany
```

Figure 7-4   *DHCP Setup for the 700 Series Router*

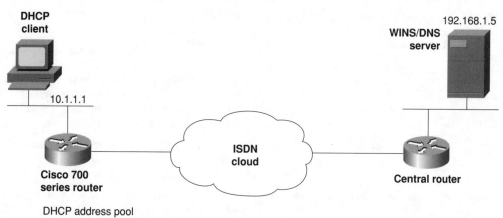

The **set dhcp server** command declares that the router be used as the DHCP server. The address pool and network mask are then declared. The syntax for the address pool is different from the syntax used to specify a pool in the IOS command set.

The address (in this case, 10.1.1.2) is the first address in the pool. The second number (252) declares the number of addresses that are assigned internally for the DHCP pool. Hence, the pool in this case uses the IP addresses 10.1.1.2 through 10.1.1.253. The gateway that is given to all DHCP clients is the 700 Ethernet interface. The DNS and WINS servers are defined as 192.168.1.5, and the domain sent to all clients is "mycompany".

The key issue is that the 700 series router is assigning itself as the gateway for the clients on its Ethernet segment. In this fashion, it becomes the router for all clients. To become successful with the CCNP material, you should focus on the flexibility of the 700 series router and not on the details of the syntax.

Foundation Summary

The Foundation Summary is a collection of tables and figures that provides a convenient review of many key concepts in this chapter. For those of you already comfortable with the topics in this chapter, this summary could help you recall a few details. For those of you who just read this chapter, this review should help solidify some key facts. For any of you doing your final preparation before the exam, these tables and figures will hopefully be a convenient way to review the day before the exam.

Table 7-4 summarizes the commands used for the three basic Cisco 700 series router profiles.

Table 7-4 *Command Summary for Cisco 700 Series Router Profile Configuration*

Profile	Command	Description
System	**set switch**	This command declares the switch type for the 700 series router. Valid choices would be DMS100, 5ESS, NI1, and so on. Because the 700 series router only supports a single BRI interface, there is no need for further definition of the switch type.
	set encapsulation	This command declares the encapsulation method for the BRI connection. The choices here are PPP and CPPP. PPP would be the most common setting.
	set ppp authentication incoming	This command declares the authentication type for an incoming call. The choices are CHAP, PAP, or NONE. This feature is unique to the 700 IOS and enables the authentication to take on a direction.
	set ppp authentication outgoing	This command is similar to the incoming authentication, but declares the method of authentication for calls leaving the 700 series router. Again, the method choices are CHAP, PAP, and NONE.
	set ppp secret	This command declares the password for the 700 series router that is used for all calls leaving the 700. This password would be used by PAP or CHAP as declared by the **set ppp authentication outgoing** command.
	set active	This command activates the profile. This can be accomplished by a router reboot after the configuration is complete.
LAN	**set bridging off**	This command does what it suggests—it turns off bridging on the LAN interface. Only those protocols (IP or IPX) that are routed are passed.
	set ip	This command declares the IP address for the LAN interface.

Table 7- 4   *Command Summary for Cisco 700 Series Router Profile Configuration (Continued)*

Profile	Command	Description
	set ip netmask	This command declares the IP address mask for the LAN interface.
	set ip routing on	This command turns on IP routing for the interface.
User	**set user CorpOFF**	This command creates the user profile called CorpOFF. This profile name is used (along with the password specified by the **set ppp host** command) for authentication in the inbound direction. This command is not used after the profile has been created. Once a profile is created, the command **cd** is used to change it.
	set bridging off	This device enables bridging to be turned off in the profile for the BRI port.
	set ip 10.33.33.1	The ip address 10.33.33.1 is used for the BRI interface when this profile is used.
	set ip netmask 255.255.255.0	The mask for the IP address is set to 24 bits.
	set ip routing on	This command enables ip routing on the interface. This does not enable the sending of RIP updates; it simply allows routing to take place over the interface.
	set number 5551212	The phone number 5551212 is called when this profile is used.
	set ip route destination 0.0.0.0/0 gateway	This is a default route inside the CorpOFF profile. This route causes this profile to be used whenever an ip packet does not have an explicit route to take.

Table 7-5 summarizes the commands used for managing Cisco 700 series router profiles.

Table 7- 5 *Command Summary for Cisco 700 Series Router Profile Management*

Command	Description
set user	This command initially creates the profile (or subdirectory) for the connection called user. Selecting the name "user" for a connection is similar to naming a router "router". Generally, the name of the connection is something that is meaningful to the connection.
upload	This command writes the configuration to the monitor screen. The configuration is presented on the screen without page breaks. It is necessary to use a monitor program (such as hyperterminal) to view the entire configuration by using the scroll arrows on your keyboard.
set default	This command is similar to doing an erase startup-config and then issuing a **reload** command on an IOS router. Care should be taken with this command because it does NOT prompt the user that the configuration will be set back to factory defaults. The use of this command could be a career-ending event if there is no saved hardcopy of the configuration.
reset	This command simply reloads and reinitializes the router.

Q&A

The questions and scenarios in this book are more difficult than what you will experience on the actual exam. The questions do not attempt to cover more breadth or depth than the exam; however, they are designed to make sure that you know the answer. Rather than enabling you to derive the answer from clues hidden inside the question itself, the questions challenge your understanding and recall of the subject.

Questions from the "Do I Know This Already?" quiz from the beginning of the chapter are repeated here to ensure that you have mastered the chapter's topic areas. Hopefully, mastering these questions will help you limit the number of exam questions on which you narrow your choices to two options and then guess.

If you incorrectly answer one of the following questions, review the answer and ensure that you understand the reason(s) why your answer is incorrect. If you are confused by the answer, refer to the text in the chapter to review.

The answers to these questions can be found in Appendix A, on page 397.

1 What are the three permanent profiles for the 700 series router?

_____

_____

_____

2 Which one of the following statements is true?

a. Any protocol routed in the LAN must be routed in the user profile.

b. Any protocol routed in the LAN cannot be routed in the user profile.

c. Any protocol routed in the LAN must be bridged in the user profile.

d. Any protocol routed in the LAN cannot be bridged in the internal profile.

3 What must be true for the 700 series router to be IP pingable?

_____

_____

_____

4 For what is the internal profile used?

_____

_____

_____

5   How many user profiles can be created?

_____

_____

_____

6   Under which mode or profile is the ISDN switch type declared?

_____

_____

_____

7   What is declared in the LAN profile?

_____

_____

_____

8   Define the acronyms SOHO and RO.

_____

_____

_____

9   Can an ISP support DDR and BoD with a 700 series router? If not, why?

_____

_____

_____

10   What command would you use to declare the use of CHAP authentication when a 700 series router calls a remote site?

_____

_____

_____

11   What does the command **set system 700MLP** do?

_____

_____

_____

12   What is the mechanism that points the 700 series router to the ISP?

_____

_____

_____

13   Which of the following protocols are supported by the 700 series router: PAP, CHAP, MPPP, IGRP, ISP, and PAT?

_____

_____

_____

14   What routing protocols can be configured on the 700 series router?

_____

_____

_____

15   What command is used to display the 700 configuration?

_____

_____

_____

16   What is the command required for a soft boot on a 700 series router?

_____

_____

_____

17   What command would you use to configure the 700 series router as a DHCP relay agent?

_____

_____

_____

18 What does the following command do: **set dhcp address 10.1.1.5 12**?

_____

_____

_____

19 Which of the following routed protocols can be used on the 700 router: IGRP, IPX, RIP, IP, OSPF, and static routes?

_____

_____

_____

20 When configuring the 700 series router for a DHCP server, how do you set up the default gateway for the client?

_____

_____

_____

Scenarios

The following scenario and questions are designed to draw together the content of the chapter and exercise your understanding of the concepts. There is not necessarily a right answer to the scenario. The thought process and practice in manipulating the related concepts is the goal of this section.

Scenario 7-1

You're a home user with an ISDN connection and would like to connect to your ISP and to your corporate office, which is using the private 192.168.4.0/24 network. Your connection to the corporate office is 192.168.4.12.

1 What router platform might you select?

2 How many user profiles do you need to create?

3 What would the route statements look like in the profiles created?

4 Could you be on the Internet and communicate with your office at the same time?

Scenario Answers

The answers provided in this section are not necessarily the only possible correct answers. They merely represent one possibility for the scenario. The intention is to test your base knowledge and understanding of the concepts discussed in this chapter.

Should your answers be different (as they likely will be) consider the differences. Are your answers in line with the concepts of the answers provided and explained here? If not, go back and read the chapter again, focusing on the sections related to the problem scenario.

Scenario 7-1 Answers

1 You might select the 700 series router. Although it is true that many router platforms would do, the 700 series router is priced for the home user market.

2 You would need to create two profiles—one for each destination that you want to reach.

3 The route statement in the ISP profile would be the default route or the following:

```
set ip route destination 0.0.0.0/0 gateway 0.0.0.0
```

The route statement in the profile used to connect to the corporate office would be

```
set ip route destination 192.168.4.0 gateway 192.168.4.12
```

where **192.168.4.12** is the ISDN interface of the router you are calling.

4 Yes. With two B channels, it would be possible to have both calls on line at the same time.

This chapter covers the following topics that you need to master as a CCNP:

- **X.25 basics**—From its emergence in the early 1970s to present day implementation strategies, X.25 remains one of the most (if not *the* most) deployed technologies in the internetworking world.

- **X.25 layered model**—X.25 employs an implementation model similar to the OSI model. This section discusses the layers of the X.25 model.

- **X.25 configuration options**—For configuration options to be supported globally, there are some configuration parameters that might need to be altered from their default settings. This section details some of those settings.

CHAPTER 8

Establishing an X.25 Connection

The CCNP Remote Access Exam requires you to be familiar with the implementation options associated with X.25. You must understand the basic deployment of X.25 as well as the optional configuration parameters.

X.25 is similar in some respects to ISDN. The basic functionality of the two is based on the same technology, and the Public Switched Telephone Network (PSTN) still provides the necessary switching facilities. X.25 is similar not only to ISDN for switched virtual circuits (SVCs) but also to Frame Relay. In addition, the frame format is almost identical to High-Level Data Link Control (HDLC). It is imperative that you understand the relationship between DCE and DTE devices. The relationship is discussed throughout the chapter.

The exam requires an understanding of various deployment configuration options, including window sizes, packet sizes, and communications windows.

How to Best Use This Chapter

By taking the following steps, you can make better use of your study time:

• Keep your notes and answers for all your work with this book in one place for easy reference.

• Take the "Do I Know This Already?" quiz and write down your answers. Studies show retention is significantly increased through writing facts and concepts down, even if you never look at the information again.

• Use the diagram in Figure 8-1 to guide you to the next step.

Figure 8-1   *How To Use This Chapter*

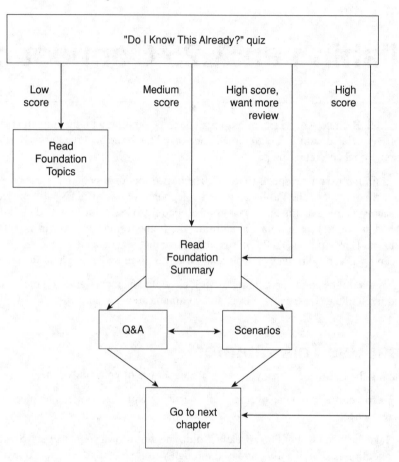

"Do I Know This Already?" Quiz

The purpose of the "Do I Know This Already?" quiz is to help you decide what parts of this chapter to use. If you already intend to read the entire chapter, you do not necessarily need to answer these questions now.

The 12-question quiz helps you make good choices about how to spend your limited study time. The quiz is sectioned into smaller, four-question "quizlets," each of which corresponds to the three major topic headings in the chapter. Use the scoresheet in Table 8-1 to record your scores.

Table 8-1   *Scoresheet for Quizlets and Quiz*

Quizlet Number	Foundation Topics Section Covered by These Questions	Questions	Score
1	X.25 Basics	1–4	
2	X.121 Addressing	5–8	
3	X.25 Configuration Examples	9–12	
All questions		1–12	

1 Name the Layer 2 of X.25.

_____

_____

_____

2 Name the Layer 3 of X.25.

_____

_____

_____

3 In X.25, what are the two possible roles that a router can play?

_____

_____

_____

4 What is the function of a PAD in an X.25 network?

_____

_____

_____

5 The addressing scheme in X.25 is known as what kind of address?

_____

_____

_____

6 List the parts of the addressing scheme from Question 5.

_____

_____

_____

7 How many digits constitute each of the parts of the address from Question 5?

_____

_____

_____

8 From where are the addresses used in configuring X.25 obtained?

_____

_____

_____

9 List the possible types of circuits available in an X.25 network deployment.

_____

_____

_____

10 What effect does changing the default ips and/or ops have on a X.25 transmission?

_____

_____

_____

11 What effect does changing the default win and/or wout have on a X.25 transmission?

_____

_____

_____

12 What is a modulo and what are the possible values?

_____

_____

_____

The answers to the "Do I Know This Already?" quiz are found in Appendix A, "Answers to the 'Do I Know This Already?' Quizzes and Q&A," on page 397. The suggested choices for your next step are as follows:

- **You correctly answered six or fewer questions overall**—Read the chapter. This includes the "Foundation Topics," "Foundation Summary," and "Q&A" sections, as well as the scenarios at the end of the chapter.

- **You correctly answered two or fewer questions on any quizlet**—Review the subsections of the "Foundation Topics" part of this chapter, based on the information that you entered in Table 8-1. Then move into the "Foundation Summary" and "Q&A" sections and the scenarios at the end of the chapter.

- **You correctly answered seven, eight, or nine questions overall**—Begin with the "Foundation Summary" section and then go to the "Q&A" section and the scenarios at the end of the chapter.

- **You correctly answered ten or more questions overall**—If you want more review on these topics, skip to the "Foundation Summary" section, and then go to the "Q&A" section and the scenarios at the end of the chapter. Otherwise, move to the next chapter.

Foundation Topics

X.25 Basics

In the 1970s, a suite of protocols was needed to provide WAN connectivity across public data networks (PDNs), which had already been deployed with great success.

Standardization in the deployment of PDNs was lacking. Industry participants at the time thought that standardization would increase the number of clients who would subscribe to PDN services, if a way could be found to decrease cost while increasing functionality. The result of this development effort was the X.25 specification, which includes X.3, X.75 and X.29. These, however, are a bit beyond our discussion at this time.

X.25 was developed primarily by telco service providers. The specifications were designed to work well in a multivendor environment. End-users can order lines from these telcos and make use of the public packet-switched networks (PSNs).

Fees charged for this service are usually fixed recurring charges; however, the billing can also be based on negotiated usage-based rates. In modern deployments, however, a number of package offerings exist, each with differing feature sets. Billing is structured in a manner similar to the billing of leased lines and the number of packets sent across those lines, as well as the duration of the connection.

X.25 and its related protocols are administered by an agency of the United Nations called the International Telecommunications Union (ITU-T). The ITU Telecommunication Standardization Sector is the committee responsible for voice and data communications.

The ITU-T has created and evolved the standards for X.25 over the last 30 years or so. The ITU-T specifications detail connections between DTE and DCE for remote terminal access and computer communications. These X.25 standards include the creation of a layered model for X.25.

The X.25 layered model defines Link Access Procedure, Balanced (LAPB) as the Layer 2 protocol and Packet Layer Protocol (PLP) as the Layer 3 protocol. Many representations of the X.25 model show X.25 as the Layer 3 protocol and we will do the same. However, you should understand that technically, PLP is the Layer 3 protocol.

The specifications for X.25 are updated regularly. Normally the update cycle is every four years. The specifications dated 1980 and 1984 are the most commonly deployed versions.

The ISO has produced ISO 7776:1986 as a comparable standard to the LAPB standard. Also, ISO 8208:1989 was created to be the equivalent to the ITU-T 1984 X.25 recommendation.

Cisco's X.25 software follows (but not completely) the ITU-T 1984 X.25 recommendation. Cisco has created its own implementation by combining the high points of both the ITU-T recommendations and the ISO recommendation. The implementation details are as follows:

- **LAPB**—LAPB is a protocol that comprises Layer 2 of the X.25 Model. LAPB specifies methods for exchanging frames, monitoring frame sequence, missing frames, and executing frame acknowledgements and retransmission when necessary.

- **LAPB datagram transport**—OSI Layer 3 datagrams are carried over a reliable LABP connection. These datagrams can be encapsulated in a proprietary protocol and transported over the LAPB connection. LAPB is a derivative of HDLC and follows HDLC frame formats. An LAPB connection can carry a single protocol or multiple protocols, depending on the configuration. Mapping X.25 addresses to protocol addresses enables a Layer 3 protocol to be routed through an X.25 network.

- **Defense Data Network (DDN) and Blacker Front-End (BFE) X.25**—The DDN X.25 Standard Service is a required protocol used in conjunction with DDN Packet Switched Nodes (PSNs). The Defense Communications Agency (DCA) has certified Cisco Systems' DDN X.25 Standard Service implementation for attachment to the DDN. Cisco's DDN implementation also includes Blacker Front-End Encryption and Blacker Emergency Mode operation. These options are beyond the scope of our discussions. For further information, check out www.cisco.com.

- **X.25 MIB**—SNMP network management capabilities for X.25 are specified in RFC 1381 and RFC 1382. Collection of information regarding LAPB XID Table, X.25 Cleared Circuit Table, and X.25 Call Parameter Table is not implemented. All SNMP community values are read-only. Refer to the NMS documentation of your specific platform for further information on supported values.

In the past, only larger corporations made use of WAN connections. Now modern communications have evolved to include the widespread use of WAN technologies. With the bandwidth cost reductions over the past few years, WAN connections are no longer cost prohibitive. These newer WAN installations can extend the functionality of X.25. For example, X.25 can be implemented on an ISDN D channel. In addition, a BRI 0 B+D implementation, rather than the traditional 2 B+D implementation, can be ordered specifically for this type of X.25 deployment.

The X.25 network utilizes an addressing scheme that can be equated to a phone number dial plan. There are specific pieces that have specific meaning. For example, 410-555-1212 has specific a specific format. For instance, 410 is the area code and is shared by all phones in a particular geographic area. The 555 is a prefix. It too is a shared number; however, the number of devices sharing it are less than the number of devices sharing 410. The last number, 1212, is a user-specific identifier. Although any one of the three divisions of the previous phone number is reusable, the entire ten-digit string is globally unique.

X.25 utilizes a hierarchical structure that is similar to the phone number structure. This hierarchical structure is discussed later in this chapter. The overall similarities between this and other technologies are also touched on because the configuration of X.25 is very much the same as the configuration of ISDN and/or Frame Relay. The obvious differences lie in the technology-specific parameters necessary for proper configuration of the router.

DTE and DCE

Data terminal equipment (DTE) and data circuit-terminating equipment (DCE) are the key players in any data communication. They identify the role and responsibilities of two X.25 communicating devices. However, the roles are not necessarily defined by physical characteristics as is traditionally thought. The X.25 DTE/DCE (that is, the Layer 2 DTE/DCE) relationship has nothing to do with the electrical characteristics of the interface (that is, the Layer 1 DTE/DCE). Although it is possible that a device can simultaneously play the role of the physical DTE or DCE while performing the role of X.25 DTE/DCE, the two are independent of each other.

The X.25 DTE typically refers to the router or PAD. The X.25 DCE typically acts as a boundary to the PDN within a switch. In a lab situation, the setup might have two routers in a back-to-back configuration; one router must be DTE and the other DCE. This configuration is in addition to the setting of the clock rate on one router and the utilization of a back-to-back serial cable with specific electrical characteristics. When the clock rate is set, that device becomes the DCE physically. It is also possible for the other router to be specified as the X.25 DCE.

The PAD receives data from terminals and transmits that data across the X.25 network in X.25 packet form. At the same time, the PAD receives transmissions from the X.25 network and forwards them on to data terminals. The communications between the PAD and the X.25 network edge device are defined by ITU specifications X.3, X.28, X.29, and X.75. Table 8-2 describes each specification.

Table 8-2   *ITU PAD Specifications*

Specification	Description
X.3	This specification provides parameters for terminal functions such as flow control, baud rate, and so on, used in X.25 host connections.
X.28	This specification provides user interface specifications for controlling a PAD locally. This specification defines the keystrokes for PAD setup similar to modem **AT** commands.
X.29	This specification provides the protocol that is defined to allow X.3 parameter configuration through network connections. Upon connect, a remote host can request changes in terminal configuration parameters.
X.75	This specification specifies the signaling convention utilized between two separate PDNs. Essentially, this is a type of inter-carrier interconnect (ICI) also known as a public Network to Network Interface (NNI).

The X.25 DCE, as mentioned previously, does not necessarily refer to the electrical nature of the device. Typically the DCE refers to a switch or concentrator within the PDN. Figure 8-2 depicts the DTE/DCE relationship.

Figure 8-2   *X.25 DTE/DCE*

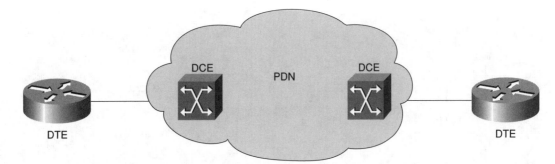

X.25 Layered Model

X.25 employs a three-layered model. Figure 8-3 compares the model to the OSI model.

The X.25 specification maps to Layers 1 through 3 of the OSI reference model. Layer 3, X.25, describes packet formats and packet exchange procedures between peer Layer 3 entities. LAPB defines Layer 2 of the X.25 layered model and performs packet framing for the DTE/DCE link. Layer 1 of the X.25 layered model defines the electrical and mechanical procedures for activating and deactivating the physical connection between the DTE and the DCE.

X.25 Layer

Layer 3 of the X.25 layered model utilizes virtual circuits (VCs). These VCs fall into two categories, permanent and switched. Permanent virtual circuits (PVCs) are nailed up connections that are always active. Switched virtual circuits (SVCs) are set up and torn down as needed.

PVC deployments are very common across many of the WAN technologies in use today. They are nailed up connections and are always active. PVCs require an extremely high level of maintenance due to their static nature.

PVCs can be equated to static routes in an IP environment. Imagine maintaining every route in every router manually. With that in mind, it is very easy to imagine the issues that arise in a PVC environment. They are essentially, after all, static routes. Any failure in the pathway causes the entire circuit to come down. There is no dynamic rerouting. The circuits must be manually reconfigured to go around a failure.

Figure 8-3   *The X.25 Layered Model*

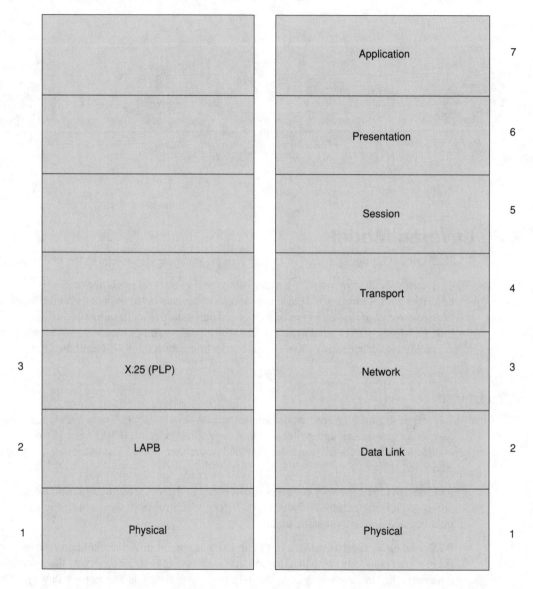

SVC deployments are significantly less maintenance intense. An SVC is simply a phone call from one point to another. As mentioned, SVC implementations are dynamically set up and torn down. They are not nailed up connections. They do tear down after some time of inactivity and must be reestablished if additional data must traverse the link.

In an SVC deployment, the provider incurs significantly less overhead. The circuits are not permanently nailed up, so bandwidth is more efficiently utilized. This fact also makes it possible to dynamically route around network failures with no manual intervention. In addition, downtime is decreased in the event of a failure. SVC implementations are similar to ISDN calls—there is a call setup, data transfer, and a call release.

When a VC is established, the DTE sends a packet to the other end of the connection using the proper VC. The DCE examines the VC identifier to make a routing determination to get the packet through the X.25 network. The Layer 3 X.25 protocol enables the DCE to MUX data from all the DTEs on the destination side of the network.

X.25 supports multiple variations for VC configuration. A single X.25 interface can support up to 4095 individual VCs. The options available are as follows:

- **Single Protocol Single Circuit**—A single protocol is sent across the X.25 link utilizing a single VC.

- **Single Protocol Multiple Circuit**—A single protocol is multiplexed over multiple VCs. SVCs can be combined to improve throughput for a given protocol.

- **Multiple Protocol Single Circuit**—Multiple protocols are multiplexed across a single circuit. Up to nine protocols can be sent across a single VC.

- **Multiple Protocol Multiple Circuit**—Multiple protocols are sent across multiple VCs. This deployment can utilize a single VC per protocol, or multiplexed protocols across multiple VCs.

X.121 Addressing

The X.25 header at Layer 3 comprises a general format identifier (GFI), a logical channel identifier (LCI), and a packet type identifier (PTI). GFI is a four-bit field. The LCI is 12 bits and is locally significant at the DTE/DCE interface. The PTI field identifies one of X.25's 17 packet types. Those packet types are beyond our scope at this time.

Addressing fields in call setup packets contain the source and destination DTE addresses. These addresses are used to establish the VCs that make X.25 communication possible.

ITU-T recommendation X.121 specifies the source and destination address formats. X.121 addresses (also known as *international data numbers*, or IDNs) vary in length and can be up to 14 decimal digits long. The forth byte in the call setup packet specifies the source DTE and destination DTE address lengths.

The first four digits of an IDN are called the data network identification code (DNIC). The DNIC is divided into two parts, the first three digits specifying the country and the last digit specifying the PSN itself. The remaining digits are called the national terminal number (NTN) and are used to identify the specific DTE on the PSN. Figure 8-4 depicts the addressing format.

Figure 8-4   *X.121 Address Format*

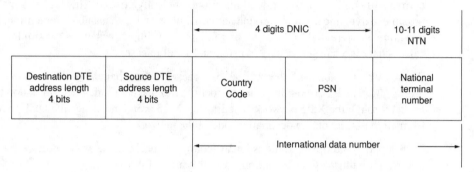

LAPB Layer

LAPB distinguishes between two types of hosts: DTE and DCE. At Level 2, LAPB enables orderly and reliable exchange of data between a DTE and a DCE. As mentioned earlier, a router using LAPB encapsulation can perform the role of a DTE or DCE device at the protocol level, which is different from the physical DTE or DCE.

Using LAPB in noisy conditions can result in greater throughput than using HDLC encapsulation in similar conditions. When LAPB detects a missing frame, the router retransmits the frame instead of waiting for the higher layers to recover the lost information. This behavior is good only if the host timers are relatively slow. In the case of quickly expiring host timers, however, you will discover that LAPB is spending much of its time transmitting host retransmissions. When using long delay satellite links, the modulo for the link should be increased to 128 from 8. This is discussed later in the chapter.

LAPB uses three frame format types:

- **Information (I) frames**—These frames carry upper-layer information and some control information (necessary for full-duplex operations). Send and receive sequence numbers and the poll final (P/F) bit perform flow control and error recovery. The send sequence number refers to the number of the current frame. The receive sequence number records the number of the frame to be received next. In bidirectional conversation, both parties keep send and receive sequence numbers. The poll bit is used to force a final bit message in response, which is used for error detection and recovery.

- **Supervisory (S) frames**—These frames provide control information. They request and suspend transmission, report on status, and acknowledge the receipt of I frames.

- **Unnumbered (U) frames**—These frames, as the name suggests, are not sequenced. They are used for control purposes.

Figure 8-5 depicts the LAPB frame structure.

Figure 8-5   *LAPB Frame*

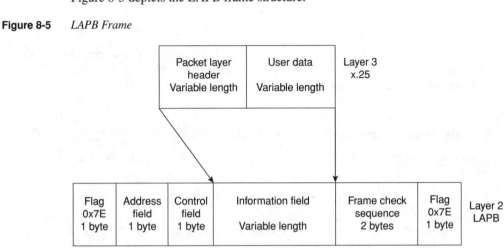

Note that Figure 8-5 also includes a depiction of the Layer 3 X.25 packet and where it fits into the frame structure. The user data is simply encapsulated into an X.25 packet, which is placed into the LAPB frame for transport through the physical layer.

X.25 Physical Layer

The physical layer of X.25 is really no different from other technologies. X.25 is a WAN technology, so it is obviously implemented on serial interfaces at varying speeds. Physical implementation of any serial-based technology requires the use of a transition cable purchased separately from the router. The cable must be specific to the type of serial interface installed in the router (EIA/TIA-232, V.35, and so on) as well as the type of interface on the CSU/DSU (DB-25, Winchester Block, and so on). Once the physical cabling is in place, the serial interface can be configured appropriately.

Configuring X.25

The configuration of X.25 is very similar to the configuration of other WAN protocols. It involves the gathering of information that is needed to properly initialize the X.25 interface and enable communication. The following tasks are necessary:

Step 1   Set the encapsulation of the interface and specify DCE or DTE. If no specification is made, the setting defaults to DTE.

Step 2   Configure the X.121 address as assigned by the PDN service provider.

> **Step 3**   Map the appropriate next logical hop protocol address to its X.121
> address. This function maps the L3 protocol address to the L2
> X.121 address.

There are other interface configuration values that can be configured to control the flow of
information. These values can be set to specify packet sizes, window sizes, and modulo sizes.
The VC ranges and types need be configured as well.

Step 1: Setting the Interface Encapsulation, Specifying DCE or DTE

The encapsulation is set at the interface configuration mode prompt. The command is entered
as follows:

```
Router(config-if)#encapsulation x25 [dte ¦ dce]
```

As stated previously, **dte** is the default setting. If the encapsulation is altered from **dce** to **dte**,
or vice versa, the interface settings are lost and reset to default values. The **dce** option is used
in environments in which the router might be used as a switch.

Step 2: Configuring the X.121 Address

The assignment of X.121 addresses is a simple process. The hardest part is usually getting the
address from the provider. Once the addresses are allocated to you by the service provider, use
the following syntax to assign it to the proper interface:

```
Router(config-if)#x25 address x.121-address
```

Step 3: Mapping the Appropriate Next Logical Hop Protocol Address to its X.121 Address

Once the address has been assigned, it is necessary to associate the remote addresses. This is
done with a map statement. Again, this function is similar to dialer map and frame-relay map
statements used with ISDN and Frame Relay respectively. The syntax is as follows:

```
Router(config-if)#x25 map protocol address x.121 address [options]
```

The *protocol* keyword refers to the upper layer protocol being routed across the X.25 network
(for example, IP, IPX, AppleTalk, and so on). The *address* keyword is referring to the upper
layer protocol next logical hop (remote end) address. The *x.121 address* refers to the x.121
address assigned to the destination.

In essence the configuration informs the router that it can reach a specific next logical hop
address by utilizing the designated x.121 address to get across the X.25 network. The previous
syntax assumes a single protocol is going across a particular circuit. If the configuration

includes multiple protocols crossing a single circuit, you can make use of the following command structure:

```
Router(config-if)#x25 map protocol address
              [protocol2 address2] [protocol3 address3] x.121 address [options]
```

In the previous command, up to nine protocol and address specifications can be made in a single command. This utilizes the multiprotocol encapsulation specified in RFC 1356. All the logical next hop protocol addresses are mapped to a single x.121 address.

X.25 Configuration Examples

Once the encapsulation is specified (and the X.121 address is entered and the X.25 maps are completed), the basic configuration for X.25 SVC connectivity is complete. Figure 8-6 depicts the network example that is utilized in the rest of this discussion.

Figure 8-6   *X.25 Network Example*

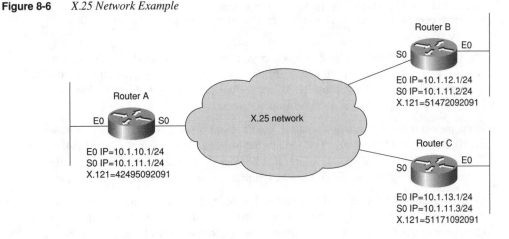

The SVC configuration for this example is a fully meshed network. You need to create separate **x25 map** statements on each router to each destination. IP is currently the only protocol transported across the X.25 network. Example 8-1 shows the RouterA configuration followed by Example 8-2 and 8-3, which show the RouterB and RouterC configurations, respectively.

Example 8-1   *RouterA X.25 Configuration*

```
RouterA(config)#interface ethernet 0
RouterA(config-if)#ip address 10.1.10.1 255.255.255.0
RouterA(config-if)#interface serial 0
RouterA(config-if)#encapuslation x25
RouterA(config-if)#ip address 10.1.11.1 255.255.255.0
RouterA(config-if)#x25 address 42495092091
RouterA(config-if)#x25 map ip 10.1.11.2 51472092091 broadcast
RouterA(config-if)#x25 map ip 10.1.11.3 51171092091 broadcast
```

Example 8-2 *RouterB Configuration*

```
RouterB(config)#interface ethernet 0
RouterB(config-if)#ip address 10.1.12.1 255.255.255.0
RouterB(config-if)#interface serial 0
RouterB(config-if)#encapuslation x25
RouterB(config-if)#ip address 10.1.11.2 255.255.255.0
RouterB(config-if)#x25 address 51472092091
RouterB(config-if)#x25 map ip 10.1.11.1 42495092091 broadcast
RouterB(config-if)#x25 map ip 10.1.11.3 51171092091 broadcast
```

Example 8-3 *RouterC Configuration*

```
RouterC(config)#interface ethernet 0
RouterC(config-if)#ip address 10.1.13.1 255.255.255.0
RouterC(config-if)#interface serial 0
RouterC(config-if)#encapuslation x25
RouterC(config-if)#ip address 10.1.11.3 255.255.255.0
RouterC(config-if)#x25 address 51171092091
RouterC(config-if)#x25 map ip 10.1.11.2 51472092091 broadcast
RouterC(config-if)#x25 map ip 10.1.11.1 42495092091 broadcast
```

The configuration in Examples 8-1–8-3 uses X.25 SVCs to transport IP only. As mentioned, you can deal with multiple protocols in different ways. For instance, the configuration can be implemented using multiple **map** statements for one protocol per VC, or multiple protocol addresses can be specified in a single **map** statement.

In the previous examples, note the use of the keyword **broadcast**. X.25 is a nonbroadcast multiaccess (NBMA) network. This means that broadcast traffic is not allowed in the network. The **broadcast** keyword tells the router that broadcasts should be sent across the individual circuits to remote routers. Without this keyword, routing updates do not traverse the cloud.

In cases in which SVCs are not permitted or desirable, PVC configurations can be put in place. The idea behind PVC configuration is very similar to that of SVCs. The configuration makes use of circuit identification numbers in this scenario. Rather than **x25 map** statements, the PVC implementation uses **x25 pvc** commands. The syntax is as follows:

```
Router(config-if)#x25 pvc circuit protocol address
    [protocol2 address2] x.121-address [option]
```

The *circuit* keyword refers to the circuit identifier mentioned previously. You should note that these circuit identifiers are locally significant. PVC identifiers are likely altered multiple times throughout the transmission across the X.25 cloud. Therefore, it is very likely that the PVC identifiers are different at both ends of the circuit. The remainder of the command is identical to the **x25 map** command discussed in the last section.

Example 8-4 shows RouterA's configuration for deployment in a PVC role. Note that RouterB and RouterC would need to be similarly configured.

Example 8-4   *RouterA PVC Configuration*

```
RouterA(config)#interface ethernet 0
RouterA(config-if)#ip address 10.1.10.1 255.255.255.0
RouterA(config-if)#interface serial 0
RouterA(config-if)#encapuslation x25
RouterA(config-if)#ip address 10.1.11.1 255.255.255.0
RouterA(config-if)#x25 address 42495092091
RouterA(config-if)#x25 pvc 2 ip 10.1.11.2 51472092091 broadcast
RouterA(config-if)#x25 pvc 5 ip 10.1.11.3 51171092091 broadcast
```

The configuration of the **x25 pvc** command can be expanded to include up to nine protocols in a single **pvc** statement or configured for one protocol per circuit.

Additional Configuration Options

In some cases, you must tweak the default settings of an X.25 installation based on service provider mandates or customer requests. There are a number of items that can be configured to change the way in which X.25 operates:

- **Range of VCs**—Incoming, outgoing, and two-way circuits are possible options.

- **Packet size**—Inbound and outbound packet size can be specified on the interface.

- **Window size**—Inbound and outbound window size can be specified on the interface.

- **Window modulus**—This is the limit of the sequence number counter.

Configuring the Range of Virtual Circuits

As mentioned, X.25 can be implemented using both PVCs and SVCs. Table 8-3 describes the VC ranges and options.

Table 8-3   *VC Ranges*

VC Type	Range	Default	Command
PVC	1–4095	None, but must be >0	**x25 pvc** *circuit*
SVC (incoming only)	1–4095	0	**x25 lic** *circuit*
	1–4095	0	**x25 hic** *circuit*
SVC (outgoing only)	1–4095	0	**x25 loc** *circuit*
	1–4095	0	**x25 hoc** *circuit*
SVC (two-way)	1–4095	1	**x25 ltc** *circuit*
	1–4095	1024	**x25 htc** *circuit*

In Table 8-3, the command structure looks a bit strange until it is pointed out the l's and h's mean "low" and "high," respectively. The i's, o's and t's are "incoming," "outgoing," and "two-way," respectively. So, **ltc** means "low two-way circuit." The rest is easy to figure out. The rule of circuit numbering specify that PVCs must have a circuit number that has a value that is lower than any SVC range. When entering a range of circuit numbers, the low circuit must be lower than the high circuit. If both low and high are 0, the range is unused.

To function properly, both sides of the X.25 connection must be configured identically. Otherwise, when X.25 sees an event from a VC in a nonspecified range, it considers it an error and therefore ignores it.

Configuring Packet Size

The maximum inbound and outbound packet sizes can be specified. The default value is 128 bytes; however, based on customer requests or carrier mandates, the size can be altered. Valid values are 16, 32, 64, 128, 256, 512, 1024, 2048, and 4096 bytes. The commands to specify packet size are as follows:

To set the inbound packet size, use the **x25 ips** command:

```
Router(config-if)#x25 ips size
```

To set the outbound packet size, use the **x25 ops** command:

```
Router(config-if)#x25 ops size
```

CAUTION   *The inbound and outbound packet size values should match unless otherwise specified by the carrier.* If different, the network must be able to support asymmetric transmission; otherwise, a conflict occurs.

Configuring Window Size

The default window size in the X.25 network can be modified as needed. The default window size is two packets. It is easy to see where the need might arise to modify this number. As with **ips** and **ops**, this parameter must be supported by the carrier and must match at both ends to avoid conflict. The range of valid sizes is equal to or 1 less than the modulus size. Modulus size is discussed in the next section. The commands to specify window size are as follows:

To set the inbound window size, use the **x25 win** command:

```
Router(config-if)#x25 win no. of packets
```

To set the outbound window size, use the **x25 wout** command:

```
Router(config-if)#x25 wout no. of packets
```

CAUTION   Both ends of the X.25 link must agree on the window size or conflicts can occur.

Configuring Window Modulus

The modulus is the packet counting mechanism for X.25. The command to define the counter limit is as follows:

```
Router(config-if)#x25 modulo modulus
```

The value specified using this command dictates the number of packets that can be sent before the counter must reset. The default value of 8 is widely used and enables seven packets to be sent (0 isn't a packet, but 1–7 are packets). The only other valid value is 128. However, a modulo of 128 is quite rare except in cases involving satellite communications.

CAUTION   Both ends of the X.25 link must agree on the window modulus or conflicts can occur.

X.25 Final Configuration

Example 8-5 illustrates the full X.25 configuration, including optional parameters.

Example 8-5   *X.25 Configuration with Optional Parameters*

```
RouterA(config)#interface ethernet 0
RouterA(config-if)#ip address 10.1.10.1 255.255.255.0
RouterA(config-if)#interface serial 0
RouterA(config-if)#encapuslation x25
RouterA(config-if)#ip address 10.1.11.1 255.255.255.0
RouterA(config-if)#x25 address 42495092091
RouterA(config-if)#x25 pvc 2 ip 10.1.11.2 51472092091 broadcast
RouterA(config-if)#x25 pvc 5 ip 10.1.11.3 51171092091 broadcast
RouterA(config-if)#x25 ltc 10
RouterA(config-if)#x25 htc 100
RouterA(config-if)#x25 ips 256
RouterA(config-if)#x25 ops 256
RouterA(config-if)#x25 win 7
RouterA(config-if)#x25 wout 7
RouterA(config-if)#x25 modulo 8
```

Foundation Summary

X.25 is said to be a dying technology. However, it is still a widely deployed technology throughout the world. Banks, credit card companies, and many other businesses utilize X.25 for transaction processing needs that do not require extremely high bandwidth. This chapter shows the configuration parameters necessary for configuring X.25 as well as for passing the CCNP Remote Access Exam.

Q&A

The questions and scenarios in this book are more difficult than what you will experience on the actual exam. The questions do not attempt to cover more breadth or depth than the exam; however, they are designed to make sure that you know the answer. Rather than enabling you to derive the answer from clues hidden inside the question itself, the questions challenge your understanding and recall of the subject.

Questions from the "Do I Know This Already?" quiz from the beginning of the chapter are repeated here to ensure that you have mastered the chapter's topic areas. Hopefully, these questions will help you limit the number of exam questions on which you narrow your choices to two options and then guess.

The answers to these questions can be found in Appendix A, on page 397.

1 Name the Layer 2 of X.25.

_____

_____

_____

2 Name the Layer 3 of X.25.

_____

_____

_____

3 In X.25, what are the two possible roles that a router can play?

_____

_____

_____

4 What is the function of a PAD in an X.25 network?

_____

_____

_____

5 The addressing scheme in X.25 is known as what kind of address?

_____

_____

_____

6 List the parts of the addressing scheme from Question 5.

_____

_____

_____

7 How many digits constitute each of the parts of the address from Question 5?

_____

_____

_____

8 From where are the addresses used in configuring X.25 obtained?

_____

_____

_____

9 List the possible types of circuits available in an X.25 network deployment.

_____

_____

_____

10 What effect does changing the default ips and/or ops have on a X.25 transmission?

_____

_____

_____

11 What effect does changing the default win and/or wout have on a X.25 transmission?

_____

_____

_____

12 What is a modulo and what are the possible values?

_____

_____

_____

13 What was the driving force behind the creation of X.25?

---

14 What entity governs the X.25 standards evolution?

---

15 What is the difference between X.25 DCE and DTE?

---

16 List the X.25 layers.

---

17 X.121 addresses are considered to be at which layer of the X.25 model?

---

18 List the three LAPB frame formats.

---

19 Does the X.25 DCE have to be the physical DCE?

---

20 List a configuration suitable for configuring for basic functionality the network in Figure 8-7.

_____

_____

_____

Figure 8-7 *Configure the Network*

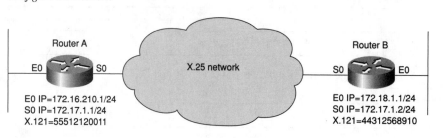

21 List a configuration for the following:

Parameter	Value
Window size incoming	127
Window size outgoing	127
Input packet size	4096
Output packet size	4096
Modulus	128

22 List a configuration for the following:

Parameter	Range
Incoming circuits	1–8
Two-way circuits	9–21
Outgoing circuits	22–25

Scenarios

The following scenarios and questions are designed to draw together the content of the chapter and exercise your understanding of the concepts. There is not necessarily a right answer to each scenario. The thought process and practice in manipulating the related concepts is the goal of this section.

Scenario 8-1: X.25 Initial Configuration

In this scenario, you must configure the Dallas and San Jose routers for X.25 connectivity. Use Figure 8-8 to assist you in the scenarios. All necessary parameters are listed there. Use the configurations in Examples 8-6 and 8-7 to answer the questions that follow.

Figure 8-8   *Scenario Topology*

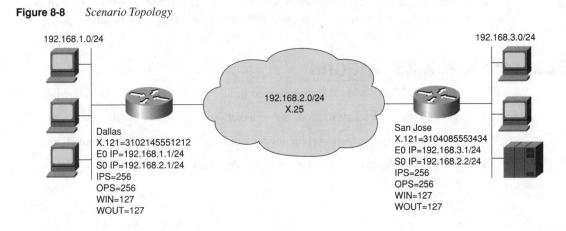

192.168.1.0/24

192.168.3.0/24

192.168.2.0/24
X.25

Dallas
X.121=3102145551212
E0 IP=192.168.1.1/24
S0 IP=192.168.2.1/24
IPS=256
OPS=256
WIN=127
WOUT=127

San Jose
X.121=3104085553434
E0 IP=192.168.3.1/24
S0 IP=192.168.2.2/24
IPS=256
OPS=256
WIN=127
WOUT=127

Example 8-6   *Dallas Configuration for Scenario 8-1*

```
interface ethernet 0
ip address 192.168.1.1 255.255.255.0
interface serial 0
encapuslation x25
ip address 192.168.2.1 255.255.255.0
x25 address 3102145551212
x25 map ip 192.168.2.1 3104085553434 broadcast
x25 ltc 10
x25 htc 100
```

Example 8-7 *San Jose Configuration for Scenario 8-1*

```
interface ethernet 0
ip address 192.168.3.1 255.255.255.0
interface serial 0
encapuslation x25
ip address 192.168.2.2 255.255.255.0
x25 address 3104085553434
x25 map ip 192.168.2.1 3102145551212 broadcast
x25 ltc 90
x25 htc 100
```

1 Is this implementation using PVCs or SVCs for X.25 connectivity? How can you tell?

2 Will the Dallas and San Jose routers experience connectivity problems with the configuration provided by Example 8-6 and 8-7? If so, why?

3 Make changes to the configuration in Example 8-6 and 8-7 that correct issues with the existing configuration only. Do not add additional lines to the configuration.

Scenario 8-2: X.25 Options

Refer to Figure 8-8. Use the settings specified to fulfill the requirements of the following:

1 Expand the configurations to include the packet size parameters listed in the figure.

2 Expand the configuration to include the windows size parameters listed in the figure.

3 Expand the configuration to include the appropriate modulo. Note that the modulo is not provided in the figure.

Scenario Answers

The answers provided in this section are not necessarily the only possible correct answers. They merely represent one possibility for each scenario. The intention is to test your base knowledge and understanding of the concepts discussed in this chapter.

Should your answers be different (as they likely will be), consider the differences. Are your answers in line with the concepts of the answers provided and explained here? If not, go back and read the chapter again, focusing on the sections related to the problem scenario.

Scenario 8-1 Answers

1 Because the **x25 pvc** command is not specified and the **x25 ltc** and **x25 htc** parameters are specified, this is a SVC implementation.

2 Yes, there will be problems. The Dallas router has mapped its own IP address to the next hop X.121 address and the X.25 SVC ranges do not match. The SVC ranges must be identical on both sides.

3 Examples 8-8 and 8-9 correct issues with the existing configurations in Examples 8-6 and 8-7:

Example 8-8 *Corrected Dallas Configuration for Scenario 8-1*

```
interface ethernet 0
ip address 192.168.1.1 255.255.255.0
interface serial 0
encapuslation x25
ip address 192.168.2.1 255.255.255.0
x25 address 3102145551212
x25 map ip 192.168.2.2 3104085553434 broadcast
x25 ltc 10
x25 htc 100
```

Example 8-9 *Corrected San Jose Configuration for Scenario 8-1*

```
interface ethernet 0
ip address 192.168.3.1 255.255.255.0
interface serial 0
encapuslation x25
ip address 192.168.2.2 255.255.255.0
x25 address 3104085553434
x25 map ip 192.168.2.1 3102145551212 broadcast
x25 ltc 10
x25 htc 100
```

Scenario 8-2 Answers

1 The configurations in Examples 8-10 and 8-11 expand the configurations in Examples 8-6 and 8-7 to include the packet size parameters listed in Figure 8-8.

Example 8-10 *Dallas Configuration Including Packet Size Parameters*

```
interface ethernet 0
ip address 192.168.1.1 255.255.255.0
interface serial 0
encapuslation x25
ip address 192.168.2.1 255.255.255.0
x25 address 3102145551212
x25 map ip 192.168.2.2 3104085553434 broadcast
x25 ltc 10
x25 htc 100
x25 ips 256
x25 ops 256
```

Example 8-11 *San Jose Configuration Including Packet Size Parameters*

```
interface ethernet 0
ip address 192.168.3.1 255.255.255.0
interface serial 0
encapuslation x25
ip address 192.168.2.2 255.255.255.0
x25 address 3104085553434
x25 map ip 192.168.2.1 3102145551212 broadcast
x25 ltc 10
x25 htc 100
x25 ips 256
x25 ops 256
```

2 The configurations in Examples 8-12 and 8-13 expand the configurations in Examples 8-6 and 8-7 to include the window size parameters listed in Figure 8-8.

Example 8-12 *Add-on to Dallas Configuration to Include Window Size Parameters*

```
interface serial 0
x25 win 127
x25 wout 127
```

Example 8-13 *Add-on to San Jose Configuration to Include Window Size Parameters*

```
interface serial 0
x25 win 127
x25 wout 127
```

3 The **win/wout** parameter is always in a range from 1 to 1 less than the modulus. So, with a **win/wout** of 127, the modulo must be 128. Examples 8-14 and 8-15 expand the configurations in Examples 8-6 and 8-7 to include the appropriate modulo.

Example 8-14 *Add-on to Dallas Configuration to Include Appropriate Modulo*

```
interface serial 0
x25 modulo 128
```

Example 8-15 *Add-on to San Jose Configuration to Include Appropriate Modulo*

```
interface serial 0
x25 modulo 128
```

This chapter covers the following topics that you need to master as a CCNP:

- **Understanding Frame Relay**—This section examines the underlying technology of Frame Relay and its components.

- **Frame Relay topologies**—This section explores some of the implementation options available in Frame Relay deployments.

- **Frame Relay configuration**—This section covers the configuration of Frame Relay, including basic configuration, subinterfaces, and point-to-point and multipoint options.

- **Frame Relay traffic shaping**—This section discusses rate enforcement and traffic behavior modification capabilities in Frame Relay.

- **Frame Relay traffic shaping configuration**—This section covers the configuration of the traffic shaping options discussed in this chapter.

CHAPTER 9

Frame Relay Connection Controlling Traffic Flow

The CCNP Remote Access exam requires you to have an in depth understanding of various WAN technologies. This chapter discusses the basics of Frame Relay as well as how to tweak it to maximize traffic control and throughput. Although Frame Relay is not a new technology by any means, it is still widely implemented around the world. Even with the advent of newer (and faster) broadband technologies, Frame Relay continues to remain popular in the workplace.

Frame Relay is a high-performance WAN protocol that operates at Layers 1 and 2 of the OSI reference model. Frame Relay originally was designed for use with ISDN interfaces. It is now used over a variety of other network interfaces as well.

Frame Relay is a nonbroadcast multiaccess (NBMA) network. In an NBMA, broadcasts are not allowed inside the network itself. Instead, for any two points to communicate, there must be a specific connection between them. In other words, for broadcasts to propagate through the Frame Relay network, they must traverse virtual circuits. In contrast, broadcast multiaccess networks (BMA), such as Ethernet, require that transmissions be placed on the wire for all stations to process.

Frame Relay is a packet-switched network. Packet-switched networks enable the dynamic sharing of network resources. Most of today's popular LANs, such as Ethernet and Token Ring, are packet-switched networks.

Frame Relay is often described as a streamlined version of X.25 because it offers fewer of the robust capabilities, such as windowing and retransmission of lost data, than does X.25. Frame Relay typically operates over WAN facilities that offer more reliable connection services.

How to Best Use This Chapter

By taking the following steps, you can make better use of your study time:

- Keep your notes and answers for all your work with this book in one place for easy reference.

- Take the "Do I Know This Already?" quiz and write down your answers. Studies show retention is significantly increased through writing facts and concepts down, even if you never look at the information again.

- Use the diagram in Figure 9-1 to guide you to the next step.

Figure 9-1 *How to Use This Chapter*

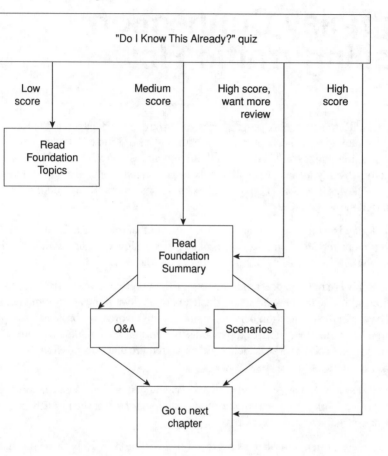

"Do I Know This Already?" Quiz

The purpose of the "Do I Know This Already?" quiz is to help you decide what parts of this chapter to use. If you already intend to read the entire chapter, you do not necessarily need to answer these questions now.

The 15-question quiz helps you make good choices about how to spend your limited study time. The quiz is sectioned into smaller, three-question "quizlets," each of which corresponds to the five major topic headings in the chapter. Use the scoresheet in Table 9-1 to record your scores.

Table 9-1   *Scoresheet for Quizlets and Quiz*

Quizlet Number	Foundation Topics Section Covered by These Questions	Questions	Score
1	Understanding Frame Relay	1–3	
2	Frame Relay Topologies	4–6	
3	Frame Relay Configuration	7–9	
4	Frame Relay Traffic Shaping	10–12	
5	Frame Relay Traffic Shaping Configuration	13–15	
All questions		1–15	

1 Is Frame Relay connection-oriented or connectionless?

_____

_____

_____

2 Frame Relay virtual circuits come in two flavors. What are those flavors?

_____

_____

_____

3 Frame Relay virtual circuits are logically defined by a DLCI. What is the range of valid DLCIs for user traffic?

_____

_____

_____

4 The Frame Relay star topology is also known as what?

_____

_____

_____

5 In a 40-route Frame Relay network running in a full mesh topology, how many connections exist?

_____

_____

_____

6 What is an advantage of a partial mesh network?

_____

_____

_____

7 Split horizon can cause reachability issues in Frame Relay networks. List two ways in which you can deal with split horizon problems.

_____

_____

_____

8 If connecting to non-Cisco routers on the other side of a Frame Relay network, what must be specified in the configuration?

_____

_____

_____

9 Frame Relay subinterfaces can be created with two different personalities. What are those personalities?

_____

_____

_____

10 In Frame Relay traffic shaping, what is Committed Information Rate (CIR)?

_____

_____

_____

11 If CIR is 64,000 bps, what should be the value of MinCIR?

12 List the steps in defining a map class for Frame Relay traffic shaping.

13 In map class configuration mode, what command enables the router to respond to BECN requests?

14 In map class configuration mode, what command specifies the CIR if you want CIR set to 512,000 bps?

15 In periods of congestion, what is the percentage drop of throughput experienced with each BECN?

The answers to the "Do I Know This Already?" quiz are found in Appendix A, "Answers to the 'Do I Know This Already?' Quizzes and Q&A," on page 397. The suggested choices for your next step are as follows:

- **You correctly answered six or fewer questions overall**—Read the chapter. This includes the "Foundation Topics," "Foundation Summary," and "Q&A" sections and the scenarios at the end of the chapter.

- **You correctly answered two or fewer questions overall**—Based on your answers in Table 9-1, review the subsection(s) of the "Foundation Topics" section of this chapter. Then move into the "Foundation Summary" and "Q&A" sections and the scenarios at the end of the chapter.

- **You correctly answered seven, eight, or nine questions overall**—Begin with the "Foundation Summary" section and then go to the "Q&A" section and the scenarios at the end of the chapter.

- **You correctly answered ten or more questions overall**—If you want more review on these topics, skip to the "Foundation Summary," and then go to the "Q&A" section and scenarios at the end of the chapter. Otherwise, move to the next chapter.

Foundation Topics

Understanding Frame Relay

Frame Relay is a connection-oriented, Layer 2 networking technology. It operates at speeds from 56 kpbs to 45 Mbps. It is very flexible and offers a wide array of deployment options.

Frame Relay operates by statistically multiplexing multiple data streams over a single physical link. Each data stream is known as a *virtual circuit (VC)*.

Frame Relay VCs come in two flavors, permanent and switched. Permanent Virtual Circuits (PVCs) are, just as the name implies, permanent, nailed up circuits. They don't tear down or reestablish dynamically. Switched Virtual Circuits (SVCs) are just the opposite. With SVCs, a data connection is made only when there is traffic to send across the link. Frame Relay SVCs are established dynamically and can reroute around network failures.

NOTE	Frame Relay SVCs are beyond the scope of this book (as well as the exam) and are not covered in detail.

Each VC is tagged with an identifier to keep it unique. The identifier, known as a Data Link Connection Identifier (DLCI), is determined on a per-leg basis during the transmission. In other words, it is locally significant. It must be unique and agreed upon by two adjacent Frame Relay devices. As long as the two agree, the value can be any valid number, and the number doesn't have to be the same end to end (that is, from router to router across a telco network).

Valid DLCI numbers are 16–1007. For DLCI purposes, 0–15 are reserved, as are 1008–1023. The DLCI also defines the logical connection between the Frame Relay (FR) switch and the customer premises equipment (CPE). DLCIs are a constant subject of discussion throughout this chapter.

Device Roles

Frame Relay devices fall into one of two possible roles, data terminal equipment (DTE) or data circuit-terminating equipment (DCE). DCE is sometimes known as data communications equipment as well. Both terms are correct.

It is important to understand that the DTE/DCE relationship is a Layer 2 (data link) layer relationship. DTE and DCE relationships are normally electrical (that is, Layer 1). The DTE/DCE relationship at Layer 1 is independent of that at Layer 2. In other words, just because a router is a Layer 1 DCE doesn't mean it is also the Layer 2 DCE.

DTEs are generally considered to be terminating equipment for a specific network and are located at the customer premises. The customer typically owns the DTEs. Examples of DTE devices are terminals, personal computers, routers, and LAN switches.

DCEs are carrier-owned internetworking devices. DCE equipment provides clocking and switching services in a network; they are the devices that actually transmit data through the WAN. In most cases, the devices are packet switches.

Figure 9-2 depicts the roles of Frame Relay devices as discussed to this point.

Figure 9-2   *Frame Relay Device Roles*

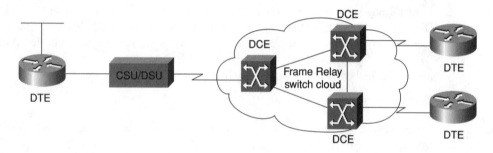

Frame Relay LMI

Local Management Interface (LMI) is the means by which Frame Relay edge devices maintain keepalive messages. The Frame Relay switch is responsible for maintaining the status of the CPE device(s) to which it is attached. LMI is the communication by which the switch monitors status.

LMI implements a keepalive mechanism that verifies connectivity between DCE and DTE and the fact that data can flow. A LMI multicast capability, in conjunction with an LMI multicast addressing mechanism, enables attached devices to learn local DLCIs as well as provide global, rather than local, significance to those DLCIs. Finally, LMI provides a status indicator that is constantly exchanged between router and switch.

The LMI setting is configurable; however, the router still tries to figure out the type on its own. (This statement is true as of IOS 11.2. Prior to 11.2 IOS, the LMI setting was manually configured based on telco requirements.)

There are three supported types of LMI (can you guess the default?):

- **Cisco**—Created by the "gang of four," this type was defined by a joint effort between Cisco, StrataCom, Nortel, and DEC. Cisco LMI uses DLCI 1023.

- **ANSI**—This type is also known as Annex D. (Actually, the full version of the name is ANSI standard T1.617 Annex D.) ANSI LMI uses DLCI 0.

- **Q933a**—This type, defined by the ITU, is known as Annex A. (Its full name is actually ITU-T Q.933 Annex A.)

Figure 9-3 depicts LMI communication between the Frame Relay switch and the CPE router.

Figure 9-3   *LMI Exchange*

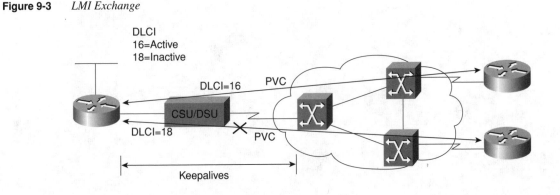

Frame Relay Topologies

Frame Relay supports connectivity of remote sites through one of three topological strategies. Each has its own advantages and disadvantages, as pointed out in the following list:

- **Hub and spoke**—Also known as the star topology, this is the dominant method of deploying Frame Relay. It consists of a single central site acting as a connection point for all remote offices. Routing between two satellite offices is accomplished through the central site. Routing through the central site tends to be the low-cost solution; however, it is also the least redundant (that is, fault tolerant) strategy.

- **Full mesh**—Also called "full mess" due to its resemblance to a spider web, this topology has a large number of connections and is very expensive to operate; however, it is the most fault tolerant. Because each site is connected to every other site, the number of connections can be large and expensive. The number of connections that are required is derived through the following formula, where *n* is the number of devices you wish to connect: $n(n - 1) \div 2$. For example, if you have 20 routers to connect, you would need $20(20 - 1) \div 2 = 190$ connections to provide a VC from each site to every other site.

- **Partial mesh**—This implementation deploys hub and spoke with redundancy. With this implementation, the cost of full mesh is avoided, and the lack of fault tolerance of hub and spoke is minimized. Although a central site is utilized, redundant connections are installed between critical sites. In essence, it is possible to create a backup central site. This is particularly useful in networks in which delay reductions are necessary because getting to a destination without traversing a central router can decrease delay significantly.

Figure 9-4 depicts the three topologies.

Figure 9-4 *Frame Relay Topologies*

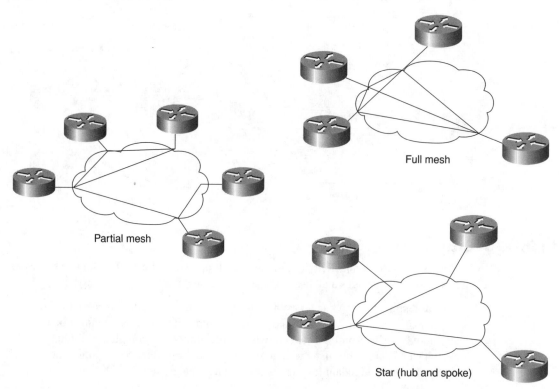

A topology has some affect on the manner in which routers are configured. By default, Frame Relay encapsulated interfaces are multipoint in nature. In environments in which the connection is a single end-to-end PVC with no other connections, there should be no problems. However, in hub and spoke or partial mesh environments, routing update problems can arise.

Issues When Connecting Multiple Sites Through a Single Router Interface

When a single physical interface is utilized on a central router to connect multiple remote sites, routing problems arise. These problems are caused by *split horizon*. Split horizon is a rule in routing protocol operation that is designed to eliminate routing loops by not allowing routing updates to be sent out of the interfaces through which they were received.

Consider the situation in which one serial interface serves multiple remote sites. In this scenario, split horizon effectively shuts down the passing of routing updates regarding networks on the far side of the remote sites. Although the central site can receive the updates through Serial 0, process them, and then make appropriate changes to the routing table, when the time comes to send them back out Serial 0 to other remote sites, split horizon does not allow it. The end result is that the central site knows all routes, but the remote sites are unable to reach each other because the central site is not allowed to send updates to them. Figure 9-5 illustrates the concept of split horizon.

Figure 9-5   *Split Horizon*

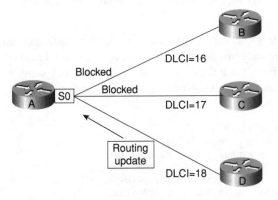

Another problem that arises on a single interface servicing multiple VCs is the issue of broadcast traffic. NBMA networks do not enable the propagation of broadcasts through the network. Therefore, the broadcast must be transmitted over each individual VC. In other words, the broadcast goes into a broadcast queue and is sent one time for each circuit being serviced (10 VCs = 10 broadcasts). These broadcasts can consume large amounts of bandwidth in a short time, depending on the volume of broadcast traffic being sent.

Many Frame Relay deployments begin as hub and spoke and then evolve into a partial mesh. Based on traffic patterns and utilization of links, you can add additional connections between remote sites and increase the bandwidth available to each site. This can assist in dealing with broadcast traffic as well as other high-volume traffic types.

Resolving Split Horizon Problems

To solve the problems created by split horizon, the first impulse is to turn it off. This is not, however, the correct action to take because turning off split horizon can be difficult. In fact, IP is usually the only protocol that allows it to be disabled. By default, IPX and AppleTalk don't allow split horizon to be disabled; however, with EIGRP as the routing protocol for IPX and AppleTalk, it is possible (but problematic) to disable split horizon. Unfortunately, once split horizon is disabled, routing loops can easily occur and cause routes to be erroneously advertised.

The easy way out of the split horizon problem is through the use of *subinterfaces*. A subinterface is a logical division of a physical interface (hereafter known as a major interface).

Theoretically, almost any number of subinterfaces can be placed on a single major interface. The limit lies in the number of Interface Descriptor Blocks (IDBs) available to the router. This number varies depending on the router series and Cisco IOS Software release.

A logical subinterface should be treated almost the same as a physical interface. It can be configured for multiple protocols, shut down, or anything else common on other interfaces with one notable exception—you cannot set encapsulation on a subinterface. Encapsulation must be defined at the major interface.

The configuration of subinterfaces solves the split horizon issue by creating multiple logical interfaces where before existed only one physical interface. Split horizon has no problem with updates leaving through interfaces other than the one through which they were received. Example 9-1 shows the necessary commands for creating a subinterface.

Example 9-1 *Creating a Frame Relay Subinterface*

```
RouterA(config)#interface serial 0
RouterA(config-if)#encapsulation frame-relay
RouterA(config-if)#interface serial 0.1 point-to-point
RouterA(config-subif)#ip address 10.1.1.1 255.255.255.0
RouterA(config-subif)#interface serial 0.2 point-to-point
RouterA(config-subif)#ip address 10.1.2.1 255.255.255.0
RouterA(config-subif)#interface serial 0.3 point-to-point
RouterA(config-subif)#ip address 10.1.3.1 255.255.255.0
```

Figure 9-6 depicts the same network scenario from Figure 9-5, but with subinterfaces implemented.

Figure 9-6 *Frame Relay Subinterfaces*

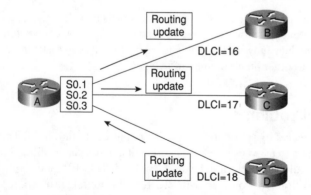

Note that the routing updates can now flow easily. However, using subinterfaces involves a trade-off. In exchange for the proper function of split horizon as well as the passing of routing updates, additional subnets are necessary. In addition, each interface has to have its own unique subnet, no matter which protocol(s) are configured.

In configuring a subinterface, you must specify whether it is point-to-point or multipoint. Point-to-point subinterfaces establish a single PVC between two end points. Each interface is its own subnet and has a single DLCI configured. Broadcasts do not present an issue here because the routers treat the subinterface as a dedicated circuit between the two points.

Multipoint subinterfaces can be used with multiple PVC configurations on a single subinterface. All participating PVC connections are members of a common subnet. Multiple DLCIs would be configured here. However, split horizon dictates that no routing updates can pass in from and then out of the same subinterface.

Frame Relay Configuration

The basic configuration of Frame Relay is quite simple. In many cases, the configuration can be as simple as setting the encapsulation and putting an IP address on the interface. This enables inverse-ARP to dynamically configure the DLCI and discover neighboring routers across the cloud. However, configurations are rarely that simple. Although basic functionality can be achieved in this manner, more complex procedures are necessary for hub and spoke subinterface configurations dealing with point-to-multipoint implementations.

Configuration of Frame Relay can be accomplished in a few steps, as follows:

Step 1   Determine the interface to be configured.

Step 2   Configure Frame Relay encapsulation.

Step 3   Configure protocol specific parameters.

Step 4   Configure Frame Relay characteristics.

Step 1: Determine the Interface to Be Configured

The first step is to decide which interface should be configured for Frame Relay functionality. This should be a fairly easy decision. The interface that interfaces the Frame Relay network is obviously the one needing the configuration. Once the interface has been selected, you should change to the appropriate interface configuration mode in the router.

Now is the time to decide whether subinterfaces should be implemented. For a single point-to-point implementation, it might not be necessary to use subinterfaces; however, this implementation does not scale. If future sites are planned, it is best to use subinterfaces from the beginning.

To create a subinterface, simply enter the command to change to the desired interface, and the interface is created. For example, to create subinterface 1 on Serial 0, use the command **interface serial 0.1**. Once this command is entered, the interface is created and the router prompt is **Router(config-subif)#**.

You must also determine the nature, or *cast type*, of the subinterface to be created. In other words, you must decide if the subinterface acts as a point-to-point connection or a point-to-multipoint connection. If not specified, the subinterface defaults to a multipoint connection.

To specify the cast type, simply add the keywords **point-to-point** or **multipoint** to the end of the interface designation when it's created. For example, **interface serial0.1 point-to-point** creates a point-to-point subinterface and **interface serial0.1 multipoint** creates a point-to-multipoint subinterface.

Step 2: Configure Frame Relay Encapsulation

To enable Frame Relay on the interface, simply issue the command **encapsulation frame relay**. The encapsulation of the interface determines the way it should act because each encapsulation is technology-specific.

The encapsulation specified at this point dictates the Layer 2 framing characteristics of the packet passed to this specific interface from Layer 3. Once the Layer 2 framing is established, the resulting frame can be passed down to the physical layer for transmission.

Step 3: Configure Protocol-Specific Parameters

For each protocol to be passed across the Frame Relay connection, you must configure appropriate addressing. This addressing must be planned in advance.

For point-to-point connections, each individual circuit should have its own subnetwork addressing and two available host addresses. In the instance of IP, each subinterface is assigned a separate (and of course, unique) IP subnet. For IPX, each subinterface must have a unique IPX network number, and so on. As with any other addressing scheme, each side of the link must have a unique host address.

For point-to-multipoint connections, each subinterface also must have unique addressing. However, a point-to-multipoint connection can (by its very nature) connect to multiple remote sites. Thus, all sites sharing the point-to-multipoint connection are members of the same subnetwork, no matter the number of connections or the protocol.

The cast type of the interface also dictates the manner in which DLCIs are assigned to the Frame Relay interface. The next section covers this topic in detail.

Step 4: Configure Frame Relay Characteristics

You must define specific parameters for Frame Relay operation. The parameters include LMI and DLCI configuration.

If you're using a release of IOS Software earlier than 11.2, you must specify the LMI type that is being implemented. The Frame Relay service provider, or telco, should provide the LMI information. For IOS Software Release 11.2 and later, you need not configure the LMI type. To disable LMI completely, use the **no keepalive** command to cease to transmit and receive LMI. However, keepalives must also be disabled at the switch.

At this point, you can configure address mapping, if necessary. In the case of point-to-point connections, mapping of protocol addresses to DLCIs is dynamic and requires no intervention (usually). However, if point-to-multipoint connections are in use, manual mapping is necessary.

Mapping is quite the same from protocol to protocol, so IP was the only one discussed in this section of the chapter. Figure 9-7 depicts a sample topology.

Figure 9-7 *Configuration Topology Example*

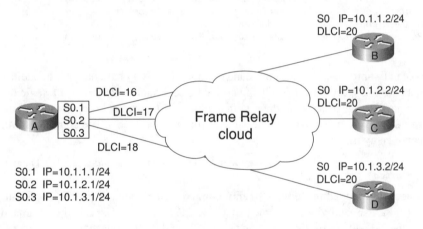

Figure 9-7 shows three point-to-point subinterfaces that require the creation of three individual subnets. The central router in this configuration is RouterA.

Although Example 9-1 covered the basic configuration for RouterA, the PVCs still need to be defined. In addition, because Example 9-1 already uses point-to-point interfaces, the only thing lacking is the DLCI, which the configuration in Example 9-2 provides.

Example 9-2 *Frame Relay Subinterfaces Configuration (Point-to-Point)*

```
RouterA(config)#interface serial 0
RouterA(config-if)#encapsulation frame-relay
RouterA(config-if)#interface serial 0.1 point-to-point
RouterA(config-subif)#ip address 10.1.1.1 255.255.255.0
RouterA(config-subif)#frame-relay interface-dlci 16
RouterA(config-fr-dlci)#interface serial 0.2 point-to-point
RouterA(config-subif)#ip address 10.1.2.1 255.255.255.0
RouterA(config-subif)#frame-relay interface-dlci 17
RouterA(config-fr-dlci)#interface serial 0.3 point-to-point
RouterA(config-subif)#ip address 10.1.3.1 255.255.255.0
RouterA(config-subif)#frame-relay interface-dlci 18
```

Example 9-3 details the same basic configuration. The difference is that the interfaces were created as multipoint interfaces. In other words, each subinterface is capable of connecting to more than one remote location. This was not the case in the previous example.

Example 9-3   *Frame Relay Subinterface Configuration (Multipoint)*

```
RouterA(config)#interface serial 0
RouterA(config-if)#encapsulation frame-relay
RouterA(config-if)#interface serial 0.1 multipoint
RouterA(config-subif)#ip address 10.1.1.1 255.255.255.0
RouterA(config-subif)#frame-relay map ip 10.1.1.2 16 broadcast
RouterA(config-subif)#interface serial 0.2 multipoint
RouterA(config-subif)#ip address 10.1.2.1 255.255.255.0
RouterA(config-subif)#frame-relay map ip 10.1.2.2 17 broadcast
RouterA(config-subif)#interface serial 0.3 multipoint
RouterA(config-subif)#ip address 10.1.3.1 255.255.255.0
RouterA(config-subif)#frame-relay map ip 10.1.3.2 18 broadcast
```

Note in Example 9-3 that the command defining the circuit has changed. In addition, although Example 9-2 specified the DLCI and nothing else, Example 9-3 created a static mapping that associated the next-hop IP address with the local DLCI that had been created by the telco. The **frame-relay map** command is the same as for other protocols. The command structure for **frame-relay map** is

```
Router(config-if)#frame-relay map protocol protocol-address dlci [broadcast][ietf
| cisco]
```

Protocols supported in the **frame-relay map** command include IP, IPX, AppleTalk, CLNS, DECnet, XNS, and Vines, to name just a few. The *protocol-address* in the command is the next hop logical address for the router on the remote end of the connection. The *dlci* argument represents the *local* DLCI, not that of the remote end. You should always map the local DLCI to the next-hop address.

In the **frame-relay map** command, the **broadcast** keyword specifies that routing updates traverse the network through this circuit. The final option in the command specifies which Frame Relay implementation to utilize in communications with the remote router. When communicating with a Cisco device on the remote side, the default value (**cisco**) can be utilized. However, when communicating with non-Cisco gear on the remote end, it can be necessary to specify that the IETF implementation of Frame Relay be used.

Verifying Frame Relay Configuration

The most useful method of verifying configurations is through the use of the **show** and **debug** commands. The examples in the following subsections show sample command output.

show frame-relay pvc Command

Example 9-4 shows output from the **show frame-relay pvc** command. This command is useful for viewing the status of statically or dynamically defined PVCs.

Example 9-4   **show frame-relay pvc** *Command Output*

```
RouterA#show frame-relay pvc
PVC Statistics for interface Serial0/0 (Frame Relay DTE)

                Active      Inactive      Deleted       Static
  Local           2            0             0            0
  Switched        0            0             0            0
  Unused          9            6             0            0

DLCI = 16, DLCI USAGE = LOCAL, PVC STATUS = ACTIVE, INTERFACE = Serial0/0.102

  input pkts 1            output pkts 2211        in bytes 34
  out bytes 489614        dropped pkts 0          in FECN pkts 0
  in BECN pkts 0          out FECN pkts 0         out BECN pkts 0
  in DE pkts 0            out DE pkts 0
  out bcast pkts 2211      out bcast bytes 489614
  pvc create time 21:15:39, last time pvc status changed 21:00:59

DLCI = 17, DLCI USAGE = LOCAL, PVC STATUS = ACTIVE, INTERFACE = Serial0/0.103

  input pkts 2101         output pkts 2220        in bytes 461204
  out bytes 492080        dropped pkts 0          in FECN pkts 0
  in BECN pkts 0          out FECN pkts 0         out BECN pkts 0
  in DE pkts 0            out DE pkts 0
  out bcast pkts 2220      out bcast bytes 492080
  pvc create time 21:14:39, last time pvc status changed 21:14:39

DLCI = 18, DLCI USAGE = UNUSED, PVC STATUS = ACTIVE, INTERFACE = Serial0/0

  input pkts 0            output pkts 0           in bytes 0
  out bytes 0             dropped pkts 0          in FECN pkts 0
  in BECN pkts 0          out FECN pkts 0         out BECN pkts 0
  in DE pkts 0            out DE pkts 0
  out bcast pkts 0        out bcast bytes 0          Num Pkts Switched 0
  pvc create time 21:32:09, last time pvc status changed 18:44:30
```

Note in the output that each PVC is detailed. The highlighted portion shows the DLCI of the circuit being detailed, the status of the PVC (ACTIVE, INACTIVE, or DELETED), and the interface with which the particular PVC is associated.

The output also gives information on each circuit that specifies the receipt or transmission of FECN/BECN packets. FECN and BECN deal with congestion in the Frame Relay network, so obviously, a low number (0 is good) is preferable. The output also details the number of discard eligible (DE) packets received. Again, the lower the number, the better.

show frame-relay lmi Command

Along with checking the status of individual PVCs, you can monitor the communication status between the router and the switch. Example 9-5 shows the output from the **show frame-relay lmi** command, which shows the number of LMI messages sent and received across the link between the router and the switch.

Example 9-5 **show frame-relay lmi** *Command Output*

```
RouterA#show frame-relay lmi

LMI Statistics for interface Serial0 (Frame Relay DTE) LMI TYPE = CISCO
    Invalid Unnumbered info 0        Invalid Prot Disc 0
    Invalid dummy Call Ref 0         Invalid Msg Type 0
    Invalid Status Message 0         Invalid Lock Shift 0
    Invalid Information ID 0          Invalid Report IE Len 0
    Invalid Report Request 0         Invalid Keep IE Len 0
    Num Status Enq. Sent 8060        Num Status msgs Rcvd 8061
    Num Update Status Rcvd 0         Num Status Timeouts 0

LMI Statistics for interface Serial1 (Frame Relay DTE) LMI TYPE = CISCO
    Invalid Unnumbered info 0        Invalid Prot Disc 0
    Invalid dummy Call Ref 0         Invalid Msg Type 0
    Invalid Status Message 0         Invalid Lock Shift 0
    Invalid Information ID 0          Invalid Report IE Len 0
    Invalid Report Request 0         Invalid Keep IE Len 0
    Num Status Enq. Rcvd 6711        Num Status msgs Sent 6711
    Num Update Status Sent 0         Num St Enq. Timeouts 2
```

The shaded line highlights an important aspect of this output: The LMI type can be specified differently for each interface, so the type is specified in the output.

Another critical piece of this output is the LMI input/output information. This is shown in the second highlighted line. If the number of sent enquiries is incrementing, but the number of received messages remains at 0, LMI is not being received from the switch. As long as both numbers are greater than zero and continue to increment on a regular basis (every few seconds), LMI is being exchanged. The output also shows timeouts, errors, and so on.

debug frame-relay lmi Command

Probably the most useful tool in verifying and troubleshooting Frame Relay comes in the form of the **debug frame-relay lmi** command, as demonstrated by Example 9-6.

Example 9-6   debug frame-relay lmi *Command Output*

```
RouterA#debug frame-relay lmi
Frame Relay LMI debugging is on
Displaying all Frame Relay LMI data
1d18h: Serial1(in): StEnq, myseq 85
1d18h: RT IE 1, length 1, type 1
1d18h: KA IE 3, length 2, yourseq 86, myseq 85
1d18h: Serial1(out): Status, myseq 86, yourseen 86, DTE up
1d18h: Serial0(out): StEnq, myseq 162, yourseen 161, DTE up
1d18h: datagramstart = 0x3001754, datagramsize = 13
1d18h: FR encap = 0xFCF10309
1d18h: 00 75 01 01 01 03 02 A2 A1
1d18h:
1d18h: Serial0(in): Status, myseq 162
1d18h: RT IE 1, length 1, type 1
1d18h: KA IE 3, length 2, yourseq 162, myseq 162
1d18h: Serial1(in): StEnq, myseq 86
1d18h: RT IE 1, length 1, type 1
1d18h: KA IE 3, length 2, yourseq 87, myseq 86
1d18h: Serial1(out): Status, myseq 87, yourseen 87, DTE up
1d18h: Serial0(out): StEnq, myseq 163, yourseen 162, DTE up
1d18h: datagramstart = 0x34D25B4, datagramsize = 13
1d18h: FR encap = 0xFCF10309
1d18h: 00 75 01 01 00 03 02 A3 A2
```

Using the **debug frame-relay lmi** command makes it possible to watch the real-time
communication between the router and the switch. Each request sent from the router to the
switch is noted as MySeq, and the counter is incremented by 1 with each request. LMIs sent
from the switch to the router by the telco are noted as Yourseen and also are incremented by 1
with each request. As long as both numbers are greater than 0, the router should be happy and
functioning normally at Layers 1 and 3. (Layer 3 connectivity is up to the administrator doing
the configuration.) You should also watch the "DTE up" note at the end of the outbound LMI
status lines.

show frame-relay map Command

The **show frame-relay map** command is used to view the DLCI mappings that have been
created. They can be static or dynamic and are noted as such in the command output.
Example 9-7 shows the output from this command.

Example 9-7   show frame-relay map *Command Output*

```
RouterA#show frame-relay map
Serial0.1 (up): point-to-point dlci, dlci 16(0x10,0x400), broadcast
          status defined, active
Serial0.2 (up): point-to-point dlci, dlci 17(0x0A,0x401), broadcast
          status defined, active
Serial0.3 (up): point-to-point dlci, dlci 18(0x0B,0x402), broadcast
          status defined, active
```

Frame Relay Traffic Shaping

Frame Relay traffic shaping is a means of controlling the output of traffic across the Frame Relay network. Whether the goal is to meet service contract obligations or to control output speed to slower links, traffic shaping can provide granular control of outbound data. Traffic shaping can provide per-VC rate enforcement, BECN support, and queuing (WFQ, PQ, or CQ) at the VC level.

Frame Relay traffic shaping is supported only on fast switching and process switching paths. Therefore, to use it, other switching methods must be disabled on all interfaces that send traffic to the serial interface.

Frame Relay Traffic Parameters

To properly understand the concepts of traffic shaping, it is important to have a firm grasp of the various traffic parameters in the Frame Relay Network. In particular, you should know that some (such as CIR and Be (Excessive Burst)) are commonly used, but misunderstood. Table 9-2 details the traffic parameters.

Table 9-2 *Frame Relay Traffic Parameters*

Parameter	Description
CIR	The average rate you want to transmit. This is generally not the same as the CIR provided by the telco. This is the amount you want to send in periods of noncongestion.
Be (Excessive Burst)	The amount of excess data allowed to be sent during the first interval once credit is built up. Transmission credit is built during periods of no transmission. The credit is the burst size. Full credit is typically CIR ÷ 8.
Bc (Committed Burst)	The amount of data to send in each Tc interval.
Tc (Committed Rate Measurement Interval)	The Bc ÷ CIR time interval. The time interval shouldn't exceed 125 ms (almost always 125 ms).
MinCIR (Minimum CIR)	The minimum amount of data to be sent during periods of congestion. This is usually what you get from the telco. MinCIR defaults to one-half of CIR.
PIR (Peak Information Rate)	Highest possible rate of transmission on a given interface.
MIR (Minimum Information Rate)	Slowest rate of transmission on a given interface.
Interval	Bc ÷ CIR. The maximum is 125 ms, or 1/8 second.
Byte Increment	Bc ÷ 8. This value must be greater than 125.
Limit	Byte Increment + Be ÷ 8 (in bytes).

The information in Table 9-2 can be easily misunderstood. For instance, consider the details around a 128-kbps Frame Relay link:

- The CIR would have a value of 128,000 bps, but that's not necessarily the guaranteed throughput value provided by the telco.

- MinCIR is usually the guaranteed value and it defaults to one-half of CIR, so MinCIR would be 64,000 bps.

- The Bc is the CIR ÷ 8, so it would be 16,000 bps.

- The byte increment is Bc ÷ 8, so it should be 2000 bps.

- Finally, the Tc would be 125 ms, which is where it should normally sit.

All parameters might or might not be utilized in the course of traffic shaping. The parameters are more related to Backward Explicit Congestion Notification (BECN) response network congestion. BECN is explained more thoroughly in the next section of this chapter.

FECN and BECN

Frame Relay's traffic shaping capabilities rely largely on the capability to detect congestion. To that end, Forward Explicit Congestion Notification (FECN) and BECN are implemented in today's Frame Relay networks.

If a Frame Relay switch senses congestion in the network, it sets the FECN bit to 1 in the Frame Relay header for traffic moving toward the destination device. This number indicates a congestive situation. Once received, the destination device flips the BECN bit in return traffic to the source. This informs the source device of the congestion in the network and that it should reduce the transmission rate.

Once congestion has been experienced, any traffic moving through the network in violation of the negotiated CIR that has been flagged as Discard Eligible (DE) can be dropped. Retransmission of dropped traffic is left to the Layer 4 protocol of the end devices (for example, to TCP).

If the router receives BECNs during the current time interval, it decreases the transmission rate by 25 percent. The rate continues to drop with each BECN (limit one drop per time interval) until the traffic rate gets to the minimum acceptable incoming or outgoing committed information rate (MINCIR). At this point, the decline in throughput is halted.

Once the traffic rate has declined involuntarily, it takes 16 time intervals without the receipt of BECNs to start to increase traffic flow again. Traffic increases by (Be + Bc) ÷ 16, or more accurately, the byte limit that shows up when the **show frame-relay pvc** command is divided by 16.

It takes significantly longer to get back up to CIR than it did to drop. To shorten the length of time, set Be to a value seven times the value of Bc. Continuing the example from Table 9-2, note that the Bc is 16000 bps. If the Be is set to 7(16,000) = 112,000, the traffic increase is

(Be + Bc) ÷ 16, or (112,000 + 16,000) ÷ 16 = 8000, bps per time interval. This forces it back to CIR (128,000 bps) immediately after the 16 (16(8000)) time intervals with no BECN.

This behavior only occurs when Frame Relay traffic shaping is active. If traffic shaping is not active, the transmission increment is fixed even though BECNs are not being received.

Using Frame Relay Traffic Shaping

There are a number of instances in which Frame Relay traffic shaping can be useful. For instance, if your network consists of high-bandwidth links exclusively, traffic shaping can be beneficial. In mixed bandwidth environments, traffic shaping can also be beneficial. In addition, any environment in which Voice over Frame Relay is being implemented requires the use of traffic shaping to adequately configure the network for voice traffic.

In mixed bandwidth environments, traffic shaping can be utilized to protect the lower-speed links. For example, a T1 link transmitting data to a site in which the bandwidth is only 56 kbps can be forced into a congestive state quite easily. If traffic shaping is implemented on the faster side, specifically on the VC directing traffic to that specific site, congestion can be stopped before it begins.

Frame Relay Traffic Shaping Configuration

Frame Relay traffic shaping is accomplished through the creation of a map class. This map class can be associated with one or more PVCs. The map class defines the traffic parameters for any circuits to which it is applied. The command structure for defining the map class is as follows:

```
RouterA(config)#map-class frame-relay name
```

The *name* parameter is an arbitrary value. This is the parameter that is used to tie the map class to one or more PVCs.

Once the **map-class** command has been entered, the prompt changes. At this point, it is time to define the traffic parameters. The average and peak transmission rates can be configured at this point along with defining whether the router should respond to BECN requests. It is also possible to define queues to prioritize PVCs. The command structure for defining peak and average rates is as follows (the peak rate is optional):

```
RouterA(config-map-class)#frame-relay traffic-rate average [peak]
```

The average rate is measured in bps (bps) and should be set to the contracted CIR. The peak rate is also measured in bps. Do not use the **frame-relay traffic-rate** command if you are enabling the **adaptive-shaping becn** command (discussed in the next paragraph). Instead, you should enable a BECN response.

To specify that the router should respond to BECN requests for throughput reduction, use the **frame-relay adaptive-shaping becn** command. Its command structure is as follows:

```
RouterA(config-map-class)#frame-relay adaptive-shaping becn
```

There are no configurable options; you simply issue the command. Use this command over the **frame-relay traffic-rate** command whenever possible. In addition, note that the **frame-relay adaptive-shaping becn** command makes the **frame-relay becn-response-enable** command obsolete.

The preceding commands have not addressed the issues of defining CIR, Bc, Be, and MinCIR. As you could probably guess, each parameter has an associated command. The command structure for the **frame-relay cir** command for the map class is as follows:

```
RouterA(config-map-class)#frame-relay cir [in |out] bits
```

The rate in the **frame-relay cir** command is expressed in bps and should be the rate at which transmission should be sent in periods with no congestion.

Use the **frame-relay bc** command to define the committed burst size for the map class:

```
RouterA(config-map-class)#frame-relay bc [in |out] bits
```

The Bc is the amount to be transmitted per interval in bytes (usually CIR ÷ 8).

Use the **frame-relay be** command to define excessive burst for a map class:

```
RouterA(config-map-class)#frame-relay be [in |out] bits
```

The Be is the additional amount to be sent in the first interval. If CIR = port speed, set Be to 0 because no additional bandwidth is available for a burst.

Use the **frame-relay mincir** command to specify the MinCIR for the map class:

```
RouterA(config-map-class)#frame-relay mincir [in |out] bits
```

Note that the MinCIR in this command is the CIR that was negotiated with the telco. It is usually one-half the actual CIR.

Example 9-8 brings it all together in a configuration that implements all the commands.

Example 9-8   *Frame Relay Traffic Shaping*

```
RouterA(config)#map-class frame-relay EM&AM
RouterA(config-map-class)#frame-relay adaptive-shaping becn
RouterA(config-map-class)#frame-relay cir 128000
RouterA(config-map-class)#frame-relay bc 16000
RouterA(config-map-class)#frame-relay be 0
RouterA(config-map-class)#frame-relay mincir 64000
RouterA(config-map-class)#exit
RouterA(config)#interface serial 0
RouterA(config-if)#encapsulation frame-relay
RouterA(config-if)#frame-relay traffic-shaping
RouterA(config-if)#interface serial 0.1 point-to-point
RouterA(config-subif)#ip address 10.1.1.1 255.255.255.0
RouterA(config-subif)#frame-relay interface-dlci 16
RouterA(config-fr-dlci)#class EM&AM
```

As has been mentioned throughout this section, Frame Relay traffic shaping can provide granular, per-VC flow control. However, it can also provide per-interface flow control. If applied to an interface rather than a specific circuit, it shapes all circuits defined on that interface. It can be placed on the major interface or the subinterface, or both.

Example 9-9 shows the same configuration as in Example 9-8, but applied to the major interface.

Example 9-9 *Frame Relay Traffic Shaping on the Interface*

```
RouterA(config)#map-class frame-relay EM&AM
RouterA(config-map-class)#frame-relay adaptive-shaping becn
RouterA(config-map-class)#frame-relay cir 128000
RouterA(config-map-class)#frame-relay bc 16000
RouterA(config-map-class)#frame-relay be 0
RouterA(config-map-class)#frame-relay mincir 64000
RouterA(config-map-class)#exit
RouterA(config)#interface serial 0
RouterA(config-if)#encapsulation frame-relay
RouterA(config-if)#frame-relay traffic-shaping
RouterA(config-if)#frame-relay class EM&AM
RouterA(config)#interface serial 0.1 point-to-point
RouterA(config-subif)#ip address 10.1.1.1 255.255.255.0
RouterA(config-subif)#frame-relay interface-dlci 16
```

To verify the operation of the Frame Relay traffic shaping configuration, use the **show frame-relay pvc** command. Example 9-10 shows output from the command.

Example 9-10 show frame-relay pvc *Command Output Verifies the Operation of Frame Relay Traffic Shaping*

```
RouterA#show frame-relay pvc
PVC Statistics for interface Serial0.1 (Frame Relay DTE)
DLCI = 16, DLCI USAGE = LOCAL, PVC STATUS = ACTIVE, INTERFACE =
Serial0.1
  input pkts 0          output pkts 0           in bytes 0
  out bytes 0           dropped pkts 0          in FECN pkts 0
  in BECN pkts 0        out FECN pkts 0         out BECN pkts 0
  in DE pkts 0          out DE pkts 0
  out bcast pkts 0       out bcast bytes 0
  Shaping adapts to BECN
  pvc create time 23:34:33, last time pvc status changed 23:34:33
  cir 128000    bc 16000      be 0      limit 10000  interval 125
  mincir 64000      byte increment 1000  BECN response yes
  pkts 0          bytes 0          pkts delayed 0        bytes delayed 0
  shaping inactive
  Serial0.1 dlci 50 is first come first serve default queueing

  Output queue 0/40, 0 drop, 0 dequeued
```

Note how the output has changed dramatically as compared with the listing in Example 9-4. With traffic shaping turned on, all configured parameters are listed. Other useful commands include **show traffic-shape** and **show traffic-shape statistics**. However, those are not covered in this book.

Foundation Summary

Frame Relay is a highly versatile technology. It supports data in varying degrees and speeds, and it supports voice traffic. In addition, it can tell the difference between the two traffic types.

At this point, your understanding of Frame Relay is slightly better than it was when you began the chapter. For the exam, however, you must thoroughly understand the operation of Frame Relay technology. Thus, it would be worth the time involved to go back and read the chapter again to make sure the finer points of traffic parameter manipulation have been cemented in.

Table 9-3 shows a review of the Frame Relay LMI types supported by Cisco routers.

Table 9-3 *LMI Types*

LMI Type	Also Known As	Defined by
Cisco	Gang of Four	Cisco, StrataCom, NortTel, and DEC
ANSI	Annex D	T1.617 Annex D
Q933a	Annex A	Q.933 Annex A

Table 9-4 provides review information regarding Frame Relay topologies.

Table 9-4 *Frame Relay Topologies*

Topology	Description
Hub and Spoke (a.k.a. Star)	This is the dominant method of deploying Frame Relay. It consists of a single central site acting as a connection point for all remote offices. Routing between two satellite offices is accomplished through the central site. This tends to be the lowest cost solution; however, it is also the least redundant (that is, fault tolerant) strategy.
Full Mesh	This topology consists of a large number of connections. It is very expensive to operate; however, it is the most fault tolerant. Because each site is connected to every other site, the number of connections can quickly grow and become expensive. The formula for deriving the number of required connections is $n(n-1) \div 2$, where n is the number of devices you wish to connect.
Partial Mesh	This implementation is hub and spoke with redundancy. The cost of full mesh is avoided and the lack of fault tolerance of hub and spoke is minimized. A central site is still utilized; however, redundant connections are installed between critical sites. In essence, it is possible to create a backup central site. This is particularly useful in networks in which delay reductions are necessary because the capability to get to a destination without traversing a central router decreases delay significantly.

Table 9-5 revisits the topic of Frame Relay traffic shaping. This table is a near duplicate of Table 9-2 and is placed here for review purposes.

Table 9-5   *Frame Relay Traffic Parameters*

Parameter	Description
CIR	The average rate you want to transmit. This is generally not the same as the CIR provided by the telco. This is the amount you want to send in periods of noncongestion.
Be	The amount of excess data allowed to be sent during the first interval once credit is built up. Transmission credit is built during periods of no transmission. The credit is the burst size. Full credit is typically CIR ÷ 8.
Bc	The amount of data to send in each Tc interval.
Tc	The Bc ÷ CIR time interval. The time interval shouldn't exceed 125 ms (almost always 125 ms).
MinCIR	The minimum amount of data to be sent during periods of congestion. This is usually what you get from the telco. MinCIR defaults to one-half of CIR.
PIR	Highest possible rate of transmission on a given interface.
MIR	Slowest rate of transmission on a give interface.
Interval	Bc ÷ CIR. The maximum is 125 ms, or 1/8 second.
Byte Increment	Bc ÷ 8. This value must be greater than 125.
Limit	Byte Increment + Be ÷ 8 (in bytes).

Table 9-6 reviews the commands to implement Frame Relay traffic shaping.

Table 9-6   *Frame Relay Traffic Shaping Commands*

Command	Function
frame-relay traffic-shaping	Enables traffic shaping on a Frame Relay interface. This command should be issued at the major interface.
map-class frame-relay *name*	Used to define a profile for the traffic parameters for any circuits to which it is applied. The *name* is case-sensitive when applied to a circuit.
frame-relay traffic-rate *average [peak]*	Defines average and peak transmission rates for any circuit to which the map class containing this command is applied.
frame-relay adaptive-shaping becn	Enables the router to respond to inbound frames with BECN markers. Once a BECN frame is received, the transmission rate is reduced.
frame-relay cir [in | out] *bits*	Defines the CIR for a map class.
frame-relay bc [in | out] *bits*	Defines the Bc for a map class.
frame-relay be [in | out] *bits*	Defines the Be for a map class.

continues

Table 9-6   *Frame Relay Traffic Shaping Commands (Continued)*

**frame-relay mincir [in	out]** *bits*	Defines the MinCIR for a map class.
class *name*	Associates a map class with a specific PVC or subinterface.
frame-relay class *name*	Associates a map class with a major interface.

Table 9-7 provides a review of the show and debug commands mentioned in the chapter for Frame Relay verification.

Table 9-7   *Useful Frame Relay* **show** *and* **debug** *Commands*

Command	Function
show frame-relay pvc	Displays status information for PVCs, including DLCI, LMI counts, FECN/BECN counts, and PVC state (ACTIVE, INACTIVE or DELETED).
show frame-relay lmi	Displays LMI traffic statistics for both inbound LMI packets and outbound LMI packets.
show frame-relay map	Displays the protocol to DLCI mappings for PVCs as well as whether the mapping is static or dynamic.
show traffic-shape	Displays general traffic shaping information and statistics.
show traffic-shape statistics	Displays only traffic shaping statistics.
debug frame-relay lmi	Enables the real-time logging and monitoring of LMI packets sent and received. It also monitors the state of the Frame Relay connection (DTE up or DTE down). This is arguably the most valuable troubleshooting command for new Frame Relay connections.

Q&A

The questions and scenarios in this book are more difficult than what you will experience on the actual exam. The questions do not attempt to cover more breadth or depth than the exam; however, they are designed to make sure that you know the answer. Rather than enabling you to derive the answer from clues hidden inside the question itself, the questions challenge your understanding and recall of the subject.

Questions from the "Do I Know This Already?" quiz from the beginning of the chapter are repeated here to ensure that you have mastered the chapter's topic areas. Hopefully, mastering these questions will help you limit the number of exam questions on which you narrow your choices to two options and then guess.

The answers to these questions can be found in Appendix A, on page 397.

1 Is Frame Relay connection-oriented or connectionless?

_____

_____

_____

2 Frame Relay virtual circuits come in two flavors. What are those flavors?

_____

_____

_____

3 Frame Relay virtual circuits are logically defined by a DLCI. What is the range of valid DLCIs for user traffic?

_____

_____

_____

4 The Frame Relay star topology is also known as what?

_____

_____

_____

5 In a 40-route Frame Relay network running in a full mesh topology, how many connections exist?

_____

_____

_____

6 What is an advantage of a partial mesh network?

_____

_____

_____

7 Split horizon can cause reachability issues in Frame Relay networks. List two ways in which you can deal with Split Horizon problems.

_____

_____

_____

8 If connecting to non-Cisco routers on the other side of a Frame Relay network, what must be specified in the configuration?

_____

_____

_____

9 Frame Relay subinterfaces can be created with two different personalities. What are those personalities?

_____

_____

_____

10 In Frame Relay traffic shaping, what is CIR?

_____

_____

_____

11 If CIR is 64,000 bps, what should the value of MinCIR be?

_____

_____

_____

12 List the steps in defining a map class for Frame Relay traffic shaping.

_____

_____

_____

13 In map-class configuration mode, what command enables the router to respond to BECN requests?

_____

_____

_____

14 In map class configuration mode, what command specifies the CIR if you want CIR set to 512,000 bps?

_____

_____

_____

15 In periods of congestion, what is the percentage drop of throughput experienced with each BECN?

_____

_____

_____

16 You are concerned that LMI is not flowing between the router and the switch. What command could you use to watch the real-time exchange of LMI traffic?

_____

_____

_____

17 Users have reported issues with network reachability. What command could be utilized to view the status of PVCs?

_____

_____

_____

18 Write out a basic Frame Relay configuration including two point-to-point subinterfaces off of Serial 0, using IP only. The DLCI for Serial 0.1 should be 24 and for Serial 0.2, the DLCI should be 95.

_____

_____

_____

19 Create the same configuration from Question 18, but use multipoint interfaces instead.

_____

_____

_____

20 Once the router has decreased throughput due to BECN requests, how long must it wait prior to increasing throughput once again?

_____

_____

_____

21 Increasing throughput once every 16 time intervals can mean that some time passes before CIR speed is regained. How can the router be configured to force the speed back to CIR immediately after the congestion has cleared?

_____

_____

_____

22 What happens to LMI traffic if the command **no keepalive** is issued on the router interface?

_____

_____

_____

23 What types of LMI are supported by Cisco routers?

_____

_____

_____

24 What is the advantage of a hub and spoke topology over a full mesh topology?

_____

_____

_____

25 What is the result of using a single serial interface to provide access to multiple remote sites?

_____

_____

_____

Scenarios

The following case studies and questions are designed to draw together the content of the chapter and exercise your understanding of the concepts. There is not necessarily a right answer to each scenario. The thought process and practice in manipulating the related concepts is the goal of this section.

Scenario 9-1

Consider Figure 9-8 for purposes of this scenario. This is a new network deployment and care must be taken to ensure that all routers have full reachability information available to them at all times.

Figure 9-8   *Scenario Topology*

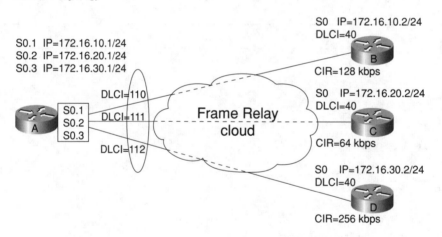

1 Configure Router A for basic Frame Relay connectivity. Use the addressing and DLCIs noted in Figure 9-8. Assume the use of the default LMI type.

2 Configure Router B for basic Frame Relay connectivity.

3 Configure Router C for basic Frame Relay connectivity.

4 Configure Router D for basic Frame Relay connectivity.

Scenario 9-2

The Frame Relay configurations from the previous scenario have been placed on each router. However, the PVCs still show as inactive.

1 List the **show** commands used in troubleshooting the configuration.

2 List the **debug** commands used in troubleshooting the configuration.

3 It has been determined that there is no LMI traversing the link between the router and the switch. What are the possible causes and cures?

Scenario 9-3

Now that the basic configurations are complete and the PVCs are active, it has been determined that Routers B, C, and D are being overloaded with traffic from Router A.

1 Implement traffic shaping on Router A so that it cannot overload the remote routers.

2 Configure all four routers so that they respond to BECN requests to step down transmission rates.

3 On Routers B, C, and D, configure CIR, MinCIR, Be, and Bc appropriately.

Scenario Answers

The answers provided in this section are not necessarily the only possible correct answers. They merely represent one possibility for each scenario. The intention is to test your base knowledge and understanding of the concepts discussed in this chapter.

Should your answers be different (as they likely will be), consider the differences. Are your answers in line with the concepts of the answers provided and explained here? If not, go back and read the chapter again, focusing on the sections related to the problem scenario.

Scenario 9-1 Answers

1 The configuration for Router A is as follows:

```
RouterA(config)#interface serial 0
RouterA(config-if)#encapsulation frame-relay
RouterA(config-if)#interface serial 0.1 point-to-point
RouterA(config-subif)#ip address 172.16.10.1 255.255.255.0
RouterA(config-subif)#frame-relay interface-dlci 110
RouterA(config-fr-dlci)#interface serial 0.2 point-to-point
RouterA(config-subif)#ip address 172.16.20.1 255.255.255.0
RouterA(config-subif)#frame-relay interface-dlci 111
RouterA(config-fr-dlci)#interface serial 0.3 point-to-point
RouterA(config-subif)#ip address 172.16.30.1 255.255.255.0
RouterA(config-subif)#frame-relay interface-dlci 112
```

2 The configuration for Router B is as follows:

```
RouterB(config)#interface serial 0
RouterB(config-if)#encapsulation frame-relay
RouterB(config-if)#ip address 172.16.10.2 255.255.255.0
RouterB(config-if)#frame-relay interface-dlci 40
```

3 The configuration for Router C is as follows:

```
RouterC(config)#interface serial 0
RouterC(config-if)#encapsulation frame-relay
RouterC(config-if)#ip address 172.16.20.2 255.255.255.0
RouterC(config-if)#frame-relay interface-dlci 40
```

4 The configuration for Router D is as follows:

```
RouterD(config)#interface serial 0
RouterD(config-if)#encapsulation frame-relay
RouterD(config-if)#ip address 172.16.30.2 255.255.255.0
RouterD(config-if)#frame-relay interface-dlci 40
```

Scenario 9-2 Answers

1 Some (not all) possible **show** commands include:

```
show frame-relay pvc
show frame-relay map
show frame-relay lmi
show interfaces
```

2 Some (not all) possible **debug** commands include:

```
debug frame-relay lmi
debug frame-relay packet
debug frame-relay events
```

3 If LMI is not traversing the link between the router and the switch, check the LMI type configured on the router. If the LMI type is correct (that is, it's what the telco told you to use), a call to the telco can be in order. It's possible that your circuit is in loopback or experiencing other issues beyond your control.

Scenario 9-3 Answers

1 The configuration for Router A is as follows:

```
RouterA(config)#map-class frame-relay emma
RouterA(config-map-class)#frame-relay cir 128000
RouterA(config-map-class)#frame-relay bc 16000
RouterA(config-map-class)#frame-relay be 0
RouterA(config-map-class)#frame-relay mincir 64000
RouterA(config)#map-class frame-relay amanda
RouterA(config-map-class)#frame-relay cir 64000
RouterA(config-map-class)#frame-relay bc 8000
RouterA(config-map-class)#frame-relay be 0
RouterA(config-map-class)#frame-relay mincir 32000
RouterA(config)#map-class frame-relay beth
RouterA(config-map-class)#frame-relay cir 256000
RouterA(config-map-class)#frame-relay bc 64000
RouterA(config-map-class)#frame-relay be 0
RouterA(config-map-class)#frame-relay mincir 128000
RouterA(config-map-class)#exit
RouterA(config)#interface serial 0
RouterA(config-if)#encapsulation frame-relay
RouterA(config-if)#frame-relay traffic-shaping
RouterA(config-if)#interface serial 0.1 point-to-point
RouterA(config-subif)#ip address 172.16.10.1 255.255.255.0
RouterA(config-subif)#frame-relay interface-dlci 110
RouterA(config-fr-dlci)#class emma
RouterA(config-fr-dlci)#interface serial 0.2 point-to-point
RouterA(config-subif)#ip address 172.16.20.1 255.255.255.0
RouterA(config-subif)#frame-relay interface-dlci 111
RouterA(config-fr-dlci)#class amanda
```

```
RouterA(config-fr-dlci)#interface serial 0.3 point-to-point
RouterA(config-subif)#ip address 172.16.30.1 255.255.255.0
RouterA(config-subif)#frame-relay interface-dlci 112
RouterA(config-fr-dlci)#class beth
```

2 The configuration for Router A is as follows:

```
RouterA(config)#map-class frame-relay emma
RouterA(config-map-class)#frame-relay adaptive-shaping becn
RouterA(config)#map-class frame-relay amanda
RouterA(config-map-class)#frame-relay adaptive-shaping becn
RouterA(config)#map-class frame-relay beth
RouterA(config-map-class)#frame-relay adaptive-shaping becn
RouterA(config-map-class)#exit
RouterA(config)#interface serial 0
RouterA(config-if)#encapsulation frame-relay
RouterA(config-if)#frame-relay traffic-shaping
RouterA(config-if)#interface serial 0.1 point-to-point
RouterA(config-subif)#frame-relay interface-dlci 110
RouterA(config-fr-dlci)#class emma
RouterA(config-fr-dlci)#interface serial 0.2 point-to-point
RouterA(config-subif)#frame-relay interface-dlci 111
RouterA(config-fr-dlci)#class amanda
RouterA(config-fr-dlci)#interface serial 0.3 point-to-point
RouterA(config-subif)#frame-relay interface-dlci 112
RouterA(config-fr-dlci)#class beth
```

The configuration for Router B is as follows:

```
RouterB(config)#map-class frame-relay grace
RouterB(config-map-class)#frame-relay adaptive-shaping becn
RouterB(config)#interface serial 0
RouterB(config-if)#encapsulation frame-relay
RouterB(config-if)#frame-relay traffic-shaping
RouterB(config-if)#frame-relay class grace
```

The configuration for Router C is as follows:

```
RouterC(config)#map-class frame-relay brooke
RouterC(config-map-class)#frame-relay adaptive-shaping becn
RouterC(config)#interface serial 0
RouterC(config-if)#encapsulation frame-relay
RouterC(config-if)#frame-relay traffic-shaping
RouterC(config-if)#frame-relay class brooke
```

The configuration for Router D is as follows:

```
RouterD(config)#map-class frame-relay geek
RouterD(config-map-class)#frame-relay adaptive-shaping becn
RouterD(config)#interface serial 0
RouterD(config-if)#encapsulation frame-relay
RouterD(config-if)#frame-relay traffic-shaping
RouterD(config-if)#frame-relay class geek
```

3 The configuration for Router B is as follows:

```
RouterB(config)#map-class frame-relay grace
RouterB(config-map-class)#frame-relay adaptive-shaping becn
RouterB(config-map-class)#frame-relay cir 128000
RouterB(config-map-class)#frame-relay bc 16000
RouterB(config-map-class)#frame-relay be 0
RouterB(config-map-class)#frame-relay mincir 64000
RouterB(config)#interface serial 0
RouterB(config-if)#encapsulation frame-relay
RouterB(config-if)#frame-relay traffic-shaping
RouterB(config-if)#frame-relay class grace
```

The configuration for Router C is as follows:

```
RouterC(config)#map-class frame-relay brooke
RouterC(config-map-class)#frame-relay adaptive-shaping becn
RouterC(config)#map-class frame-relay amanda
RouterC(config-map-class)#frame-relay adaptive-shaping becn
RouterC(config-map-class)#frame-relay cir 64000
RouterC(config-map-class)#frame-relay bc 8000
RouterC(config-map-class)#frame-relay be 0
RouterC(config-map-class)#frame-relay mincir 32000
RouterC(config)#interface serial 0
RouterC(config-if)#encapsulation frame-relay
RouterC(config-if)#frame-relay traffic-shaping
RouterC(config-if)#frame-relay class brooke
```

The configuration for Router D is as follows:

```
RouterD(config)#map-class frame-relay geek
RouterD(config-map-class)#frame-relay adaptive-shaping becn
RouterD(config-map-class)#frame-relay cir 256000
RouterD(config-map-class)#frame-relay bc 64000
RouterD(config-map-class)#frame-relay be 0
RouterD(config-map-class)#frame-relay mincir 128000
RouterD(config)#interface serial 0
RouterD(config-if)#encapsulation frame-relay
RouterD(config-if)#frame-relay traffic-shaping
RouterD(config-if)#frame-relay class geek
```

This chapter covers the following topics that you need to master as a CCNP:

- **Queuing overview**—This section discusses when to use queuing and which queuing technique to use.

- **Weighted Fair Queuing (WFQ)**—This section discusses the most commonly deployed queuing methodology—WFQ. WFQ is a simple technique that gives low volume traffic priority on the link.

- **Priority queuing**—This section discusses how to manipulate specific protocols and traffic types on a link by giving those protocols or traffic types higher priority access to WAN bandwidth.

- **Custom queuing**—This section discusses a queuing technique that enables all protocols and traffic types to share a WAN link. In this queuing, each protocol and traffic type is allocated a specific amount of bandwidth.

- **Compression techniques**—This section addresses the need for compression in enterprise networks and discusses when such techniques are a good idea.

CHAPTER 10

Managing Network Performance with Queuing and Compression

The CCNP Remote Access exam requires you to have an in depth understanding of various WAN technologies. In this chapter the discussion focuses on queuing techniques offered in Cisco IOS.

Many industry participants believe that queuing is a necessary configuration on all routers. In fact, it is not. This chapter discusses the concepts behind queuing, when to use queuing, and which type of queuing is best for a particular situation.

How to Best Use This Chapter

By taking the following steps, you can make better use of your study time:

- Keep your notes and answers for all your work with this book in one place for easy reference.

- Take the "Do I Know This Already?" quiz and write down your answers. Studies show retention is significantly increased by writing facts and concepts down, even if you never look at the information again.

- Use the diagram in Figure 10-1 to guide you to the next step.

Figure 10-1   *How to Use This Chapter*

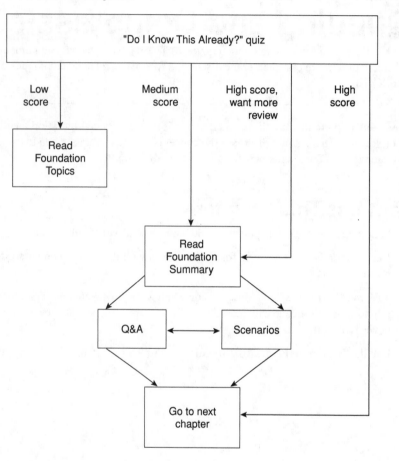

"Do I Know This Already?" Quiz

The purpose of the "Do I Know This Already?" quiz is to help you decide which parts of this chapter to use. If you already intend to read the entire chapter, you do not necessarily need to answer these questions now.

The 15-question quiz helps you make good choices about how to spend your limited study time. The quiz is sectioned into smaller, three-question "quizlets," each of which corresponds to the five major topic headings in the chapter. Use the scoresheet in Table 10-1 to record your scores.

Table 10-1   *Scoresheet for Quizlets and Quiz*

Quizlet Number	Foundation Topics Section Covered by These Questions	Questions	Score
1	Queuing Overview	1–3	
2	FIFO/Weighted Fair Queuing	4–6	
3	Priority Queuing	7–9	
4	Custom Queuing	10–12	
5	Compression Overview	13–15	
All questions		1–15	

1 Where on a router is queuing implemented?

_____

_____

_____

2 When should queuing be considered a viable implementation?

_____

_____

_____

3 Should a queuing strategy be implemented on all WAN interfaces?

_____

_____

_____

4 When is WFQ enabled by default?

_____

_____

_____

5 What is the configurable parameter of WFQ?

_____

_____

_____

6 What type of traffic gets the highest priority with WFQ?

_____

_____

_____

7 How many queues are available in priority queuing?

_____

_____

_____

8 If a default queue is not specified in the configuration, in which queue are traffic types that are not defined in the priority list placed?

_____

_____

_____

9 What happens to traffic in the low-priority queue if there is always traffic in the high-priority queue?

_____

_____

_____

10 How many queues are available in custom queuing?

_____

_____

_____

11 How is traffic dispatched in a custom queuing implementation?

_____

_____

_____

12 How can a higher priority be assigned to a particular queue?

_____

_____

_____

13 List the types of compression supported by most Cisco routers.

_____

_____

_____

14 When should link compression be implemented?

_____

_____

_____

15 Which type of compression should be utilized on virtual circuit-based WAN deployments?

_____

_____

_____

The answers to the "Do I Know This Already?" quiz are found in Appendix A, "Answers to the 'Do I Know This Already?' Quizzes and Q&A," on page 397. The suggested choices for your next step are as follows:

- **You correctly answered six or fewer questions overall**—Read the chapter. This includes the "Foundation Topics," "Foundation Summary," and "Q&A" sections and the scenarios at the end of the chapter.

- **You correctly answered two or fewer questions on any quizlet**—Review the subsection(s) of the "Foundation Topics" section of this chapter, based on Table 10-1. Then move into the "Foundation Summary" and "Q&A" sections and the scenarios at the end of the chapter.

- **You correctly answered seven, eight, or nine questions overall**— Begin with the "Foundation Summary" section, and then go to the "Q&A" section and the scenarios at the end of the chapter.

- **You correctly answered ten or more questions**—If you want more review on these topics, skip to the "Foundation Summary" section, and then go to the "Q&A" section and the scenarios at the end of the chapter. Otherwise, move to the next chapter.

Foundation Topics

The process that handles the movement of data through a router is protocol dependent. With the many variations in protocol needs and activities in the typical internetworking environment, traffic sometimes needs to be prioritized. Anytime prioritization takes place, latency is added to the transfer time. In addition, prioritization of critical traffic can come at the expense of less critical traffic. This chapter explains what to do when prioritization is needed and how to decide the degree to which prioritization should be implemented.

Along with a discussion of traffic prioritization, the topic of compression is also addressed in this chapter. Compression is a somewhat misunderstood tool. Although compression has a number of circumstances in which it is useful, it has just as many circumstances in which it is detrimental.

Queuing Overview

The misconception that queuing is a necessary part of any router configuration is a topic that needs to be dealt with straight away. As mentioned earlier, implementation of any queuing strategy results in higher delay in the network. This happens because of a higher per packet processor requirement. In other words, each traffic type must be sorted out and dealt with according to the defined parameters of the queue. This is the trade-off for assuring that your critical traffic passes through the router.

Queuing is only necessary when existing traffic flow is having problems getting through the router. If all traffic is going through properly and no packet drops are occurring, leave it alone. Simply put, in the absence of congestion, do not implement a queuing strategy and leave the default setting alone. Depending on the interface type and speed, a queuing strategy might already be in place. Again, if it works, don't change it. That point cannot be stressed enough.

There are four types of queuing discussed in this chapter:

- First in, first out (FIFO)
- WFQ
- Priority queuing
- Custom queuing

Once the queuing discussion is complete, our focus shifts to data compression techniques as well as where and when to use them.

It may seem an obvious fact, but queuing is most effectively implemented on WAN links. Bursty traffic and low data rates can combine to create a congestive situation that can require administrative oversight to correct. Depending on the maximum transmission units (MTUs) of the surrounding media, queuing is most effective when applied to links with T1 (1.544 Mbps) or E1 (2.048 Mbps) bandwidth speeds or lower.

If congestion is temporary, queuing can be a proper remedy to the situation. If the congestion is chronic, queuing can compound the issue by introducing additional delay. At this point, it's time to accept the fact that a bandwidth upgrade (and possibly a router upgrade) is in order. For this type of congestion, the price and time involved in the upgrade is the better choice.

The establishment of a queuing policy assists the network administrator with handling individual traffic types. The goal, typically, is to maintain the stability of the overall network, even in the face of numerous traffic needs and types. Much time, unfortunately, can be spent supporting traffic types that are not in line with company goals. "The traffic exists, we have to transport it, so let's deal with it" mantra is a common one in today's enterprise networks.

The engineering and design of the network might need to be reevaluated. You can make minute (or significant) changes to the overall design that remedy the issues causing the delay. For instance, if the core routers are overloaded while the distribution routers are hardly utilized, it might be time to offload some traffic.

Queuing is, in essence, a band-aid. It is meant to prioritize traffic and keep it flowing long enough for an upgrade to be planned and put in place. Queuing itself is not the goal.

Once the decision has been made to implement a queuing strategy, you must decide which queuing strategy should be utilized. Figure 10-2 serves as a fundamental map to assist in that decision.

Figure 10-2   *Which Queuing Strategy?*

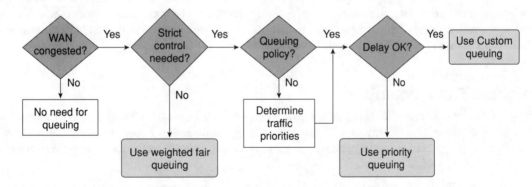

As shown in the figure, you must determine whether the level of congestion constitutes a condition that requires queuing. Once that determination is made, another decision awaits. How strictly should the control of the queuing policy be enforced? Are the defaults OK, or should a more granular approach be applied?

FIFO

FIFO is the most basic of strategies. In essence, it is the first-come, first-served approach to data forwarding. In FIFO, packets are transmitted in the order in which they are received.

Until recently, FIFO was the default queuing strategy for all interfaces on a router. However, should it become necessary for the traffic to be reordered in any way, another strategy must be invoked because FIFO gives no regard to one type of traffic over another. It simply dispatches data as it receives it. Figure 10-3 illustrates the FIFO methodology.

Figure 10-3   *FIFO*

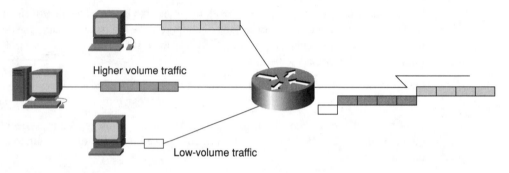

FIFO is not really queuing; it is more along the lines of buffering. The packets are routed to the interface and stored in router memory until transmittal. The transmission order is based on the arrival order of the first bit of the packet. Essentially, the packet's outbound buffer is selected as soon as its outbound interface is selected.

Weighted Fair Queuing

As mentioned, FIFO is often not ideal. Fortunately, WFQ enables Telnet and other interactive traffic to have priority over FTP and other large transfers, thus improving overall throughput. The FTP packets get through with relatively little delay, and Telnet users see improved response times.

In WFQ, traffic is sorted by high- and low-volume conversations. The traffic in a session is kept within one conversation (session), and the records are handled FIFO within a particular conversation. The lower volume interactive traffic is given a priority and flows first. The necessary bandwidth is allocated to the interactive traffic, and the high-volume conversations equally share whatever bandwidth is left over.

WFQ is the default on interfaces of less than 2 MB because at higher speeds, queuing is usually not necessary. In addition, WFQ is on by default for interfaces that support it. That being said, you should note that WFQ is not used by default on Link Access Procedure on the B channel (LAPB) for X.25, compressed Point-to-Point Protocol (PPP), or Synchronous Data Link Control (SDLC) interfaces.

Discrimination of traffic conversations is based on source and destination packet header addresses. Other factors such as source and destination MAC addresses, source and destination port or socket numbers, data-link connection identifier (DLCI) in Frame Relay deployments, Quality of Service (QoS) values, and Type of Service (ToS) values also provide discriminatory criteria to the WFQ process. Figure 10-4 illustrates the WFQ concept.

Figure 10-4   *Weighted Fair Queuing*

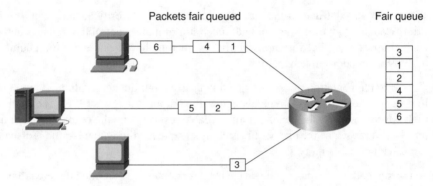

Note that in Figure 10-4, there are three conversations in progress. Two of the conversations constitute a higher volume of traffic. With WFQ, the low-volume traffic is given the priority on the outbound interface. Therefore, the number 3 packet is given dispatch priority.

Configuring WFQ

Configuring WFQ involves issuing a command to adjust the queue limits. To keep some conversations from overwhelming the circuit, you can configure the maximum number of records that any high-volume conversation allows into the queue. The default setting is 64 records (packets), but the supported range is from 1–4096. If a conversation reaches the queue limit, no further records are queued for that conversation until the percentage of the entries in the queue for that conversation drops. Essentially, all new packets for the over-queue-limit conversation are dropped and lost.

TCP window sizes control the amount of data that can be transmitted between two hosts without an acknowledgement. A larger window size enables a higher transmission threshold. Conversations using TCP that suffer a packet drop retransmit automatically as part of the Layer 4 flow control process. As a consequence, the communicating parties in the TCP conversation are forced to reduce their window sizes.

A WFQ configuration utilizes the **fair-queue** command. As stated, the command requires the discard threshold parameter. The command to configure WFQ is as follows:

```
RouterA(config-if)#fair-queue [congestive-discard-threshold]
```

Standard IOS practice dictates that default values not be shown in the configuration. To that end, it should be noted that the **fair-queue** command does not show up in the router configuration unless it has been modified from the default of 64, or disabled using the **no fair-queue** command.

Priority Queuing

When absolute control over the throughput is necessary, priority queuing can be utilized. Priority queuing gives the network administrator granular control that reduces network delay for high-priority traffic. Variations of priority queuing have been in use for a number of years in differing vendor implementations.

Cisco's implementation of priority queuing utilizes four queues: high, medium, normal, and low. For traffic placed in individual queues, the output strategy is FIFO. The traffic defined as high priority receives the benefit of all available resources on the output interface until the queue is empty. Once the high queue is complete, the medium queue traffic is dispatched in the same manner until empty.

At this stage, the high queue is again checked for content and emptied if there is any new traffic. If there are no entries in the high queue after servicing the medium queue, the normal queue is emptied. Once normal traffic has been dispatched, the high queue is checked again, followed by the medium and normal queues. If all three are empty, the low queue is serviced. The result is that high-priority traffic always suffers the shortest delay in awaiting dispatch. Figure 10-5 illustrates the concept of priority queuing.

The low-priority traffic (in the normal and low queues) has no choice but to wait until it can be serviced. The traffic can even age out and be purged from memory if the queue overflows. Once an overflow occurs, all new packets for that queue are dropped until space is freed up in the queue. Each queue has a fixed length, which is configurable. The defaults are as follows:

- **High**—20 records
- **Medium**—40 records
- **Normal**—60 records
- **Low**—80 records

Note that the lower priority queues are larger, by default, than the higher priority queues. This is due to the queuing algorithm and the fact that the lower priority queues might wait longer to be serviced. During the wait, a traffic jam of sorts can build up. To keep the queue from overflowing and dropping traffic, a larger queue size is necessary.

As stated, these default queue values can be defined by the user. However, as is the general rule in this industry, if it works, don't mess with it.

Figure 10-5   *Priority Queuing Process*

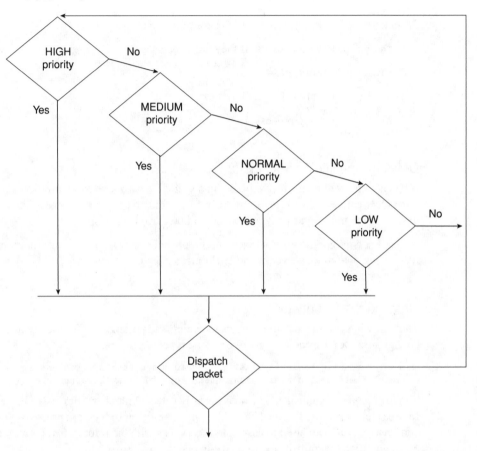

Configuring Priority Queuing

As with any task, the configuration of priority queuing can be quite simple, or it can be a rather lengthy process. In the most basic of configurations, each protocol that traverses a particular WAN link is configured to enter a specific queue. In more advanced configurations, standard or extended access lists can be defined for specific traffic types and applied to a queue configuration.

In priority queuing, the **priority-list** commands are read in the order of their appearance until a matching protocol or interface type is found. When a match is found, the packet is assigned to the appropriate queue and the search ends. In addition, the additional lines that might exist after the line in which the match was found are not processed.

With the priority queuing nuances in mind, it is apparent that some planning needs to go into the creation of the list. Packets that do not match other assignment rules are assigned to the default queue. The tasks involved in the configuration are as follows:

1 Define specific access lists (if they are to be used).

2 Create the priority list.

3 Apply the priority list to the interface.

4 Verify the queuing process.

Defining Specific Access Lists

If it is necessary to queue traffic based on a specific network address, protocol, or application, access lists can be put in place to sort the traffic. Standard or extended access lists can be defined to specify the traffic type or types that should be placed into a specific queue.

Access list configuration is not discussed in this book. For additional information on access lists, check out www.cisco.com and perform a search on "access-list."

Creating the Priority List

The following command syntax shows the command parameters for priority queue configuration for a specific protocol or traffic type:

```
RouterA(config)#priority-list list-number protocol protocol-name
{high ¦ medium ¦ normal ¦ low} queue-keyword keyword-value
```

The *list-number* argument can be an arbitrarily selected number from 1–16; however, all lines for a particular priority list must have the same *list-number* to function properly. *queue-keyword* and *keyword-value* are used to associate access lists with the priority list. Example 10-1 shows a configuration that utilizes the **priority-list** command.

Example 10-1 **priority-list** *Configuration with Access Lists*

```
RouterA(config)#access-list 101 permit tcp any any eq telnet
RouterA(config)#priority-list 1 protocol ip high list 101
RouterA(config)#priority-list 1 protocol ip medium
RouterA(config)#priority-list 1 protocol ipx medium
RouterA(config)#priority-list 1 protocol Appletalk normal
RouterA(config)#interface serial 0
RouterA(config-if)#priority-group 1
```

The **access-list** line in Example 10-1 specifies Telnet as the specific traffic type for which to search. The **priority-list** specifies that any traffic matching access list 101 should be placed into the high-priority queue.

There is another way to assign specific traffic to a particular queue. Example 10-2 places Telnet into the high queue, but without the use of access lists.

Example 10-2 priority-list *Configuration without Access Lists*

```
RouterA(config)#priority-list 1 protocol ip high tcp 23
RouterA(config)#priority-list 1 protocol ip medium
RouterA(config)#priority-list 1 protocol ipx medium
RouterA(config)#priority-list 1 protocol Appletalk normal
RouterA(config)#interface serial 0
RouterA(config-if)#priority-group 1
```

The keyword **tcp** and the value **23** specify Telnet traffic without having to utilize an access list. Other valid keywords are as follows:

- **gt**—Signifies that values greater than or equal to the specified number should be considered a match for the priority list line.

- **lt**—Signifies that values less than or equal to the specified number should be considered a match for the priority list line.

- **List**—Checks the access list number as specified in this line.

- **tcp**—Dictates that the specified Transmission Control Protocol (TCP) port number should be considered a match for this priority list line.

- **udp**—Dictates that the specified User Datagram Protocol (UDP) port number should be considered a match for this priority list line.

All other IP traffic (that is, non-Telnet) is placed in the medium queue, as is IPX. AppleTalk is placed in the normal queue. The queue does not activate until applied to the serial interface.

You can also specify that any traffic that entered the router through a particular interface be placed into a particular queue by using the following command structure:

```
RouterA(config)#priority-list list-number interface interface-type
    interface-number {high ¦ medium ¦ normal ¦ low}
```

NOTE   The positioning of commands is imperative. The queue list is processed line by line. The first time a packet matches a line in the list, it is sorted based on that line. In Example 10-3, for example, if the line placing IP in the medium queue was entered prior to the lines placing Telnet in the high queue, all Telnet traffic would be placed in the medium queue rather than in the high queue.

The easiest way to explain the use of this command is with a example. Example 10-3 shows the use of this command in conjunction with the configuration in Example 10-1.

Example 10-3 *Interface-Based Queuing Example*

```
RouterA(config)#access-list 101 permit tcp any any eq telnet
RouterA(config)#priority-list 1 protocol ip high list 101
RouterA(config)#priority-list 1 interface Ethernet 0 high
RouterA(config)#priority-list 1 protocol ip medium
RouterA(config)#priority-list 1 protocol ipx medium
RouterA(config)#priority-list 1 protocol Appletalk normal
RouterA(config)#interface serial 0
RouterA(config-if)#priority-group 1
```

The highlighted line is the only change in the configuration. The line specifies that any traffic that entered the router through interface Ethernet 0 be placed in the high-priority queue, regardless of the traffic type.

As mentioned, any traffic that does not match any line in a priority list is placed in the default queue. For priority queuing, the default queue is normal if not specified. The command structure for assigning a default queue is as follows:

```
Router(config)#priority-list list-number default {high | medium | normal | low}
```

Example 10-4 expands on the configuration in Example 10-3 by specifying the default queue value.

Example 10-4 *Default Queue Configuration*

```
RouterA(config)#access-list 101 permit tcp any any eq telnet
RouterA(config)#priority-list 1 protocol ip high list 101
RouterA(config)#priority-list 1 interface Ethernet 0 high
RouterA(config)#priority-list 1 protocol ip medium
RouterA(config)#priority-list 1 protocol ipx medium
RouterA(config)#priority-list 1 protocol Appletalk normal
RouterA(config)#priority-list 1 default low
RouterA(config)#interface serial 0
RouterA(config-if)#priority-group 1
```

The highlighted line specifies that any traffic not matching the other lines in the list be moved to the low-priority queue.

It is possible to alter the size of each individual queue. The process is very simple. It involves the use of a command in the priority list definition:

```
RouterA(config)# priority-list list-number queue-limit [high-limit [medium-limit
   [normal-limit [low-limit]]]
```

As mentioned, the defaults for the high, medium, normal, and low queues are 20, 40, 60, and 80, respectively. Example 10-5 shows the use of this command, again added to our existing configuration in Example 10-3.

Example 10-5 *Modifying Queue Limits*

```
RouterA(config)#access-list 101 permit tcp any any eq telnet
RouterA(config)#priority-list 1 protocol ip high list 101
RouterA(config)#priority-list 1 interface Ethernet 0 high
RouterA(config)#priority-list 1 protocol ip medium
RouterA(config)#priority-list 1 protocol ipx medium
RouterA(config)#priority-list 1 protocol Appletalk normal
RouterA(config)#priority-list 1 default low
RouterA(config)#priority-list 1 queue-limit 10 40 60 90
RouterA(config)#interface serial 0
RouterA(config-if)#priority-group 1
```

The highlighted command specifies that the high queue has been reduced to a capacity of 10 records, the medium and normal have not been altered, and the low queue has been increased in capacity to 90 records. This enables faster processing of the high queue and more potential holding space for the low queue.

Applying the Priority List to the Interface

Once the priority list is created, it must be associated with an interface. In the preceding examples, this was evident. The priority list was activated on the interface once the **priority-group** command was entered. Note that the priority list number was the same as the priority group number. Although it is possible to apply the same priority list to multiple interfaces, it is not possible to configure multiple priority groups on a single interface.

Verifying Priority Queuing

Verifying your queuing configuration is relatively simple. The most useful command is **show queueing.** It shows the detail of the priority lists configured on the router and the appropriate details of each list. Example 10-6 shows the command output for **show queueing**.

Example 10-6 **show queuing priority** *Command Displays Priority List Details*

```
RouterA(config)#show queueing priority
Current priority queue configuration:
List   Queue   Args
1      low     default
1      high    protocol ip              list 101
1      medium  protocol ip
1      medium  protocol ipx
1      normal  protocol appletalk
1      high    limit 10
1      low     limit 90
```

NOTE   Notice that the word "queuing" is misspelled as "queueing." The Cisco IOS has contained that particular typographical error for a number of years.

Example 10-6 notes the default queue and then line-by-line details about the remainder of the queue configuration. Note that the changes that were made to the queue sizes are given and that the sizes for the medium and normal queues are not listed because they've been left at the default settings.

Custom Queuing

Custom queuing enables the sharing of available bandwidth evenly (or not) across all types of traffic. This technique allocates a percentage of bandwidth to each of the various traffic types. The difference between this approach and priority queuing is that the queues are processed in round-robin sequence (in essence, they are multiplexed). Therefore, it is possible that high-priority traffic would not be serviced quickly enough because although each type of traffic would get *some* bandwidth, no traffic would be designated with a higher priority than the rest.

Custom queuing employs 17 queues. Queue 0, the system queue, is used (as the name implies) for the system. Queue 0 is the only queue that has a higher priority than the remaining queues and that might not have traffic assigned to it. The traffic serviced by queue 0 is as follows:

- ISO IGRP hellos
- ESIS hellos
- IS-IS hellos
- DECnet hellos
- SLARP address resolution
- EIGRP hellos
- OSPF hellos
- Router syslog messages
- Spanning Tree keepalives

The administrator configures the remaining queues, 1–16, which are served on a round-robin basis.

With priority queuing, the lower priority traffic types can starve out and be dropped due to latency because if the high and medium queues are active at all times, no traffic from the low and normal queues are serviced. Custom queuing alleviates this condition by allocating bandwidth evenly.

By default, queues evenly balance traffic. There are two thresholds by which queues are measured: *queue limit* and *byte count*. The queue limit default is 20 records. The byte count limit default is 1500 bytes. Whichever limit is hit first signifies the end of a particular queue's time with the processor.

Note that the router does not fragment a packet just to meet queue limit or byte count conditions. For instance, if the byte count limit is reached during the transmission of a packet, the entire packet is dispatched, not just cut short. Figure 10-6 illustrates the custom queuing concept.

Figure 10-6   *Custom Queuing*

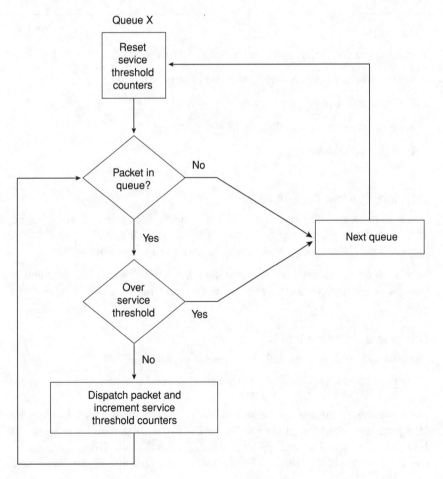

To provide what is in essence a higher priority to any particular traffic type, the limits for that queue can be increased. For instance, if FTP is a high priority, the queue limit and byte count can be increased to give it a higher percentage of bandwidth and processor time.

Configuring Custom Queuing

As with priority queuing, the configuration of custom queuing involves the creation of a list and associating a group with an interface. Traffic in the queues can be configured based on a specific traffic type, protocol, or input interface. Access lists can be configured to place specific traffic types into a particular queue, and traffic not designated to a particular queue can be placed in a default queue.

NOTE   To implement custom queuing on a Frame Relay interface, Frame Relay traffic shaping must be disabled.

The tasks involved in the configuration are as follows:

1   Define specific access lists (if they are to be used).

2   Create the queue list.

3   Apply the queue list to the interface.

4   Verify the queuing process.

Defining Specific Access Lists

If you want queue traffic to be based on a specific network address, protocol, or application, access lists can be put in place to sort the traffic. Standard or extended access lists can be defined to specify the traffic types that should be placed into a specific queue.

Access list configuration is not discussed in this book. For additional information on access lists, check out www.cisco.com and perform a search on "access-list."

Creating the Queue List

The command structure for custom queuing is as follows:

```
RouterA(config)#queue-list list-number protocol protocol-name queue-number
    queue-keyword keyword-value
```

The *list-number* argument can be an arbitrarily selected number from 1–16; however, all lines for a particular queue list must have the same *list-number* to function properly. The *queue-keyword* and *keyword-value* arguments are utilized in the association of access lists with the queue list. Example 10-7 shows a configuration example utilizing this command.

Example 10-7 *Custom Queue Configuration with Access Lists*

```
RouterA(config)#access-list 101 permit tcp any any eq ftp
RouterA(config)#access-list 101 permit tcp any any eq ftp-data
RouterA(config)#queue-list 1 protocol ip 1 list 101
RouterA(config)#queue-list 1 protocol ip 2
RouterA(config)#queue-list 1 protocol ipx 3
RouterA(config)#queue-list 1 protocol Appletalk 4
RouterA(config)#interface serial 0
RouterA(config-if)#custom-queue-list 1
```

In Example 10-7, access list 101 defines FTP traffic as a specific traffic type. The first **queue-list** command in the example specifies that any match to access list 101 be placed into queue 1.

As was the case in priority queuing, custom queuing can assign specific traffic to a queue without the use of access lists. You need only specify the protocol (TCP or UDP) and the port number. Example 10-8 shows the same configuration as in Example 10-7, but without the use of access lists.

Example 10-8 *Custom Queue Configuration without Access Lists*

```
RouterA(config)#queue-list 1 protocol ip 1 tcp 20
RouterA(config)#queue-list 1 protocol ip 1 tcp 21
RouterA(config)#queue-list 1 protocol ip 2
RouterA(config)#queue-list 1 protocol ipx 3
RouterA(config)#queue-list 1 protocol Appletalk 4
RouterA(config)#interface serial 0
RouterA(config-if)#custom-queue-list 1
```

In Example 10-8, all FTP traffic (TCP ports 20 and 21) is assigned to queue 1. All additional IP traffic goes into queue 2. IPX traffic goes into queue 3, and AppleTalk goes into queue 4. You can activate the custom queue by applying it to an interface using the **custom-queue-list** command.

It is also possible to specify that any traffic that entered the router through a particular interface be placed into a particular queue, using the following command structure:

```
RouterA(config)#queue-list list-number interface interface-type
    interface-number queue-number
```

The easiest way to explain the use of this command is with a command example. Example 10-9 shows the use of this command in conjunction with the configuration in Example 10-7.

Example 10-9 *Interface-Based Custom Queuing Example*

```
RouterA(config)#access-list 101 permit tcp any any eq ftp
RouterA(config)#access-list 101 permit tcp any any eq ftp-data
RouterA(config)#queue-list 1 interface ethernet 0 6
RouterA(config)#queue-list 1 protocol ip 1 list 101
RouterA(config)#queue-list 1 protocol ip 2
RouterA(config)#queue-list 1 protocol ipx 3
RouterA(config)#queue-list 1 protocol Appletalk 4
RouterA(config)#interface serial 0
RouterA(config-if)#custom-queue-list 1
```

The highlighted line specifies that any traffic that enters the router through interface E0 be placed in queue 6, regardless of the type of traffic it happens to be. It is placed at the top of the list so that it is the first line processed in the list.

The processing of a queue list is line-by-line. Once a match has been found, processing of the list stops. If the interface specific line was placed at the end of the list in Example 10-9, all traffic entering through E0 would have been placed in other queues rather than the one specified.

As mentioned, any traffic that does not match any lines in a priority list is placed in the default queue. For custom queuing, the default queue is queue 1, if not otherwise specified. The command structure for assigning a default queue is as follows:

```
Router(config)#queue-list list-number default queue-number
```

Example 10-10 expands the configuration in Example 10-9 by adding the command to assign a default queue.

Example 10-10 *Default Queue Configuration*

```
RouterA(config)#access-list 101 permit tcp any any eq ftp
RouterA(config)#access-list 101 permit tcp any any eq ftp-data
RouterA(config)#queue-list 1 interface ethernet 0 6
RouterA(config)#queue-list 1 protocol ip 1 list 101
RouterA(config)#queue-list 1 protocol ip 2
RouterA(config)#queue-list 1 protocol ipx 3
RouterA(config)#queue-list 1 protocol Appletalk 4
RouterA(config)#queue-list 1 default 5
RouterA(config)#interface serial 0
RouterA(config-if)#custom-queue-list 1
```

The highlighted command specifies that any traffic not matching the other lines in the list be moved to queue 5.

The amount of data a queue can service before having to move on to the next queue is known as a service threshold. You can alter the size of each individual queue. The command structure for resizing a queue's record limit service threshold is as follows:

```
RouterA(config)#queue-list list-number queue queue-number limit limit-number
```

This command alters the number of records the queue can process in a given cycle. Valid entries are 0–32, 767. The command structure for altering the byte-count service threshold is as follows:

```
RouterA(config)#queue-list list-number queue queue-number
   byte-count byte-count-number
```

As mentioned, the defaults for queue limits are 20 records or 1500 bytes, whichever comes first. Example 10-11 shows the use of the commands to resize a queue's record limit service threshold and to alter the byte-count service threshold. Example 10-11 builds on the configuration in Example 10-10.

Example 10-11 *Modifying Queue Limits*

```
RouterA(config)#queue-list 1 protocol ip 1 tcp 20
RouterA(config)#queue-list 1 protocol ip 1 tcp 21
RouterA(config)#queue-list 1 protocol ip 2
RouterA(config)#queue-list 1 protocol ipx 3
RouterA(config)#queue-list 1 protocol Appletalk 4
RouterA(config)#queue-list 1 default 5
RouterA(config)#queue-list 1 queue 1 limit 60
RouterA(config)#queue-list 1 queue 1 byte-count 4500
RouterA(config)#interface serial 0
RouterA(config-if)#custom-queue-list 1
```

The highlighted lines specify that queue 1 services 60 records or 4500 bytes prior to moving on to the next queue. This triples the size of queue 1, which was defined in the queue list as containing FTP traffic. Therefore, queue 1 has a higher percentage of overall bandwidth and, in essence, a higher priority.

Applying the Custom Queue List to the Interface

Once the queue list is created, it must be associated with an interface. The queue list is activated on the interface once the **custom-queue-list** command is entered. Note that the queue list number is the same as the custom queue list number. Although you can apply the same queue list to multiple interfaces, you cannot configure multiple custom queue lists on single interface.

Verifying Custom Queuing

Verifying your queuing configuration is relatively simple. The most useful command is **show queueing**. It shows the detail of the custom lists configured on the router and the appropriate details of each list. Example 10-12 shows the command output.

Example 10-12 show queueing custom *Command Output*

```
RouterA#show queueing custom
Current custom queue configuration:
List   Queue   Args
1      5       default
1      6       interface Ethernet 0
1      1       protocol ip tcp port ftp
1      1       protocol ip tcp port ftp-data
1      2       protocol ip
1      3       protocol ipx
1      4       protocol appletalk
1      1       queue-limit 60
1      1       byte-count 4500
```

Example 10-12 notes the default queue and then line-by-line details about the remainder of the queue configuration. Note that the changes that were made to the queue sizes are noted along with the queue that was altered.

Compression Overview

Various types of compression algorithms are in use in the world today. Many are well conceived and utilized. Others, well, let's just say they're the opposite.

For compression, a scope needs to be set ahead of time. There are compression methods for data, links, hard drives, and so on. Our discussion in this chapter focuses on compression across WAN links.

Whether data is already compressed when WAN links begin to process it affects the router's capability to further compress that data. If data is already compressed, recompressing can actually make the data larger. The discussion in this chapter focuses on what happens at the WAN interface, regardless of the type of data being transported.

Compression is but one technique for squeezing every possible bit of bandwidth from an existing internetwork deployment. Compression, like queuing, is meant to provide critical time to plan and deploy network upgrades and to reduce overall utilization of a WAN link. However, nothing is free. The execution of the compression algorithm adds a significant amount of cycles to the CPU. Unfortunately, the additional load on the CPU might not be something it can handle.

In compression, CPU utilization of the router increases considerably. However, the WAN link utilization drops considerably. It's a trade-off because all that has been accomplished is the displacement of utilization from the WAN to the router. Obviously, the effects of compression vary based on the algorithm implemented, but, hopefully, the point is made.

As technology advances, compression will move from a software function to a hardware function. This is already a reality in some router models with the addition of newly available modules specifically geared toward performing data compression in hardware. Not only is this much faster than software compression, it is less costly for the CPU (generally).

The effects of compression must be taken into account prior to any implementation. If your routers are already at 80 percent or more CPU utilization, it's not a good idea to implement compression. Doing so can result in a catastrophic outage.

Data compression makes efficient use of bandwidth and increases WAN throughput by reducing the size of the frame being transported. Compression is best utilized on slower WAN links. There will come a point when the router can send the data faster than the router can compress, send, and then decompress the data.

Cisco supports a number of compression types:

- Link

- Payload

- TCP Header

- Microsoft Point-to-Point

Microsoft's Point-to-Point compression, which is an algorithm, is out of scope for our purposes and is not discussed further in this book.

Figure 10-7 illustrates where various types of compression make transmission more efficient.

Figure 10-7   *Compression Methods*

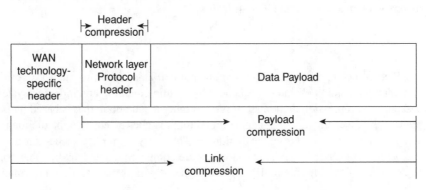

Link Compression

Link compression (also known as *per-interface compression*) is the compression of the entire transported entity. In other words, it compresses the header and the payload.

Link compression is not dependent on any particular protocol function. Cisco supports two algorithms on its router chassis to compress traffic: STAC and Predictor. For HDLC links, STAC is the only available choice.

For data transmission over point-to-point dedicated connections, use link compression. In link compression, the complete packet is compressed and any header information specific to WAN switching technologies is not available to the network.

STAC

You might remember that a few years ago, a company known as STAC electronics successfully sued Microsoft for illegal use of a disk compression utility. That utility was DoubleSpace, and it was initially included with DOS 5.0. After the lawsuit, Microsoft altered the algorithm, purchased a substantial stake in STAC Electronics, and released the DriveSpace compression utility. That same STAC electronics provides the STAC compression algorithm for Cisco routers. (The algorithm is also known as stacker.) Fortunately, Cisco legally utilizes the algorithm.

STAC is based on an algorithm known as Lempel-Ziv (LZ), which searches the data stream for redundant strings and replaces them with a token. The token is an information pointer that is significantly shorter than the string it replaces. If LZ cannot find any duplicated strings in the data, no compression occurs and transmission occurs as if the link had no compression activated.

There are cases, such as the sending of encrypted data, in which compression actually expands the size of a transmission. In such cases, the original transmission is sent untouched. The STAC compression algorithm tends to be quite CPU-intensive and should not be implemented on routers with an already high CPU utilization.

Predictor

The Predictor compression method is rightly named. This Cisco-proprietary algorithm attempts to predict the coming character sequences by an implementing and indexing system that is based on a compression dictionary. It is essentially a code book that is based on possible data sequences. If a character string can be found that matches an entry in the dictionary, the string is replaced with the entry from the dictionary. That entry comprises a much shorter sequence of characters. At the remote end, the characters are compared to the data dictionary once again to be decoded. The strings are looked up and replaced with the appropriate information.

The Predictor compression method is like sign language. Rather than spelling out each individual word (no compression), a single hand motion utilizes an entire word or concept (compression). Because both parties understand the hand motions, successful communication occurs. Conversely, when one of the people involved in the communication does not understand sign language, communication does not occur. This same lack of communication occurs with compression. If one side is using a compression algorithm, so too must the other side. (Need it be mentioned that the algorithm must be the same at both sides?)

The concept behind this type of algorithm is utilized in compression methods outside the data realm as well. Many voice compression implementations, for instance, make use of G.729 and G.729a (CSA-CELP) implementations that provide 8-kbps voice compression, down from 64-kpbs, across a WAN. These implementations are directly based on the code book/dictionary prediction methodology.

Although STAC is CPU-intensive, Predictor tends to be extremely memory intensive. Therefore, if the router has not been outfitted with a good amount of RAM, don't even think about implementing Predictor. If RAM is plentiful, it is a consideration that can be beneficial.

Payload Compression

Payload compression is exactly what its name implies. Also known as per-VC compression, payload compression compresses only the data portion of the transmission. All headers are left intact.

It cannot be assumed that customer WAN links are all dedicated point-to-point connections. To that end, payload compression might need to be implemented if compression is needed on a WAN link. WAN technologies such as Frame Relay, ATM, X.25, and SMDS require that the header information be untouched so that it can be read by the individual switches that the transmission crosses. Any implementation of virtual circuits disallows link compression. In these cases, payload compression is appropriate.

TCP Header Compression

RFC 1144 defines the Van Jacobson algorithm. In doing so, it also defines the algorithm for TCP/IP header compression. The 20-byte IP header is compressed to 2 or 4 bytes to reduce overhead across the network. The Layer 2 header remains intact so that it can be utilized by the appropriate Layer 2 transport.

This type of compression is most beneficial when used with implementations transmitting small packets, such as voice over IP, Telnet, and so forth. This type of compression can be done on just about any WAN implementation (X.25, Frame Relay, ISDN, and so on).

Compression Issues

Specific issues arise during specific network implementations. In selecting the algorithm that will be utilized for a particular deployment, the following should be considered:

- **Modem compression**—Some modems implement compression. Modems making use of MNP5 and V.42bis are not compatible. Although each offers 2 and 4 times compression, they cannot communicate with each other. If you use modem compression, make sure that the modems at both ends of the connection are using a common protocol. If compression is being performed by the modem, do not attempt to configure compression at the router level.

- **Data encryption**—Encryption occurs at the network layer where compression is a Layer 2 function. The purpose of encryption is security, obviously. Encryption requires the removal of anything that looks like a pattern. In other words, when LZ tries to run, there are no redundant strings for it to replace with a token. Therefore, the compression is unsuccessful and can actually expand the traffic it was attempting to compress. In such a case, the traffic is sent uncompressed. If you don't want to send traffic uncompressed, you can implement compression and encryption at Layer 3 using IPComp (IP Compression Protocol) and IPSec (IP Security Protocol), respectively.

- **CPU and memory**—Some algorithms are memory-intensive and some are CPU-intensive. Thus, before planning or implementing compression, you must know the physical configuration of your router (that is, its RAM and CPU) before ordering additional hardware.

Configuring Compression

To configure compression, there are a number of commands. Most are technology-specific. The technology-specific commands are not what one would consider intuitive overall. For software compression, use the **compress** command:

```
RouterA(config-if)#compress [predictor ¦ stac ¦ mppc]
```

For Frame Relay deployments, use the **frame-relay payload-compress** command to enable STAC compression on an interface or a subinterface. There are no additional configuration parameters for use with this command, as illustrated by the following command structure:

```
RouterA(config-if)#frame-relay payload-compress
```

For X.25 deployments, use the **x25 map compressdtcp** command to enable TCP header compression.This enables the mapping of compressed TCP headers to X.121 addresses.

To enable TCP header compression for a given interface, use the **ip tcp header-compression**. Its command structure is as follows:

```
RouterA(config-if)#ip tcp header-compression [passive]
```

The **passive** keyword at the end of the command specifies that compression be performed only if packets received on that interface are compressed on arrival.

Foundation Summary

The Foundation Summary is a collection of tables and figures that provides a convenient review of many key concepts in this chapter. For those of you already comfortable with the topics in this chapter, this summary could help you recall a few details. For those of you who just read this chapter, this review should help solidify some key facts. For any of you doing your final preparation before the exam, these tables and figures will hopefully be a convenient way to review the day before the exam.

Table 10-2 summarizes the various queuing techniques discussed in this chapter.

Table 10-2   *Queuing Summary*

FIFO	Weighted Fair	Priority	Custom
No configuration	No queue lists; defines congestive discard threshold	Four queues: high, medium, normal, and low	Seventeen queues; sixteen configurable queues
No priority traffic	Low-volume traffic has priority	High queue serviced first; lower priority queues serviced when higher queues are empty	Round-robin
Traffic dispatched on first-come, first-served basis	Traffic dispatched based on conversation	Packet dispatching	Service threshold dispatching

Table 10-3 summarizes the various queuing techniques discussed in this chapter.

Table 10-3   *Queuing Command Summary*

Weighted Fair Queuing	
Command	**Function**
fair-queue [*congestive-discard-threshold*]	Enables WFQ on an interface; optionally, a congestive discard threshold can be specified; range = 1–4096; default = 64.
Priority Queuing	
Command	**Function**
priority-list *list-number* **protocol** *protocol-name* {**high** I **medium** I **normal** I **low**} *queue-keyword keyword-value*	Creates a protocol-specific entry for priority queuing; optionally, a tcp/udp port number can be specified for added control

continues

Table 10-3   *Queuing Command Summary (Continued)*

Priority Queuing (Continued)	
Command	**Function**
priority-list *list-number* **interface** *interface-type interface-number* {**high** I **medium** I **normal** I **low**}	Creates an interface-specific entry for priority queuing; all traffic entering the router through the specified interface is placed in the specified queue
priority-list *list-number* **default** {**high** I **medium** I **normal** I **low**}	Creates a default priority queue for traffic not matching any priority queue definition; if not specified, default = normal
priority-list *list-number* **queue-limit** [**high-limit** [**medium-limit** [**normal-limit** [**low-limit**]]]	Alters the number of entries a specific priority queue can hold; higher priority queues should hold fewer entries than lower priority queues
priority-group *group-number*	Applies a priority list to an interface to activate it
Custom Queuing	
Command	**Function**
queue-list *list-number* **protocol** *protocol-name queue-number queue-keyword keyword-value*	Creates a protocol-specific entry for custom queuing; optionally, a tcp/udp port number can be specified for added control
queue-list *list-number* **interface** *interface-type interface-number queue-number*	Creates an interface-specific entry for custom queuing; all traffic entering the router through the specified interface is placed in the specified queue
queue-list *list-number* **default** queue-number	Creates a default priority queue for traffic not matching any priority queue definition
queue-list *list-number* **queue** *queue-number* **limit** *limit-number*	Alters the service threshold for the number of records processed in a particular queue prior to processing of the next queue; default = 20
queue-list *list-number* **queue** *queue-number* **byte-count** *byte-count-number*	Alters the service threshold for a number of bytes processed in a particular queue prior to processing of the next queue; default = 1500
custom-queue-list *list-number*	Applies the custom queue list to an interface to activate it

Q&A

The questions and scenarios in this book are more difficult than what you will experience on the actual exam. The questions do not attempt to cover more breadth or depth than the exam; however, they are designed to make sure that you know the answer. Rather than enabling you to derive the answer from clues hidden inside the question itself, the questions challenge your understanding and recall of the subject.

Questions from the "Do I Know This Already?" quiz from the beginning of the chapter are repeated here to ensure that you have mastered the chapter's topic areas. Hopefully, mastering these questions will help you limit the number of exam questions on which you narrow your choices to two options and then guess.

The answers to these questions can be found in Appendix A, on page 397.

1 Where on a router is queuing implemented?

_____

_____

_____

2 When should queuing be considered a viable implementation?

_____

_____

_____

3 Should a queuing strategy be implemented on all WAN interfaces?

_____

_____

_____

4 When is WFQ enabled by default?

_____

_____

_____

5 What is the configurable parameter of WFQ?

_____

_____

_____

6 What type of traffic gets the highest priority with WFQ?

_____

_____

_____

7 How many queues are available in priority queuing?

_____

_____

_____

8 If a default queue is not specified in the configuration, in which queue are traffic types not defined in the priority list placed?

_____

_____

_____

9 What happens to traffic in a low-priority queue if there is always traffic in the high-priority queue?

_____

_____

_____

10 How many queues are available in custom queuing?

_____

_____

_____

11 How is traffic dispatched in a custom queuing implementation?

_____

_____

_____

12 How can a higher priority be assigned to a particular queue?

_____

_____

_____

13 List the types of compression supported by most Cisco routers.

_____

_____

_____

14 When should link compression be implemented?

_____

_____

_____

15 Which type of compression should be utilized on virtual circuit-based WAN deployments?

_____

_____

_____

For the remaining questions, refer to Figure 10-8 for the existing network topology.

Figure 10-8   _Q&A Network Topology_

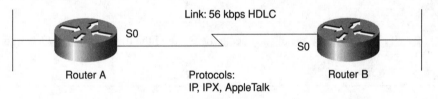

Link: 56 kbps HDLC

S0   S0

Router A   Router B

Protocols:
IP, IPX, AppleTalk

16 At first look, is this network a good candidate for queuing implementation? Why?

_____

_____

_____

17 Configure both routers for WFQ. Use a congestive discard threshold of 256.

_____

_____

_____

18 Configure both routers for priority queuing. Place any ICMP traffic in the high queue. IP should be in the medium queue, followed by IPX and AppleTalk in the normal queue. Any unspecified traffic should be placed in the low queue.

_____

_____

_____

19 If a default queue is not specified, where would the traffic go in the configuration for Question 18?

_____

_____

_____

20 Configure both routers for custom queuing. All TFTP traffic should be in queue 1. Queue 1 should have 4 times the default service thresholds. All other IP should go to queue 2, followed by IPX in queue 3 and AppleTalk in queue 4. Unspecified traffic should go into queue 5.

_____

_____

_____

21 If a default queue is not specified, where would the traffic go in the Question 20 configuration?

_____

_____

_____

22 What is the best type of compression to use for the network topology in Question 20?

_____

_____

_____

23 Configure the compression technique from Question 22. You must decide the parameters to be used, if any.

_____

_____

_____

24 Change the encapsulation of interface Serial 0 on each router to Frame Relay. Now what is the best compression technique?

_____

_____

_____

25 Configure the compression technique from Question 22. You must decide the parameters to use, if any.

_____

_____

_____

Scenarios

The following case studies and questions are designed to draw together the content of the chapter and exercise your understanding of the concepts. There is not necessarily a right answer to each scenario. The thought process and practice in manipulating the related concepts is the goal of this section.

Figure 10-9 provides the topology for all scenarios in this chapter.

Figure 10-9   *Scenario Topology*

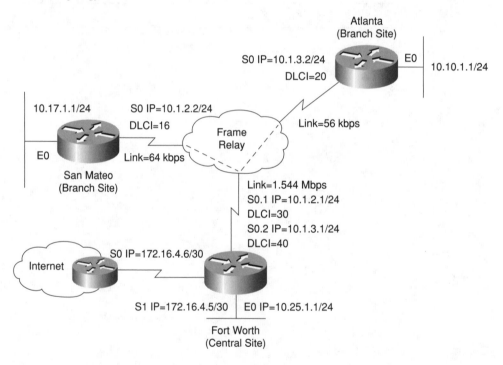

Scenario 10-1

Some congestion has been experienced over the Frame Relay network. It has been decided that a queuing strategy might be appropriate to deploy at this time. Refer to Figure 10-9 in completing the following tasks:

1   Configure WFQ on the Fort Worth router's serial 0 interface only. Make sure that the congestive discard threshold is eight times larger than the default setting.

2 Configure WFQ on the Atlanta router. Configure an appropriate congestive discard threshold.

3 Configure WFQ on the San Mateo router. Configure an appropriate congestive discard threshold.

Scenario 10-2

It seems that the WFQ deployment in San Mateo didn't provide congestion relief. Refer to Figure 10-9 in completing the following tasks:

1 Decide on a queuing strategy for the San Mateo router that allows all applications some CPU time, no matter the type of traffic.

2 Because most traffic originating from this site is Internet traffic, make sure that FTP, Telnet, TFTP, and HTTP are allocated 5 times the default service threshold.

3 Ensure that IP, IPX, and AppleTalk have their own service queues.

4 Include the configuration of a default queue.

Scenario 10-3

The Atlanta router seems to be experiencing many of the same symptoms as the San Mateo router. However, the queuing strategy utilized in San Mateo doesn't seem to work for the nature of the Atlanta traffic flow. Refer to Figure 10-9 in completing the following tasks:

1 Decide on a queuing strategy that allows specific traffic prioritization so that critical traffic gets through, even at the expense of lesser traffic.

2 DNS, FTP, Telnet, TFTP, and HTTP are the most critical traffic types. Make sure they get through.

3 The remaining IP traffic is fairly high-priority. However, it should not interfere with the core traffic types listed in the previous task. Configure accordingly.

4 IPX and AppleTalk should be configured so that they are transmitted after any other IP traffic has been sent.

5 Include the configuration of a default queue. Any traffic not listed should be considered of nominal importance.

Scenario 10-4

The decision has been made to implement a compression algorithm in hopes of further alleviating the congestion that has been plaguing the network. Refer to Figure 10-9 in completing the following tasks:

1 Implement an appropriate compression technique on the Fort Worth router.

2 Implement an appropriate compression technique on the Atlanta router.

3 Implement an appropriate compression technique on the San Mateo router.

Scenario Answers

The answers provided in this section are not necessarily the only possible correct answers. They merely represent one possibility for each scenario. The intention is to test your base knowledge and understanding of the concepts discussed in this chapter.

Should your answers be different (as they likely will be), consider the differences. Are your answers in line with the concepts of the answers provided and explained here? If not, go back and read the chapter again, focusing on the sections related to the problem scenario.

Scenario 10-1 Answers

   1 Example 10-13 details the Fort Worth router configuration for WFQ.

Example 10-13 *Fort Worth Router Fair Queuing Configuration*

```
Interface serial 0
fair-queue 512
```

   2 Example 10-14 details the Atlanta router configuration for WFQ.

Example 10-14 *Atlanta Router Fair Queuing Configuration*

```
Interface serial 0
fair-queue 256
```

   3 Example 10-15 details the San Mateo router configuration for WFQ queuing.

Example 10-15 *San Mateo Router Fair Queuing Configuration*

```
Interface serial 0
fair-queue 256
```

Scenario 10-2 Answers

   1 To meet the requirements of this scenario, a custom queuing implementation is necessary.

   2 Example 10-16 details the configuration necessary to fulfill the requirements of this task. The default byte-count threshold is 1500. The default queue limit is 20 records. The task calls for 5 times the service thresholds. Therefore, 7500 bytes (1500×5) and 100 records (20×5) are necessary to meet the requirements. The appropriate protocol and ports have been added to the configuration to meet the needs of the network.

   3 Example 10-16 includes the necessary configuration for this task. Each protocol specified has its own queue.

4 Example 10-16 includes the necessary configuration for this task. The default queue is configured last.

Example 10-16 *Scenario Configuration for the San Mateo Router*

```
queue-list 1 protocol ip 1 tcp 20
queue-list 1 protocol ip 1 tcp 21
queue-list 1 protocol ip 1 tcp 23
queue-list 1 protocol ip 1 tcp 80
queue-list 1 protocol ip 1 udp 69
queue-list 1 protocol ip 2
queue-list 1 protocol ipx 3
queue-list 1 protocol appletalk 4
queue-list 1 queue-limit 100
queue-list 1 byte-count 7500
queue-list 1 default 5
interface serial 0
custom-queue-list 1
```

Scenario 10-3 Answers

1 To meet the needs specified by this scenario, a priority queuing implementation is necessary.

2 Example 10-17 details the configuration for this task. DNS, FTP, Telnet, TFTP, and HTTP are placed into the high-priority queue.

3 Example 10-17 details the configuration for this task. The remaining IP traffic is placed into the medium queue to meet the requirement that it be a high priority, but not as high as the protocols mentioned in Task 2.

4 Example 10-17 details the configuration for this task. IPX and AppleTalk are placed into the normal queue so that they are serviced when all IP has been dispatched.

5 Example 10-17 details the configuration for this task. The default queue is set to low. Any traffic not specified in the list is placed there.

Example 10-17 *Scenario Configuration for the Atlanta Router*

```
priority-list 4 protocol ip high tcp 53
priority-list 4 protocol ip high udp 53
priority-list 4 protocol ip high tcp 20
priority-list 4 protocol ip high tcp 21
priority-list 4 protocol ip high udp 69
priority-list 4 protocol ip high tcp 80
priority-list 4 protocol ip medium
priority-list 4 protocol ipx normal
priority-list 4 protocol appletalk normal
priority-list 4 default low
interface serial 0
priority-group 4
```

Scenario 10-4 Answers

1 This scenario actually ends up as a fairly straight-forward configuration. With VC-based technologies, link compression cannot be implemented because the Layer 2 headers are compressed. Frame Relay implementations have specific compression commands that enable payload compression. Therefore, that is the task for this entire scenario. Example 10-18 shows the configuration of compression on the Fort Worth router. Note that the compression is configured on the *major* interface, not the subinterface. Frame Relay traffic shaping is not enabled by default. It is simply mentioned as a reminder that you cannot compress and traffic shape at the same time.

Example 10-18 *Compression Configuration on the Fort Worth Router*

```
interface serial 0
encapsulation frame-relay
no frame-relay traffic-shaping
frame-relay payload-compress
```

2 As mentioned, compression options are limited with VC-based deployments. Example 10-19 shows the configuration of compression on the Atlanta router.

Example 10-19 *Compression Configuration on the Atlanta Router*

```
interface serial 0
encapsulation frame-relay
no frame-relay traffic-shaping
frame-relay payload-compress
```

3 Finally, the San Mateo router must be configured. By now, you should have the idea. Example 10-20 shows the configuration on the San Mateo router.

Example 10-20 *Compression Configuration on the San Mateo Router*

```
interface serial 0
encapsulation frame-relay
no frame-relay traffic-shaping
frame-relay payload-compress
```

This chapter covers the following topics that you need to master as a CCNP:

- **Characteristics of NAT**—This section covers Network Address Translation (NAT), which is a tool that enables administrators to use the RFC 1918 private address space for internal network numbering.

- **Simple NAT translation**—In this section, you learn that a simple NAT translation replaces the outbound or inbound destination address with another address.

- **Overloading**—Overloading the address space is used with Internet connectivity. Overloading NAT translates or replaces not only the IP address, but also the port number in the TCP header. In this fashion, a single IP address can be used again and again. The port number is used to map the translation, and the address space is thus conserved. This method has become a very common method for Internet connectivity.

- **Overlapping networks**—This section covers how overlapping networks using the same IP addresses can be connected by doing a double translation of address space on a single router.

- **TCP load distribution**—NAT is also capable of doing a simple TCP load distribution. NAT does this by advertising a single IP address and translating it to a pool of addresses when the IP address is the inbound destination. In this fashion, multiple hosts can be advertised as a single IP address.

- **NAT definitions**—This section covers the four NAT address classes: Inside Local, Inside Global, Outside Local, and Outside Global. All are used throughout the discussion and should be well understood by the successful CCNP candidate.

- **NAT configurations**—This section explores the four configurations of NAT: simple, overload, overlap, and TCP load distribution.

- **Verfication of NAT translation**—The administrator must verify the translations that occur using NAT. For this purpose, the **show ip nat translation** command is available.

- **Port address translation**—This section covers port address translation (PAT), which is a form of NAT that translates the port address as well as the network layer address.

CHAPTER 11

Scaling IP Addresses with NAT

It is imperative for a CCNP candidate to understand the use of NAT. This information is needed in today's network environment as well; NAT is a standard deployment for almost all enterprise networks.

In the last few years, much ado has been given to IP Version 6 as a way to alleviate the current IP Version 4 address limitations. IP Version 6 proposes the use of 128 bits for address space compared to the current IP Version 4 space of 32 bits.

The prolific use of NAT has ameliorated the necessity of transitioning to this larger address space. Most companies now embrace the idea of using the private address space, defined in RFC 1918, and using NAT to access the Internet.

The use of NAT enables a large corporation to utilize their own selected address space and still gain access to the Internet. Whatever address space is used on the inside of a private network, NAT can provide the necessary numbering for Internet access in a much more efficient manner.

Overloading an IP address enables a private company to use a single legitimate address as a proxy for hundreds and thousands of private addresses. This feature is discussed in the "Foundation Topics" section of this chapter, along with the other features of NAT. This topic is not only germane to obtaining a CCNP or CCDP, but also relevant in a real-world sense.

How to Best Use This Chapter

By taking the following steps, you can make better use of your study time:

- Keep your notes and answers for all your work with this book in one place for easy reference.

- Take the "Do I Know This Already?" quiz and write down your answers. Studies show retention is significantly increased through writing facts and concepts down, even if you never look at the information again.

- Use the diagram in Figure 11-1 to guide you to the next step.

Figure 11-1 *How to Use This Chapter*

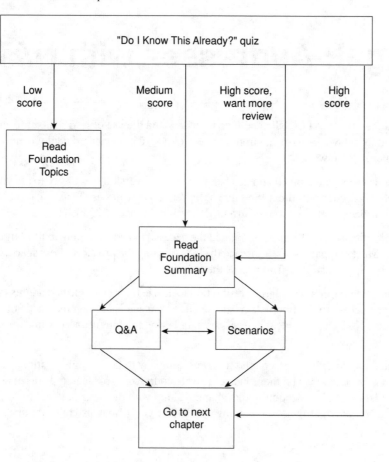

"Do I Know This Already?" Quiz

The purpose of the "Do I Know This Already?" quiz is to help you decide what parts of this chapter to use. If you already intend to read the entire chapter, you do not necessarily need to answer these questions now.

The fifteen-question quiz helps you determine how to spend your limited study time. The quiz is sectioned into smaller "quizlets," each of which corresponds to the nine major topic headings in the chapter. Use the scoresheet in Table 11-1 to record your scores.

Table 11-1   *Scoresheet for Quizlets and Quiz*

Quizlet Number	Foundation Topics Section Covered by These Questions	Questions	Score
1	Characteristics of NAT	1–2	
2	Simple NAT Translation	3–4	
3	Overloading	5–6	
4	Overlapping Networks	7–8	
5	TCP Load Distribution	9	
6	NAT Definitions	10–11	
7	NAT Configurations	12	
8	Verification of NAT Translation	13	
9	Port Address Translation	14–15	
All questions		1–15	

1 What are the benefits of NAT?

_____

_____

_____

2 What are the disadvantages of NAT?

_____

_____

_____

3 Using simple NAT translation, what TCP header information is altered?

_____

_____

_____

4 What private address space is available from RFC 1918?

_____

_____

_____

5 What does it mean when a NAT translation is overloaded?

_____

_____

_____

6 What TCP header information is altered by using NAT overload?

_____

_____

_____

7 When should NAT overlap be deployed?

_____

_____

_____

8 What NAT translation is generally used for overlapped networks? Why?

_____

_____

_____

9 Briefly describe the use of NAT TCP load distribution.

_____

_____

_____

10 List the four NAT address descriptions and a brief definition of each.

_____

_____

_____

11 An inside local address is translated to what in a simple NAT translation?

_____

_____

_____

12 What are the four types of NAT translations or configurations?

_____

_____

_____

13 What command is used to erase all current NAT-translated sessions?

_____

_____

_____

14 Port address translation is used on what router series only?

_____

_____

_____

15 Is PAT a subset of NAT? Defend your answer.

_____

_____

_____

The answers to the "Do I Know This Already?" quiz are found in Appendix A, "Answers to the 'Do I Know This Already?' Quizzes and Q&A," on page 397. The suggested choices for your next step are as follows:

- **You correctly answered six or fewer questions overall**—Read the chapter. This includes the "Foundation Topics," the "Foundation Summary," and the "Q&A" sections, as well as the scenarios at the end of the chapter.

- **You correctly answered seven, eight, or nine questions overall**—Begin with the "Foundation Summary" section and then go to the "Q&A" section and the scenarios at the end of the chapter.

- **You correctly answered ten or more questions overall**—If you want more review on these topics, skip to the "Foundation Summary" section, and then go to the "Q&A" section and the scenarios at the end of the chapter. Otherwise, move to the next chapter.

Foundation Topics

Characteristics of NAT

NAT enables nonregistered IP addresses, or the RFC 1918 private address space, to be used inside a private network and to gain access to a public network, such as the World Wide Web. The edge router connected to the public network uses NAT to translate the private network addresses to a registered public address. The translation can be statically or dynamically done.

In the case of a simple translation, each nonregistered IP address is translated to a unique public address. This enables access from networks that are using nonregistered addressing (or a private address space) to the WWW. In this scenario, the administrator would first have to find an Internet service provider (ISP) to supply a block of addresses for use. This may be monetarily difficult for all but the largest of companies.

To conserve the use of address space, a private space can be "overloaded" to a single or small number of addresses by using the source IP address plus the source port of the packet to further distinguish the sending address. Figure 11-2 illustrates the packet header.

Figure 11-2   *Packet Header Information*

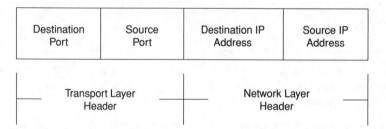

The disadvantages to NAT implementation are the increased latency, the address accountability, and the loss of certain application functionality, as defined in the following list:

- **Latency**—An increased latency is due to the introduction of a translation step (a Layer 7 application used for the translation) in the switching path.

- **Accountability**—Some may perceive the hiding of internal addresses from the external world as advantageous. However, this can be problematic when trying to determine which internal IP address is responsible for what traffic. Constantly monitoring the NAT connections or providing *only* static NAT translations would help your workload, but would also detract from the ease of use provided by a dynamic NAT implementation.

- **Functionality**—Some applications that require a specific source port or source address would not be able to function in a NAT environment that provides randomly selected address and port assignments. For example, a specialized database that uses IP addresses for access to specific records would not function. Functionality could be restored, however, by using statically mapped translations, but again the dynamic functionality of NAT would be lost.

Another reason that a specific source port or source address would not be able to function in a NAT environment is that some applications embed IP address information at the application layer, in addition to the IP packet addressing; when this happens, NAT is unable to identify the situation that is producing a mismatch between the information included in the IP packet and the information included at the application layer. Oracle and other relational databases are common examples of applications that embed IP address information.

NAT conserves legal addresses, reduces overlap dysfunctionality, increases Internet flexibility, and eliminates network renumbering in a changed environment, as described in the following list:

- **Conservation**—Legally registered addresses can be conserved using the private address space and NAT to gain access to the Internet.

- **Overlap dysfunction**—In an overlapped network situation, NAT can enable immediate connectivity without renumbering. In the case in which two companies have merged and are both using the same private address space, overlap dysfunction can be temporarily alleviated with NAT. The key here is the word *temporary*. This solution is not a design example but a Band-Aid for a quick resolution of the problem. In addition, if a service provider has connectivity to multiple clients that are using the same private address space, it may be necessary to allow connection to multiple clients that have elected to use the same private address space.

- **Flexibility**—Connecting to an Internet provider or changing providers can be accomplished with only minor changes to the NAT configuration. Becoming disgruntled or unenamored with an ISP provider is not uncommon. With NAT, changing ISPs is simply a matter of changing the pool of addresses that have been assigned. Because the NAT function occurs at the edge of the network, the router is the only device that requires a reconfiguration. If the customer accepts a nonprivate block of addresses from a provider and uses these on the inside network, changing ISPs would require renumbering the entire network.

- **Eliminated renumbering**—As network changes are made, the cost of immediate renumbering can be eliminated by using NAT to allow the existing address scheme to remain. The renumbering effort can be gradually implemented or relegated to a DHCP server in an incremental fashion rather than all at once.

Simple NAT Translation

NAT translation (in its original form) replaced the source IP address with a publicly legitimate address. The replacement address came from a pool of addresses that were defined on the NAT device. These replacement addresses were, of course, publicly valid in the Internet address space. NAT is an application layer process that inserts the legitimate address into the packet header and maintains a table of translated addresses, as shown in Figure 11-3.

Figure 11-3 *NAT in Operation*

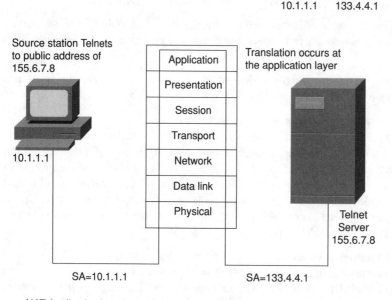

Translation table
10.1.1.1   133.4.4.1

Source station Telnets
to public address of
155.6.7.8

| Application |
| Presentation |
| Session |
| Transport |
| Network |
| Data link |
| Physical |

10.1.1.1

Translation occurs at
the application layer

Telnet
Server
155.6.7.8

SA=10.1.1.1   SA=133.4.4.1

NAT Application has the address range of 133.4.4.1 through 133.4.4.254

Overloading

Overloading uses the source port to further distinguish which sending station is transmitting. In this fashion, a single legitimate IP address can be used for many senders. The source port is a number greater than 1024 and is a software addressable port at the transport layer. The first 1024 port numbers are well-known ports, which are assigned by RFC 1400.

The terms socket and port are often used interchangeably. This is incorrect. A socket is the **IPaddress:Portnumber** pair that is unique to an IP addressable device. The port refers to a numbered entity that is addressable by software. For example, every device has a port number of 23 for telnet (regardless of whether it is in use). In contrast, only one device has the socket of 122.5.7.8:23. In other words, the socket refers to a specific location on the network whereas a port is simply a reference point that could exist on any device.

The overloading feature of NAT uses the entire socket to track the sender; thus, the same IP address can be substituted for many sending addresses, as illustrated in Figure 11-4.

Figure 11-4 *Overloading of Substitute Addresses*

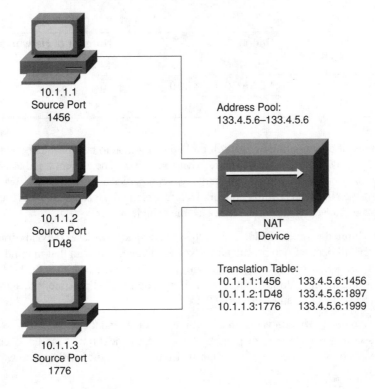

Each device that is sending through the NAT device in Figure 11-4 is translated and given a new socket number. The new socket number has a unique port number known by the router or NAT device and a common IP address for each translation. In this fashion, only one legitimate address is required for the translation. The use of the port to make the translation unique is called PAT. With PAT, the entire socket is replaced.

Overlapping Networks

Another use of NAT occurs when two networks are overlapped, or using the same numbering scheme. If they are merged, the IP address scheme fails because of the overlap. This NAT function is *not* something that should be designed into a network.

NAT overlap aids the administrator when a merger occurs. The two entities, without the renumbering of each end station, can be consolidated. In this fashion, the administrator can focus on putting a renumbering plan in place.

Overlapping networks can occur for a number of reasons, such as a merger, the consolidation of company resources that are tied with newly installed WAN components, and so on. Many companies have chosen to use the private address space defined by RFC 1918, which reserves the address ranges for the private network space shown in Table 11-2.

Table 11-2   *Private Address Ranges*

Class	Range	Number of Networks
A	10.0.0.0	1
B	172.16.0.0–172.31.0.0	16
C	192.168.0.0–192.168.255.0	255

The overlapping of network numbering will probably continue to be a problem due to the extensive use of private address space in the private sector and the current trend toward inter- and intra-company connectivity. You can merge two companies using the same private address space by using the NAT **overlapping** network feature; essentially, each network is translated to the other. This double translation can take place on a single router.

The use of the limited number of addresses in the private space increases the odds dramatically that an overlap will occur if two private networks are merged. It is with that in mind that most design guidelines dictate that if using the private space, *do not* start with the 10.1.0.0 network because others are likely to do just that as well. The recommended practice is to start in the middle, such as 10.128.0.0, and work from there.

The drawback to this restriction is that most technical people read the same literature and go to the same classes and talk to the same pundits. Therefore, the next time a merger occurs, they will not have to worry about the overlap of the 10.1.0.0 network; they will have to worry about the overlap of the 10.128.0.0 network.

Another area in which overlapping can occur is when a company elects to use a nonprivate address for their own purposes with the idea that they will never connect to the Internet. This is a very bad assumption in today's e-commerce driven world. Common sense would dictate that an Internet connection would eventually be required in this e-age and consequently, renumbering would be needed. With NAT, you have an interim fix for overlap.

TCP Load Distribution

NAT can be used for *TCP load distribution*. This works in a form that is somewhat reversed from other translations. In the other three uses of NAT, the sender uses a nonlegitimate source address in a packet destined for the outside world. In contrast, load distribution takes advantage of the NAT function by allowing a site to advertise an address but when you send a packet to the advertised address, it is rerouted to another set of addresses.

Load distribution occurs, for example, when a large hardware company has multiple mirrored servers on their internal web site and has advertised through DNS that to access their server, you must attach to 122.17.17.128. In reality, however, the server is addressed as 122.17.17.1, 122.17.17.2, and so on. In this fashion, as each request comes in, it would be sent in a rotary or round-robin fashion to each of the mirrored servers. Figure 11-5 shows an example of this configuration.

Cisco offers the Local Director software product, which can accomplish the same load distribution, but in a much more resilient fashion. The use of NAT for load distribution can be likened to a "poor-man's" solution. However, given a small shop, this feature can provide a cost effective solution.

Figure 11-5   *TCP Load Distribution Using NAT*

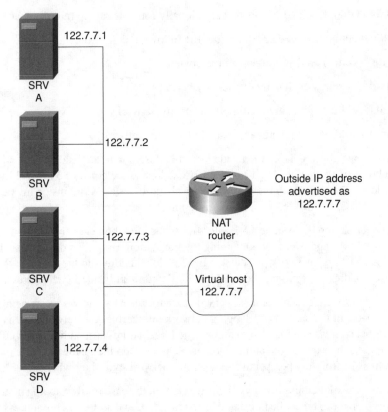

The ubiquitous use of the private space and the proficiency of NAT and PAT have greatly reduced the short supply of address space available on the Internet. This has not stopped the development of IP Version 6 (or IP Next Generation IPNG), but has slowed the implementation of it dramatically.

NAT Definitions

The addresses used for NAT translation can be summed up in four categories:

- **Inside Local**—IP addresses that are unique to the host inside the network, but not globally significant. They are generally allocated from RFC 1918 or randomly picked.

- **Inside Global**—IP addresses that are assigned by the IANA or service provider. They are legitimate in the global address space or Internet. The Inside Local addresses are translated to the Inside Global address for Internet use.

- **Outside Local**—IP addresses of a host on an outside network that is presented to the inside network and that is legitimate to the local network. These addresses *do not* have to be globally significant. They are generally selected from RFC 1918 or randomly picked.

- **Outside Global**—IP addresses that are globally routable on the Internet space.

To make the thought process easier, consider the following definitions:

- **Inside**—Addresses that are inside my network

- **Outside**—Addresses that are outside my network

- **Local**—Addresses that are legitimate inside my network

- **Global**—Addresses that are legitimate outside my network

Simple NAT translation replaces the inside local IP address with an inside global address. To say it another way, the neither-legal-or-RFC1918 addresses are converted to legal Internet-routable addresses, where both the global and local addresses are valid inside my network. In the previous scenario, "inside my network" is a point of perspective.

The use of overloading is the same as simple NAT translation; however, the same Inside Global address is used over and over by maintaining the translation using the port address. For TCP load distribution, "my" network presents an Inside Global address to the Internet. When Internet users address this global address, it is translated to an Inside Local address.

The need for the "outside local address" category occurs when two networks are using the same IP address space. In the case of overlapping network numbering, the network that is using an Outside Global address is translated to an Outside Local address. In addition, the outside address could be the same as the address that is being used on the inside, because the Outside Global address is, from my perspective, not-on-my-network-but-okay-where-it-is.

Because this network address is okay-where-it-is but, in the case of overlapping networks, not-okay-on-my-network, it must be translated to an Outside Local address. This address is outside my network but okay-when-it-gets-in.

Figure 11-6 shows each category of address and its location relative to "my network." The terms inside and outside are relative to the network being discussed; hence, what is outside my network is inside to the far side.

Figure 11-6 *Overlapping Address Definitions*

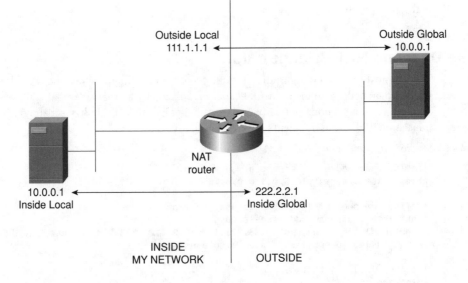

In Figure 11-6, both networks are using the 10.0.0.0/24 network. "My Network" is being translated to the 222.2.2.0/24 network, and the "Other Network" is being translated to the 111.1.1.0/24 network.

NAT Configurations

There are five general configurations that are used for NAT—simple, static, overload, overlap, and load distribution. In all cases, you should recognize that the general syntax is essentially the same for each configuration. In addition, though, you should pay particular attention to the arguments that are added to indicate which configuration is being used. As a sample configuration, assume that you need to convert a simple translation to an overloaded translation. To do this, you would add the keyword **overload** to the end of the NAT translation statement.

Overall, each configuration shown in the sections that follow has the same elements:

Step 1   Declare the address pool that will be used for the translation.

Step 2   Define the translation.

Step 3   Define the interfaces that will participate in NAT.

Step 4   Define the addresses that will be translated.

Again, the successful CCNP candidate should review each of the configurations presented. While reviewing the configurations here, it can be helpful to identify each of the four elements in the configurations.

Simple Dynamic NAT Configuration

The simplest form of configuration is a one-to-one translation in which the IP address of the Inside Local address in the network header is replaced by an Inside Global address. The replacement can be done statically or dynamically. Example 11-1 shows a simple NAT translation with the assignments done dynamically.

Example 11-1 *Simple NAT Translation*

```
!define what addresses are to be converted
access-list 1 permit 10.0.0.1 0.0.0.255

!define the pool of addresses to use for translation and
!what interfaces and addresses to use
ip nat pool simple-nat-pool 123.123.123.1 123.123.123.254 netmask 255.255.255.0
ip nat inside source list 1 pool simple-nat-pool

!declare inside interfaces
interface e0
  ip address 10.0.0.1 255.255.255.0
  ip nat inside

!declare outside interface
interface s0
  ip address 144.144.144.1 255.255.255.0
  ip nat outside
```

The access list defines what addresses to translate using the **permit** statement. The two key commands are **ip nat pool** and **ip nat inside**. The **ip nat pool** statement can be read as:

> **ip nat** uses the **pool** called **simple-nat**-**pool**, which has the addresses **123.123.123.1**— **123.123.123.254** and which uses a network mask of **255.255.255.0**.

Each address that matches the criteria stipulated by the access list can use the pool of addresses specified in the previous statement. To decide which addresses are to be translated, the **ip nat inside** (or **outside**) statement is used. This statement can be read as:

> **ip nat**, if an interface is declared as **inside**, and the **source** address of a packet matches the **access-list 1, then** use the **pool** called **my-natpool** to replace the IP address when the traffic destination is located beyond an interface that has been declared **outside**.

The following conditions dictate the use of NAT translation:

- *Only* on interfaces that are declared inside or outside can packets be translated.

- *Only* traffic from an outside to an inside (or vice versa) is translated.

- Packets received on an outside interface destined for an outside interface *are not* translated.

- Packets received on an inside interface destined for an inside interface *are not* translated.

The definition of inside and outside can be arbitrary. Declaring the S0 interface to be an inside interface with the E0 being the outside interface can be done. The **ip nat inside** command is simply changed to **ip nat outside**. The question then would be, why? The answer is that maintaining the concept of inside and outside as it is used with the address definitions lends itself to using the correct declarations of inside and outside.

A key concept to keep in mind is that *only* traffic from an inside to an outside (or vice versa) is translated. A packet that is inbound to an inside interface and that has as a routed destination an outside interface is a candidate for translation. The command **ip nat inside source list 1 pool simple-nat-pool** then states that if the source address is on list 1, the declared pool should be used. The selection of inside versus outside and source versus destination is up to the administrator. The following examples use inside and outside in relation to the owned network, which is the preferred methodology.

Static NAT Configuration

It is possible, and sometimes desirable, to configure NAT statically. A classic example of this configuration would be a resource on the inside of a network that must be accessed from the outside world at a specific location. In this situation, the advertised location of the resource is propagated to the world through DNS, and the inside resource must *always* carry in the outside world the same translated address and *always* be reachable at the same Inside Global address.

Static translation is done using the following command:

```
ip nat inside source static 10.0.0.1 108.77.2.1
```

This command says the following:

> **ip nat,** if the packet is inbound to a NAT **inside** interface destined for a NAT **outside** interface, always (**statically**) changes the address 10.0.0.1 to the address **108.77.2.1**.

If a group of requestors is being translated using a pool and one of the internal devices is a resource (10.0.0.1), the configuration from Example 11-1 is changed to that shown in Example 11-2.

Example 11-2 *Static NAT Configuration*

```
access-list 1 permit 10.0.0.0 0.0.0.255

ip nat pool natpool 222.12.12.2 222.12.12.254 netmask 255.255.255.0
ip nat inside source static 10.0.0.1 222.12.12.1
ip nat inside source list 1 pool natpool

!declare inside interfaces
interface e0
  ip address 10.0.0.1 255.255.255.0
  ip nat inside

!declare outside interface
interface s0
  ip address 144.14.14.1 255.255.255.0
  ip nat outside
```

Note that the range of available addresses does not contain the statically assigned address. The resource has a uniquely defined address in the outside world. The 222.12.12.0 network is legitimate in the Internet community and would be advertised there. The 222.12.12.1 inside address is addressable and entered into the DNS tables for the Internet community. In this way, the device that is statically (and *always*) translated to the 222.12.12.1 address is available to the outside world.

NAT Overloading Configuration

To convert the configuration for simple NAT translation to overload, the administrator must use the **overload** argument. Overloading an Inside Global address uses the same syntax as the simple NAT translation, but with the extra argument, the router knows to track the port numbers for the translation table.

The configuration in Example 11-3 extends simple NAT translation to an overload implementation.

Example 11-3 *NAT Overload Implementation*

```
!define what addresses are to be converted
access-list 1 permit 10.0.0.1 0.0.0.255

!define the pool of addresses to use for translation and
!what interfaces and addresses to use
ip nat pool natpool 123.123.123.1 123.123.123.2 netmask 255.255.255.0
ip nat inside source list 1 pool natpool overload
```

Example 11-3 *NAT Overload Implementation (Continued)*

```
!declare inside interfaces
interface e0
  ip address 10.0.0.1 255.255.255.0
  ip nat inside

!declare outside interface
interface s0
  ip address 144.14.14.1 255.255.255.0
  ip nat outside
```

The change to the configuration is extremely minor; an extra argument was added to the simple NAT translation. However, in an overload configuration, only a single IP address is needed to front for a large number of clients.

NAT Overlapping Configuration

NAT can deal with overlapping networks, even though it is not desirable to create an overlapped network. The overlapping of networks typically occurs during a merger of two companies that are using the same private address space. The overlap configuration is put in place as a stopgap while renumbering takes place.

The following configuration uses the addresses designated as Outside Global and Outside Local with reference, albeit arbitrary, to one or the other networks. One network is declared as the inside space and one is declared as the outside space.

Figure 11-7 shows a scenario in which two networks that are both using the 10.0.0.0 address space are merged using an overlap configuration. It should be pointed out that the same overall effect could be accomplished by doing a simple translation on the edge router and leaving each of the networks intact; however, with the overlap configuration, the translation is done on one router platform only. This provides a single point for the configuration and a single point for maintenance of the address space.

Figure 11-7 *Overlapped Networks*

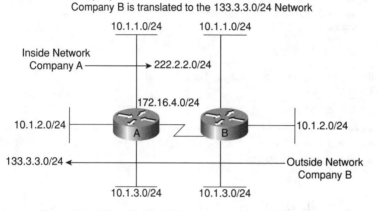

Company A is translated to the 222.2.2.0/24 Network
Company B is translated to the 133.3.3.0/24 Network

10.1.1.0/24   10.1.1.0/24

Inside Network
Company A ──────────→ 222.2.2.0/24

172.16.4.0/24

10.1.2.0/24 ──────┤   A   B   ├── 10.1.2.0/24

133.3.3.0/24 ◄─────────────────────── Outside Network
                                        Company B

10.1.3.0/24   10.1.3.0/24

Router A handles both translations.

Example 11-4 accomplishes the double translation on Router A.

Example 11-4 *Overlapping Network NAT Implementation*

```
!declare the address pools
ip nat pool coming-in 133.3.3.1 133.3.3.254 prefix-length 24
ip nat pool going-out 222.2.2.1 222.2.2.254 prefix-length 24

!declare the translations
ip nat outside source list 1 pool coming-in
ip nat inside source list 1 pool going-out

!specify which addresses will use the pool
access-list 1 permit 10.1.0.0 0.0.255.255

!specify the interfaces
interface serial 0
  ip  address 172.16.4.1 255.255.255.0
  ip nat outside
!
interface ethernet 0
  ip address 10.1.1.1 255.255.255.0
  ip nat inside
!
interface ethernet 1
  ip address 10.1.2.1 255.255.255.0
  ip nat inside
!
interface ethernet 2
  ip address 10.1.3.1 255.255.255.0
  ip nat inside
```

The configuration in Example 11-4 declares that all addresses beginning with 10.1 be translated. The key is which pool is used. For those source addresses that arrive on an outside interface and that are destined for an inside interface, the translation uses the pool called **coming-in**. The source addresses that arrive on an inside interface destined for the outside interface use the pool called **going-out**. The access list that dictates which addresses are matched and must use the designated pool is the same for both because all 10.1 addresses require translation before crossing from an inside to an outside interface, or vice versa.

NAT TCP Load Distribution Configuration

NAT can be used as a simple tool for TCP load balancing. Figure 11-8 illustrates a classic example for TCP load balancing. In the figure, Company A has four mirrored Web servers. They advertise that users can download beta copies of their software for testing at www.companya.com, which is found at 188.88.88.88 on the Internet. The address 188.88.88.88 is a legitimate address that Company A obtained from their service provider. NAT translates incoming requests for 188.88.88.88 in a round-robin or rotary fashion to balance the requests across the mirrored servers.

Figure 11-8   *NAT TCP Load Distribution*

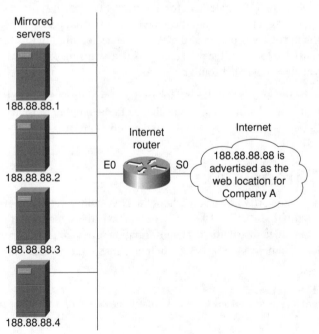

The configuration is straightforward. Any packet that arrives at Company A's Internet router, which has a destination for the 188.88.88.88 host, is translated in a rotary fashion to one of the four mirrored servers. The configuration in Example 11-5 shows the syntax for this implementation.

Example 11-5 *NAT TCP Load Distribution Implementation*

```
!declare the pool
ip nat pool company-A 188.88.88.1 188.88.88.4 prefix-length 24

!declare the translation
ip nat outside destination list 1 pool company-A rotary

!declare the access-list for translation candidates
access-list 1 permit 188.88.88.88 0.0.0.0

!declare the interfaces
interface S0
  ip nat outside

interface E0
  ip nat inside
```

You should note that the declaration statement for the translation specifies that the **destination** address should be checked against list 1, not the source address as in previous configurations. In addition, the argument **rotary** is placed at the end of the declaration. In this fashion, each incoming packet is translated to one of the pool members in a recurring sequential fashion; thus, a load distribution is achieved over the four servers.

You should note that the router does not keep track of the availability of the destination addresses assigned to it in the "pool"; hence, any change to the number of rotary members or the internal configuration *must* be reflected in the router definitions.

Verification of NAT Translation

There are two commands to verify and troubleshoot the NAT configuration: **show ip nat translation** and **show ip nat statistics**. The translation table is the same format for simple, overload, overlapped, and load distribution. The information provided is different depending upon the configuration. Example 11-6 shows the output for a simple translation.

Example 11-6 *Verifying NAT Translation*

```
Router#show ip nat translation
Pro     Inside global    Inside local    Outside local    Outside global
---     156.8.34.1       10.15.0.1       ---              ---
---     156.8.34.2       10.15.0.2       ---              ---
---     156.8.34.3       10.15.0.3       ---              ---
```

Because this is a simple translation, only the information that is relevant is put into the table. The concept of outside local and outside global is not used, and therefore not presented when a simple NAT translation is configured. If an overloaded translation has been configured, the output from the **show ip nat translation** command would be as demonstrated in Example 11-7.

Example 11-7 *NAT Overloaded Translation Output*

Pro	Inside global	Inside local	Outside local	Outside global
tcp	143.4.23.1:1098	10.1.0.1:1098	73.4.5.6:23	73.4.5.6:23
tcp	143.4.23.1:1345	10.1.0.2:1345	73.4.5.6:23	73.4.5.6:23
tcp	143.4.23.1:1989	10.1.0.3:1989	73.4.5.7:21	73.4.5.7:21

Notice that the Outside Local address and the Outside Global address are the same. Because the router is not performing an overlapped configuration, the Outside Global address is not known.

When an overlapping configuration is being used, the router has knowledge of the Outside Global address, so the output from a **show ip nat translation** command would appear as demonstrated in Example 11-8.

Example 11-8 *NAT Overlapping Translation Output*

Pro	Inside global	Inside local	Outside local	Outside global
tcp	133.3.3.1:1098	10.1.0.1:1098	173.4.5.6:23	10.1.0.23:23
tcp	133.3.3.2:1345	10.1.0.2:1345	173.4.5.6:23	10.1.0.23:23
tcp	133.3.3.3:1989	10.1.0.3:1989	173.4.5.7:21	10.2.0.45:21

Because the router is performing both translations, the Outside Global address is known.

The **show ip nat statistics** command is also useful in troubleshooting a NAT installation, as demonstrated in Example 11-9.

Example 11-9 *Troubleshooting NAT Installation with* **show ip nat statistics**

```
Router#show ip nat statistics
Total translations: 1 (0 static, 1 dynamic; 0 extended)
Outside interfaces: Serial0Inside interfaces: Ethernet0Hits: 1  Misses: 0
Expired translations: 2Dynamic mappings:-- Inside Source
access-list 1 pool my-pool refcount 2 pool my-pool: netmask 255.255.255.0
        start 172.3.4.1 end 172.3.4.7
        type generic, total addresses 7, allocated 1 (14%), misses 0
```

The **show ip nat statistics** command displays which interfaces are inside and which are outside, the pool name, and the addresses that are with the mask. The hits and misses refer to the number of times a translation lookup succeeded or failed.

To troubleshoot NAT, you can use the **debug ip nat** command. The output from this command shows which addresses were translated and, for a TCP connection, what the transaction numbers are. The output in Example 11-10 shows a sample output from a NAT debug.

Example 11-10 *Troubleshooting a NAT Installation with* **debug ip nat**

```
Router#debug ip nat
NAT: s=10.1.0.1->12.1.3.2, d=155.5.5.5 [1]
NAT: s=155.5.5.5, d=12.1.3.2->10.1.0.1 [1]
NAT: s=10.1.0.1->12.1.3.2, d=155.5.5.5 [2]
NAT*: s=155.5.5.5, d=12.1.3.2->10.1.0.1 [2]
!Additional output omitted............
```

The translation is shown clearly from the source address to the destination and the reverse communications. The * indicates that the translation was done in the fast path or by using cache. To watch and debug this output in real time would be daunting at best. The number in brackets indicates the sequencing number for a TCP session that could be useful for debugging a protocol analyzer trace of the session.

The administrator can shut down a translated session using the **clear** command for **ip nat**. The syntax for clearing a simple NAT translation is as follows:

    clear ip nat translation inside global-ip-address local-ip-address

The administrator must type the addresses without error to clear the correct translation session. Any typographical error in the command syntax can clear the wrong session! It is also possible to clear *all* current translated sessions on the router by using this command:

    clear ip nat translation *

The use of the asterisk (*) as a wildcard clears *all* currently established NAT sessions. The use of this command might be needed on a periodic basis to clear out any hung NAT sessions. It is common practice at some sites to clear all translations at the end of Friday to allow all tables a chance to reset.

Port Address Translation

PAT is a form of NAT in which the port is also replaced at the translating device. PAT is the only address translation feature for the Cisco 700 series router. Only a minor treatment of the PAT syntax was discussed in both the CMTD and BCRAN course material. In addition, PAT was not discussed in the 700 series router chapter, so some additional 700 series commands need to be discussed here.

The concept behind PAT is the same as for NAT. A pool of addresses is not needed because only one address services all devices. The two commands that are needed for the 700 to use PAT are

```
set ip pat on
set ip pat porthandler port ip-address
```

where *port* is the transport layer port for the application and *ip-address* is the local address of the device.

Once you enter the **set ip pat on** command, the single address that is used for the translation is included in the port handler assignment. The port handler is unique to the 700 series router. The port handler declares which ports are translated. Earlier, the chapter explained how an access list declares which traffic will be translated for Cisco IOS Software-based routers. In our current situation, however, the selection is done on a port basis; up to 15 port handler statements can be on a 700 series router. Figure 11-9 shows the port handler in use.

Figure 11-9   *Using the Port Handler for PAT*

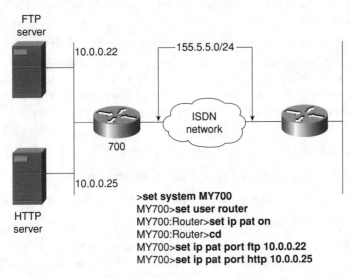

```
>set system MY700
MY700>set user router
MY700:Router>set ip pat on
MY700:Router>cd
MY700>set ip pat port ftp 10.0.0.22
MY700>set ip pat port http 10.0.0.25
```

The FTP and HTTP servers are translated when they are sent using the Router profile. The address to which they are translated is the address of the interface that is in use at the time. In the example in the figure, FTP packets from the outside world that are destined for 155.5.5.2 (the 700 series router's ISDN interface address) are translated to 10.0.0.22—the inside FTP server. Likewise, HTTP packets addressed to the 155.5.5.2 address are translated to 10.0.0.25—the HTTP server.

Turning PAT on is a system-wide command to the 700 series router. The definition for the port-handler function is done within a profile. There are a number of limitations that must be addressed while using this technology:

- **ping** from an outside host ends at the router. Hence, end-to-end connectivity testing is not possible.

- Only one inside web server, FTP server, Telnet server and so forth is supported because *all* port traffic is defined by a single **ip porthandler** command.

- Only 15 port handlers are supported in a single configuration.

The limitations specified should not be a deterrent to the use of PAT on a 700 series router. You should remember the market positioning of this device and realize that small remote offices can take advantage of the translation function to share resources on a larger network.

The two commands associated with PAT on the 700 series router are **set ip pat on**, which is a global command that requires no arguments, and **set ip pat porthandler**, which has the following arguments:

```
default | telnet | ftp | smtp | wins | http | port ip-address | off
```

The **telnet, ftp, smtp, wins**, and **http** arguments declare the well-known ports for those protocols. The key arguments are **default** and *port ip-address*. The **default** argument specifies any port that is not declared by another (there are up to 15) **set ip pat porthandler** command. The *port ip-address* is used when the administrator must specify a port other than the defined ports—Telnet, FTP, SMTP, WINS, and HTTP.

The limiting numbers for the 700 series router are as follows:

- 400 PAT entries are allocated for sharing among the inside machines.

- Only 15 port handler addresses can be used.

- 1500 maximum MAC addresses can be supported.

The bottom line is that the 700 series router can be configured for a lot more than a 128-kbps ISDN line can handle. The limitation is not what the device can do, but what can be done on the resource that the device uses.

Foundation Summary

The Foundation Summary is a collection of information that provides a convenient review of many key concepts in this chapter. For those of you already comfortable with the topics in this chapter, this summary could help you recall a few details. For those of you who just read this chapter, this review should help solidify some key facts. For any of you doing your final preparation before the exam, these tables and figures will hopefully be a convenient way to review the day before the exam.

The addresses used for NAT translation can be summed up in four categories:

- **Inside Local**—IP addresses that are unique to the host inside the network, but not globally significant. They are generally allocated from RFC 1918 or randomly picked.

- **Inside Global**—IP addresses that are assigned by the IANA or service provider. They are legitimate in the global address space or Internet. The Inside Local addresses are translated to the Inside Global address for Internet use.

- **Outside Local**—IP addresses of a host on an outside network that is presented to the inside network and that is legitimate to the local network. These addresses *do not* have to be globally significant. They are generally selected from RFC 1918 or randomly picked.

- **Outside Global**—IP addresses that are globally routable on the Internet space.

To make the thought process easier, consider the following definitions::

- **Inside**—Addresses that are inside my network

- **Outside**—Addresses that are outside my network

- **Local**—Addresses that are legitimate inside my network

- **Global**—Addresses that are legitimate outside my network

Table 11-3   *Private Address Space Ranges*

Address Class	Range	Number of Networks
A	10.0.0.0	1
B	172.16.0.0–172.31.0.0	16
C	192.168.0.0–192.168.255.0	255

Q&A

The questions and scenarios in this book are more difficult than what you will experience on the actual exam. The questions do not attempt to cover more breadth or depth than the exam; however, they are designed to make sure that you know the answer. Rather than allowing you to derive the answer from clues hidden inside the question itself, the questions challenge your understanding and recall of the subject.

Questions from the "Do I Know This Already?" quiz from the beginning of the chapter are repeated here to ensure that you have mastered the chapter's topic areas. Hopefully, these questions will you help limit the number of exam questions on which you narrow your choices to two options and then guess.

The answers to these questions can be found in Appendix A, on page 397.

1 What are the benefits of NAT?

_____

_____

_____

2 The Outside Global address is converted to which NAT address class?

_____

_____

_____

3 What are the disadvantages of NAT?

_____

_____

_____

4 Using simple NAT translation, what TCP header information is altered?

_____

_____

_____

5 What private address space is available from RFC 1918?

_____

_____

_____

6 What does it mean when a NAT translation is overloaded?

_____

_____

_____

7 Which commands would you use for an overloaded NAT translation using a defined pool of addresses called **transpool** for outbound traffic?

_____

_____

_____

8 What TCP header information is altered using NAT overload?

_____

_____

_____

9 When should NAT overlap be deployed?

_____

_____

_____

10 What NAT translation is generally used for overlapped networks? Why?

_____

_____

_____

11 What command would show which interfaces have been declared as outside or inside?

_____

_____

_____

12 Briefly describe the use of NAT TCP load distribution.

_____

_____

_____

13 List the four NAT address descriptions and provide a brief definition for each.

_____

_____

_____

14 An inside local address is translated to what in a simple NAT translation?

_____

_____

_____

15 What are the four types of NAT translations or configuration?

_____

_____

_____

16 The port handler for the 700 series router allows which of the following?

a. up to 15 port-handler addresses

b. multiple ports for a single inside service

c. only one inside port per service supported

d. up to 400 ports maximum to be open for the port handler

e. up to 1500 ports

17 An Inside Local address _____. (Choose two answers.)

a. is unique to the inside network and can be routed internally

b. is unique to the inside network, but can not be routed internally

c. is always selected from RFC 1918 private address space

d. is not routable on the internet

e. can use a private address or an IANA-assigned address space

18 What command is used to erase all the currently NAT translated sessions?

_____

_____

_____

19 Port address translation is used on what router series?

_____

_____

_____

20 Given the following output, what type of translation is being used on this router?

```
Pro     Inside global     Inside local      Outside local     Outside global
tcp     103.32.32.1:1098   10.1.0.1:1098     13.43.5.6:23      13.43.5.6:23
tcp     103.32.32.1:1345   10.1.0.2:1345     13.43.5.6:23      13.43.5.6:23
tcp     103.32.32.1:1989   10.1.0.3:1989     13.43.5.7:21      13.43.5.7:21
```

_____

_____

_____

21 Given the following router configuration information which of the subsequent statements is true? (Choose three answers.)

```
access-list 1 permit 10.0.0.0 0.0.0.255

ip nat pool natpool 222.12.12.2 222.12.12.10 netmask 255.255.255.0
ip nat inside source static 10.0.0.1 222.2.2.1
ip nat inside source list 1 pool natpool
```

a. All addresses belonging to the 10.0.0.0/8 network are translated by the router.

b. The translation uses an overload technique.

c. The translation is a simple NAT technique.

d. The address 10.0.0.1 can be pinged from the outside network.

e. The address 222.2.2.1 can be pinged from the outside network.

f. The pool can support up to nine translations.

g. The pool can support translations of up to 64 K per assigned address.

22 What differentiates PAT from NAT?

_____

_____

_____

Scenarios

The following scenarios and questions are designed to draw together the content of the chapter and exercise your understanding of the concepts. There is not necessarily a right answer to each scenario. The thought process and practice in manipulating each of the concepts is the goal of this section.

Scenario 11-1

Your company, a medium-sized law firm, has been dialing up from individual PCs to receive information from a data warehouse service.

It has recently been decided to network the PCs, which are running Windows 98 or 95, to gain access to the data through the Internet. You have contacted a local ISP and will maintain a leased line to their POP. You have approximately 15 lawyers and 20 support staff members with which to deal. Internet usage will be tolerated *only* for the lawyers on staff and certain research assistants.

The ISP has given you a single IP address—187.202.4.6. Based on this information, answer or complete the following questions and tasks.

  1 What router would you select for the office?

  2 What would be your IP address scheme?

  3 Create the NAT configuration that would be used for this connection.

  4 Describe your solution to the Internet access policy that is described for the lawyers and office staff.

Scenario 11-2

Your company has merged with a smaller entity. You will provide their Internet access over a newly installed T1 facility. Their IP address scheme uses three private Class C addresses—192.168.11.0/24, 192.168.22.0/24, and 192.168.33.0/24. You are currently using the 10.0.0.0 network.

The newer, smaller company currently has no Internet access. Your provider has given you a CIDR block of 103.112.8.24/29. You are currently using 103.112.8.25—103.112.8.29 for addresses on your DMZ. You have been using 103.112.8.30 for your 10.0.0.0 NAT translation. Based on this information, answer or complete the following questions and tasks.

  1 What can you do to enable translation of the new company's address space?

  2 Create the NAT configuration that would be used for this connection.

  3 What recommendation would you have for the consolidation of address space?

Scenario 11-3

Your company has merged with another company of equal size and you have both been using the 10.0.0.0 network as a base for your internal network numbering. Management has promised a bonus if you can get minimal communication between the ABCServer and the XYZServer by this weekend. The ABCServer is on your network, and the XYZServer is on the other network. The address in your space for the ABCServer is 10.1.0.1/24, and the address in the new company's space is 10.1.0.18/24.

Users in the ABC network should be able to talk to the XYZServer, and the users in the XYZ network should be able to talk to the ABCServer. For simplicity, assume that all addresses are 10.1.0.x/24. Based on this information, answer or complete the following questions and tasks.

1   Explain what you will do to quickly complete the overall task.

2   Create the NAT configuration that would be used for this connection.

3   What considerations, other than NAT, must be addressed to allow the configuration to happen?

4   What is your long-term recommendation for the configuration and how can you implement it?

Scenario Answers

The answers provided in this section are not necessarily the only possible correct answers. They merely represent one possibility for each scenario. The intention is to test your base knowledge and understanding of the concepts discussed in this chapter. Should your answers be different (as they likely will be), consider the differences. Are your answers in line with the concepts of the answers provided and explained here? If not, go back and read the chapter again, focusing on the sections related to the problem scenario.

Scenario 11-1 Answers

1 Given the fact that only 15 or so people would be using the connection at a given time can lead you to select a 1600 series router. However, some consideration should be given to using a 3620, which would provide a higher degree of scalability for the situation.

2 Any IP address scheme would work in this situation, however, strictly adhering to the private address space number would be recommended. Given the size of the office, you can choose a Class C address space and use a 24-bit mask to keep it simple.

3 The following NAT configuration could be used, given a selection of 192.168.1.0/24 as the internal addresses used:

```
access-list 1 permit 192.168.1.0 0.0.0.255

ip nat pool lawpool 187.202.4.6 187.202.4.6 netmask 255.255.255.0
ip nat inside source list 1 pool lawpool overload

!declare inside interface
interface e0
  ip address 192.168.1.1 255.255.255.0
  ip nat inside

!declare outside interface
interface s0
!address assigned to the interface by the ISP
  ip address 112.18.23.2 255.255.255.250
  ip nat outside
```

4 There are a number of ways to allow only the lawyers and certain others to use this connection. One way would be to apply an access list on the inbound Ethernet to block unwanted users from routing through the router. This would be highly CPU-intensive, but with such light usage, it might not be a problem. After all, the only time that these users would try to get through the router is when they were trying to do something that they were not authorized to do anyway.

It would also be possible to use different portions of the Class C address for the lawyers and those that could use the Internet and then translate only that group of addresses. An access list could be placed on the outbound side of the serial port to block all nontranslated addresses. Although this would be easier to accomplish from a CPU perspective than would the previously discussed solution, either way would work.

Scenario 11-2 Answers

1 To allow translation of the new addresses, additional match criteria can be added to the NAT translation access list. This scenario is simply an addition of more addresses for translation. Because the companies were not using the same address space, nothing else need be done.

2 The following NAT configuration could be used:

```
access-list 1 permit 10.0.0.0 0.0.0.255
access-list 1 permit 192.168.11.0 0.0.0.255
access-list 1 permit 192.168.22.0 0.0.0.255
access-list 1 permit 192.168.33.0 0.0.0.255

ip nat pool bigpool 103.112.8.30 103.112.8.30 netmask 255.255.255.0
ip nat inside source list 1 pool bigpool overload

!declare inside interface
interface e0
  ip address 10.0.0.1 255.255.255.0
  ip nat inside

!declare outside interface
interface s0
!address assigned to the interface by the ISP
  ip address 156.108.213.2 255.255.255.250
  ip nat outside
```

3 Not enough information is given to lead one to believe that anything should be done to consolidate address space. As it stands, both companies are using the private space which is easily controlled and routed. As they say, if it ain't broke, don't fix it.

Scenario 11-3 Answers

1 To provide immediate connectivity, you can use the overlap feature in NAT. This would enable the ABC and XYZ companies to coexist during a transition.

2 The following NAT configuration could be used, given a selection of 192.168.1.0/24 as the internal addresses used:

```
ip nat pool XYZ-in 192.168.1.2 192.168.1.254 prefix-length 24
ip nat pool ABC-out 192.168.2.2 192.168.2.254 prefix-length 24
```

```
!declare the translations
ip nat outside source list 1 pool XYZ-in
ip nat inside source list 1 pool ABC-out
!declare the static translation so the servers can be reached
!these lines give an constant 'known' translation to the
!server addresses
ip nat inside source static 10.1.0.1 192.168.1.1
ip nat outside source static 10.1.0.18 192.168.2.1
!specify which addresses will use the pool
access-list 1 permit 10.1.0.0 0.0.255.255

!specify the interfaces
interface serial 0
   ip  address 172.16.4.1 255.255.255.0
   ip nat outside
!
interface ethernet 0
   ip address 10.1.0.2 255.255.255.0
   ip nat inside
```

3 The primary consideration, other than NAT, is the sharing of the server address information between the two entities. The static NAT declarations provide the capability for the two companies to have unique addresses in each other's space for their servers; however, it would be necessary to provide a DNS service for the users to be able to contact the other side easily.

4 The long-term recommendation would be to implement some sort of IP renumbering and then remove the translation between the companies.

This chapter covers the following topics that you need to master as a CCNP:

- **AAA Overview**—Authentication, authorization, and accounting (AAA) describes a global security setup for a RAS or network environment. There is no AAA per se, but several pieces of software that comprise the way of doing business we call AAA.

- **Interface Types**—This topic is needed to determine from where a user is coming into the router. Fortunately, AAA can be used to make a decision based on the inbound connection method. In this section of the chapter, the different connection methods are discussed. In a nutshell, you will learn that a connection can be physical to the router, for example, the console (CON) or AUX port, or it can be a vty session or dial-up session. AAA is able to discern these types of connections and must be configured to authenticate based on the connection type.

- **AAA Configuration**—AAA configuration is explored for the various methods of connection for authentication of the user being presented to the router.

- **AAA Authorization**—This section discusses AAA configuration for authorizing resource use after a user has been authenticated.

- **AAA Accounting**—This section presents AAA configuration for accounting by focusing on how much data is needed for a given environment.

- **Virtual Profiles**—This section covers virtual profiles, which are the next generation of a dialer profile. The specific user information needed for a call can be stored in the AAA server and centrally managed.

CHAPTER 12

Using AAA to Scale Access Control in an Expanding Network

With the evolving large networks of today, it is imperative that the successful CCNP candidate be able to monitor the access and use of the network. AAA provides the capability to track not just access and usage, but also the level of access and use of today's large-scale networks.

You must be able to document the type of access for a number of reasons. Usage, to some extent, represents the need for the network. The tracking of the command usage and the access method can be a predictor for future growth in a network.

Without AAA or some other tracking mechanism, an administrator that sees a network that "works" today might be faced with a network that is "down" tommorrow. Tracking proactively determines if the current growth is about to stretch beyond the current resources.

Any design requires a comprehensive management plan. AAA provides this component and enables the administrator to successfully predict when an adjustment is needed. Failure to properly implement a management plan that tracks network usage and access can leave an administrator in the lurch when the resources are stretched to a point that they break. It is easier to "sell" an upgrade to management with significant and appropriate data than it is to wait until management asks why you are not doing your job.

Career-level decisions are made every day. Implementing AAA to provide proactive tracking and supervision of the network resources should be an easy decision to make.

How to Best Use This Chapter

By taking the following steps, you can make better use of your study time:

- Keep your notes and answers for all your work with this book in one place for easy reference.

- Take the "Do I Know This Already?" quiz and write down your answers. Studies show that retention is significantly increased through writing facts and concepts down, even if you never look at the information again.

- Use the diagram in Figure 12-1 to guide you to the next step.

Figure 12-1 *How to Use This Chapter*

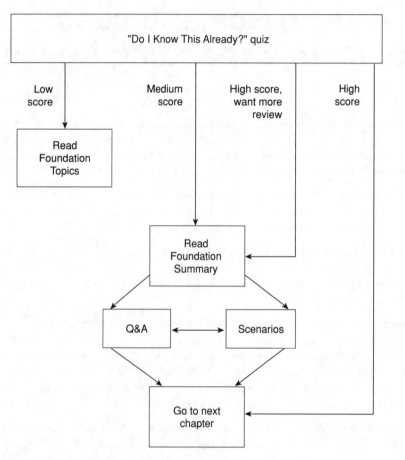

"Do I Know This Already?" Quiz

The purpose of the "Do I Know This Already?" quiz is to help you decide what parts of this chapter to use. If you already intend to read the entire chapter, you do not necessarily need to answer these questions now.

The eleven-question quiz helps you determine how to spend your limited study time. The quiz is sectioned into smaller "quizlets," each of which corresponds to the six major topic headings in the chapter. Use the scoresheet in Table 12-1 to record your scores.

Table 12-1   *Scoresheet for Quizlets and Quiz*

Quizlet Number	Foundation Topics Section Covered by These Questions	Questions	Score
1	AAA Overview	1–2	
2	Interface Types	3–4	
3	AAA Configuration	5–7	
4	AAA Authorization	8	
5	AAA Accounting	9–10	
6	Virtual Profiles	11	
All questions		1–11	

1 For what does AAA stand?

_____

_____

_____

2 What is authentication?

_____

_____

_____

3 What is the difference between character mode and packet mode?

_____

_____

_____

4 What communication method—packet or character—is used on the console port of a router?

_____

_____

_____

5 What are the five authentication modes on a router?

_____

_____

_____

6 What authentication method is used on an interface without an AAA-defined method?

_____

_____

_____

7 What is the command to enable AAA using Remote Authentication Dial-In User Service (RADIUS)?

_____

_____

_____

8 What is *authorization*?

_____

_____

_____

9 What does the argument *start-stop* mean when using AAA accounting?

_____

_____

_____

10 What commands when tracked should use the *wait-start* argument?

_____

_____

_____

11 What is stored in a virtual profile?

_____

_____

_____

The answers to the "Do I Know This Already?" quiz are found in Appendix A, "Answers to the 'Do I Know This Already?' Quizzes and Q&A Sections," on page 397. The suggested choices for your next step are as follows:

- **You correctly answered six or fewer questions overall**—Read the chapter. This includes the "Foundation Topics," the "Foundation Summary," and the "Q&A" sections, as well as the scenarios at the end of the chapter.

- **You correctly answered seven, eight, or nine questions overall**—Begin with the "Foundation Summary" section and then go to the "Q&A" section and the scenario at the end of the chapter.

- **You correctly answered ten or more questions overall**—If you want more review on these topics, skip to the "Foundation Summary" section, and then go to the "Q&A" section and the scenario at the end of the chapter. Otherwise, move to the next chapter.

Foundation Topics

AAA Overview

AAA provides a method for setting up access control on a router. Access control provides a means to declare who (authentication) can access the network, what (authorization) the users can do, and what (tracking or accounting) the user has done. AAA provides a method to control and configure these three independent security functions.

CiscoSecure ACS (Access Control Server) provides authentication, authorization, and accounting and is used in many of the BCRAN classes as the AAA server. This does *not* mean that CiscoSecure is the only AAA server. CiscoSecure is only one of the AAA server software packages that is available. CiscoSecure comes bundled with the following:

- **AAA Server**—This is the basic AAA functionality for authentication, authorization, and accounting.

- **Netscape Fastrack Server**—This piece of software provides an interface function to the GUI Admin Client. Admin Client enables the administrator to manage the CiscoSecure ACS database through Netscape or Internet Explorer. The Web-based interface enables logins to the ACS database to perform system administrator tasks. ACS stores these modifications in its relational database management system (RDBMS) (or in another supported RDBMS).

- **An RDBMS**—The ACS server can operate with an external RDBMS or the Oracle and Sybase Enterprise database applications because it uses the open database connectivity (ODBC) interface. The RDBMS that is bundled with the CiscoSecure package is SQLAnywhere and is a nonscalable RDBMS.

Authentication

Authentication identifies users. During the authentication process, the user login (name) and password are checked against the AAA database. Also, depending on the protocol, AAA supports encryption.

Authentication determines who the user is. Passing the authentication test enables access to the network. This process is only one of the components for user control with AAA. Once the userid and password are accepted, AAA can be used to define what the user is then authorized to do.

Authorization

Authorization enables the administrator to control authorization on a one-time, per-service, per-user list, per-group, or per-protocol basis. AAA lets the administrator create attributes that describe the functions that the user is allowed to use.

AAA authorization works by assembling a set of attributes that describe what the user is authorized to perform. These attributes are compared to the information contained in a database for a given user and the result is returned to AAA to determine the user's actual capabilities and restrictions. This requires that the database be in constant communication with the AAA server during the connection to the RAS device.

Accounting

Accounting enables the administrator to collect information such as start and stop times for user access, executed commands, traffic statistics, and resource usage and then store that information in the RDBMS. In other words, accounting enables the tracking of service and resources that are "consumed" by the user. The key point to accounting is the capability of the administrator to proactively track and predict service and resource usage. This information can then be used for client billing, internal billing, network management, or audit trails.

Interface Types

An understanding of the communication method on each port or port definition is important to understanding and performing a successful configuration of AAA.

Character mode is used on the TTY, VTY, AUX, and CON ports. These are the control ports on the router. On the other hand, packet mode is used on the async, group-async, BRI, PRI, serial, dialer profiles, and dialer rotaries. These are the communication ports on the router.

The concept of control versus communication is a fine distinction. The use of the term *control* indicates a character communication connection that enables control or configuration of the router. The term *communication* indicates that the port is being used to access another source other than the router.

Control ports are ports in which router configuration would normally take place. Character mode sends keystrokes to the router through the TTY, VTY, AUX and CON ports for configuration or query commands.

Communication ports are ports in which communication to another device occurs or where traffic is passing through the router to another device. These ports are WAN ports. Packet mode uses interface mode or a link protocol session to communicate with a device other than the router. The defined interfaces on the router are async, group-async, BRI, PRI, serial, dialer profiles, and dialer rotaries. Interfaces become important to the configuration of AAA. Each of the authentications and authorizations is tied to one of the interfaces.

It should be noted that the key thing to keep in mind is packet vs character mode, not the physical port itself. The AUX port, for instance, can be used in both modes. After enabling AAA, each attachment to the router, whether it is character or packet mode, must be declared for authentication. Failure to declare a method for a connection results in a failed authentication.

AAA Configuration

AAA configuration is implemented in three steps:

Step 1   Enable AAA Configuration on the router. During the declaration of AAA, the router must be told if it will be "speaking" with a Terminal Access Control Access Control System (TACACS) or RADIUS server.

Step 2   Define who will be authenticated, what they are authorized to do, and what will be tracked in the database.

Step 3   Enable or define the method on the interface.

The following sections detail how to turn on AAA (Step 1), how to define the methods for authentication, authorization and accounting (Step 2), and how to declare AAA on an interface (Step 3).

It should be noted that once AAA is turned on for a router, any interface and connection method *must* be defined or access is not permitted. Therefore, it is important to leave a "backdoor" or local access method available during initial deployment to guard against loss of router access due to coding mistakes. This is discussed in the sections on authentication for each of the access methods: login, enable, PPP, ARAP, and NASI.

Enabling AAA

To enable AAA on the router, use this command:

```
aaa new-model
```

The **no** form of this command disables AAA on the router. Once AAA is enabled, the router must point to the source of the AAA server. For a TACACS, the command is as follows:

```
tacacs-server host ip-address [single-connection]
```

The *ip-address* parameter designates the location of the CiscoSecure server or another TACACS server. The optional **single-connection** parameter tells the router to maintain a single connection for the duration of the session between the router and the AAA device. The alternative is to open and close a TCP connection for each session. The opening and closing of a connection is the default. Cisco recommends the single-connection feature for improved performance.

A shared password is used between the access router and the AAA server for security. The command to establish this password on the router is as follows:

```
tacacs-server key password
```

The password must be configured on the AAA server also. The passwords are case-sensitive.

The first steps for the configuration of AAA used on a RADIUS server are similar to the TACACS implementation: "tacacs" is replaced by "radius". The following example is the initial command set for a RADIUS implementation:

```
aaa new-model
radius-server host 115.55.43.1
radius-server key specialname
```

In the command set, the IP address is 115.55.43.1 and the shared password is **specialname**.

AAA Authentication

Once AAA has been enabled on the router, the administrator must declare the methods by which authentication can take place. The key issue is to ensure that the administrator has a way to gain access to the router if the AAA server is down. Failure to provide a backdoor interface can result in lost communications to the router and the necessity to break in through the console port. Care should be taken to always configure a local access method during any implementation of AAA.

The syntax for configuring AAA on the router can be daunting at first glance. Breaking it down keeps it simpler. Each of the modes listed (**login**, **enable**, **arap**, and so on) is a method by which a user might gain access to or through the router.

Do you remember the packet and character mode designation from the previous section? The global configuration commands enable the administrator to declare the method that is used for authentication, regardless of the access mode being used. These methods, which are shown later, include **enable**, **line**, **local**, **none**, and so on and are checked in the order in which they are specified in the command. The generic form for the authentication command is as follows:

```
aaa authentication [login | enable | arap | ppp | nasi] method
```

This example does not include specifics for the method by which the access is evaluated. It is clearer to show each of the commands and then discuss the method that can be added to the command.

Each command in the following list can stand alone and each declares a command definition for the authentication command. In addition, each command is used for a specific access purpose. These purposes were discussed previously.

- **aaa authentication login**—This command answers this question: How do I authenticate the login dialog?

- **aaa authentication enable**—This command answers this question: Can the user get to the privileged command prompt?

- **aaa authentication arap**—This command answers this question: Does the AppleTalk Remote Access Protocol (ARAP) user use RADIUS or TACACS+? (One must be selected.)

- **aaa authentication ppp**—This command answers this question: What method should be used if a user is coming over a PPP connection?

- **aaa authentication nasi**—This command answers this question: What method should be used if a user is coming over NASI?

AAA Authentication Login

What method of authentication is going to be used during the login procedure? The answer to this question is defined by this interface command:

```
aaa authentication login [default | listname]
```

The declaration of **default** tells the router what to do if no listname has been declared on the interface. If a listname has been declared, that listname controls the login. For example, the global command

```
aaa authentication login myway argument argument argument …
```

declares how the **myway** list is interpreted. On each interface that is declared to use authentication **myway**, one or more of the following arguments is used for the authentication:

```
[enable | line | local | none | tacacs+ | radius | guest]
```

Each of the previous arguments declares a method of authentication, and they can be listed one after another on the command line. Example 12-1 shows this concept.

Example 12-1 *Declaring a Method of AAA Authentication*

```
Router(config)#aaa authentication login myway tacacs+ radius local
Router(config)#aaa authentication login default tacacs+
Router(config)#line 1 12
Router(config-line)#login authentication myway
```

The first statement declares that list **myway** use TACACS+, and then RADIUS, and then local username/password pairs for authentication. The fourth statement declares on lines 1–12 that anyone attempting to log in to these interfaces is authenticated using the order specified in the list **myway**. Note that if someone attaches to the console port, he or she is authenticated by TACACS+ only because that is the default and because there is not a login authentication statement on the console port.

The term *listname* (defined as **myway** in Example 12-1) refers to the list of methods that will be used, not to a list of people that will be authenticated. In Example 12-1, the term can be interpreted as "my people will use this list for authentication."

The order of the authentication arguments is important. In Example 12-1, if the *user* fails authentication with TACACS+, he or she is denied access. If the *router* fails to access TACACS+, the router tries to contact a RADIUS server. The key issue is that a secondary method is used only if a previous method is unavailable to the router.

This key issue is important to remember because if **tacacs+** is the only option to verify a login and the TACACS+ service is unavailable or down, *nobody* can log in. If the authentication methods were set as **tacacs+** and **local**, administration username/password pairs could be placed on the router so that even if TACACS+ were down, an administrator can still gain access to the router.

It is important to maintain a proper order for the methods. You should make local a last resort method so that access to the router is maintained by at least a local username/password pair.

The following list describes each of the methods for login authentication. You should memorize this list for the exam.

- **line**—This method says to use the password that is on the line that is being attached to. This is done using the line command **login** (ask for a password) and the command **password** *xxx*, where *xxx* is the password for the line.

- **enable**—This method says to use the enable password for authentication on the interface. The authentication is compared against the enable password on the router.

- **local**—This method says to use the **username** *yyyy* **password** *xxxx* pairs that are on the router for authentication.

- **none**—This method says to not use an authentication method.

- **tacacs+**—This method says to use the TACACS server declared by the **tacacs-server host** *ip-address* statement on the router.

- **radius**—This method says to use the RADIUS server declared by the **radius-server host** *ip-address* statement on the router.

AAA Authentication Enable

What method is used if a user tries to access privileged mode on the router? If no AAA methods are set, the user must have the enable password. This password is demanded by the IOS. If AAA is being used and *no* default is set, the user also needs the enable password for access to the privileged mode.

The construct for AAA is similar to the login authentication commands. The following example shows the implementation of AAA authentication enable:

```
Router(config)#aaa authentication enable thefolks tacacs+ enable
```

This command declares that to gain access to privileged mode, TACACS+ is checked first and then only if TACACS+ returns an error or is unavailable is the enable password used. With all the lists that are set for AAA, the secondary methods are used only if the subsequently listed methods return an error or are unavailable. If the returned message is a "fail," the router does not try to authenticate using the subsequent method in the list.

The following list describes each of the methods for enabling authentication. You should memorize this for the exam.

- **enable**—This method says to use the enable password for authentication on the interface. The authentication is compared against the enable password on the router.

- **line**—This method says to use the password that is on the line that is being attached to. This is done using the line command **login** (ask for a password) and the command **password *xxx***, where *xxx* is the password for the line.

- **none**—This method says to not use an authentication method.

- **tacacs+**—This method says to use the TACACS server declared by the **tacacs-server host** *ip-address* statement on the router.

- **radius**—This method says to use the RADIUS server declared by the **radius-server host** *ip-address* statement on the router.

AAA Authentication ARAP

The **aaa authentication arap** command is used in conjunction with the **arap authentication** line configuration command. This describes the methods that are tried when AppleTalk Remote Access (ARA) users attempt to gain access to the router. Example 12-2 shows the configuration.

Example 12-2 *Declaring AAA Authentication with ARAP*

```
Router(config)#aaa authentication arap applefolk tacacs+ local
Router(config)#line 1 12
Router(config-line)#arap authentication applefolk
```

The first statement declares that TACACS+ and then the local username/password pairs are used if TACACS+ returns an error or is unavailable. On lines 1 through 12, the list points back to the AAA declaration in the first statement.

The following list describes each of the methods for authentication using AAA for ARAP. You should memorize this for the exam.

- **line**—This method says to use the password that is on the line that is being attached to. This is done using the line command **login** (ask for a password) and the command **password *xxx***, where *xxx* is the password for the line.

- **local**—This method says to use the **username** *yyyy* **password** *xxxx* pairs that are on the router for authentication.

- **tacas+**—This method says to use the TACACS server declared by the **tacacs-server host** *ip-address* statement on the router.

- **guest**—This method says to allow a login if the username is guest. This option is only valid using ARAP.

- **auth-guest**—This method says to allow the guest login only if the user has already logged into the EXEC process on the router and has now started the ARAP process.

It should be noted that by default, guest logins through ARAP are disabled when you initialize AAA. The **aaa authentication arap** command with either the **guest** or **auth-guest** keyword is required for guest access when using AAA.

AAA Authentication PPP

The **aaa authentication ppp** command is used in conjunction with the **ppp authentication** line configuration command to describe the methods that are tried when point-to-point (PPP) users attempt to gain access to the router. Example 12-3 shows this configuration.

Example 12-3 *Declaring AAA Authentication with PPP*

```
Router(config)#aaa authentication ppp pppfolk tacacs+ local
Router(config)#line 1 12
Router(config-line)#ppp authentication pppfolk
```

The same type of syntax is used throughout all AAA commands. With the **ppp** command, set the interface command **is ppp authentication** *option(s)*, where the options are the standard non-AAA options of **pap**, **chap**, **pap chap**, **chap pap**, or **ms-chap**. In addition, the AAA command methods can be used. In the previous example, the authentication is first TACACS+ and then local username/password pairs if TACACS+ is unavailable or returns an error.

The following list describes each of the methods for authentication using AAA for PPP. You should memorize this for the exam.

- **local**—This method says to use the **username** *yyyy* **password** *xxxx* pairs that are on the router for authentication.

- **none**—This method says to not use an authentication method.

- **tacacs+**—This method says to use the TACACS server declared by the **tacacs-server host** *ip-address* statement on the router.

- **radius**—This method says to use the RADIUS server declared by the **radius-server host** *ip-address* statement on the router.

- **krb5**—This method says that the Kerberos 5 method is available only for PPP operations, and communications with a Kerberos security server must be established. Kerberos login authentication works with PPP Password Authentication Protocol (PAP) only. The name Kerberos comes from Greek mythology and is the name of the three-headed dog that guarded the entrance of Hades.

- **if-needed**—This is another PPP-only option. It stops authentication if the user has been authenticated previously on the TTY line.

AAA Authentication NASI

The **aaa authentication nasi** command is used with the **nasi authentication** line configuration command to specify a list of authentication methods that are tried when a NASI user attempts to gain access to the router. Example 12-4 shows this configuration.

Example 12-4 *Declaring AAA Authentication with NASI*

```
Router(config)#aaa authentication nasi novellfolk tacacs+ local
Router(config)#line 1 12
Router(config-line)#nasi authentication novellfolk
```

As with the other access methods, when a user is using NASI, this example would require TACACS+ authentication and then would use the username/password pair if TACACS+ was unavailable.

The following list describes each of the methods for authentication using AAA for NASI. You should memorize this for the exam.

- **line**—This method says to use the password that is on the line that is being attached to. This is done using the line command **login** (ask for a password) and the command **password** *xxx*, where *xxx* is the password for the line.

- **enable**—This method says to use the enable password for authentication on the interface. The authentication is compared against the enable password on the router.

- **local**—This method says to use the **username** *yyyy* **password** *xxxx* pairs that are on the router for authentication.

- **none**—This method says to not use an authentication method.

- **tacacs+**—This method says to use the TACACS server declared by the **tacacs-server host** *ip-address* statement on the router.

When AAA is turned on, all lines and ports on the router use AAA; hence, the default group should be configured for any access method that the router will see.

AAA Authorization

Once a user has been authenticated, he or she can be further restricted in what he or she is allowed to do. This is done using the **aaa authorization** command. These restrictions can be applied to activities or services offered on the router.

As with the authentication, it is easier to see an example before diving into each option available. The syntax is quite simple and declares which activity or service (network, exec, command level, config-commands, and reverse-access) is being attempted and which method of authorization is to be used (**local**, **none**, **radius**, **tacacs+**, or **krb5**). Example 12-5 demonstrates the syntax for AAA authorization.

Example 12-5 *Applying Restrictions with AAA Authorization*

```
Router(config)#aaa new-model
Router(config)#aaa authentication login myfolk tacacs+ local
Router(config)#aaa authorization exec tacacs+ local
Router(config)#aaa authorization command 1 tacacs+ local
Router(config)#aaa authorization command 15 tacacs+ local
```

In the example, AAA is turned on with **aaa new-model,** and the authentication method is declared for the list called "myfolk". The third line declares that if one of the logged in users wants to gain access to the EXEC mode, TACACS+ is contacted to see if the user is allowed to perform that function.

The last two lines are similar. The logged in user is tested against the TACACS database for authorization to run level 1 and level 15 commands; the router IOS commands are either level 1 or level 15 commands. It is possible to change the level of each command on the router to allow for a more controlled access environment for the users.

The AAA has power, but the administrative overhead to use this power can be daunting to most administrators. In addition, this level of control can be unnecessary for most installations. As an example of this overhead, consider a common scenario in which AAA is set up so that subadministrators can have access to configuration mode, but with the ability to use only a subset of the commands. Although possible, the configuration on the router to change the level for each command can become less than productive.

The generic form of the authorization command is as follows:

aaa authorization *do-what? check-how?*

The *do-what?* arguments can be any of the following:

- **network**—This argument uses the *check-how?* method for authorization to perform all network-related service requests, that is, SLIP, PPP, and ARAP protocol.

- **exec**—This argument uses the *check-how?* method for authorization to determine if the user is allowed to create and run the router EXEC shell. If TACACS+ or RADIUS is being used, it is possible that the database could return autocommand information, such as menu system, to the user.

- **command level**—This argument uses the *check-how?* method for authorization of all commands at the specified privilege level. The level can be set to values of 1–15.

- **reverse-access**—This argument uses the *check-how?* method for authorization of reverse access connections such as reverse Telnet.

The *check-how?* arguments are the same as those used for authentication. *check-how?* simply points to where the authentication should be done. The *check-how?* arguments can be any of the following:

- **tacacs+**—In this argument, TACACS+ authorization is done by associating attribute-value (AV) pairs to individual users. The AV pair associates a function that the user is authorized to do. When a user attempts to do a *do-what?*, the TACACS database is checked.

- **if-authenticated**—In this argument, if the user has been authenticated, he or she is allowed to perform the function. Notice that we are not checking authorization, but whether the user is in the database and is valid.

- **none**—In this argument, the router does not request authorization information for the *do-what?*. Authorization is not performed and a query is not sent to the database.

- **local**—In this argument, the router or access server consults its local database, as defined by the use of the username/password pairs that are configured in global configuration mode on the router.

- **radius**—In this argument, RADIUS authorization is done by associating attributes to a username on the RADIUS server. Each username and the associated attributes are stored within the RADIUS database.

- **krb5-instance**—In this argument, the router queries the Kerberos server for authorization. The authorizations are stored on the Kerberos server.

In general, authorization can be implemented in many ways. The issue is finding which database or resource that has the AV pair or attribute or map to provide the router with the answer to the authorization query.

AAA Accounting

AAA accounting can supply information concerning user activity back to the database. This concept was especially helpful in the early days of Internet service when many ISPs offered 20 or 40 hours per week at a fixed cost and hourly or minute charges in excess of the specified timeframe. Today it is much more common for the ISP charge to be set for an unlimited access time. This does not, however, minimize the power of accounting to enable the administrator to track unauthorized attempts and proactively create security for system resources. In addition, accounting can be used to track resource usage to better allocate system usage.

Accounting is generally used for billing and auditing purposes and is simply turned on for those events that are to be tracked. As with explaining any authentication or authorization, an example is a good way to start. Syntactically, the commands follow this general syntax:

```
aaa accounting what-to-track how-to-track where-to-send-the-information
```

The *what-to-track* arguments are as follows:

- **network**—With this argument, network accounting logs the information, on a user basis, for PPP, SLIP, or ARAP sessions. The accounting information provides the time of access and the network resource usage in packet and byte counts.

- **connection**—With this argument, connection accounting logs the information about *outbound* connections made from the router or RAS device, including Telnet and rlogin sessions. The key word is outbound; it enables the tracking of connections made from the RAS device and where those connections were established.

- **exec**—With this argument, EXEC accounting logs the information about when a user creates an EXEC terminal session on the router. The information includes the IP address and telephone number, if it is a dial-in user, and the time and date of the access. This information can be particularly useful for tracking unauthorized access to the RAS device.

- **system**—With this argument, system accounting logs the information about system-level events. System-level events include AAA configuration changes and reloads for the device. Again, this information would be useful to track unauthorized access or tampering with the router.

- **command**—With this argument, command accounting logs information regarding which commands are being executed on the router. The accounting record contains a list of commands executed for the duration of the EXEC session, along with the time and date information.

As you can see, the amount of information that can be tracked is substantial. It is important that the administrator track only that information that is useful. Tracking of unwanted information can create a large overhead on the network resource.

The *how-to-track* argument can be any of the following:

- **start-stop**—The **start-stop** option sends an accounting record when the process begins. This is sent as a background process and the user request is begun without delay. When the user process is completed, the stop time and information is sent to the AAA database. This option is needed when an elapsed time of usage is required.

- **stop-only**—The **stop-only** option sends aggregated information based on the *what-to-track* at the end of the user process. This option can be used when only the *what-to-track* information is needed.

- **wait-start**—As mentioned, the **wait-start** option does not allow the user process to start until an acknowledgement is received from the accounting database engine by the RAS device. **wait-start** is particularly important when the tracked event can cause a loss of connectivity with the accounting database.

The last piece of information needed for the router or RAS is where to send the information that is being tracked. The *where-to-send-the-information* argument can be either of the following locations:

- **tacacs+**—When this option is used, the information is sent to the TACACS+ server defined by the **tacacs-server host** *ip-address* command.

- **radius**—When this option is used, the information is sent to the RADIUS server database defined by the **radius-server host** *ip-address* command. The current Cisco implementation does not support the command accounting feature.

Example 12-6 shows a simple accounting setup.

Example 12-6 *AAA Accounting Setup*

```
Router(config)#aaa accounting command 15 start-stop tacacs+
Router(config)#aaa accounting connection start-stop tacacs+
Router(config)#aaa accounting system wait-start tacacs+
```

In the first line, accounting has been activated for all level 15 commands to show when the command began and when it ended for the user that initiated the command. The second line logs to the database when the user's connection began and when it ended. In the last statement, any system-level events, such as a reload or configuration change, are tracked by start and end time.

The **wait-start** argument assures that the logging of the start of the system event is acknowledged before the event is allowed to start. The key issue here is that if the event is a reload of the router, it is imperative that the event be logged and acknowledged before the router reloads. If the message is missed or lost in transmission, the event would go unrecorded.

The basics of accounting are that the accounting records are sent to a TACACS+ server or a RADIUS server. In addition, the records that are to be tracked should be recorded to the router with the AAA accounting commands.

Accounting is a powerful tool for proactive management of network resources; however, it is a double-edged sword. The more accounting, the more resources are used to accomplish the accounting. It is generally recommended that the **stop-only** argument be used if an elapsed time is not needed.

The format of accounting records depends on the AAA software that is being used. The treatment of AAA within the confines of the BCRAN class is intended to give the student a basic understanding of AAA. All AAA software engines can provide the same or similar functionality; it is impossible to describe the intricacies of an individual software suite as the standard for AAA.

Virtual Profiles

The next evolution of the dialer profile is the creation of a virtual profile. Virtual profile information can be kept on an AAA server and associated with a user. The key elements to the virtual profile are as follows:

- **The physical interface specification**—This information is maintained on the router or RAS device and is generic for any outbound connection.

- **The generic information about a connection that is stored in a template on the router or access device**—This enables the physical interface to be divorced from the connection-specific information.

- **The user-specific information that is stored on the AAA server**—This information is specific to the user and the connection and can be managed and maintained in a central location, as shown in Figure 12-2

Figure 12-2   *Virtual Profile Components*

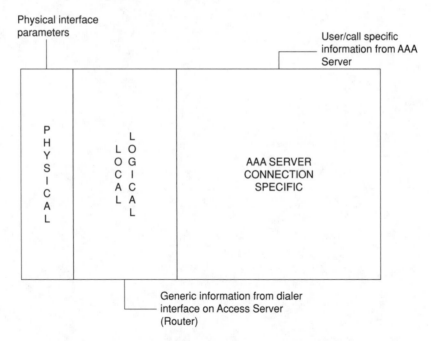

When a user has gained access to the RAS device and initiates an outbound connection, the AAA server can provide detailed information on how to handle the user-specific connection. The evolution is then complete. The router maintains the resource, and the AAA server provides the information about the connection on a user-by-user basis. In this way, the router administrator need only provide a resource and not the details regarding the use of it.

Once the user has gained access to the remote access server by passing authentication, the user then requests an interface to create a session. If the authorization is passed, the AAA server provides the virtual template on behalf of the user, and the connection is established with the user-specific connection information.

Virtual profiles provide the latest evolution for remote access. Throughout this book, the connections made from an access server have gone from a unique phone number assigned to an interface to a group of numbers associated with an interface with the **dialer-map** command to dialer profiles. The last step, virtual profiles, completely disassociates the router from maintaining the information about a remote connection.

For more information on virtual profiles, the Cisco Firewall and Securities class offers an in-depth discussion of this topic. For independent study, you can turn to "Dial Solutions Command Reference," for Cisco IOS Release 12.0, on the Cisco Documentation CD.

Foundation Summary

The Foundation Summary is a collection of information that provides a convenient review of many key concepts in this chapter. For those of you already comfortable with the topics in this chapter, this summary could help you recall a few details. For those of you who just read this chapter, this review should help solidify some key facts. For any of you doing your final preparation before the exam, these tables and figures will hopefully be a convenient way to review the day before the exam.

The general syntax for AAA authentication is as follows:

```
aaa authentication [login | enable | arap | ppp | nasi] method
```

Each of the arguments for the **aaa authentication command** specifies how the user is accessing the router. Is it locally through a physical port (login) or is it through a dial facility encapsulated for Novell, Apple, or PPP (NASI, ARAP, or PPP)?

The list that follows documents each valid command argument and the question that is being answered by that argument:

- **aaa authentication login**—How do I authenticate the login dialog?

- **aaa authentication enable**—Can the user get to the privileged command prompt?

- **aaa authentication arap**—This command answers this question: Does the AppleTalk Remote Access Protocol (ARAP) user use RADIUS or TACACS+? (One must be selected.)

- **aaa authentication ppp**—What method should be used if a user is coming over a PPP connection?

- **aaa authentication nasi**—What method should be used if a user is coming over NASI?

The general syntax for the **aaa authorization** command is as follows:

```
aaa authorization do-what? check-how?
```

The *do-what?* arguments can be any of the following:

- network

- exec

- command level

- reverse-access

The *check-how?* arguments can be any of the following:

- if-authenticated

- tacacs+

- none
- local
- radius
- krb5-instance

The general syntax for the **aaa accounting** command is as follows:

```
aaa accounting what-to-track how-to-track where-to-send-the-information
```

The *what-to-track* arguments are as follows:

- network
- connection
- exec
- system

The *how-to-track* argument can be any of the following:

- start-stop
- stop-only
- wait-start

The *where-to-send-the-information* argument can be either of the following locations:

- tacacs+
- radius

The two types of access methods into a router are as follows:

- **Character mode**—This method sends keystrokes to the router through the TTY, VTY, AUX, and CON ports for configuration or query commands.

- **Packet mode**—This method uses interface mode or a link protocol session to communicate with a device other than the router. These defined interfaces are async, group-async, BRI, PRI, serial, dialer profiles, and dialer rotaries.

Q&A

The questions and scenarios in this book are more difficult than what you should experience on the actual exam. The questions do not attempt to cover more breadth or depth than the exam; however, they are designed to make sure that you know the answer. Rather than allowing you to derive the answer from clues hidden inside the question itself, the questions challenge your understanding and recall of the subject.

Questions from the "Do I Know This Already?" quiz from the beginning of the chapter are repeated here to ensure that you have mastered the chapter's topic areas. Hopefully, these questions will help limit the number of exam questions on which you narrow your choices to two options and then guess.

The answers to these questions can be found in Appendix A, on page 397.

1 What does AAA stand for?

   _____

   _____

   _____

2 What ports operate in character mode on the router?

   _____

   _____

   _____

3 When enabling AAA for TACACS+, what does the argument *single-connection* do?

   _____

   _____

   _____

4 What is *authentication*?

   _____

   _____

   _____

5 What is the difference between character mode and packet mode?

   _____

   _____

   _____

6 What does the command **aaa authentication enable** do on the router?

_____

_____

_____

7 AAA has been enabled for the router, but there is no authentication method declared on the console port. What is the result?

_____

_____

_____

8 What communication method—packet or character—is used on the console port of a router?

_____

_____

_____

9 What are the five authentication modes on a router?

_____

_____

_____

10 What authentication method is used on an interface without an AAA-defined method?

_____

_____

_____

11 What is the consequence of not having an authorization statement for level 15 commands if AAA has been enabled on the router?

_____

_____

_____

12 To ensure that the use of the **shutdown** command is recorded to the AAA database, what command should you use?

_____

_____

_____

13 What is the command to enable AAA using RADIUS?

_____

_____

_____

14 What is *authorization*?

_____

_____

_____

15 What does the argument *start-stop* mean when using AAA accounting?

_____

_____

_____

16 What command is used to enable AAA on a router?

_____

_____

_____

17 What is Kerberos?

_____

_____

_____

18 What commands, when tracked, should use the *wait-start* argument?

_____

_____

_____

19 Virtual profiles enable the router administrator to...

a. provide a resource without knowing details about the connection

b. check the AAA server to see if a connection should be made

c. back up interface parameters on a TACACS server

_____

_____

_____

20 What is stored in a virtual profile?

_____

_____

_____

Scenarios

The following scenario and questions are designed to draw together the content of the chapter and exercise your understanding of the concepts. There is not necessarily a right answer. The thought process and practice in manipulating each of the concepts is the goal of this section.

Scenario 12-1

You are the administrator of a RAS and you want to ensure that all users that are using the router to gain access to the network are authenticated on an AAA device using RADIUS. In addition, you want anyone who has console or AUX access that might be configuring the router to be authenticated on the AAA device unless communication to the AAA device fails. In addition, you want to ensure a backdoor for administrators.

All level 15 commands should be tracked when used. Administrators should gain access through the console, through AUX, and occasionally through Telnet. Users should only attach to the router using PPP. Given this setup, answer the questions that follow.

1   What would be the router configuration given an AAA address of 123.123.123.123 using a password of AAAsecret?

2   You now have to allow access to a group of users that will be accessing a Novell service using the NASI client software. What additional commands need to be added to your original configuration?

3   You now have to allow the database to track the connection time for all PPP users. What additional commands need to be added to your configuration?

Scenario Answers

The answers provided in this section are not necessarily the only possible correct answers. They merely represent one possibility for the scenario. The intention is to test your base knowledge and understanding of the concepts discussed in this chapter.

Should your answers be different (as they possibly will be), consider the differences. Are your answers in line with the concepts of the answers provided and explained here? If not, go back and read the chapter again, focusing on the sections related to the problem scenario.

Scenario 12-1 Answers

1 The router configuration given an AAA address of 123.123.123.123 using a password of AAAsecret would be as follows:

```
Router(config)#aaa new-model
Router(config)#radius-server host 123.123.123.123
Router(config)#radius-server key AAAsecret

Router(config)#aaa authentication login admins radius local
Router(config)#aaa authentication login default radius
Router(config)#aaa authentication ppp default radius
Router(config)#aaa accounting command 15 wait-start radius
Router(config)#line 1 5
Router(config-line)#aaa authentication admins
Router(config)#line con 0
Router(config-line)#aaa authentication admins
Router(config)#line aux 0
Router(config-line)#aaa authentication admins
```

2 To allow access to a group of users that will be accessing a Novell service using the NASI client software, you would add the following command to your original configuration:

```
Router(config)#aaa authentication nasi default radius
```

3 To allow the database to track the connection time for all PPP users, you would add the following command to your original configuration:

```
Router(config)#aaa accounting connection start-stop radius
```

Answers to the "Do I Know This Already?" Quizzes and Q&A Sections

Answers to Chapter 2 "Do I Know This Already?" Quiz

1 *What are the selection criteria for selecting a router platform?*

Availability, bandwidth, cost, ease of management, applications and traffic patterns, backup needs and QOS, and access control requirements are the selection criteria.0.

2 *Which of the following does not affect the installation of a router?*

a. availability

b. reliability

c. cost

d. router port density

e. security requirements

f. bandwidth usage

The answer is d, router port density. The router, and thus its port density, is selected after the requirements are established.

3 *In routing, what is meant by the term* availability?

Availability describes whether a WAN service is offered in a given area and whether it can be selected for use. For instance, if ISDN is not offered in a location, it is not available, even though it is a valid choice.

4 *In routing, what is meant by the term* reliability?

Reliability is the term for how often a WAN service must be available. For instance, do you require a backup link in the case of a primary link failure? Does dial-on-demand routing (DDR) suffice for a particular application? These questions should be asked when evaluating reliability from a design perspective.

5 *Name two important issues that you must consider when selecting a product for a SOHO.*

You must consider cost and availability. Cost is always a factor to the smaller office, and availability dictates what service is possible.

6 *What product would you select for a central office facility that had to support three to five branch offices using Frame Relay circuits from 64–256 Kbps and that had 20–30 occasional dial-up users?*

The best choice is the 3600 series router. For instance, the 3640 router with a PRI and a Mica modem bank would satisfy the occasional dial-in users and enable the Frame Relay connections.

Answers to Chapter 2 Q&A Section

1 *What are the selection criteria for selecting a router platform?*

Availability, bandwidth, cost, ease of management, applications and traffic patterns, backup needs and QOS, and access control requirements are the selection criteria.

2 *Which of the following does not affect the installation of a router?*

a. availability

b. reliability

c. cost

d. router port density

e. security requirements

f. bandwidth usage

The answer is d, router port density. The router, and thus its port density, is selected after the requirements are established.

3 *Of the 3600, 4800, 5300, and 7100 series routers, which provides a high dial-up port density for an ISP?*

The 3600 provides a high dial-up port density for an ISP.

4 *Which of the following statements is true?*

a. All interface cards used in the 2600 can be used in the 1600.

b. All interface cards used in the 1600 can be used in the 2600.

c. All interface cards used in the 3600 can be used in the 1600.

d. All interface cards used in the 3600 can be used in the 2600.

The answer is b. All interface cards used in the 1600 can be used in the 2600.

5 *In routing, what is meant by the term* availability?

Availability describes whether a WAN service is offered in a given area and whether it can be selected for use. For instance, if ISDN is not offered in a location, it is not available, even though it is a valid choice.

6 *In routing, what is meant by the term* reliability?

Reliability is the term for how often a WAN service must be available. For instance, do you require a backup link in the case of a primary link failure? Does DDR suffice for a particular application? These questions should be asked when evaluating reliability from a design perspective.

7 *Backup is a consideration when looking at which of the following criteria: availability, reliability, traffic patterns, or QoS?*

Backup is a consideration when looking at reliability.

8 *What WAN connection method affords the most control for the consumer?*

Leased lines offer the most control for the consumer because they never produce a busy signal. In addition, the only data that travel over the link are the customer's data.

9 *Name two important issues in the selection of a product for a SOHO.*

Cost and availability are important issues. Cost is always a factor to the smaller office, and availability dictates what service is possible.

10 *What WAN methods offer the least control to the customer?*

Asynchronous communications and dialup do not provide a method to circumvent a busy condition. If the remote location is not answering, the calling location has no way to break into the location. It is important to remember that the concept of control is not local, but remote, and the customer will want to control the far end availability. With a leased line, the consumer owns both ends of the facility and they can't be used for other purposes. With a dial-up facility, the user can only make a call and hope the other end answers.

11 *What product would you select for a central office facility that had to support three to five branch offices using Frame Relay circuits from 64–256 Kbps and that had 20–30 occasional dial-up users?*

The best choice is the 3600 series router. For instance, the 3640 router with a PRI and a Mica modem bank would satisfy the occasional dial-up users and enable the Frame Relay connections.

12 *What router would be appropriate for a SOHO user who is using ISDN and who is very cost-conscious?*

The 700 series router would be appropriate.

13 *A branch office must connect to the central site over Frame Relay at 64 kbps. No growth is expected for the next two years, at which time Frame Relay connectivity for two satellite sites will be added at 64 kbps. What router platform would you recommend?*

The 3600 series router is recommended.

14 *The administration is considering supplying routers for all their ISDN dial-up users. The network administrators are comfortable with the IOS and must implement the dialup for 20 users over the next few months. What equipment would you propose for the central office and the SOHOs?*

800s at the SOHOs and a 3600 at the central office are recommended.

Answers to Chapter 3 "Do I Know This Already?" Quiz

1 *Which router is best used as a central site router: 2611, 3640, or 1004?*

The 3640 router provides more power than the 2611 or 1004. Therefore, it is the best choice of the three for a central site router.

2 *Which router best serves as a small office or home office (SOHO) router for telecommuters: 7200, 700, or 7500?*

The 700 router is best suited for the role of a SOHO router. The 7200 and 7500 routers are suited for roles as core routers.

3 *Which WAN technology is best suited for providing high-density dial-up access for remote users?*

Primary Rate Interface (PRI) is best suited due to the number of independent access channels it makes available to users.

4 *Which WAN technology is best suited for variable bandwidth (low-speed to high-speed) deployments that enable the connection of multiple branch offices to a central site?*

Frame Relay is typically deployed in a hub and spoke topology and allows for 56-kbps to 45-Mbps connectivity.

5 *What does a green LINK LED signify on an Ethernet interface?*

A green LINK LED signifies that the connection to the Ethernet network has been properly established.

6 *On a 1600 router, what is the CD LED?*

The CD LED is the Carrier Detect indicator. This light signifies that the service provider signal is being received on the interface.

Answers to Chapter 3 Q&A Section

1 *Which router is best used as a central site router: 2611, 3640, or 1004?*

The 3640 router provides more power than the 2611 or 1004. Therefore, it is the best choice of the three for a central site router.

2 *Which router best serves as a small office or home office (SOHO) router for telecommuters: 7200, 700, or 7500?*

The 700 router is best suited for the role of a SOHO router. The 7200 and 7500 routers are suited for roles as core routers.

3 *Which WAN technology is best suited for providing high-density dial-up access for remote users?*

Primary Rate Interface (PRI) is best suited due to the number of independent access channels it makes available to users.

4 *Which WAN technology is best suited for variable bandwidth (low-speed to high-speed) deployments that enable the connection of multiple branch offices to a central site?*

Frame Relay is typically deployed in a hub and spoke topology and enables 56-kbps to 45-Mbps connectivity.

5 *What does a green LINK LED signify on an Ethernet interface?*

A green LINK LED signifies that the connection to the Ethernet network has been properly established.

6 *On a 1600 router, what is the CD LED?*

The CD LED is the Carrier Detect indicator. This light signifies that service provider signal is being received on the interface.

7 *List four routers that would be suitable for use as central site routers.*

The suitable routers are 7200, 3640, 4000, AS5300, and 12000 (although not discussed).

8 *List three routers that would be suitable for use as branch office routers.*

The suitable routers are 1600, 1700, 2500, 2600, and 3620. There are others.

9 *List a possible cause of an OK LED not being green on a 1600 router.*

If the OK LED is not green, this indicates that the router failed one or more portions of the boot sequence and is possibly functioning improperly.

10 *List a possible cause of a LINK LED not being lit on an Ethernet interface.*

If there is no LINK light, the cause is fairly simple. Either there is no cable attached, or the cable is bad. Another possible cause is lack of power to the hub or switch to which the router is attached.

Answers to Chapter 4 "Do I Know This Already?" Quiz

1 *What pins are used for modem control?*

Pins 6, 8, and 20 are used for modem control.

2 *What is the standard for DCE/DTE signaling?*

The standard is EIA/TIA 232.

3 *In character mode using reverse Telnet, what is the command to connect to the first async port on a 2509 router that has a loopback interface of 192.168.1.1?*

telnet 192.168.1.1 2001

4 *What port range is reserved for accessing an individual port using binary mode?*

The port range is 6000–6999.

5 *If a four-port serial (A/S) module is in the second slot on a 3640 router, what are the line numbers for each port?*

The second slot would be slot 1 because the slots are counted 0, 1, 2, and then 3. Therefore, the ports would be 33, 34, 35, and 36.

6 *What is the AUX port line number on a 3620 series router?*

The AUX port would be line 65.

7 *What does the **physical-line async** command do and on what interfaces would you apply it?*

The **physical-line async** command places a serial (A/S) interface into asynchronous mode so that it can be used for dialing. It would be used only on an A/S interface.

8 *In what configuration mode must you be to configure the physical properties of an asynchronous interface?*

You must be in line configuration mode.

9 *When should **modem autoconfigure discovery** be used? What happens when you use it?*

modem autoconfigure discovery should be used only when you are physically not near the modem and do not know what type it is. After autoconfigure learns the modem type, the modem should be configured to reduce the CPU usage on the router.

10 *Which of the following commands would you use to add an entry to a modemcap database called newmodem?*

a. **edit modemcap newmodem**

b. **modemcap edit newmodem**

    c. **modemcap edit type newmodem**

    d. **modemcap add newmodem**

The answer is c, **modemcap edit type newmodem**.

11 *List four reasons why you would use a chat script.*

You would use it to initialize a modem, provide a modem with a dial string, log in to a remote system, or execute a set of commands on a remote system.

12 *Which of the following would trigger a chat script start?*

    a. Line reset

    b. DDR

    c. Line activation

    d. Manual

The answer is a, b, c, and d.

Answers to Chapter 4 Q&A Section

1 *What pins are used for modem control?*

Pins 6, 8, and 20 are used for modem control.

2 *What is the standard for DCE/DTE signaling?*

The standard is EIA/TIA 232.

3 *If the user wants to terminate a call, what pin does the DTE device drop to signal the modem?*

It drops the DTR pin.

4 *What must be done to terminate a reverse Telnet session with an attached modem?*

You must press Ctrl+Shift+6, press x, and then execute a disconnect.

5 *In character mode using reverse Telnet, what is the command to connect to the first async port on a 2509 router that has a loopback interface of 192.168.1.1?*

telnet 192.168.1.1 2001

6 *Which interface is line 97 on a 3640 series router?*

    a. S 0/97

    b. S 3/1

    c. S 2/1

    d. S 097

Line 97 corresponds to slot 3, line 1, which is written as S 2/1. The answer is c.

7 *What port range is reserved for accessing an individual port using binary mode?*

The 6000–6999 range is reserved.

8 *When flow control is enabled, which pins are used?*

The RTS and CTS pins are used.

9 *If a four-port serial (A/S) module is in the second slot on a 3640 router, what are the line numbers for each port?*

The second slot would be slot 1 because the slots are counted 0, 1, 2, and then 3. Therefore, the ports would be 33, 34, 35, and 36.

10 *What is the **AT** command to return a router to factory default settings?*

    a. **AT Default**

    b. **AT@F**

    c. **AT&F**

    d. **ATZ**

The answer is c, the **AT&F** command

11 *What is the AUX port line number on a 3620 series router?*

The AUX port line number would be line 65.

12 *Which of the following commands configure a router for use with a Viva modem?*

    a. **modem autoconfigure viva**

    b. **modem configure type viva**

    c. **modem autoconfigure type viva**

    d. **modem autoconfigure discovery type viva**

The answer is c, the **modem autoconfigure type viva** command

13 *What does the **physical-line async** command do and on what interfaces would you apply it?*

The **physical-line async** command places a serial (A/S) interface into asynchronous mode so that it can be used for dialing. It would be used only on an A/S interface.

14 *In what configuration mode must you be to configure the physical properties of an asynchronous interface?*

You must be in line configuration mode.

15 *What does it mean when the signal pin RTS is asserted?*

It means that the DTE has available buffer space.

16 *What is the command to manually begin a chat script named remcon?*

start-script remcon

17 *When should modem autoconfigure discovery be used, and what are the ramifications of doing so?*

modem autoconfigure discovery should be used only when you are physically not near the modem and do not know what type it is. After autoconfigure learns the modem type, the modem should be configured to reduce the CPU usage on the router.

18 *What command would you use to add an entry to the modemcap database called newmodem?*

modemcap edit type newmodem

19 *Which interface type provides clocking for a line?*

DCE provides clocking for a line.

20 *List four reasons why you would use a chat script.*

You would use it to initialize a modem, provide a modem with a dial string, log in to a remote system, or execute a set of commands on a remote system.

21 *What command can be used to determine whether Serial 0 is the DCE or DTE?*

show controller S0

22 *What command lists the transmit and receive speeds for the asynchronous ports on the router?*

show line

23 *On which pins does the DTE device send and receive?*

It transmits on pin 2 and receives on pin 3.

24 *Which of the following would trigger a chat script start?*

a. Line reset

b. DDR

c. Line activation

d. Manual

The answer is a, b, c, and d.

Answers to Chapter 5 "Do I Know This Already?" Quiz

1 *Where is PPP typically implemented?*

PPP is typically implemented on ISDN lines; however, it is also used in point-to-point dedicated circuits.

2 *What is the function of the LCP?*

The PPP LCP provides a method of establishing, configuring, maintaining, and terminating a point-to-point connection.

3 *What is the difference between interactive and dedicated asynchronous implementations?*

Interactive asynchronous (async) implementations enable the dial-up user to see and access the router prompt. Dedicated asynchronous implementations force the connection directly into a PPP session.

4 *List the four PPP LCP negotiable options.*

The four options are Authentication, Callback, Compression and Multilink.

5 *List the two supported authentication types with PPP.*

The two types are PAP and CHAP.

6 *In PPP Callback implementations, which router is in charge of the authentication challenge as well as the disconnect of the initial call?*

The server router issues the authentication challenge and disconnects the call so that the callback can be placed.

7 *What command shows the status of individual B channels at any given time?*

show dialer

8 *What command enables the real-time viewing of CHAP communications?*

debug ppp authentication

9 *What command enables the real-time viewing of dial events?*

debug dialer

Answers to Chapter 5 Q&A Section

1 *Where is PPP typically implemented?*

It is typically implemented on ISDN lines; however, it is also used in point-to-point dedicated circuits.

2 *What is the function of the LCP?*

The PPP LCP provides a method of establishing, configuring, maintaining, and terminating a point-to-point connection.

3 *What is the difference between interactive and dedicated asynchronous implementations?*

Interactive async implementations enable the dial-up user to see and access the router prompt. Dedicated async implementations force the connection directly into a PPP session.

4 *List the 4 PPP LCP negotiable options.*

The four options are Authentication, Callback, Compression, and Multilink.

5 *List the two supported authentication types with PPP.*

The two types are PAP and CHAP.

6 *In PPP Callback implementations, which router is in charge of the authentication challenge as well as the disconnect of the initial call?*

The server router issues the authentication challenge and disconnects the call so that the callback can be placed.

7 *What command shows the status of individual B channels at any given time?*

show dialer

8 *What command enables the real-time viewing of CHAP communications?*

debug ppp authentication

9 *What command enables the real-time viewing of dial events?*

debug dialer

10 *Describe the PPP Callback procedure.*

The client initiates a call to the server. The server answers and issues an authentication challenge. If successful, the server disconnects and dials the client back. Once again, authentication takes place. If successful, the call proceeds and data transfer can begin.

11 *What are the supported compression types on Cisco routers?*

The supported types are Stac, Predictor, MPPC, and TCP header compression.

12 *Which command, used with callback, ensures that a callback is made only to a properly configured client?*

dialer callback-secure

13 *What command informs a router that it is to be a callback client?*

ppp callback request

14 *What command informs a router that it is to be a callback server?*

ppp callback accept

15 *What is the default time interval between CHAP challenges?*

Two minutes

16 *In the event of PPP authentication failure, what happens to the call?*

The call is immediately disconnected.

Answers to Chapter 6 "Do I Know This Already?" Quiz

1 *List the two most common implementations of ISDN.*

The two most common implementations of ISDN are BRI and PRI.

2 *List the number of bearer channels for BRI, T1 PRI, and E1 PRI.*

The numbers are BRI = 2, T1 PRI = 23, and E1 PRI = 30.

3 *What type of information is carried over the D channel?*

Signaling (and sometimes data, depending on the implementation) is carried over the D channel.

4 *List the specifications that define Layer 2 and Layer 3 of ISDN.*

The specifications are Layer 2 = Q.921 and Layer 3 = Q.931.

5 *When is it necessary to use **dialer in-band** in an ISDN BRI configuration?*

When the router does not have a native BRI interface, a terminal adapter must be placed between it and the NT1. The **dialer in-band** command must be used to utilize bandwidth from each B channel for signaling.

6 *What is the difference between a router with a BRI S/T interface and one with a BRI U interface?*

BRI S/T interfaces do not have an integrated NT1, whereas BRI U interfaces do include an integrated NT1.

7 *Write out the commands to define only Telnet and FTP as interesting traffic for DDR.*

The following commands define only Telnet and FTP as interesting traffic for DDR:

```
access-list 100 permit tcp any any eq 23
access-list 100 permit tcp any any eq 20
access-list 100 permit tcp any any eq 21
dialer-list 1 protocol ip list 100
```

8 *List two of the most common encapsulations available for use on BRI interfaces.*

Two of the most common encapsulations available for use on BRI interfaces are PPP and HDLC.

9 *An interface that has been configured not to send routing updates is known as what type of interface?*

The interface is a passive interface.

10 *When using rotary groups, what should determine the dialer interface number?*

The logical dialer interface number must match the rotary-group number defined on each physical interface.

11 *What technology is used to provide redundancy for WAN links?*

Dial backup is used to provide redundancy.

12 *DDR traditionally involves the use of static routes. If static routes are not desired, what technology can be implemented?*

You can implement snapshot routing.

13 *What information is required of the telco to implement PRI implementations?*

The telco must provide the switch type, the framing, and the line code.

14 *List the options available for T1 and E1 framing and line code configuration.*

The available options are T1 = AMI/B8ZS and SF/ESF, E1 = AMI/HDB3, and CRC4/No-CRC4.

15 *List the command to have the router forward all incoming voice calls to internal MICA technology modems.*

isdn incoming-voice modem

Answers to Chapter 6 Q&A Section

1 *List the two most common implementations of ISDN.*

The two most common implementations are BRI and PRI.

2 *List the number of bearer channels for BRI, T1 PRI and E1 PRI.*

The numbers are BRI = 2, T1 PRI = 23, and E1 PRI = 30.

3 *What type of information is carried over the D channel?*

Signaling (and sometimes data, depending on the implementation) is carried over the D channel.

4 *List the specifications that define Layer 2 and Layer 3 of ISDN.*

The specifications are Layer 2 = Q.921 and Layer 3 = Q.931.

5 *When is it necessary to use* **dialer in-band** *in an ISDN BRI configuration?*

When the router does not have a native BRI interface, a terminal adapter must be placed between it and the NT1. The **dialer in-band** command must be used to utilize bandwidth from each B channel for sigaling.

6 *What is the difference between a router with a BRI S/T interface and one with a BRI U interface?*

BRI S/T interfaces do not have an integrated NT1; whereas, BRI U interfaces do include an integrated NT1.

7 *Write out the commands to define only Telnet and FTP as interesting traffic for DDR.*

The following commands define only Telnet and FTP as interesting traffic for DDR:

```
access-list 100 permit tcp any any eq 23
access-list 100 permit tcp any any eq 20
access-list 100 permit tcp any any eq 21
dialer-list 1 protocol ip list 100
```

8 *List two of the most common encapsulations available for use on BRI interfaces.*

Two of the most common encapsulations available for use on BRI interfaces are PPP and HDLC.

9 *An interface that has been configured not to send routing updates is known as what type of interface?*

The interface is a passive interface.

10 *When using rotary groups, what should determine the dialer interface number?*

The logical dialer interface number must match the rotary-group number defined on each physical interface.

11 *What technology is used to provide redundancy for WAN links?*

Dial backup is used to provide redundancy.

12 *DDR traditionally involves the use of static routes. If static routes are not desired, what technology can be implemented?*

You can implement snapshot routing.

13 *What information is required of the telco to implement PRI implementations?*

The telco must supply the switch type, the framing, and the line code.

14 *List the options available for T1 and E1 framing and line code configuration.*

The available options are T1 = AMI/B8ZS and SF/ESF, E1 = AMI/HDB3, and CRC4/No-CRC4.

15 *List the command to have the router forward all incoming voice calls to internal MICA technology modems.*

isdn incoming-voice modem

16 *Describe the key difference between Cisco's bandwidth on demand and Multilink PPP.*

BOD does not make use of a standardized implementation; it is Cisco-proprietary. The implementation of BOD simply requires the entry of a **dialer load-threshold** command. PPP Multilink is a standardized implementation of load sharing technologies. Once the **dialer load-threshold** command has been entered, enter the **ppp multilink** command to activate the standardized version.

17 *Create an access list that specifies HTTP and any ICMP traffic as interesting.*

```
access-list 100 permit tcp any any eq http
access-list 100 permit icmp any any
dialer-list 1 protocol ip list 100
```

Use Figure A-1 to answer the remaining questions.

18 *Configure router A such that any IP traffic causes an ISDN call to be placed.*

```
dialer-list 1 protocol ip permit
```

Figure A-1 *Network Diagram for Use with Q&A*

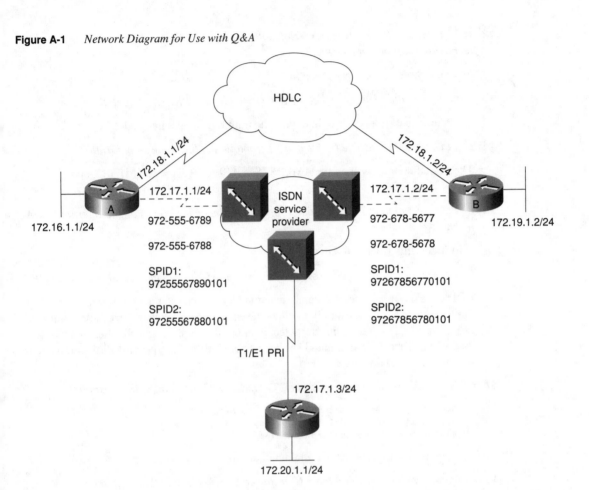

19 *Configure both routers A and B for dynamic routing using RIP and for static routing between networks 172.16.1.0 and 172.19.1.0. Assume the use of only the ISDN network at this time. Make sure no dynamic routes are being sent out the BRI0 interface.*

```
!RouterA
ip route 172.19.1.0 255.255.255.0 172.17.1.2
router rip
network 172.16.0.0
network 172.17.0.0
network 172.18.0.0
passive-interface bri0

!RouterB
ip route 172.16.1.0 255.255.255.0 172.17.1.1
router rip
network 172.17.0.0
network 172.18.0.0
network 172.19.0.0
passive-interface bri0
```

20 *Configure both routers A and B for basic DDR connectivity using dialer maps. Use basic-ni1 for the switch type. Include the configuration parameters from Questions 3 and 4.*

```
!RouterA
isdn switch-type basic-ni1
interface e0
ip address 172.16.1.1 255.255.255.0
interface bri0
encapsulation ppp
ip address 172.17.1.1 255.255.255.0
dialer map ip 172.17.1.2 broadcast 9726785677
dialer map ip 172.17.1.2 broadcast 9726785678
ppp Multilink
isdn spid1 97255567890101 9724446789
isdn spid2 97255567880101 9725556788
router rip
network 172.16.0.0
network 172.17.0.0
network 172.18.0.0
passive-interface bri0
exit
ip route 172.19.1.0 255.255.255.0 172.17.1.2
dialer-list 1 protocol ip permit

!RouterB
isdn switch-type basic-ni1
Interface e0
ip address 172.19.1.2 255.255.255.0
interface bri0
encapsulation ppp
ip address 172.17.1.2 255.255.255.0
dialer map ip 172.17.1.1 broadcast 9725556789
dialer map ip 172.17.1.1 broadcast 9725556788
ppp Multilink
isdn spid1 97267856770101 9726785677
isdn spid2 97267856780101 9726785678
exit
router rip
network 172.17.0.0
network 172.18.0.0
network 172.19.0.0
passive-interface bri0
exit
ip route 172.16.1.0 255.255.255.0 172.17.1.1
dialer-list 1 protocol ip permit
```

21 *Configure both routers A and B so that a second B channel is initialized if the first reaches 50 percent saturation in either direction. Also, the call should disconnect after 30 seconds of idle time. Note: This is not a dial backup situation.*

```
!RouterA
interface bri0
dialer load-threshold 127
dialer idle-timeout 30

!RouterB
interface bri0
dialer load-threshold 127
dialer idle-timeout 30
```

22 *Configure Router C for T1 PRI connectivity using B8ZS and ESF. Configure the appropriate IP addressing on interface S 0:23.*

```
!RouterC
controller t1 0
framing esf
linecode b8zs
pri-group timeslots 1-23
interface s0:23
ip address 172.17.1.3 255.255.255.0
```

23 *Now assume that Router C is being implemented in an E1 environment using the default settings for framing and linecode. Make the appropriate configuration changes.*

```
!RouterC
controller e1 0
framing crc4
linecode hdb3
pri-group timeslots 1-30
interface s0:15
ip address 172.17.1.3 255.255.255.0
```

24 *Remove the static routes between A and B. Implement a solution that enables dynamic routing without keeping the link up constantly.*

```
!RouterA
isdn switch-type basic-ni1
Interface e0
ip address 172.16.1.1 255.255.255.0
interface bri0
encapsulation ppp
ip address 172.17.1.1 255.255.255.0
dialer map ip 172.17.1.2 broadcast 9726785677
dialer map ip 172.17.1.2 broadcast 9726785678
dialer load-threshold 127
snapshot server 5 dialer
dialer map snapshot 1 name RouterB 9726785677
ppp Multilink
isdn spid1 97255567890101 9725556789
isdn spid2 97255567880101 9725556788
```

```
router rip
network 172.16.0.0
network 172.17.0.0
network 172.18.0.0
passive-interface bri0
exit
dialer-list 1 protocol ip permit

!RouterB
isdn switch-type basic-ni1
Interface e0
ip address 172.19.1.2 255.255.255.0
interface bri0
encapsulation ppp
ip address 172.17.1.2 255.255.255.0
dialer map ip 172.17.1.1 broadcast 9725556789
dialer map ip 172.17.1.1 broadcast 9725556788
dialer load-threshold 127
snapshot client 5 720 dialer
dialer map snapshot 1 name RouterA 9725556789
ppp Multilink
isdn spid1 97267856770101 9726785677
isdn spid2 97267856780101 9726785678
exit
router rip
network 172.17.0.0
network 172.18.0.0
network 172.19.0.0
passive-interface bri0
exit
dialer-list 1 protocol ip permit
```

25 *Configure Router A and B so that the ISDN link is activated only in cases in which the HDLC link is down or has reached 85 percent capacity. The backup timers for failure are at your discretion.*

```
!RouterA
interface serial 0
ip address 172.18.1.1 255.255.255.0
backup interface bri 0
backup delay 5 60
backup load 85 4
interface bri0
encapsulation ppp
ip address 172.17.1.1 255.255.255.0
dialer map ip 172.17.1.2 broadcast 9726785677
dialer map ip 172.17.1.2 broadcast 9726785678
dialer load-threshold 127
ppp Multilink
isdn spid1 97255567890101 9724446789
isdn spid2 97255567880101 9725556788

!RouterB
interface serial 0
ip address 172.18.1.2 255.255.255.0
```

```
backup interface bri 0
backup delay 5 60
backup load 85 4
interface bri0
encapsulation ppp
ip address 172.17.1.2 255.255.255.0
dialer map ip 172.17.1.1 broadcast 9725556789
dialer map ip 172.17.1.1 broadcast 9725556788
dialer load-threshold 127
ppp Multilink
isdn spid1 97267856770101 9726785677
isdn spid2 97267856780101 9726785678
```

Answers to Chapter 7 "Do I Know This Already?" Quiz

1 *Define the acronyms SOHO and RO.*

They stand for small office/home office and remote office. The difference between them is slight: the 700 is positioned for a SOHO and not generally positioned for a RO. This should be remembered when selecting equipment during the test.

2 *What are the three permanent profiles for the 700 series router?*

The profiles are LAN, standard, and internal.

3 *For what is the internal profile used?*

The internal profile is used when routing is enabled and provides the configuration parameters to pass data between the bridge engine and the IP/IPX route engine.

4 *How many user profiles can be created?*

Sixteen user profiles can be created. A total of 20 profiles is allowed on the device; however, the LAN, standard, internal, and system profiles also count toward the 20.

5 *Can an ISP support dial-on-demand (DDR) routing and bandwidth-on-demand (BoD) with a 700 series router? If not, why?*

Both DDR routing and BoD are supported on the device, not the ISP. DDR is controlled by the 700, and BoD is supported with the Multilink PPP option, if negotiated during the LCP setup. This question is tricky.

6 *What is the mechanism that points the 700 to the ISP?*

The static route that is in the profile that dials the ISP is the mechanism that enables the 700 series router to route packets to the ISP. In general, the route to the ISP would be the default, or all 0s, route.

7 *What routing protocols can be configured on the 700 series router?*

The RIP-1 and RIP-2 routing protocols can be configured on the 700 series router.

8 *How would you configure a 700 series router as a DHCP relay agent?*

You could configure it using the **set dhcp relay** *ip-address* command, where *ip-address* is the address of the DHCP server.

9 *When configuring the 700 series router for a DHCP server, how do you set up the default gateway for the client?*

You don't. The key here is to recognize that when the 700 is declared as the DHCP server (**set dhcp server**), the router hands out an address when it sets itself as the default gateway. All DHCP requests from the Ethernet are resolved by the 700 series router.

Answers to Chapter 7 Q&A Section

1 *What are the three permanent profiles for the 700 series router?*

The profiles are LAN, standard, and internal.

2 *Which one of the following statements is true?*

a. Any protocol routed in the LAN must be routed in the user profile.

b. Any protocol routed in the LAN cannot be routed in the user profile.

c. Any protocol routed in the LAN must be bridged in the user profile.

d. Any protocol routed in the LAN cannot be bridged in the internal profile.

The answer is a. Any protocol routed in the LAN must be routed in the user profile.

3 *What must be true for the 700 series router to be IP pingable?*

IP must be turned on for the internal profile.

4 *For what is the internal profile used?*

The internal profile is used when routing is enabled and provides the configuration parameters to pass data between the bridge engine and the IP/IPX route engine.

5 *How many user profiles can be created?*

Sixteen user profiles can be created. A total of 20 profiles is allowed on a device; however, the LAN, standard, internal, and system profiles count toward the 20.

6 *Under which mode or profile is the ISDN switch type declared?*

It is declared in the system profile.

7 *What is declared in the LAN profile?*

The IP address, the IPX address, and the IP subnet mask are declared in the LAN profile.

8 *Define the acronyms SOHO and RO.*

They stand for small office/home office and remote office. The difference between them is slight: the 700 is positioned for a SOHO and not generally positioned for a RO. This should be remembered when selecting equipment during the test.

9 *Can an ISP support DDR and BoD with a 700 series router? If not, why?*

Both DDR routing and BoD are supported on the device, not the ISP. DDR is controlled by the 700, and BoD is supported with the Multilink PPP option, if negotiated during the LCP setup. This question is tricky.

10 *What command would you use to declare the use of CHAP authentication when a 700 series router calls a remote site?*

set ppp auth out chap

11 *What does the command **set system 700MLP** do?*

It changes the system name to 700MLP.

12 *What is the mechanism that points the 700 series router to the ISP?*

The static route that is in the profile that dials the ISP is the mechanism that enables the 700 series router to route packets to the ISP. In general, the route to the ISP would be the default, or all 0's, route.

13 *Which of the following protocols are supported by the 700 series router: PAP, CHAP, MPPP, IGRP, ISP, and PAT?*

PAP, CHAP, MPPP, and PAT are supported.

14 *What routing protocols can be configured on the 700 series router?*

RIP-1 and RIP-2 can be configured on the 700 series router.

15 *What command is used to display the 700 configuration?*

upload

16 *What is the command required for a soft boot on a 700 series router?*

reset

17 *What command would you use to configure the 700 series router as a DHCP relay agent?*

You would use **set dhcp relay** *ip-address*, where *ip-address* is the IP address of the DHCP server.

18 *What does the following command do: **set dhcp address 10.1.1.5 12**?*

The command sets a DHCP address range between 10.1.1.5 and 10.1.1.16.

19 *Which of the following routed protocols can be used on the 700 router: IGRP, IPX, RIP, IP, OSPF, and static routes?*

You can use IPX and IP.

20 *When configuring the 700 series router for a DHCP server, how do you set up the default gateway for the client?*

You don't. The key here is to recognize that when the 700 is declared as the DHCP server (**set dhcp server**), the router hands out an address when it sets itself as the default gateway. All DHCP requests from the Ethernet will be resolved by the 700 series router.

Answers to the Chapter 8 "Do I Know This Already?" Quiz

1 *Name the Layer 2 of X.25.*

The Layer 2 is LAPB.

2 *Name the Layer 3 of X.25.*

The Layer 3 is X.25.

3 *In X.25, what are the two possible roles that a router can play?*

The roles are DCE and DTE.

4 *What is the function of a Packet Assembler/Disassembler (PAD) in an X.25 network?*

The PAD is a device that collects data from asynchronous terminals and outputs that data encapsulated inside X.25 packets.

5 *The addressing scheme in X.25 is known as what kind of address?*

It is known as X.121 addressing.

6 *List the parts of the addressing scheme from Question 5.*

The parts are DNIC and NTN.

7 *How many digits constitute each of the parts of the address from Question 5?*

The DNIC has four digits, and the NTN has 8–11 digits.

8 *From where are the addresses used in configuring X.25 obtained?*

They are obtained from the PDN provider.

9 *List the possible types of circuits available in an X.25 network deployment.*

The circuit types include PVC, SVC incoming only, SVC outgoing only, and SVC two-way.

10 *What effect does changing the default ips and/or ops have on a X.25 transmission?*

Altering the input packet size or the output packet size changes the maximum size of the X.25 packet at the ingress/egress point of the network. The sizes must match in most situations.

11 *What effect does changing the default win and/or wout have on a X.25 transmission?*

Altering the window incoming size or the window outgoing size settings changes the number of packets that can be sent in a single window. The sizes must match on both ends of the connection.

12 *What is a modulo and what are the possible values?*

The modulo is a counter that specifies the packet numbering modulus. The default is 8, and the only other possible value is 128.

Answers to the Chapter 8 Q&A Section

1 *Name the Layer 2 of X.25.*

The Layer 2 is LAPB.

2 *Name the Layer 3 of X.25.*

The Layer 3 is X.25.

3 *In X.25, what are the two possible roles that a router can play?*

The roles are DCE and DTE.

4 *What is the function of a PAD in an X.25 network?*

The PAD is a device that collects data from asynchronous terminals and outputs that data encapsulated inside of X.25 packets.

5 *The addressing scheme in X.25 is known as what kind of address?*

It is known as X.121 addressing.

6 *List the parts of the addressing scheme from Question 5.*

The parts are DNIC and NTN.

7 *How many digits constitute each of the parts of the address from Question 5?*

The DNIC has four digits, and the NTN has 8–11 digits.

8 *From where are the addresses used in configuring X.25 obtained?*

They are obtained from the PDN provider.

9 *List the possible types of circuits available in an X.25 network deployment.*

The circuit types include PVC, SVC incoming only, SVC outgoing only, and SVC two-way.

10 *What effect does changing the default ips and/or ops have on a X.25 transmission?*

Altering the input packet size or the output packet size changes the maximum size of the X.25 packet at the ingress/egress point of the network. The sizes must match in most situations.

11 *What effect does changing the default win and/or wout have on a X.25 transmission?*

Altering the window incoming size or the window outgoing size settings changes the number of packets that can be sent in a single window. The sizes must match on both ends of the connection.

12 *What is a modulo and what are the possible values?*

The modulo is a counter that specifies the packet numbering modulus. The default is 8, and the only other possible value is 128.

13 *What was the driving force behind the creation of X.25?*

The X.25 specifications detail connections between DTE and DCE for remote terminal access and computer communications.

14 *What entity governs the X.25 standards evolution?*

The ITU-T governs X.25. ITU is governed by the United Nations.

15 *What is the difference between X.25 DCE and DTE?*

The X.25 DCE typically acts as a boundary to the PDN within a switch. The X.25 DTE typically refers to the router or a PAD.

16 *List the X.25 layers.*

The layers are Layer 1, Physical; Layer 2, LAPB; and Layer 3, X.25.

17 *X.121 addresses are considered to be at which layer of the X.25 model?*

X.121 addresses are X.25 layer addresses.

18 *List the three LAPB frame formats.*

Information, Supervisor, and Unnumbered are the three types of LAPB frames.

19 *Does the X.25 DCE have to be the physical DCE?*

No. The physical DTE/DCE relationship is independent of the X.25 DTE/DCE relationship.

20 *List a configuration suitable for configuring for basic functionality the network in Figure A-2.*

Figure A-2   *Configure the Network*

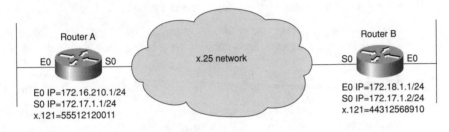

The following code creates a suitable configuration:

Example A-1   *RouterA*

```
interface ethernet 0
ip address 172.16.210.1 255.255.255.0
interface serial 0
encapuslation x25
ip address 172.17.1.1 255.255.255.0
x25 address 55512120011
x25 map ip 172.17.1.2 44312568910 broadcast
```

Example A-2   *RouterB*

```
interface ethernet 0
ip address 172.18.1.1 255.255.255.0
interface serial 0
encapsulation x25
ip address 172.17.1.2 255.255.255.0
x25 address 44312568910
x25 map ip 172.17.1.1 55512120011 broadcast
```

21 *List a configuration for the following:*

Parameter	Value
Window size incoming	127
Window size outgoing	127
Input packet size	4096
Output packet size	4096
Modulus	128

The following is an acceptable configuration:

Example A-3 *RouterA*

```
interface ethernet 0
ip address 172.16.210.1 255.255.255.0
interface serial 0
encapuslation x25
ip address 172.17.1.1 255.255.255.0
x25 address 55512120011
x25 map ip 172.17.1.2 44312568910 broadcast
x25 win 127
x25 wout 127
x25 ips 4096
x25 ops 4096
x25 modulo 128
```

Example A-4 *RouterB*

```
interface ethernet 0
ip address 172.18.1.1 255.255.255.0
interface serial 0
encapsulation x25
ip address 172.17.1.2 255.255.255.0
x25 address 44312568910
x25 map ip 172.17.1.1 55512120011 broadcast
x25 win 127
x25 wout 127
x25 ips 4096
x25 ops 4096
x25 modulo 128
```

22 *List a configuration for the following:*

Parameter	Range
Incoming circuits	1–8
Two-way circuits	9–21
Outgoing circuits	22–25

The following is an acceptable configuration:

Example A-5 *RouterA*

```
interface ethernet 0
ip address 172.16.210.1 255.255.255.0
interface serial 0
encapuslation x25
ip address 172.17.1.1 255.255.255.0
x25 address 55512120011
x25 map ip 172.17.1.2 44312568910 broadcast
x25 lic 1
x25 hic 8
x25 ltc 9
x25 htc 21
x25 loc 22
x25 hoc 25
x25 win 127
x25 wout 127
x25 ips 4096
x25 ops 4096
x25 modulo 128
```

Example A-6 *RouterB*

```
interface ethernet 0
ip address 172.18.1.1 255.255.255.0
interface serial 0
encapsulation x25
ip address 172.17.1.2 255.255.255.0
x25 address 44312568910
x25 map ip 172.17.1.1 55512120011 broadcast
x25 lic 1
x25 hic 8
x25 ltc 9
x25 htc 21
x25 loc 22
x25 hoc 25
x25 win 127
x25 wout 127
x25 ips 4096
x25 ops 4096
x25 modulo 128
```

Answers to the Chapter 9 "Do I Know This Already?" Quiz

1 *Is Frame Relay connection-oriented or connectionless?*

Frame Relay is connection-oriented.

2 *Frame Relay virtual circuits come in two flavors. What are those flavors?*

Frame Relay virtual circuits can be PVC or SVC.

3 *Frame Relay virtual circuits are logically defined by a DLCI. What is the range of valid DLCIs?*

Valid DLCIs fall in the range of 16–1007.

4 *The Frame Relay star topology is also known as what?*

It is also known as hub and spoke.

5 *In a 40-route Frame Relay network running in a full mesh topology, how many connections exist?*

You need 780 virtual circuits to fully mesh the routers in the network. The number is calculated with this formula: $n(n \times 1) \div 2$, where n is the number of routers.

6 *What is an advantage of a partial mesh network?*

A partial mesh provides a compromise between cost and redundancy. With a partial mesh, critical or high volume sites can have redundant connections and avoid traversing a central site router.

7 *Split horizon can cause reachability issues in Frame Relay networks. List two ways in which you can deal with split horizon problems.*

The two methods of dealing with split horizon issues are turning it off (not recommended) and implementing subinterfaces.

8 *If connecting to non-Cisco routers on the other side of a Frame Relay network, what must be specified in the configuration?*

If connecting in a multivendor Frame Relay environment, you must use the IETF implementation of Frame Relay. This can be done by using the **encapsulation frame-relay ietf** command, or IETF can be specified on each PVC as needed.

9 *Frame Relay subinterfaces can be created with two different personalities. What are those personalities?*

Point-to-point and multipoint are the personality options for Frame Relay subinterfaces.

10 *In Frame Relay traffic shaping, what is Committed Information Rate (CIR)?*

In Frame Relay traffic shaping, CIR is the average rate at which you want to transmit. This is generally not the same as the CIR provided by the telco, which is the amount you want to send in periods of noncongestion.

11 *If CIR is 64,000 bps, what should be the value of MinCIR?*

The recommended setting for MinCIR is one-half of CIR, so MinCIR should be 32,000 bps.

12 *List the steps in defining a map class for Frame Relay traffic shaping.*

First, create the map class at global config. Then, define the traffic parameters for the map class. Finally, associate the map class with a VC or an interface.

13 *In map class configuration mode, what command enables the router to respond to BECN requests?*

frame-relay adaptive-shaping becn

14 *In map class configuration mode, what command specifies the CIR if you want CIR set to 512000 bps?*

frame-relay cir 512000

15 *In periods of congestion, what is the percentage drop of throughput experienced with each BECN?*

The drop is 25 percent but does not exceed MinCIR.

Answers to the Chapter 9 Q&A Section

1 *Is Frame Relay connection-oriented or connectionless?*

Frame Relay is connection-oriented.

2 *Frame Relay virtual circuits come in two flavors. What are those flavors?*

Frame Relay virtual circuits can be PVC or SVC.

3 *Frame Relay virtual circuits are logically defined by a DLCI. What is the range of valid DLCIs?*

Valid DLCIs fall in the range of 16–1007.

4 *The Frame Relay star topology is also known as what?*

It is also known as hub and spoke

5 *In a 40-route Frame Relay network running in a full mesh topology, how many connections exist?*

You need 780 virtual circuits to fully mesh the routers in the network. The number is calculated with this formula: $n(n \times 1) \div 2$, where n is the number of routers.

6 *What is an advantage of a partial mesh network?*

A partial mesh provides a compromise between cost and redundancy. With a partial mesh, critical or high volume sites can have redundant connections and avoid traversing a central site router.

7 *Split horizon can cause reachability issues in Frame Relay networks. List two ways in which you can deal with split horizon problems.*

The two methods of dealing with split horizon issues are turning it off (not recommended) and implementing subinterfaces.

8 *If connecting to non-Cisco routers on the other side of a Frame Relay network, what must be specified in the configuration?*

If connecting in a multivendor Frame Relay environment, you must use the IETF implementation of Frame Relay. This can be done using the **encapsulation frame-relay ietf** command, or IETF can be specified on each PVC as needed.

9 *Frame Relay subinterfaces can be created with two different personalities. What are those personalities?*

Point-to-point and multipoint are the personality options for Frame Relay subinterfaces.

10 *In Frame Relay traffic shaping, what is CIR?*

In Frame Relay traffic shaping, CIR is the average rate at which you want to transmit. This is generally not the same as the CIR provided by the telco, which is the amount you want to send in periods of noncongestion.

11 *If CIR is 64,000 bps, what should the value of MinCIR be?*

The recommended setting for MinCIR is one-half of CIR, so MinCIR should be 32,000 bps.

12 *List the steps in defining a map class for Frame Relay traffic shaping.*

First, create the map class at global config. Then, define the traffic parameters for the map class. Finally, associate the map class with a VC or an interface.

13 *In map-class configuration mode, what command enables the router to respond to BECN requests?*

frame-relay adaptive-shaping becn

14 *In map class configuration mode, what command specifies the CIR if you want CIR set to 512000 bps?*

frame-relay cir 512000

15 *In periods of congestion, what is the percentage drop of throughput experienced with each BECN?*

The drop is 25 percent but does not exceed MinCIR.

16 *You are concerned that LMI is not flowing between the router and the switch. What command could you use to watch the real-time exchange of LMI traffic?*

debug frame-relay lmi

17 *Users have reported issues with network reachability. What command could be utilized to view the status of PVCs?*

show frame-relay pvc

18 *Write out a basic Frame Relay configuration including two point-to-point subinterfaces off of Serial 0, using IP only. The DLCI for Serial 0.1 should be 24 and for Serial 0.2, the DLCI should be 95.*

```
Router(config)#interface serial 0
Router(config-if)#encapsulation frame-relay
Router(config-if)#interface serial 0.1 point-to-point
Router(config-if)#ip address 10.1.1.1 255.255.255.0
Router(config-if)#frame-relay interface-dlci 24
Router(config-if)#interface serial 0.2 point-to-point
Router(config-if)#ip address 10.1.2.1 255.255.255.0
Router(config-if)#frame-relay interface-dlci 95
```

19 *Create the same configuration from Question 18, but use multipoint interfaces instead.*

```
Router(config)#interface serial 0
Router(config-if)#encapsulation frame-relay
Router(config-if)#interface serial 0.1 multipoint
Router(config-if)#ip address 10.1.1.1 255.255.255.0
Router(config-if)#frame-relay map ip 10.1.1.2 24 broadcast
Router(config-if)#interface serial 0.2 multipoint
Router(config-if)#ip address 10.1.2.1 255.255.255.0
Router(config-if)#frame-relay map ip 10.1.2.2 95 broadcast
```

20 *Once the router has decreased throughput due to BECN requests, how long must it wait prior to increasing throughput once again?*

The router must wait for 16 time intervals (usually about two seconds) of receiving no BECNs before increasing throughput.

21 *Increasing throughput once every 16 time intervals can mean that some time passes before CIR speed is regained. How can the router be configured to force the speed back to CIR immediately after the congestion has cleared?*

Set the Be to $7 \times$ Bc. The Bc is the amount of data sent in a time interval, usually CIR ÷ 8. The Be is the amount of excess data allowed to be sent during the first interval with credit. Because BECN has backed the speed down, a credit builds for each time interval. If CIR is 64,000, Bc is 8000. If Be is set to $7 \times$ Bc, it will be 56,000. Once 16 time intervals have passed, the throughput bursts to CIR immediately (Bc = 8000) + (Be = 56,000) ÷ 16 = 4000 bps per time interval. Successful passage of 16 time intervals with no BECN sends the value to 64,000 bps immediately rather gradually.

22 *What happens to LMI traffic if the command **no keepalive** is issued on the router interface?*

LMI traffic ceases to cross the link.

23 *What types of LMI are supported by Cisco routers?*

Cisco, ANSI, and Q933a LMI types are supported.

24 *What is the advantage of a hub and spoke topology over a full mesh topology?*

Hub and spoke topologies are less costly than full or partial mesh topologies. However, they also lack redundancy. Another advantage is ease of management. A large percentage of the network can be administered (traffic filters, route filters, and so on) from a single point.

25 *What is the result of using a single serial interface to provide access to multiple remote sites?*

In this type of point-to-multipoint deployment, split horizon causes routing information about remote sites and networks to be blocked from exiting that interface. The end result is that the remote routers and their networks are invisible to each other.

Answers to the Chapter 10 "Do I Know This Already?" Quiz

1 *Where on a router is queuing implemented?*

Queuing should be implemented on low-speed WAN interfaces only.

2 *When should queuing be considered a viable implementation?*

Queuing should be considered a solution when the router experiences more than occasional congestion. If the existing traffic flow is having problems getting through the router on a regular basis, queuing should be considered.

3 *Should a queuing strategy be implemented on all WAN interfaces?*

No. Queuing should be implemented on low-speed serial interfaces that experience regular congestive conditions. If there is no congestion, queuing is not needed.

4 *When is WFQ enabled by default?*

WFQ is enabled by default on all serial interfaces with speeds of 2.048 Mbps and lower. Some technologies disable WFQ when the encapsulation is set on the interface.

5 *What is the configurable parameter of WFQ?*

The configurable parameter in WFQ is the congestive discard threshold. This is the number of records that can exist in the queue at a given time.

6 *What type of traffic gets the highest priority with WFQ?*

Low-volume, interactive traffic gets priority on a WFQ-enabled link.

7 *How many queues are available in priority queuing?*

There are four queues: high, medium, normal, and low.

8 *If a default queue is not specified in the configuration, in which queue are traffic types that are not defined in the priority list placed?*

Unspecified traffic defaults to the normal queue unless configured otherwise. A default queue should be defined in all queue lists.

9 *What happens to traffic in the low-priority queue if there is always traffic in the high-priority queue?*

The Time To Live (TTL) for the traffic might expire and the traffic might be dropped. Also, the low-priority queue could fill up and overflow, causing dropped traffic.

10 *How many queues are available in custom queuing?*

There are 17 queues in custom queuing, 0–16. Only 1–16 are user-configurable.

11 *How is traffic dispatched in a custom queuing implementation?*

Traffic is dispatched on a round-robin basis. Each queue is serviced until its service threshold is reached.

12 *How can a higher priority be assigned to a particular queue?*

The service thresholds for that particular queue can be expanded to give it a higher percentage of the overall bandwidth.

13 *List the types of compression supported by most Cisco routers.*

Link compression, payload compression, TCP header compression, and Microsoft Point-to-Point Compression are supported by most Cisco router models. Additional types of compression are supported by other chassis models.

14 *When should link compression be implemented?*

Link compression works best on point-to-point dedicated circuits that do not require the use of header information for switching purposes.

15 *Which type of compression should be utilized on virtual circuit-based WAN deployments?*

Payload compression should be used on VC-based deployments. This leaves the Layer 2 header intact for use by the carrier network.

Answers to the Chapter 10 Q&A Section

1 *Where on a router is queuing implemented?*

Queuing should be implemented on low-speed WAN interfaces only.

2 *When should queuing be considered a viable implementation?*

Queuing should be considered a solution when the router experiences more than occasional congestion. If the existing traffic flow is having problems getting through the router on a regular basis, queuing should be considered.

3 *Should a queuing strategy be implemented on all WAN interfaces?*

No. Queuing should be implemented on low-speed serial interfaces that experience regular congestive conditions. If there is no congestion, queuing is not needed.

4 *When is WFQ enabled by default?*

WFQ is enabled by default on all serial interfaces with speeds of 2.048 Mpbs or lower. Some technologies disable WFQ when the encapsulation is set on the interface.

5 *What is the configurable parameter of WFQ?*

The configurable parameter in WFQ is the congestive discard threshold. This is the number of records that can exist in the queue at a given time.

6 *What type of traffic gets the highest priority with WFQ?*

Low-volume, interactive traffic gets the priority on a WFQ-enabled link.

7 *How many queues are available in priority queuing?*

There are four queues: high, medium, normal, and low.

8 *If a default queue is not specified in the configuration, in which queue are traffic types not defined in the priority list placed?*

Unspecified traffic defaults to the normal queue unless configured otherwise. A default queue should be defined in all queue lists.

9 *What happens to traffic in a low-priority queue if there is always traffic in the high-priority queue?*

The TTL for the traffic can expire and the traffic can be dropped. Also, the low-priority queue could fill up and overflow, causing dropped traffic.

10 *How many queues are available in custom queuing?*

There are 17 queues in custom queuing, 0–16. Only 1–16 are user-configurable.

11 *How is traffic dispatched in a custom queuing implementation?*

Traffic is dispatched on a round-robin basis. Each queue is serviced until its service threshold is reached.

12 *How can a higher priority be assigned to a particular queue?*

The service thresholds for a particular queue can be expanded to give it a higher percentage of the overall bandwidth.

13 *List the types of compression supported by most Cisco routers.*

Link compression, payload compression, TCP header compression, and Microsoft Point-to-Point Compression are supported by most Cisco router models. Other chassis models support additional types of compression.

14 *When should link compression be implemented?*

Link compression works best on point-to-point dedicated circuits that do not require the use of header information for switching purposes.

15 *Which type of compression should be utilized on virtual circuit-based WAN deployments?*

Payload compression should be used on VC-based deployments. This leaves the Layer 2 header intact for use by the carrier network.

For the remaining questions, refer to Figure A-3 for the existing network topology.

Figure A-3 *Chapter 10 Q&A Network Topology*

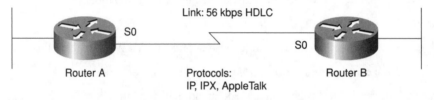

16 *At first look, is this network a good candidate for queuing implementation? Why?*

Yes. It has low bandwidth, and, because of the default characteristics of the protocols going across the link, it has a good chance of experiencing congestion.

17 *Configure both routers for WFQ. Use a congestive discard threshold of 256.*

Example A-7 *RouterA*

```
RouterA(config-if)#fair-queue 256
```

Example A-8 *RouterB*

```
RouterB(config-if)#fair-queue 256
```

18 *Configure both routers for priority queuing. Place any ICMP traffic in the high queue. IP should be in the medium queue, followed by IPX and AppleTalk in the normal queue. Any unspecified traffic should be placed in the low queue.*

Example A-9 *RouterA*

```
RouterA(config)#access-list 100 permit icmp any any
RouterA(config)#priority-list 1 protocol ip high list 100
RouterA(config)#priority-list 1 protocol ip medium
RouterA(config)#priority-list 1 protocol ipx normal
RouterA(config)#priority-list 1 protocol appletalk normal
RouterA(config)#priority-list 1 default low
RouterA(config)#interface serial 0
RouterA(config-if)#priority-group 1
```

Example A-10 *RouterB*

```
RouterB(config)#access-list 100 permit icmp any any
RouterB(config)#priority-list 1 protocol ip high list 100
RouterB(config)#priority-list 1 protocol ip medium
RouterB(config)#priority-list 1 protocol ipx normal
RouterB(config)#priority-list 1 protocol appletalk normal
RouterB(config)#priority-list 1 default low
RouterB(config)#interface serial 0
RouterB(config-if)#priority-group 1
```

19 *If a default queue is not specified, where would the traffic go in the configuration for Question 18?*

If no default queue is specified in a priority queue implementation, traffic goes into the normal queue.

20 *Configure both routers for custom queuing. All TFTP traffic should be in queue 1. Queue 1 should have 4 times the default service thresholds. All other IP should go to queue 2, followed by IPX in queue 3 and AppleTalk in queue 4. Unspecified traffic should go into queue 5.*

Example A-11 *RouterA*

```
RouterA(config)#queue-list 1 protocol ip 1 udp 69
RouterA(config)#queue-list 1 protocol ip 2
RouterA(config)#queue-list 1 protocol ipx 3
RouterA(config)#queue-list 1 protocol appletalk 4
RouterA(config)#queue-list 1 default 5
RouterA(config)#queue-list 1 queue 1 limit 80
RouterA(config)#queue-list 1 queue 1 byte-count 6000
RouterA(config)#interface serial 0
RouterA(config-if)#custom-queue-list 1
```

Example A-12 *RouterB*

```
RouterB(config)#queue-list 1 protocol ip 1 udp 69
RouterB(config)#queue-list 1 protocol ip 2
RouterB(config)#queue-list 1 protocol ipx 3
RouterB(config)#queue-list 1 protocol appletalk 4
RouterB(config)#queue-list 1 default 5
RouterB(config)#queue-list 1 queue 1 limit 80
RouterB(config)#queue-list 1 queue 1 byte-count 6000
RouterA(config)#interface serial 0
RouterA(config-if)#custom-queue-list 1
```

21 *If a default queue is not specified, where would the traffic go in the Question 20 configuration?*

If no default queue is specified in a custom queue implementation, traffic goes into queue 1.

22 *What is the best type of compression to use for the network topology in Question 20?*

Given the fact that HDLC is in use in this topology, link compression using STAC or Predictor can be utilized.

23 *Configure the compression technique from Question 22. You must decide the parameters to be used, if any.*

Example A-13 *RouterA*

```
RouterA(config-if)#compress stac
          or
RouterA(config-if)#compress predictor
```

Example A-14 *RouterB*

```
RouterB(config-if)#compress stac
          or
RouterB(config-if)#compress predictor
```

24 *Change the encapsulation of interface Serial 0 on each router to Frame Relay. Now what is the best compression technique?*

In a Frame Relay deployment, link compression cannot be utilized. Payload compression is a better choice.

25 *Configure the compression technique from Question 22. You must decide the parameters to use, if any.*

Example A-15 *RouterA*

```
RouterA(config-if)#frame-relay payload-compress
```

Example A-16 *RouterB*

```
RouterB(config-if)#frame-relay payload-compress
```

Answers to the Chapter 11 "Do I Know This Already?" Quiz

1 *What are the benefits of NAT?*

The benefits of NAT include conservation, overlap dysfunction, flexibility, and the elimination of renumbering. Addresses are conserved because "real" addresses are not needed for the private network. Overlap dysfunction occurs when two companies, which were using the same address space, merge. Renumbering occurs when a company changes ISPs and keeps the same internal address space. When this occurs, only the NAT device requires a change.

2 *What are the disadvantages of NAT?*

The disadvantages include increased latency, lesser accountability, and nonfunctionality with some applications.

3 *Using simple NAT translation, what TCP header information is altered?*

The source IP address and the subnet mask are altered.

4 *What private address space is available from RFC 1918?*

Address Class	Range	Number of Classful Networks
A	10.0.0.0	1
B	172.16.0.0–172.31.0.0	16
C	192.168.0.0–192.168.255.0	255

5 *What does it mean when a NAT translation is overloaded?*

When a NAT translation is overloaded, the same IP address is used over and over, and the tracking is done by using the source port number in addition to the source IP address.

6 *What TCP header information is altered by using NAT overload?*

The source IP address, the subnet mask, and the source port number are altered.

7 *When should NAT overlap be deployed?*

It should be deployed in a network merger in which two entities are using the same IP numbering scheme or two intranets are using the same numbering scheme.

8 *What NAT translation is generally used for overlapped networks? Why?*

Simple NAT is used because the administrator generally controls both networks that are being translated.

9 *Briefly describe the use of NAT TCP load distribution.*

Load distribution advertises a single IP address and when it is referenced, it is translated to a pool of addresses that represents a group of mirrored servers or devices.

10 *List the four NAT address descriptions and a brief definition of each.*

The NAT address descriptions are as follows:

Inside Local address classes are IP addresses that are unique to the host inside the network, but not globally significant

Inside Global address classes are IP addresses that are assigned by the Internet Assigned Numbers Authority (IANA) or service provider and that are legitimate in the global address space or Internet.

Outside Local address classes are IP addresses of a host on an outside network that is presented to the inside network and that is legitimate to the local network.

Outside Global address classes are IP addresses that are globally routable on the Internet space.

11 *An inside local address is translated to what in a simple NAT translation?*

It is translated to an Inside Global address.

12 *What are the four types of NAT translations or configurations?*

They are simple, overload, overlap, and TCP load distribution.

13 *What command is used to erase all current NAT- translated sessions?*

clear ip nat translation *

14 *Port address translation is used on what router series only?*

It is used on the Cisco 700 series routers.

15 *Is PAT a subset of NAT? Defend your answer.*

Pat is a subset of NAT within the 700 IOS code. The 700 does only PAT and does not have the flexibility that the NAT implementation the Enterprise IOS code has. In general, PAT really is a superset of NAT since PAT allows for the translation of the port number, as well as the address. But, given the definitions of PAT and NAT used in this context, PAT is a subset of the functionality that the Enterprise IOS offers.

Answers to the Chapter 11 Q&A Section

1 *What are the benefits of NAT?*

The benefits include conservation, overlap dysfunction, flexibility, and the elimination of renumbering.

2 *The Outside Global address is converted to which NAT address class?*

It is converted to an Outside Local address.

3 *What are the disadvantages of NAT?*

The disadvantages include increased latency, lesser accountability, and nonfunctionality with some applications

4 *Using simple NAT translation, what TCP header information is altered?*

The source IP address and the subnet mask are altered.

5 *What private address space is available from RFC 1918?*

Address Class	Range	Number of Classful Networks
A	10.0.0.0	1
B	172.16.0.0–172.31.0.0	16
C	192.168.0.0–192.168.255.0	255

6 *What does it mean when a NAT translation is overloaded?*

When a NAT translation is overloaded, the same IP address is used over and over, and the tracking is done by using the source port number in addition to the source IP address.

7 *Which commands would you use for an overloaded NAT translation using a defined pool of addresses called **transpool** for outbound traffic?*

ip nat inside source list 1 pool transpool overload

8 *What TCP header information is altered using NAT overload?*

The source IP address, the subnet mask, and the source port number are altered.

9 *When should NAT overlap be deployed?*

It should be deployed in a network merger in which two entities are using the same IP numbering scheme or two intranets are using the same numbering scheme.

10 *What NAT translation is generally used for overlapped networks? Why?*

Simple NAT is used because the administrator generally controls both networks that are being translated.

11 *What command would show which interfaces have been declared as outside or inside?*

show ip nat statistics

12 *Briefly describe the use of NAT TCP load distribution.*

Load distribution advertises a single IP address and when it is referenced, it is translated to a pool of addresses that represent a group of mirrored servers or devices.

13 *List the four NAT address descriptions and provide a brief definition for each.*

The NAT address descriptions are as follows:

Inside Local address classes are IP addresses that are unique to the host inside the network, but not globally significant.

Inside Global address class are IP addresses that are assigned by the IANA or service provider and that are legitimate in the global address space or Internet.

Outside Local address classes are IP addresses of a host on an outside network that is presented to the inside network and that is legitimate to the local network.

Outside Global address classes are IP addresses that are globally routable on the Internet space.

14 *An inside local address is translated to what in a simple NAT translation?*

It is translated to an Inside Global address.

15 *What are the four types of NAT translations or configuration?*

They are simple, overload, overlap, and TCP load distribution.

16 *The port handler for the 700 series router allows which of the following?*

a. up to 15 port-handler addresses

b. multiple ports for a single inside service

c. only one inside port per service supported

d. up to 400 ports maximum to be open for the port handler

e. up to 1500 ports

The answers are a and c.

17 *An Inside Local address _____. (Choose two answers.)*

a. is unique to the inside network and can be routed internally

b. is unique to the inside network, but cannot be routed internally

c. is always selected from RFC 1918 private address space

d. is not routable on the Internet

e. can use a private address or an IANA-assigned address space

The answers are a and e.

18 *What command is used to erase all the currently NAT translated sessions?*

clear ip nat translation *

19 *Port address translation is used on what router series?*

It is used on the Cisco 700 series.

20 *Given the following output, what type of translation is being used on this router?*

Pro	Inside global	Inside local	Outside local	Outside global
tcp	103.32.32.1:1098	10.1.0.1:1098	13.43.5.6:23	13.43.5.6:23
tcp	103.32.32.1:1345	10.1.0.2:1345	13.43.5.6:23	13.43.5.6:23
tcp	103.32.32.1:1989	10.1.0.3:1989	13.43.5.7:21	13.43.5.7:21

Overload translation is being used on this router.

21 *Given the following router configuration information which of the subsequent statements is true? (Choose three answers.)*

```
access-list 1 permit 10.0.0.0 0.0.0.255

ip nat pool natpool 222.12.12.2 222.12.12.10 netmask 255.255.255.0
ip nat inside source static 10.0.0.1 222.2.2.1
ip nat inside source list 1 pool natpool
```

a. All addresses belonging to the 10.0.0.0/8 network are translated by the router.

b. The translation uses an overload technique.

c. The translation is a simple NAT technique.

d. The address 10.0.0.1 can be pinged from the outside network.

e. The address 222.2.2.1 can be pinged from the outside network.

f. The pool can support up to nine translations.

g. The pool can support translations of up to 64 K per assigned address.

The answers are c, e and f.

22 *What differentiates PAT from NAT:*

PAT changes the port address; NAT does not.

Answers to the Chapter 12 "Do I Know This Already?" Quiz

1 *For what does AAA stand?*

It stands for authentication, authorization, and accounting.

2 *What is authentication?*

Authentication provides a method of identifying users. During the authentication process, the user login (name) and password are checked against the AAA database.

3 *What is the difference between character mode and packet mode?*

Character mode sends keystrokes to the router through the TTY, vty, AUX, and CON ports for configuration or query commands. Packet mode uses interface mode or a link protocol session to communicate with a device other than the router. These defined interfaces would be the async, group-async, BRI, PRI, serial, dialer profiles, and dialer rotaries.

4 *What communication method—packet or character—is used on the console port of a router?*

Character mode sends keystrokes to the router through the TTY, vty, AUX and CON ports for configuration or query commands.

5 *What are the five authentication modes on a router?*

Login, enable, Apple Remote Access Protocol (ARAP), PPP, and Netware Asynchronous Services Interface (NASI) are the five modes.

6 *What authentication method is used on an interface without an AAA-defined method?*

The default method is used. If no default method has been specified, no authentication can take place.

7 *What is the command to enable AAA using Remote Authentication Dial-In User Service (RADIUS)?*

aaa new-model

radius-server host *radius-ip-address*

radius-server key *password*

8 *What is* authorization*?*

Authorization enables the administrator to control authorization on a one-time, per-service, per-user list, per-group, or per-protocol basis.

9 *What does the argument start-stop mean when using AAA accounting?*

The *start-stop* option sends an accounting record when the process has begun. This is sent as a background process and the user request is begun without delay. When the user process is completed, the stop time and information is sent to the AAA database. This option is needed when an elapsed time of usage is required.

10 *What commands when tracked should use the wait-start argument?*

The *wait-start* option is important when the tracked event might cause a loss of connectivity with the accounting database, such as during a reload or shutdown.

11 *What is stored in a virtual profile?*

The user-specific information for a particular connection is stored in a virtual profile on the AAA server. This information is specific to the destination being called and the connection being used. The key to a virtual profile is that it can be centrally managed.

Answers to Chapter 12 Q&A Section

1 *What does AAA stand for?*

It stands for authentication, authorization, and accounting.

2 *What ports operate in character mode on the router?*

The VTY, AUX, and CON ports operate in character mode.

3 *When enabling AAA for TACACS+, what does the argument single-connection do?*

It establishes a connection that is not torn down.

4 *What is* authentication*?*

Authentication provides a method of identifying users. During the authentication process, the user login (name) and password are checked against the AAA database.

5 *What is the difference between character mode and packet mode?*

Character mode sends keystrokes to the router through the TTY, VTY, AUX, and CON ports for configuration or query commands. Packet mode uses interface mode or a link protocol session to communicate with a device other than the router. These defined interfaces are async, group-async, BRI, PRI, serial, dialer profiles and dialer rotaries.

6 *What does the command **aaa authentication enable** do on the router?*

It declares the method for privileged mode access.

7 *AAA has been enabled for the router, but there is no authentication method declared on the console port. What is the result?*

The default authentication method for login is used.

8 *What communication method—packet or character—is used on the console port of a router?*

Character mode sends keystrokes to the router through the TTY, vty, AUX, and CON ports for configuration or query commands.

9 *What are the five authentication modes on a router?*

Login, enable, ARAP, PPP, and NASI are the modes.

10 *What authentication method is used on an interface without a AAA defined method?*

The default method is used. If no default method has been specified, no authentication takes place.

11 *What is the consequence of not having an authorization statement for level 15 commands if AAA has been enabled on the router?*

Anyone in privilege mode can execute a level 15 command.

12 *To ensure that the use of the **shutdown** command is recorded to the AAA database, what command should you use?*

You should use **aaa accounting command 15 wait-start tacacs+**.

13 *What is the command to enable AAA using RADIUS?*

aaa new-model

radius-server host *radius-ip-address*

radius-server key *password*

14 *What is authorization?*

Authorization enables the administrator to control authorization on a one-time, per-service, per-user list, per-group, or per-protocol basis.

15 *What does the argument start-stop mean when using AAA accounting?*

The *start-stop* argument sends an accounting record when the process begins. This is sent as a background process, and the user request begins without delay. When the user process is completed, the stop time and information is sent to the AAA database. This option is needed when an elapsed time of usage is required.

16 *What command is used to enable AAA on a router?*

aaa new-model

17 *What is Kerberos?*

It is a security protocol that can be used for authorization.

18 *What commands, when tracked, should use the wait-start argument?*

wait-start is important when the tracked event, such as reload or shutdown, might cause a loss of connectivity with the accounting database.

19 *Virtual profiles enable the router administrator to...*

a. provide a resource without knowing details about the connection

b. check the AAA server to see if a connection should be made

c. back up interface parameters on a TACACS server

The answer is a.

20 *What is stored in a virtual profile?*

The user-specific information for a particular connection is stored in a virtual profile on the AAA server. This information is specific to the destination being called and the connection being used. The key to a virtual profile is that it can be centrally managed.

INDEX

Numerics

2B+D connections, 55
2B+D model (ISDN), 131–132
8-N-1 connections, 74
66 block, 132
700 series routers, 27, 53
    DHCP, 207–208
    IP routing, configuring, 200–201, 203
    networking, 197
    PAT (Port Address Translation), 352–354
    profiles, 198
        activating, 200
        internal profiles, 199
        standard profiles, 199
        user profiles, 201
    routing, 205–207
    routing protocol support, 198
    system profiles
        configuration command, 203–204
        management commands, 205
    telephony services, 198
800 series routers, 28, 53
1000 series routers, 28, 53
1600 series routers, 29, 52
    verifying installation, 58
1700 series routers, 52
2500 series routers, 29, 52
2600 series routers, 30, 52
3600 series routers, 30, 49
    verifying installation, 56
4000 series routers, 50
4500 series routers, 31
4700 series routers, 31
7200 series routers, 32, 51

A

AAA (Accounting, Authentication, and Authorization)
    accounting, 382–384
    authentication, 375–380
    authorization, 381–382
    enabling, 374
    shared passwords, establishing, 374
    virtual profiles, 385–386
aaa accounting command
    arguments, 383–384
    syntax, 383
aaa authentication arap command, 378–379
aaa authentication command, 376
aaa authentication enable command, 378
aaa authentication login command, 376
aaa authentication nasi command, 380
aaa authentication ppp command, 379
aaa authorization command, 381–382
access lists
    defining for custom queuing, 308
    specifying interesting traffic, 144

accounting (AAA), configuring, 382–384
activating profiles, 200
adding modems to modemcap database, 84
addressing
    DDR, 146
    ISDN Layer 2, 136
        SPIDs, 137
        TEIs, 136
    NAT, 342
    X.121 addressing, 231, 234
administrative distance, 164
aliasing, 168
allocating bandwidth, 306–307
alternative backup (DDR), 163
AMI (Alternate Mark Inversion), 170
ANSI LMIs, 258
ANSI T1.601, 135
applying, 305
    custom queue list to interfaces, 311
    SPIDs to ISDN interfaces, 148
ARA (AppleTalk Remote Access)
    authentication, 378–379
architecture of PPP (Point-to-Point
    Protocol), 101
arguments
    aaa accounting command, 383–384
    aaa authentication command, 376
    aaa authorization command, 381–382
AS5000 series routers, 31
AS5X00 series routers, 50–51
assembling WAN equipment, 54
async dynamic address command, 105
async mode interactive command, 80
asynchronous configuration, 78
asynchronous connections, 55
AT commands, 82
AT&T 5ESS switch, 134
authentication (AAA)
    AAA, configuring, 375—380
    PPP (Point-to-Point Protocol)
        CHAP, 107–108
        PAP, 105
authorization (AAA), configuring, 381–382
autoconfiguration, modems, 82–84
average transmission rates (Frame Relay), measuring, 272

B

B (bearer) channel, 131
B8ZS (Binary with 8 Zero Substitution), 170
bandwidth, allocating, 306–307
bandwidth 38 command, 80
Bc (Committed Burst), 270
Be (Excess Burst), 270
BECN (Backward Explicit Congestion Notification), 271–272
BFE (Blacker Front-End) X.25, 227

billing
  AAA accounting, configuring, 382–384
  X.25 services, 226
BOD (bandwidth on demand), DDR configuration, 153
branch office routers
  1600 series, 52
    verifying installation, 58
  1700 series, 52
  2500 series, 52
  2600 series, 52
  installation
    requirements for, 26
    verifying, 57
  selecting, 51–53
BRI (Basic Rate Interface), 131
  2B+D, 55
  66 block, 132
  CPE, 132
  Layer 1, 133–135
  Layer 2, 135
  SPIDs, 132, 137
  terminal adapters, 132
byte count, 307

C

cabling for WAN equipment, 54
call termination, 74
caller ID screening (DDR), 148
calls, ISDN
  release process, 141
  setup procedure, 139–140
cast type (subinterfaces), 264
CCDP (Cisco Certified Design Professional) certification, 3
  exams required for, 7–8
  target audience, 7
  training path, 11–12
CCIE (Cisco Certified Internetwork Expert) certification, 5
CCNP (Cisco Certified Network Professional) certification, 3
  exams required for, 7–8
  target audience, 7
  training path, 11–12
cd lan command, 202
central site routers
  3600 series, 49
    verifying installation, 56
  4000 series, 50
  7200 series, 51
  AS5X00 series, 50–51
  demarc, 48
  installing, requirements for, 26
  selecting, 48–50
  verifying installation, 56
certification
  CCDP (Cisco Certified Design Professional), 3
    exams required for, 7–8
    target audience, 7
    training path, 11–12
  CCIE (Cisco Certified Internetwork Expert), history of, 5–6
  CCNP (Cisco Certified Network Professional), 3
    exams required for, 7–8

  target audience, 7
  training path, 11–12
channels
  ISDN PRI, 131
  timeslots, 168
CHAP (Challenge Handshake Authentication Protocol), 107–108
chapters, content structure, 13
characteristics of Frame Relay, configuring, 264–266
chat scripts, 84
  REMDEVICE, 85
check-how? arguments, authorization command, 382
CIR (Committed Information Rate), 270–271
Cisco 700 series routers
  DHCP, 207–208
  IP routing, configuring, 200–201, 203
  networking, 197
  PAT (Port Address Translation), 352–354
  profiles, 198
    activating, 200
    internal profiles, 199
    standard profiles, 199
    user profiles, 201
  routing, 205–207
  routing protocol support, 198
  system profiles
    configuration command, 203–204
    management commands, 205
  telephony services, 198
Cisco LMIs, 258
Cisco Local Director, 341
Cisco Product Selection Tool, 32
Cisco router product families, 27–28, 31–32
clearing NAT translation, 352
code book/dictionary prediction
  compression, 315
commands
  aaa accounting
    arguments, 383–384
    syntax, 383
  aaa authentication, 376
  aaa authentication arap, 378–379
  aaa authentication enable, 378
  aaa authentication login, 376
  aaa authentication nasi, 380
  aaa authentication ppp, 379
  aaa authorization, 381–382
  async dynamic address, 105
  async mode interactive, 80
  bandwidth 38, 80
  cd lan, 202
  controller t1 0/0, 173
  debug dialer, 156
  debug frame-relay lmi, 268
  debug isdn q931, 140
  debug ppp authentication, 112
  debug ppp multilink, 156
  debug ppp negotiation, 112
  dialer callback-secure, 110
  dialer hold-queue, 111
  dialer idle-timeout, 146, 148, 180

dialer in-band, 132, 152
dialer load-threshold, 153
disconnect, 75
encapsulation ppp, 80
flowcontrol hardware, 81
frame-relay adaptive-shaping, 272
frame-relay bc, 273
frame-relay be, 273
frame-relay cir, 273
frame-relay mincir, 273
frame-relay payload-compress, 316
interface serial 0.1, 263
ip default network, 151
ip tcp header-compression passive, 80
ip unnumbered, 104
ip unnumbered Ethernet0, 79
isdn answer, 148
isdn incoming-voice modem, 174–175
isdn spid1, 148
isdn switch-type, 142
isdnq921, 136–137
login local, 81
modem autoconfigure, 83
modem InOut, 81
no cdp enable, 80
peer default ip address pool
    remaddpool, 80
physical-layer async, 79
ppp authentication chap, 80
ppp callback request, 110
ppp context, 104
set dhcp relay, 208
set user, 202
show dialer, 112, 155
show frame-relay lmi, 268
show frame-relay map, 269
show frame-relay pvc, 267, 274
show interface bri0, 145
show ip nat statistics, 351
show ip nat translation, 350
show ip route all, 207
show isdn status, 140, 172
show line, 76–77
show modemcap, 83
show ppp multilink, 155
start-chap, 85
x25 map compressdtcp, 316
x25 pvc, 236
communication ports, 373
company sites, requirements for, 26
comparing port types, 373
compression, 312–313
    configuring, 316
    data encryption, 316
    link compression, 314
        Predictor, 314–315
        STAC, 314
    LZ algorithm, 314
    modem compression, 316

payload compression, 315
PPP, 111
TCP header compression, 315
configuring, 172–174
    AAA
        accounting, 382–384
        authentication, 375–377, 379–380
        authorization, 381–382
    Cisco 700 series routers
        DHCP, 208
        IP routing, 200–203
        routing, 205–207
        system profiles, 203–205
    compression, 316
    DDR, 141
        addressing parameters, 146
        BOD, 153
        caller ID screening, 148
        default routes, 151–152
        dial backup, 161–164
        dialer profiles, 157–159
        encapsulation, 146
        interesting traffic, 143–144
        ISDN switch type, 142
        ML-PPP, 153–156
        passive interfaces, 149–150
        protocol addressing, 147
        rate adaptation, 152
        redistribution, 150
        rotary groups, 159–160
        snapshot routing, 165–166
        SPIDs, 148
        static routes, 145
    Frame Relay
        characteristics, 264–266
        encapsulation, 264
        interface selection, 263
        protocol-specific parameters, 264
        subinterfaces, 263
        traffic shaping, 272–275
        verification, 266–269
    modems, AT commands, 82
    NAT, 343–350
    priority queuing, 301–306
        positioning commands, 303–304
    queuing policies
        custom queuing, 308–312
        WFQ, 299
    X.25, 233
        encapsulation, 234
        examples, 235–236
        inbound/outbound packet sizes, 238
        modulus, 239
        VC ranges, 237–238
        window sizes, 238
        X.121 address, 234
    See also autoconfiguration
connections
    2B+D, 55
    8-N-1, 74

asynchronous, 55, 78
point-to-point, LCP, 104
PRI, 55
reverse Telnet, 74
connectivity, ISDN Layer 1, 133–135
control ports, 373
controller t1 0/0 command, 173
CPE (customer premise equipment), 48, 132
creating
priority lists, 302–303
profiles for Cisco 700 series routers,
198–200
custom queuing, 306–307
configuring, 308, 310–312
verifying operation, 312
customer premise equipment (CPE), 48, 132

D

D channel (PRI), 131
data encryption, 316
data link layer protocols, LAPD, 138
databases, modemcap, 83–84
DCA (Defense Communications Agency), 227
DCE (data circuit-terminating equipment), 228, 257–258
call termination, 72–74
DDN (Defense Data Network) X.25, 227
DDR (dial-on-demand routing), 141
addressing parameters, configuring, 146
BOD (bandwidth on demand),
configuring, 153
caller ID screening, 148
default routes, 151–152
dial backup, 161–162
alternative backup, 163
dynamic backup, 163
static backup, 164
dialer profiles, 157–159
encapsulation, configuring, 146
interesting traffic, specifying, 143–144
rotary groups, 159–160
snapshot routing, 165–166
DDR ISDN switch type, configuring, 142
ML-PPP, configuring, 153–156
passive interfaces, configuring, 149–150
protocol addressing, 147
rate adaptation, 152
SPIDs, configuring, 148
static routes
redistribution, 150
specifying, 145
DE (Discard Eligible) traffic, 271
debug dialer command, 156
debug frame-relay lmi command, 268
debug isdn q931 command, 140
debug ppp authentication command, 112
debug ppp multilink command, 156
debug ppp negotiation command, 112
dedicated sessions, PPP, 104
default routes, DDR configuration, 151–152

defining
access lists for custom queuing, 308
map classes, 272
demarc, 132
central site routers, 48
devices
branch office routers
1600 series, 52
1700 series, 52
2500 series, 52
2600 series, 52
central site routers
3600 series, 49
4000 series, 50
7200 series, 51
AS5X00 series, 50–51
Cisco router product families, 27–32
local exchange equipment, 142
SOHO routers
1000 series, 53
700 series, 53
800 series, 53
DHCP, 207–208
installation, requirements for, 27
selecting, 53
verifying installation, 58–59
switches, ISDN, 134
WAN equipment
assembling, 54
selecting, 48–53
verifying installation, 55–59
DHCP (Dynamic Host Configuration Protocol), 207
Cisco 700 series router configuration, 208
RFCs pertaining to, 208
dial backup, 161–162
alternative backup, 163
dynamic backup, 163
static backup, 164
dialer callback-secure command, 110
dialer hold-queue command, 111
dialer idle-timeout 180 command, 146
dialer idle-timeout command, 148
dialer in-band command, 132, 152
dialer-lists, 143
dialer load-threshold command, 153
dialer maps, ISDN addressing, 147
dialer profiles, 157–159
dial-up connections, configuring PPP
sessions, 104
disabling AAA, 374
disconnect command, 75
discovery process, modems, 83
displaying modemcap settings, 84
distance-vector routing protocols, snapshot routing, 165–166
DLCIs (Data Link Connection Identifiers), 257
DoubleSpace (STAC) utility, 314
do-what? arguments (authorization
command), 381
DSIR pins, 73

DTE (data terminal equipment), 72–74,
257–258
DTE (data terminating equipment), 228
DTR signal pins, 73
dynamic backup (DDR), 163

E

E1 lines
framing, ISDN PRI, 166, 171
line code, 172
See also T1 lines
edge devices, Frame Relay LMI, 258
editing modemcap database, 84
EIA/TIA-232, 72
enabling AAA, 374
encapsulation, configuring
DDR, 146
Frame Relay, 264
X.25, 234
encapsulation ppp command, 80
encryption, 316
ESF (Extended SuperFrame) framing, 168
establishing shared passwords (AAA), 374
exam preparation, 9
scenarios, 14–17
structure of chapter content, 13
topics covered, 9–11
examples of X.25 configuration, 235–236
exchange termination, 134
extended access lists, specifying interesting traffic, 144
extending demarc on central site routers, 48

F

FECN (Forward Explicit Congestion Notification), 271–272
fields, PPP frames, 103
FIFO (First In, First Out) queuing, 298
filtering traffic with access lists, 144
floating static routes, 164
flowcontrol hardware command, 81
Foundation Summaries, 13–14
Frame Relay
configuring
characteristics, 264–266
encapsulation, 264
interface selection, 263
protocol-specific parameters, 264
subinterfaces, 263
DCE, 257–258
DLCIs, 257
DTE, 257–258
LMI, 258
physical connections, 55
STAC compression, enabling, 316
subinterfaces, 261–262
multipoint, 263
topologies, 259
traffic shaping, 270
configuring, 272, 274–275

DE (Discard Eligible), 271
map classes, 272
parameters, 270–271
verifying operation, 274–275
VCs, 257
verifying configuration, 266–269
debug frame-relay lmi command, 268
show frame-relay lmi command, 268
show frame-relay map command, 269
show frame-relay pvc command, 267
frame-relay adaptive-shaping becn command, 272
frame-relay bc command, 273
frame-relay be command, 273
frame-relay cir command, 273
frame-relay mincir command, 273
frame-relay payload-compress command, 316
frames
LAPB, 232
PPP, 103
framing methods
ESF (Extended SuperFrame), 168
ISND layer 1, 135
full-mesh topology
Frame Relay, 259

G-H

gateway of last resort, 151
global addresses (NAT), 342
global profiles, 199
hardware selection
product families, 27–32
SOHO routers, 53
WAN equipment, 48
branch office routers, 51, 53
central site routers, 48–50
connections for remote access, 25
HDB3 (high-density bit, level 3), 172
header compression, TCP, 315
hierarchical structure of X.25, 227
history of CCIE program, 5
home offices
Cisco 700 series router configuration, 206–207
See also SOHO routers
how-to-track arguments, aaa accounting command, 383
hub-and-spoke topology
Frame Relay, 259

I-K

IDBs (Interface Descriptor Blocks), 262
I-Frames, 232
implementing DDR (dial-on-demand routing), 141–156
inbound/outbound packet sizes, X.25 configuration, 238
inside global addresses (NAT), 342
inside local addresses (NAT), 342

installing
    ISDN
        BRI, 132
        PRI, 167
    WAN equipment, verification of, 55
        branch office routers, 57
        central site routers, 56
        SOHO routers, 58–59
interactive sessions, PPP, 104
interesting traffic, 143
    DDR configuration, 143–144
interface serial 0.1 command, 263
interfaces
    Frame Relay, selecting, 263
    logical configuration, 79–80
    NT1, 132
internal profiles, Cisco 700 series routers, 199
ip default network command, 151
IP routing
    Cisco 700 series routers, 200– 203
    overlapping networks, addressing, 340
ip tcp header-compression passive
    command, 80
ip unnumbered command, 104
ip unnumbered Ethernet0 command, 79
ISDN (Integrated Services Digital
    Network), 130
    2B+D connections, 55
    BRI, 131
        66 block, 132
        CPE, 132
        SPIDs, 132
        terminal adapters, 132
    call release, 141
    call setup, 139–140
    DDR, 141
        addressing parameters, 146
        BOD (bandwidth on demand), 153
        caller ID screening, 148
        default routes, 151–152
        dial backup, 161–164
        dialer profiles, 157–159
        encapsulation, 146
        interesting traffic, specifying,
            143–144
        ML-PPP, 153–156
        passive interfaces, configuring,
            149–150
        protocol addressing, 147
        rate adaptation, 152
        rotary groups, 159–160
        snapshot routing, 165–166
        SPIDs, 148
        static routes, redistribution, 150
        static routes, specifying, 145
        switch type, configuring, 142
    Layer 1, 133–135
    Layer 2, 135
        SPIDs, 137
        TEIs, 136

    Layer 3, 138
    PRI, 55, 131, 166, 172–174
        analog calls on digital modems,
            174–175
        configuring, 172–174
        E1 framing, 171
        E1 line code, 172
        line coding, 167
        protocol layers, 172
        T1 framing, 168
        T1 line code, 170
isdn answer command, 148
isdn incoming-voice modem command,
    174–175
isdn spid1 command, 148
isdn switch-type command, 142
isdnq921 command, 136–137
ITU I.430 specification, ISDN Layer 1 framing method, 135
ITU Q.921 specification, 136
ITU Telecommunication Standardization Sector, 226
ITU X.25, PAD specifications, 228

L

LAN profiles, Cisco 700 series routers,
    configuring, 199–201
LAPB (Link Access Procedure, Balanced), 227
LAPB layer (X.25), 232–233
LAPD (Link Access Procedure on the D channel), 138
Layer 1 (ISDN), 133–135
Layer 2 (ISDN), 135
    SPIDs, 137
    TEIs, 136
Layer 3 (ISDN), 138
layered model, X.25, 229–231, 233
LCP negotiation, 105
LED indicators
    branch office routers, 57–58
    central site routers, 56
    SOHO routers, 58–59
line coding
    HDB3 (high-density bit, level 3), 172
    ISDN PRI, 167, 170
    T1, verifying, 170
line mode, physical configuration, 80–81
line numbering (routers), 75–77
link compression
    Predictor, 314–315
    STAC, 314
LMI (Local Management Interface), 258
load distribution, TCP, 340–341
local addresseses (NAT), 342
Local Director (Cisco), 341
local exchange equipment, 134, 142
local loop, NT1, 132
local termination, 134
logical configuration of routers, 79–80
logical parameters, asynchronous configuration, 78
logical subinterfaces (Frame Relay), 262

login local command, 81
LZ (Lempel-Ziv) algorithm, 314

M

map classes, 272
map statements, X.25 configuration, 234
measuring average/peak transmission rates, Frame Relay, 272
MinCIR (Minimum CIR), 270
MinCIR (minimum CIR), 271
ML-PPP (Multilink PPP), 112
    DDR configuration, 153–156
    troubleshooting, 155–156
modem autoconfigure command, 83
modem compression, 316
modem InOut command, 81
modemcap database, 83
    editing, 84
modems
    AT commands, 82
    autoconfiguration, 82–84
    call termination, 74
    chat scripts, 84–85
        REMDEVICE, 85
    discovery, 83
    DSR pins, 73
    DTR pins, 73
    signaling, 72–74
    terminal adapters, 132
modulus, X.25 configuration, 239
multiframes, 171
multipoint subinterfaces, 263

N

naming conventions, Cisco 700 series router profiles, 198
NASI authentication, 380
NAT (Network Address Translation)
    inside global addresses, 342
    inside local addresses, 342
    outside global addresses, 342
    outside local addresses, 342
    overlapping configuration, 347–349
    overlapping networks, 339–340
    overloading, 339
    overloading configuration, 346–347
    PAT (port address translation), 352–354
    sessions, clearing, 352
    simple dynamic configuration, 344–345
    static configuration, 345
    TCP load distribution, 340–341,
        349–350
    troubleshooting, 352
    verifying translation, 350–352
NBMA (nonbroadcast multiaccess)
    networks, 251

networks
    Cisco 700 series routers, profile configuration, 197–201
    NBMA, 251
    overlapping, 340
no cdp enable command, 80
nonprivate addresses, overlap, 340
Northern Telecom DMS-100 switch, 134
NT1, 132

O

outbound packet size (X.25), configuring, 238
output, isdnq921 command, 136–137
outside global addresses (NAT), 342
outside local addresses (NAT), 342
overlap configuration, NAT, 339, 347–349
overlapping networks, 340
overloading, NAT configuration, 339, 346–347

P

PAD specifications, X.25, 228
PAP (Password Authentication Protocol), 105
parameters, adjusting for Frame Relay traffic, 270–271
partial-mesh topology, Frame Relay, 259
passive interfaces, DDR configuration,
    149–150
PAT (port address translation), 352–354
payload compression, 315
peak transmission rates, measuring on Frame Relay, 272
peer default ip address pool remaddpool command, 80
per-interface compression, 314
permit statement, 344
physical configuration, 80–81
physical connections
    2B+D, 55
    asynchronous, 55
    PRI, 55
    WAN equipment, 54
physical layer (X.25), 233
physical-layer async command, 79
physical parameters of asynchronous configuration, 78
point of demarcation. *See* demarc
point-to-multipoint connections, Frame Relay, 264–265
ports, 338
    line numbering, 75–77
POTS (plain old telephone service), 130
PPP (Point-to-Point Protocol), 146
    architecture, 101
    authentication, 379
        CHAP, 107–108
        PAP, 105
    Callback, 109–111
    compression, 111
    dedicated sessions, 104
    frame structure, 103
    interactive sessions, 104
    layered model, 102

LCP, 104
troubleshooting, 112
See also ML-PPP
ppp authentication chap command, 80
ppp callback request command, 110
ppp context command, 104
Predictor compression, 314–315
preparating for Remote Access exam
scenarios, 14–17
structure of chapter content, 13
topics covered, 9–11
PRI (Primary Rate Interface), 55, 131, 166
analog calls on digital modems, 174–175
configuring, 172–174
E1 framing, 171
E1 line code, 172
line coding, 167
protocol layers, 172
T1 framing, 168
T1 line code, 170
priority lists to interface, 305
priority queuing, 300
configuring, 301–306
positioning commands, 303–304
verifying, 305
product families of routers, hardware selection for, 27–32
profiles
Cisco 700 series routers, 198
activating, 200
internal profiles, 199
standard profiles, 199
user profiles, 201
SPIDs (service profile identifiers), 132, 137, 148
virtual profiles, 385–386
protocol addressing (DDR), configuring, 147
protocol layers
ISDN PRI, 172
Layer 1, 133–135
Layer 2, 135–137
Layer 3, 138
protocol-specific parameters, Frame Relay, 264
PVCs (permanent virtual circuits), 229
multipoint subinterfaces, 263

Q

Q.921 specification (ITU), 136
Q933a LMIs, 258
queuing, 296–297
custom queuing, 306–307
configuring, 308–312
verifying operation, 312
FIFO, 298
priority queuing, 300
configuring, 301–306
positioning commands, 303–304
verifying, 305
WFQ, 298–299
quizzes, exam preparation, 13

R

R interface, 132
RAS (remote access server), modems
reverse Telnet connections, 74
signaling, 72–74
rate adaptation (DDR), 152
redistribution (DDR), 150
redundancy (DDR), dial backup, 163–165
REMDEVICE chat script, 85
remote access
routers, selecting, 23–25
WAN connections, selecting, 25
Remote Access exam, 9
preparing for, 14–17
topics covered, 9, 11
requirements
branch office installations, 26
CCDP certification, 7–8
CCNP certification, 7–8
central site installations, 26
Remote Access exam, preparation scenarios, 14–17
RO installations, 27
SOHO installations, 27
reverse Telnet connections, 74
RFCs (Requests For Comments)
DHCP-related, 208
RFC 1661 (PPP), 101
RJ-11 cables, asynchronous connections, 55
RO installations, requirements, 27
rotary groups, 159–160
routers
Cisco 700 series, 205–207
DHCP, 207–208
IP routing, 200–203
networking, 197
PAT, 352–354
profiles, 198–200
routing protocol support, 198
telephony services, 198
control ports, 373
gateway of last resort, 151
interfaces, logical configuration, 79–80
line numbering, 75–77
physical configuration, 80–81
product families, 27–32
remote access, selection criteria, 23–25
routing protocols
administrative distances, 164–165
split horizon, 260

S

S (supervisory) frames, 232
selecting
interface for Frame Relay
configuration, 263
router product family, 27–32
routers for remote access, 23–25

WAN equipment, 48
    branch office router, 51–53
    central site router, 48–50
    connections for remote access, 25
    SOHO router, 53
set dhcp relay command, 208
set user command, 202
shared passwords (AAA), establishing, 374
show dialer command, 112, 155
show frame-relay lmi command, 268
show frame-relay map command, 269
show frame-relay pvc command, 267, 274
show interface bri0 command, 145
show ip nat statistics command, 351
show ip nat translation command, 350
show ip route all command, 207
show isdn status command, 140, 172
show line command, 76–77
show modemcap command, 83
show ppp multilink command, 155
signal pins (modems), 73
signaling, modems, 72–74
simple dynamic NAT configuration, 344–345
snapshot routing, 165–166
SNMP (Simple Network Management Protocol) on X.25
    networks, 227
sockets, 338
    NAT overloading, 339
software
    Cisco Local Director, 341
    compression, configuring, 316
SOHO routers
    700 series, 53
        configuration, 206–207
    800 series, 53
    1000 series, 53
    DHCP, 207–208
    installation, requirements for, 27
    selecting, 53
    verifying installation, 58–59
source ports, 338
specialized certification, 8
specifying
    default routes (DDR), 151–152
    interesting traffic (DDR), 143–144
    static routes (DDR), 145, 150
SPIDs (service profile identifiers), 132, 137
    DDR, configuring, 148
split horizon, 260
    troubleshooting, 261–262
STAC compression, enabling, 316
STAC electronics, 314
standard AT commands, 82
standard profiles, Cisco 700 series routers, 199
star topology, Frame Relay, 259
start-chap command, 85
static backup (DDR), 164
static NAT configuration, 345
static routes
    DDR, 145

redistribution, 150
structure of chapter content, 13
subinterfaces
    cast type, 264
    Frame Relay, 261–262
SVCs (switched virtual circuits), 229, 257
switches, ISDN, 134
Sylvan Prometric testing centers, Web site, 4
syntax
    aaa accounting command, 383
    aaa authorization command, 381
    chat scripts, 84–85
    map statements, 234
system profiles
    Cisco 700 series routers, 199
        configuration commands, 203–204
        configuring, 200
        management commands, 205

T

TACACS+ (terminal access control access controller server),
    AAA authentication,
    374–380
T1 lines
    framing, 168
    line code, 170
    PRI, 166–168
target audience for CCNP/CCDP
    certification, 7
TCP (Transmission Control Protocol)
    enabling, 316
    header compression, 315
    load distribution, 340–341
        NAT, 349–350
TE1 interface, 132
TE2 interface, 132
TEIs (Terminal Endpoint Identifiers), 136
telephony services, Cisco 700 series
    routers, 198
terminal adapters, 132
Terminal Endpoint Identifier. *See* TEI
termination points
    Northern Telecom DMS-100 switch, 134
    NT1, 132
    TEIs, 136
timeslots, 168
topics covered on Remote Access exam, 9–11
topologies, Frame Relay, 259
traffic
    queuing, 296–297
        custom queuing, 306–308, 310–312
        FIFO, 298
        priority queuing, 300–306
        WFQ, 298–299
    shaping, Frame Relay, 270
        configuring, 272, 274–275
        DE, 271
        map classes, 272
        parameters, 270–271
        verifying operation, 274–275

training paths for certification, 11–12
troubleshooting
    ML-PPP, 155–156
    NAT, 352
    PPP, 112
    split horizon, 261–262

U-V

U (unnumbered) frames, 232
U interface, 132
user profiles, Cisco 700 series routers, 201
Van Jacobson algorithm, 315
VCs (virtual circuits), 257
    ranges for X.25 configuration, 237–238
verifying
    custom queuing operation, 312
    Frame Relay configuration, 266–267, 269
        debug frame-relay lmi command, 268
        show frame-relay lmi command, 268
        show frame-relay map command, 269
        show frame-relay pvc command, 267
    Frame Relay traffic shaping operation, 274–275
    NAT translation, 350, 352
    priority queuing, 305
    T1 line coding, 170
    WAN equipment installation, 55
        branch office routers, 57
        central site routers, 56
        SOHO routers, 58–59
viewing modemcap settings, 84
virtual profiles, 385–386

W

WANs
    branch office routers
        1600 series, 52, 58
        1700 series, 52
        2500 series, 52
        2600 series, 52
        installing, 26
        selecting, 51–53
        verifying installation, 57
    central site routers
        3600 series, 49, 56
        4000 series, 50
        7200 series, 51
        AS5X00 series, 50–51
        demarc, 48
        installing, requirements for, 26
        selecting, 48–50
        verifying installation, 56
    connections for remote access
        2B+D, 55
        8-N-1, 74
        asynchronous, 55, 78
        point-to-point, LCP, 104
        PRI, 55
        reverse Telnet, 74
        devices
        assembling, 54
        selecting, 25, 48

verifying installation, 55
SOHO routers
    700 series, 53
    800 series, 53
    1000 series, 53
    configuration, 206–207
    DHCP, 207–208
    installation, requirements for, 27
    selecting, 53
    verifying installation, 58–59
X.25, 226
    configuring, 233–236
    DTE/DCE, 228
    encapsulation, 234
    hierarchical structure, 227
    inbound/outbound packet sizes, 238
    LAPB, 227, 232–233
    modulus, 239
    physical layer, 233
    VC ranges, 237–238
    window sizes, 238
    X.121 address, configuring, 234
    X.25 layer, 229–231
Web sites, Sylvan Prometric testing centers, 4
well-known ports, 338
WFQ (Weighted Fair Queuing), 298–299
what-to-track arguments, aaa accounting command, 383
window sizes, X.25 configuration, 238

X-Z

X.121 addresses for X.25 networks,
    configuring, 231, 234
X.25, 226
    configuring, 233
        examples, 235–236
    DTE/DCE, 228
    encapsulation, 234
    hierarchical structure, 227
    inbound/outbound packet sizes, configuring, 238
    LAPB layer, 227, 232–233
    modulus, configuring, 239
    PAD specifications, 228
    physical layer, 233
    VC ranges, configuring, 237–238
    window sizes, 238
    X.25 sublayer, 229–230
        X.121 addressing, 231, 234
x25 map compressdtcp command, 316
x25 pvc command, 236